AF321579

this is tomorrow

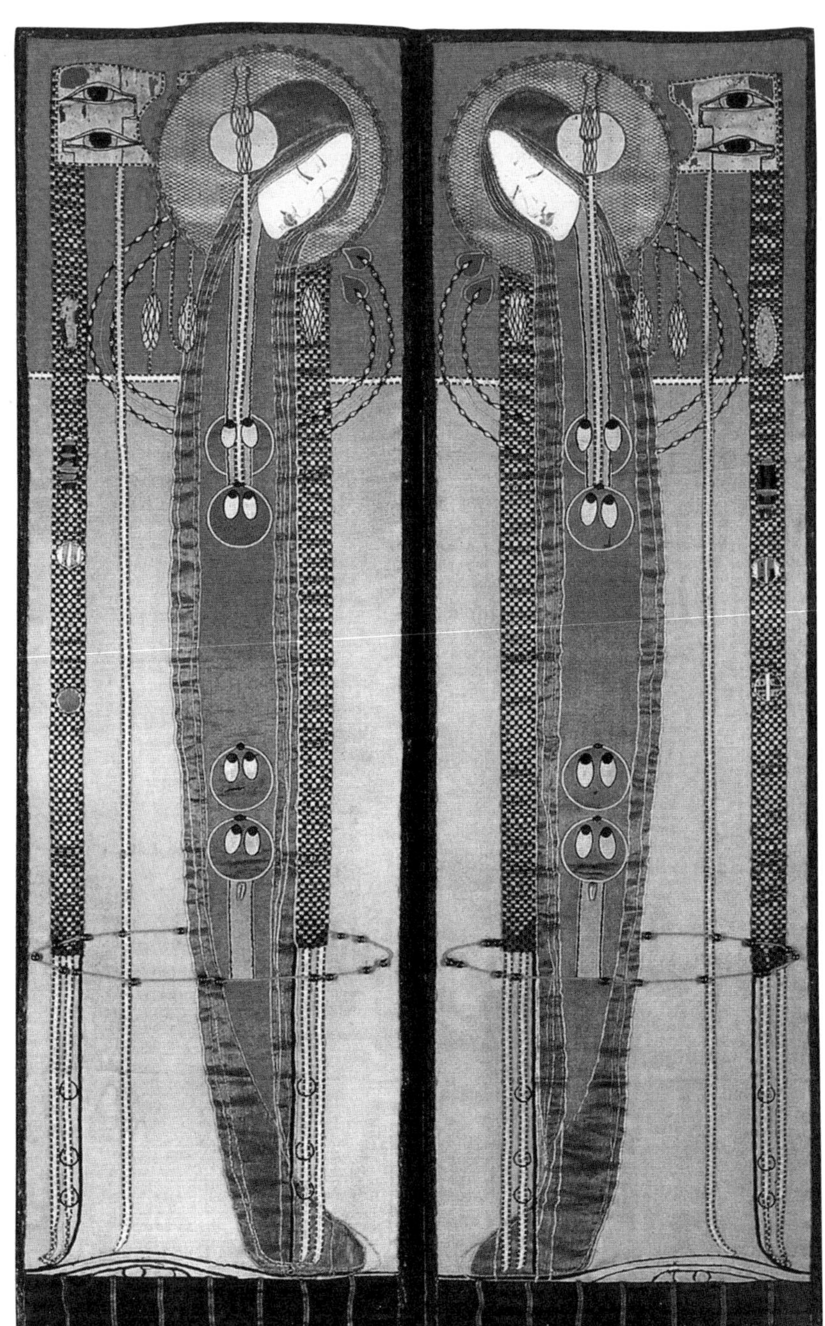

this is tomorrow

Twentieth-century Britain and its Artists

Michael Bird

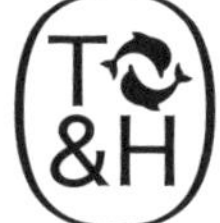

For Felicity

FRONTISPIECE
Margaret MacDonald, *Embroidered Panels*, 1902. Linen with silk braid,
ribbon, silk appliqué and bead decoration, 177 × 41 cm (69¾ × 16¼ in.)

First published in the United Kingdom in 2022 by
Thames & Hudson Ltd, 181A High Holborn, London WC1V 7QX

First published in the United States of America in 2022 by
Thames & Hudson Inc., 500 Fifth Avenue, New York, New York 10110

This is Tomorrow: Twentieth-century Britain and its Artists © 2022
Thames & Hudson Ltd, London
Text © 2022 Michael Bird

Typeset by Peter Burgess

British Library Cataloguing-in-Publication Data
A catalogue record for this book is available from the British Library

Library of Congress Control Number 2022931875

ISBN 978-0-500-02443-0

Printed in China by Shanghai Offset Printing Products Limited

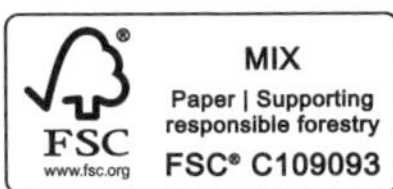

Be the first to know about our new releases,
exclusive content and author events by visiting
thamesandhudson.com
thamesandhudsonusa.com
thamesandhudson.com.au

Contents

There really is no such thing as Art. There are only artists.

Ernst Gombrich, 1950

I think the whole impulse of art and artists finding themselves, or the human being finding themselves making art...is very like being part of the earth in terms of soil, and one can analyse the soil and find all of the different minerals that are in there, and the different bacterias and the different fungi, and the earthworms and the bugs, and one tends to think of all these things as separate, but really it's one organism, just one living being.... And art is like that, and I'm just like a microbe among many others, and there's a symbiosis, it all works, and we all have to be there.

David Nash, 1995

A moving train

This is the story of twentieth-century Britain, viewed through the lens of artists' lives. I think of it less as art history than as *artists'* history, since it is through the artists' experiences that the narrative unfolds – the people, the places, the encounters and multiple individual criss-crossing trajectories. It contains its share of art-historical landmarks, such as Roger Fry's first post-impressionist show in 1910 or 'This Is Tomorrow', a determinedly future-facing exhibition at the Whitechapel Art Gallery in 1956 from which I have borrowed my title, but what I am more interested in is the wave-motion dynamic underlying all this – how the making of art (rather than, say, drafting legislation or firing a gun) is a potent, open-ended form of participation in the life of your own time.

There's much coming and going. The interwoven strands in this story pass through London, Glasgow and Leeds, Cornwall and the Caribbean, New York, Paris, Moscow and Berlin. Some artists were born in Britain but spent large parts of their working lives elsewhere. Others were born abroad but made their work in, and their mark on, Britain. The first two artists who take centre stage are James Abbott McNeill Whistler, a Paris-trained expatriate American, and his young German-born, half-Danish pupil-assistant Walter Sickert. Successive waves of immigration and surges of refugees from war and persecution have brought with them artists, and young people who would go on to become artists, along with fresh ideas and unfamiliar habits of thinking and living that would take root in Britain, in all kinds of ways, both in and beyond art. In our era of resurgent nationalism, this factor alone – the borderless, continually revitalized continuities of art – makes this a story worth telling.

The twentieth century, as Naum Gabo – a Russian-Jewish artist-exile in London – observed in 1937, 'appears in history under the sign of revolutions and disintegration'. There could be no 'stable point', no settled equilibrium 'in either the material or the ideal structure of our life'. From the 1870s onwards, in art, as in politics, technology and other areas, the rhythms of change and adaptation became embedded in collective consciousness. I look at how the work of artists in Britain reflected and refracted some of the defining changes of the period, such as the vast scale of dislocation caused by war, the effects of educational reforms, the progress of the women's movement and the emergence of modern mass media.

There are excellent books about specific phases of art and culture in twentieth-century Britain, but this is the first attempt to tell the story as a connected narrative from start to finish. In its account of what it meant to be modern – the ways in which people (not only artists) at various times saw themselves as inhabitants of a modern Britain with a modern future – it spans the 'long twentieth century', from the closing years of Queen Victoria's reign through two world wars to the social-democratic state of the post-war decades and its dismantling in the free-marketeering 1980s and 1990s. In deciding which artists and episodes to include, I have had to be selective, but what I hope emerges is a sense of interconnecting currents that flow out beyond individual careers and historical moments – the spark that kept the engine turning through 120 years or so.

Historical imagination – for me, at any rate – begins in the textures and atmosphere of everyday life. When I think of the early Yorkshire years of Barbara Hepworth and Henry Moore, there is coal smoke in the air, the rattle of pit-head gear – formative smells and sounds, these must have been. Coal is one texture, chiselled and abraded marble another, but the banked, glowing grate and the smooth holed stone share a world. A life has its texture, too. And, as historical material on which to draw, the life story has much more of a role for the last century than for previous eras. The whole period is just within reach of family memory: three of my grandparents were born in the 1890s, my parents in the 1920s, my children in the 1990s – between us we experienced life in Britain in all but the first fourteen years covered by this book. As a society, we have inherited unprecedented numbers of documented lives. Official records, diaries, letters, newsreels, home movies, oral history interviews – what were once 'hidden' histories (the lives of front-line soldiers, coal miners, steel workers and domestic servants, for example) have become the clearly audible voice of the past. 'The figure of the servant,' writes the cultural historian Alison Light, 'takes us not only inside history but inside ourselves.' The same is true of the artist – even *more* true, I would say, because of the particularly subtle, reflexive ways in which time and art are intertwined.

Art of all historical periods, given half a chance, can make us breathe the atmosphere of the time of its making as if it were happening over again. If the American essayist and activist Susan Sontag was right, that 'a society becomes "modern" when one of its chief activities is producing and consuming images', then twentieth-century visual artists defined as well as reflected their age. It has also often been noticed that artists have a way of tuning into things that have not yet happened. The great Marxist cultural historian Eric Hobsbawm wondered how it was that 'brilliant fashion designers' (he could equally have said artists) 'sometimes succeed in anticipating the shape of things to come better than professional predictors'. Near the end of a long career devoted to analysing the effects of beliefs and ideas on the course of transformative events, he had to confess that, to this particular question, 'I still don't know the answer.' One of the most famous instances of art's proleptic workings was the futurists' obsession with destruction and machines in the years preceding the First World War – a war that, as historian Niall Ferguson contends, caught professional predictors like international money-men 'almost entirely by surprise'. Artists, too, have proved reliably early adopters of new ideas and experimenters with fledgling technologies. When Eugène Manet showed the twenty-two-year-old Sickert round his eminent brother's studio in 1883, there on the easel was one of the first paintings to capture the bland glare of indoor electric lighting. At the same time, artists carry on using methods that would seem anachronistic in any other setting, behaving in their studios in ways that an ancient Greek would recognize. In all of this activity there is a continual future-facing gathering up of the past into the present.

I take this as a pattern for thinking about history, which leads to a nuanced view of what it meant to be avant-garde (a military term adopted by progressive artists in mid-nineteenth-century France and introduced into English by a *Daily Telegraph* journalist in 1910). I am sceptical about that hoary trope, 'the shock of the new'. It is true that there are plenty of accounts of audiences jeering at unfamiliar (but not necessarily new) art, as Virginia Woolf observed Londoners doing at her friend Fry's first post-impressionist show, and art critics spritzing up their copy with flourishes of spleen and mockery. But *shock*? In the century of Passchendaele, Buchenwald and the Bomb, is it possible that art retained – if it ever had – a capacity to leave us torn from our moorings, helplessly shaken? No. Incomprehension, hilarity, boredom, squeamishness, incredulity at inexplicably high prices (although not usually at unfairly low ones), feelings of exclusion and being looked down on – people have experienced all these things in the face of modern art, but seldom, surely, actual shock. Except, that is, in a purely social sense. An easy-going acceptance of polyamorousness and post-impressionist taste was felt by members of the Bloomsbury circle in the 1900s to mark them off from the shockable 'man in the street'. The twentieth century, it turned out, had far worse shocks up its sleeve.

And newness? Modernity has been marked from the outset by our readiness to assimilate the new. As millions of people adapted, without problem or protest, to new technologies and media that had, within just a few years, morphed from fantastical dreams into quotidian realities, newness per se has proved again and again its ability to be anything but shocking. And artists, even traditionalist artists, are specialists in transformation, in both an obvious physical sense (stone into sculpture) and a metaphysical one (mind into matter). This is, then, the story of a century of extraordinarily rapid change told through the working lives of a group of people whose daily engagement with transformation is, whichever way you look at it, unique. There is always another side to the equation, the non-artists who encounter and participate in art – the public, the audience, us. Our broader experience of visual culture has also changed over time, along with our responses to art. This, too, is part of the story.

Visitors to 'This Is Tomorrow' in August 1956 encountered a series of mini-installations in which young painters, sculptors, architects and designers had collaborated to realize their visions of life in a Britain of the future – a nation poised between post-war austerity and the economic and cultural boom years of the 1960s. The writer–curator Lawrence Alloway explained that the exhibition drew on 'powerful precedents for placing art in a time-perspective that relies on the future to complete it'. He also pointed out that, while vision is necessary if we are going to get anywhere, 'yesterday's tomorrow is never today'. The distant landscape looks different as we get closer, the horizon keeps changing. In this artists' history of twentieth-century Britain, history is a moving train. There are no fixed points from which to judge historic failure or success but instead a vivid series of transitions. The story begins in 1878, when the British public was first dragged into a dispute concerning modern art.

1
Fireworks

Westminster, November 1878

A winter morning, a thick London fog. In the Court of Exchequer, next to Westminster Hall, members of the special jury recruited for today's trial – men of property, Oxbridge graduates – settle on to their bench. Among the press and public, crowded shoulder to shoulder in slightly sweaty anticipation – Sir John Huddleston, the judge, likes his courtroom as warm as possible – there's an almost theatrical simmer. Everyone is here because, at an exhibition last year, a celebrated critic took a violent dislike to one particular painting. He denounced the artist for 'wilful imposture' and 'Cockney impudence'. In a lifetime of looking at art, he thundered, he 'never expected to hear a coxcomb ask 200 guineas for flinging a pot of paint in the public's face'. The artist, astonishingly, swung back. He sued for libel, demanding damages of £1,000 – a substantial, not to say punitive, sum.

———

Art and notoriety, insult and revenge – this trial was 'the talk of the moment' in London, reported the American writer and man-about-Europe Henry James to his readers on the other side of the Atlantic. For them, too, the defendant was a household name: John Ruskin, Slade Professor of Fine Art at Oxford University, the pre-eminent voice on matters of art and beauty throughout the English-speaking world. For many years, Ruskin had striven to teach his fellow men and women to live through their eyes: 'to *see* something and tell what it *saw* plainly' was 'the greatest thing a human soul ever does in this world'. Seeing, in Ruskin's sense, was 'poetry, prophecy, religion – all in one'. Gaze into 'the pure blue of a serene sky,' he counselled in his first published book, *Modern Painters* – a master already at twenty-four – 'you will see that there is variety and fullness in its very repose. It is not flat dead colour, but a deep, quivering, transparent body of penetrable air.' To read Ruskin on the wonder of the natural world and its reflection in art was, it was often felt, almost better than looking for yourself. 'I feel now as if I had been walking blindfold,' Charlotte Brontë enthused about *Modern Painters*, 'this book seems to give me eyes.'

In 1843, when he chose his book title, 'modern' simply meant 'of our times'. Ruskin's artist hero, J. M. W. Turner, was modern because he did not want to paint academically impeccable pictures but to capture the 'Truth of Space' in the here and now – the 'dazzle and indecision of distance', the mysterious drama of the weather. The 'modern folly' that goaded the older Ruskin to heartache and fury was something else. He had witnessed Britain's transformation into the world's most heavily industrialized nation and stood appalled by its human and environmental cost – by the 'frenzy of avarice' that was blighting lives and landscapes, 'drowning our sailors, suffocating our miners, poisoning our children, and blasting the cultivable surface of England into a treeless waste of ashes'. In the face of this kind of modernity, which defined itself by its eagerness to trample on the past, clear-sighted seeing was no longer enough. Ruskin became increasingly preoccupied by the need for social action.

Determined to demonstrate an alternative to industrial capitalism – a humane future that could be secured only by turning back the clock – Ruskin founded the Guild of St George. He bought land on which to establish self-sustaining rural communities, with workshops, farms, schools and educational art collections. He published a series of pamphlets, *Fors Clavigera* ('Fortune the Key-bearer'), addressed to 'the Workmen and Labourers of Great Britain'. 'If all the money of all the capitalists in the whole world were destroyed, the notes and bills burnt, the gold irrevocably buried, and all the machines and apparatus of manufactures crushed,' he claimed in the first instalment in 1871, 'the poorer population would be very little worse off than they are at this instant.' In an age of rampant mechanization, Ruskin insisted that 'No machines will increase the possibilities of life.' Railways were a particular bête noire: 'Wherever I look or travel, I see that men, wherever they can reach, destroy all beauty. They seem to have no other desire or hope but to have large houses and to be able to move fast.' He campaigned to scupper plans for a railway through the Lake District, where he lived beside Coniston Water in a sprawling mansion filled with paintings by Turner and the pre-Raphaelites, sketchbooks containing his own beautifully observed drawings, and a museum's-worth of geological specimens.

Most of those present in the Court of Exchequer and jostling in the corridors outside will have had their opinions about the plaintiff too. James Abbott Whistler was an American artist who had lived in London since 1859 ('McNeill' was a later addition to his name). Although his full-length portraits and shadowy riverscapes, to which he gave musical titles like *harmony* and *arrangement*, did not find favour at the Royal Academy, he had become a celebrity on the West End scene. If Ruskin held the moral high ground, Whistler made news – for instance, the spat in 1876 with Liverpool shipping tycoon Frederick Leyland about some altera-

John Ruskin, *Twig of Peach Bloom*, c. 1874. Watercolour and gouache on cream wove paper, 20.9 × 16.1 cm (8¼ × 6⅜ in.)

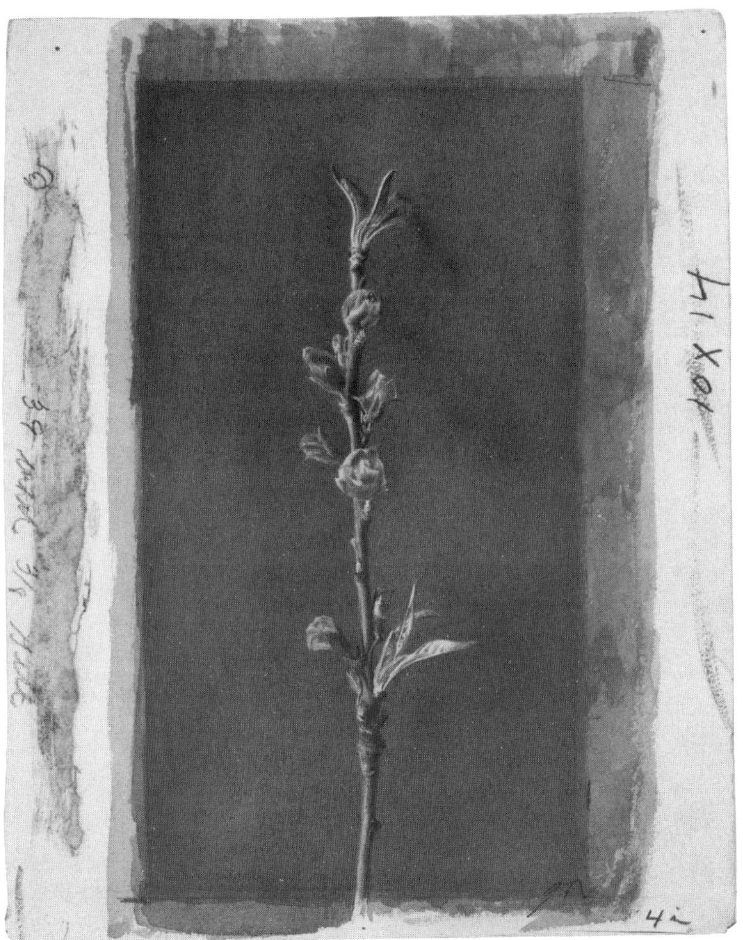

tions he had commissioned Whistler to make to the dining room of his Kensington home. While Leyland was away, Whistler did as he pleased, 'putting in every touch with such freedom – that when I came round to the corner where I started, why, I had to paint part of it over again'. On the window shutters he painted a golden pair of fighting peacocks – artist and patron duelling beak-to-claw. Incensed by the liberties Whistler had taken, Leyland refused to pay, threatening to horse-whip the artist. 'I have made you famous,' Whistler retorted. 'My work will live when you are forgotten.' And then *The Grasshopper*, a French farce adapted for the London music-hall stage by John Hollingshead, manager of the Gaiety Theatre. Instead of a parody of a Barbizon School landscape painter, Hollingshead recast the male lead as a certain 'Artist of the Future' with whom he guessed his audience would be more familiar. Whistler seemed happy to be the model for the 'harmonist in colours', Pygmalion Flippit.

According to Whistler, 'none but an artist can be a competent critic'. His line on Ruskin, 'that he preaches to young men what he cannot perform!', was a mischievous allusion to another side of Ruskin's reputation – his divorce in 1854 from the beautiful young Effie Gray on grounds of non-consummation and presumed sexual impotence. Whistler himself had a showman's instinct for public relations: in May 1878, for example, he gave a posse of journalists a tour of his Chelsea home, including the dining room he had designed, like Leyland's, in his version of the fashionable style of japonisme, 'peacock-blue, over-grown with an eruption of Japanese fans'. The *Kilburn Times* reporter noted Whistler's special sensitivity to 'colour harmonies exhibited in the dress of a fair critic', whom the artist persuaded to pose, while the group gathered round. It was a bravura performance:

> *his entire apparatus is on a large scale. His brushes are more like those of a house painter than an artist. With extraordinary rapidity, without sketching any outline, he throws, as it were, the background on the canvas, as if the figure were rather an accident than the motive of the study.... While literally 'dashing in' his work à grands coups de pinceau [with big brushstrokes], the painter is a study in himself – of combined mental and physical activity. The pace is tremendous.*

Ruskin, too, was a seasoned performer. To accommodate the large following his lectures attracted, he sometimes delivered them twice over.

In 1873, he told an Oxford audience, 'I never saw anything so impudent on the walls of any exhibition in any country as last year in London. It was a daub, professing to be a "harmony in pink and white" (or some such nonsense).' Not caring whether anyone got the 'harmony' clue to the artist's true identity, Ruskin peremptorily trashed his work: it was 'absolute rubbish' that had taken at most 'a quarter of an hour to scrawl' but was priced at 250 guineas – an hourly rate of more than £1,000.

In June 1877, visiting the newly opened Grosvenor Gallery to view work by his friend Edward Burne-Jones, Ruskin again happened on one of Whistler's 'daubs'. Founded by a couple of rich amateur artists, the debonair banker Sir Coutts Lindsay and his wife Lady Blanche FitzRoy, the Grosvenor occupied palatial purpose-built premises on New Bond Street, complete with restaurant, library and billiard room. Although some paintings on display, many of them by the Lindsays and their friends, were discreetly offered for sale, the note they aimed for was exclusive private collection rather than luxury emporium. Their formula – promoting artists who were cold-shouldered by the Royal Academy, like Burne-Jones and Whistler, while luring the eminent Academicians George Frederic Watts and John Everett Millais to show with them – met with instant success. On the day the Grosvenor opened, it received seven thousand visitors. In the course of reviewing London exhibitions for *The Nation*, Henry James watched the gallery become a high-society haunt, where people went 'with the expectation of finding something very strange and abnormal'. It is a measure of how quickly, at this time, new sensations – cultural and otherwise – were breaking on the London scene that, within a year, some found the Grosvenor passé. 'I am rather disappointed, you know,' James overheard a visitor complain. 'I expected the arrangement of the pictures would be more unusual.' Had she, he wondered, hoped to find the paintings 'hung upside down, or with their faces to the wall?'

Crossing the green marble floors, past scarlet damask-covered walls, among the swishing trains of expensive dresses, Ruskin, already irked by the ostentatious 'glitter' of his surroundings, encountered *Nocturne in Black and Gold* (1875; pl. 1). This smallish painting was one of four crepuscular Thames-side scenes, all with 'nocturne' in the title, which Whistler was showing along with three standing portraits. Ruskin stared at the clouds of soft, smoky greys and silky blue-blacks, loosely brushed in the thinnest paint, with a few figures silhouetted at the bottom. Without the subtitle, *The Falling Rocket*, the spatters of red and yellow sprinkling the smoke or sky could have been careless mess. And here again was the outrageous price tag, 200 guineas (Whistler, keen to sell a painting he had first shown two years ago, had actually reduced it by 20 per cent). Artists should be properly remunerated, Ruskin believed, but on the basis of worthwhile labour. Compared to a sunset or storm by Turner, how could fireworks – a crowd-pleasing spectacle apparently taking place in Cremorne Gardens, a Chelsea pleasure park near Whistler's house – arouse any kind of moral reflection? Where was the skill? It would take a master carpenter three years to earn what this charlatan demanded for a few insouciant minutes at his easel. Ruskin, who had made his name defending Turner, the greatest 'modern painter', from his critics, now felt summoned to protect art itself from degradation by an artist whose modernity was of the disastrous new type. In the next issue of *Fors*, on the theme of the 'free-heartedness of unselfish toil' and the corruption of the 'modern system for accumulating wealth', he excoriated Whistler in the terms that had landed them both in court.

When he took up his pen on behalf of the public, however, it wasn't the Grosvenor Gallery's clientele he had in mind. In their quest for talking points, the bored beau monde no doubt deserved the 'absolute rubbish' dished up for them by Whistler. For the 'Workmen and Labourers of Great Britain', on the other hand, Ruskin believed that 'Art-knowledge' had the power to change lives. This literate working-class public was almost as modern as Whistler's paintings: it had emerged in the slipstream of the Industrial Revolution, which in turn had set in motion a sea change in British education. In a country where being a fluent reader and writer had once been an elite accomplishment, the 1870 Elementary Education Act brought universal literacy another step closer. This was a basic requirement for the regiments of clerks and administrators, designers and engineers needed to service an advanced industrial nation and its empire, and a springboard for the new mass phenomenon of the working-class autodidact.

'*Knowledge*,' declared Samuel Smiles, who published his bestselling compilation of motivational tales, *Self-Help*, in 1859, 'is of itself one of the highest enjoyments. Every human being has a great mission to perform, noble faculties to cultivate, a vast destiny to accomplish.' In that quirk of Victorian thinking in which moral and social attributes like 'nobility' became confused, the idea gained traction that, perhaps even more than other forms of knowledge, 'Art-knowledge' enabled those who acquired it to aspire to some 'higher' state of awareness, or even, as part of a programme of self-help, higher social status. Ideas of this kind led ambitious young professionals from working-class backgrounds to spend their leisure hours in art galleries; the apprentice architect and future novelist Thomas Hardy, son of a Dorset stonemason, spent twenty minutes of every lunch-break in the National Gallery, focusing each visit on a single painting. But if art was a gateway, you first had to find the key that could make a fire-streak sunset by Turner or a creamy breast by Rubens open the door to destinies of previously unimaginable vastness. Through his writings and lectures, Ruskin was the key-bearer for countless personal epiphanies of this kind. Still, the 'Workmen and Labourers of Great Britain' might wonder why he had leapt so ferociously to their defence, given that they were unlikely ever to set eyes on *Nocturne in Black and Gold* or need shielding from flung paint of the modern kind.

Throughout the year it had taken the trial to come to court, Whistler had been picturing his triumphant showdown with Ruskin, whom he had never met face to face. In the event, however, Ruskin was unable to attend. His mental health had been fragile for some time; after a breakdown in 1878, he was debarred on doctor's orders from testifying in person. He briefed a proxy, Burne-Jones, whose 'expert' status as a professional artist concealed his own rivalrous but veiled animosity towards Whistler. As the trial got under way at half-past ten on 25 November, it was, in any case, the plaintiff's turn to take the stand. Instantly recognizable from his caricature in *Vanity Fair* – wasp-waisted coat, monocle, shock of unruly curls, Van Dyck goatee – Whistler appeared at once combative and effete, his stints at West Point military academy and in Charles Gleyre's atelier in Paris both apparent. So this was an artist; this – even more unexpected in this setting – was an American. Between 1815 and 1914, some ten million emigrants left Britain for the United States, but in 1878 native-born Americans were still a novelty in London, where the British class system was at a loss to place them. They were not quite foreigners, yet neither were they, like Australians or Canadians, subjects of the British Empire. Henry James, sensitive to snide pleasantries about the brashness of his fellow countrymen, was concerned that Whistler's confrontational swagger brought a tang of the Wild West to the proceedings. If they were taking place in 'some Western American town', he opined, they would have typified the 'provincial and barbarous' behaviour the British expected of Americans, almost guaranteed to 'vulgarise the idea of art'.

Opening for Whistler, Serjeant John Humffreys Parry conceded that his ideas about painting might seem 'eccentric' but that he was 'an unwearied worker in his profession', who did not deserve to be 'treated with contempt and ridicule by Mr Ruskin'. He submitted that Ruskin had accused Whistler of fraud in a deliberate attempt to damage his reputation. Whistler's senior counsel William Petheram then talked the artist through a presentation of his case, in which Whistler immediately contradicted Parry: he had not been born in America, he claimed, but St Petersburg. This wasn't true. His early years had been spent in a clapboard colonial house in the Massachusetts textile town of Lowell, from where his father, Major George Washington Whistler, an army engineer, moved his young family to Russia when Whistler was nine to work on the Moscow–St Petersburg railway. But Whistler believed in an artist's unconditional freedom to alter any mere, bare fact in the service of art: 'I shall be born when and where I want,' he liked to say, 'and I do not choose to be born in Lowell.'

'Will you tell us the meaning of the word "nocturne" as applied to your pictures?' Petheram prompted. He wanted the jury to understand that Whistler's paintings were serious and sincere.

'I wished to indicate an artistic interest alone, divesting the picture of any outside anecdotal interest.' A painting, said Whistler, speaking the language of French art theory, was 'a problem that I attempt to solve', 'an arrangement of line and form and colour'. In other words, an object in itself, with its own properties and laws, rather than a vehicle for storytelling.

An 'arrangement'? Ruskin's counsel, Sir John Holker, pounced. Attorney General and MP for Preston, he seldom lost a case. He was confident of tripping up this Yankee fop. What was the *subject* of *Nocturne in Black and Gold*? Was it a view that anyone would recognize? Was 200 guineas a 'stiffish price'?

'How long do you take to knock off one of your pictures?'

'Oh, I "knock one off" possibly in a couple of days.'

Snorts of laughter, irrepressible hoots.

The ponderous Lancastrian gathered himself up. 'The labour of two days is that for which you ask 200 guineas?'

'No,' countered Whistler. 'I ask it for the knowledge I have gained in the work of a lifetime.'

A burst of clapping.

Huddleston intervened. The judge was well known as a theatre-lover – he might possibly have seen *The Grasshopper* – but he would not allow his court to become 'an arena for applause'. 'If this manifestation of feeling is repeated,' he snapped, 'I shall have to clear the court.'

No one, probably, got Whistler's real point. He was not saying that a lifetime of gaining knowledge turned his time into money, like a lawyer's, but that art, for the artist, is life lived – it is what he made of being who

James Abbott McNeill Whistler, *c.* 1878, photograph by London Stereoscopic & Photographic Company

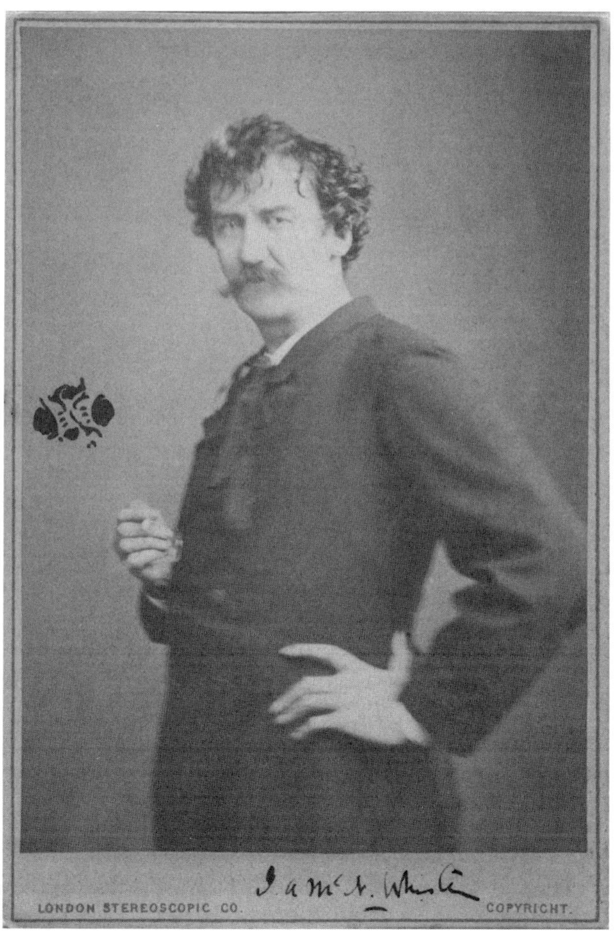

he was. The value of a painting could not be calculated without weighing the life experience of the artist. Would the public ever fully understand? This morning, in any case, there was no time to reflect.

Nocturne in Blue and Silver (*c.* 1872–75) – one of the group of riverscapes from the Grosvenor exhibition (later retitled *Nocturne: Blue and Gold – Old Battersea Bridge*) – was shown to the jury. In the foreground, a towering dark T-shape, representing a segment of the last surviving wooden bridge across the Thames, looms through the blue dusk, a palpable chill coming off the river. Whistler owned a small boat, in which he rowed out at night from the Chelsea foreshore, sometimes staying on the water until dawn. He could not paint in the boat in the dark, but in Paris he had learned how to memorize a scene: look long, turn away, turn back, check the image in your mind's eye against the real thing, point by point, then carry the picture in your head, back to the studio, every detail in place. Huddleston had no idea that this was what it took to paint as Whistler did.

'Which part of the picture is the bridge?' he asked.

More laughter. Another telling-off.

'Your lordship is too close at present to the picture to perceive the effect I intended to produce at a distance.'

Holker again: 'Do you say that this is a correct representation of Battersea Bridge?... What is that mark on the right of the picture, like a cascade? Is it a firework?... Are those figures on the top of the bridge intended as people?'

Whistler deftly returned the serve: 'They are just what you like.'

Here, in six short words, Whistler elegantly undermined the entire foundation of Victorian narrative art. In its place, he set the principle of subjectivity, the relative as opposed to the absolute truth of seeing.

'My whole scheme was only to bring about a certain harmony of colour.'

After the lunch break, *Nocturne in Black and Gold* was passed around, upside down, for the jury to inspect. Holker doggedly dragged the argument back to his chosen ground. What was this a picture *of*?

'This is Cremorne?' he asked, as if to say 'How on earth...?', provoking general laughter. How long had it taken to paint? What was its 'peculiar beauty'? 'Do you not think that anybody looking at that picture might fairly come to the conclusion that it has no peculiar beauty?'

Parry seized his chance to let Whistler restate his position. Had he actually *intended* the painting to be 'a representation of a place'? No, answered Whistler, '*Nocturne in Black and Gold* was not painted to offer the portrait of a particular place, but as an artistic impression.'

These were almost the last words Whistler spoke in court. For the rest of the afternoon, his prosecution witnesses took turns: the poet William Rossetti, brother of the pre-Raphaelite painter and poet Dante Gabriel Rossetti, and the artist Albert Moore. Holker harped persistently on the question of price. 'Would you give 200 guineas for it?' he demanded of Rossetti, who demurred, 'I am too poor to give 200 guineas for any picture.' 'If I were rich, I would buy the picture myself,' claimed Moore.

At four o'clock, in the seeping dusk – the gloomy chamber relied on candle-light – Huddleston called time. He permitted himself a witticism, a little flourish of his excellent French: 'The condition in which the court is now might be called "*nocturne*".' The trial would resume next day, with the case for the defence.

———

'Impression': at the time of the Whistler–Ruskin trial, this word had begun to divide the cultural old guard from the modern spirits like an article of faith. Its double meaning was partly responsible: on the one hand vagueness ('I have the impression'), on the other precision, as when a shape is transferred, clean and sharp, from one medium to another, like an etching inked on to paper. These contradictory meanings had troubled no one until recently, but now, impressions were contested ground: it was symptomatic that Whistler's skill as a printmaker was widely acknowledged – it was his 'impressions' in paint that caused the problem. In August 1878, the lay preacher and editor of the *Spectator* Richard Holt Hutton satirized the fashionable 'cultus of Impressionability'; he mocked its devotees, for whom 'the flux of impressions' stirred up 'every shade of namby-pamby tenderness', emasculating 'the stronger purposes to which nine men out of ten owe their usefulness'. Someone with 'sensuous susceptibilities' was like a bed of wax, which 'takes off an impression of the form that is left upon it': the form was primary, the impression secondary. In other words, for Hutton and his readership of conservative believers, the solid object equated to the real world – the world made by God. However sensitive you might be, you would be wrong – in fact, immoral – to assert that your impressions of something were more real than the thing itself.

Hutton's target, three months before the trial, was not Whistler but the Oxford don and writer Walter Pater, who sowed the word 'impression' through his work like stardust. He considered Pater a danger because of the appeal of his 'namby-pamby' ideas to certain young people, and the eloquent sleight of hand by which he made self-regarding subjectivity seem logical and even morally right, as in the preface to his book on the Italian Renaissance:

> 'To see an object as in itself it really is,' has been justly said to be the aim of all true criticism whatever, and in aesthetic criticism the first step towards seeing one's object as it really is, is to know one's own impression as it really is.... What is this song or picture, this engaging personality presented in life or in a book, to me? What effect does it really produce in me? Does it give me pleasure? and if so what sort or degree of pleasure?... The answers to these questions are the original facts with which the aesthetic critic has to do; and, as in the study of light, of morals, of number, one must realise such primary data for one's self, or not at all.

This kind of talk went with a penchant for dressing like a dandy (as Whistler did), not to mention the rumours of 'Greek love' that clung to Pater and his impressionable disciples, the 'aesthetes'. Yet, subversive though Pater's ideas might be, the aesthetes, easily identified according to the journalist Harry Quilter by their 'dishevelled hair, eccentricity of attire and general appearance of weary passion', piqued the public imagination. Their best-known and most flamboyant representative was the young poet and playwright Oscar Wilde, who had, aged twenty-two, appeared at the Grosvenor Gallery's inaugural exhibition in a cello-shaped coat. It was said that Hollingshead had inserted a song-and-dance number for Whistler, Wilde and fellow aesthete Frank Miles into a performance of *The Grasshopper*. In 1880, the librettist–composer duo W. S. Gilbert and Arthur Sullivan, scouting for a topical theme for their next comic opera, homed in on aestheticism. *Patience* premiered the following spring and ran for almost six hundred shows. Its hero, Archibald Grosvenor, an 'idyllic poet' who is cured of his narcissistic conceit ('I am a trustee for Beauty') by love, was generally believed to be modelled on Wilde.

In the deep epistemological strata below the aesthete jokes and journalistic gripes about the 'cultus of Impressionability' – the culture wars of

1878 – a tectonic shift in attitudes was under way. The Whistler–Ruskin trial straddled the fault line. On one side, the belief, underwritten by Christian faith, that 'primary data' about the world rested on a bedrock of God-given truth, static and eternal. On the other, the subjectivity of impressions, which registered a world of movement and change. Hostility to Whistler and to the aesthetes, whom Whistler himself came to view with suspicion as populists and poseurs, shared something with the outrage roused by Charles Darwin. In 1859, in *On the Origin of Species*, Darwin had proposed that, rather than being created once and for all by God, the forms of all living creatures had developed, and continued to develop, in response to the struggle for survival. In the book's sixth edition in 1873, by which time he felt that 'almost all naturalists' had accepted his theory, Darwin finally gave it a name: evolution – a word that originally described the unrolling of a scroll, a steadily changing picture.

Hutton's riposte to Darwin – that humans are different from animals, evolving through 'a higher principle of moral selection' – chimes with his attack on the moral failings of the 'cultus of Impressionability'. If Darwinian evolution painted a true picture of the world, that picture was inherently dynamic. The old idea of knowledge, as extolled by Samuel Smiles, was like putting money in the bank: its value would remain stable and continue to grow. But the 'knowledge of a lifetime' of which Whistler spoke was experiential and evolving – it entailed learning how to project your impressions back on to the world, to make them real. Maybe this was what artists had always done – Turner, for example, although not in the way Ruskin saw it: when Turner painted hazy distances, he was registering the imprint of something *out there*, which really existed. Whistler's 'artistic impressions', by contrast, appeared to him to be nothing but incomprehensible confections of paint.

Ruskin and Hutton might feel confident that, as far as the public concerned itself with such matters, they had the God-fearing, church-going public on their side, but by 1878, they were fighting a rearguard action on behalf of the objectivity of God's created universe, unable to acknowledge the speed at which the tide was turning. Across the Channel, as Whistler was certainly aware, the challenge of realizing 'one's own impression as it really is' occupied the most talented artists of the time. In May 1876, Henry James published a review in the *New York Tribune* in which he introduced a new term into English: 'impressionist'. This was his translation of the French word *impressioniste*, a critic's derogatory tag for a group of young artists whose work he had seen at art dealer Paul Durand-Ruel's gallery. The exhibition contained 240 paintings by, among others, Paul Cézanne, Edgar Degas, Claude Monet (the title of whose painting *Impression, Sunrise* had given a largely sceptical press its cue), Berthe Morisot, Camille Pissarro and Pierre-Auguste Renoir.

Les impressionistes initially failed to impress James; they made him 'think better than ever of all the good old rules which decree that beauty is beauty and ugliness ugliness'. Yet their nickname intrigued him. He had long been preoccupied by the relationship between visual art and fiction, making the hero of his early novel *Roderick Hudson* an American sculptor in Rome. By 1878, he was questioning the basis of fictional realism: if characters were defined both by the way they saw the world and by the way others saw them, at what point in this twin perspective could you situate the truth? According to the 'good old rules', impressionism initially struck James as being 'incompatible with the existence of first-rate talent'. Yet, what exactly were the impressions these artists sought to capture? They were 'partisans of unadorned reality', for whom a painting should 'give a vivid impression of how a thing happens to look, at a particular moment'. At the same time, unlike photographers, they aimed to 'send detail to the dogs and concentrate on general expression'. Impressionist paintings, then, contained two kinds of impression: the imprint of 'unadorned reality' and its expressive interpretation. James would explore impressionism's implications for the art of fiction in his later novel, *The Portrait of a Lady*. But, for now, he wondered how on earth a 'British jury of ordinary taxpayers' could make head or tail of the complex questions of aesthetics raised by the Whistler–Ruskin trial.

———

Ruskin's side of the dispute occupied the trial's second day. It was Holker's turn to play, successfully, for laughs, conjuring a picture of the Grosvenor Gallery's female clientele, in which he conflated medievalist pre-Raphaelite soulfulness and the distinctly more of-the-moment cult of aesthetic rapture. 'We would find "nocturnes", "arrangements" and "symphonies" surrounded by groups of artistic ladies – beautiful ladies who endeavour to disguise their attractions in medieval millinery', who fall into ecstasies at paintings with titles like *Moonlight in E Minor* or *Chiaroscuro in Four Flats*. 'Gentlemen,' he turned to the jury,

'you have examined *Nocturne in Blue and Silver: Old Battersea Bridge*....
But what in the world is that structure in the middle? Is that a telescope
or a fire escape?' If Whistler disliked being ridiculed, 'he should not
have subjected himself to it by publicly exhibiting such productions'.
Ruskin was entitled to take him to task: 'If a critic thinks a painting is
a daub, he has a right to say so.'

Burne-Jones was then called on as the lead witness for the defence.
What was his opinion of *Old Battersea Bridge*? Although 'really very
beautiful in colour', it was 'bewildering in its form', a sketch with no
'finish'. As for *Nocturne in Black and Gold*, 'It would be impossible to
call it a serious work of art.' Burne-Jones's testimony, delivered with
quiet authority, was a small masterpiece in backhanded praise and
crafty equivocation, yet he could not conceal his guarded admiration:
Whistler's nocturnes 'look like night – they have a beautiful tone like
night'. William Frith, a Royal Academy stalwart and painter of popular
realist scenes, had far less trouble putting the upstart in his place. Frith
had made a fortune from his panoramas of contemporary life, in which
he gave the public moral parables in paint – a platform at Paddington
Station, packed with incident and different social types, a racecourse
crowd on Derby Day. Asked whether Whistler's nocturnes were works
of art, he huffed, 'I should say not.' What about his colours? 'There is
a beautiful tone of colour in the picture of Old Battersea Bridge,' he
admitted, 'but the colour does not represent any more than you could
get from a piece of wallpaper or silk.'

Had Ruskin been present, he might have spoken up on wallpaper's
behalf. He traced the beginnings of his own aesthetic sensibility, as an
only child allowed few toys, to solitary hours spent musing on every
detail of his surroundings, during which 'the carpet, and what patterns
I could find in bed-covers, dresses, or wall-papers' had been his 'chief
resources'. Frith's notion of what qualified as art would have excluded
most of what was happening in British art schools at this time, where
young men learned drawing and painting, carving and modelling, printing and lettering, not in order to become Royal Academicians but to
earn a living designing textiles, cutlery, ceramics and other industrial
products. It had been to stimulate British industry's competitiveness
vis-à-vis its imperial rivals that Queen Victoria's late husband, Prince
Albert, had sponsored the establishment of new art schools across the
country, as well as public collections like the South Kensington Museum

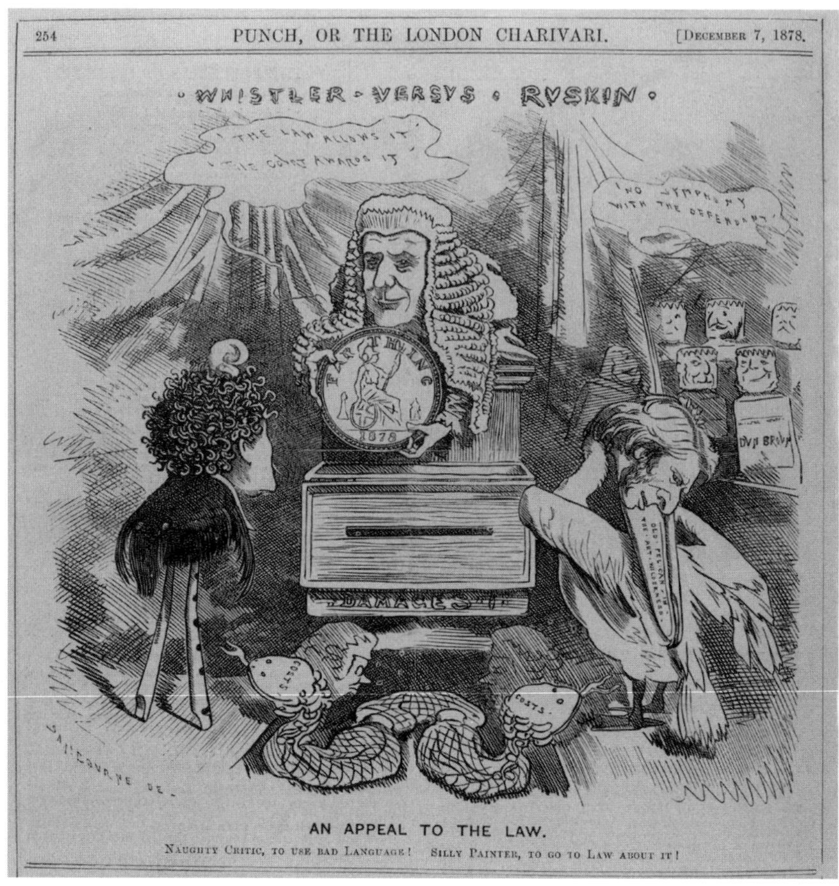

Edward Linley Sambourne, 'Whistler versus Ruskin', *Punch*, 7 December 1878

(now the V&A), where trainee industrial and commercial designers sought inspiration from illuminated manuscripts and medieval stonework – the glories of a lost agrarian world to which Ruskin hoped his Guild of St George would enable British workers to return.

At twenty to three the jury retired to consider their verdict. Huddleston sent them off with a perplexing set of instructions, delivered in a rambling forty-minute speech. Libel, he seemed to say, had been committed – but was it of a serious enough nature to bring to court? At quarter past four, the jury foreman reported that they could not agree. What they had to decide, said the judge, was whether Ruskin's criticism was 'fair and bona fide'. Ten minutes later came the verdict. Whistler had won: in accusing him of 'wilful imposture', Ruskin had gone too far. He had, thought Henry James, 'quite transgresse[d] the decencies of criticism'. It 'gratifies one's sense of justice', he observed, 'to see him brought up as a disorderly character...a general scold'. But instead of the £1,000 damages he'd claimed (about £85,000 today), Whistler was awarded just one farthing, the smallest coin. The *Punch* cartoonist Edward Linley Sambourne drew the courtroom like a scene from Lewis Carroll's *Alice Through the Looking Glass*. Huddleston grips a huge farthing; Whistler and Ruskin – the one with penny-whistle legs, a metaphor for cheapness as well as a pun on his name, the other a sad-faced 'Old Pelican in the Art Wilderness' – cower crestfallen. A two-headed snake, labelled 'Costs', hisses at them both.

The jurymen had spent two days mulling over art in a way they had never done before, peering into 'bewildering' skeins of misty blues and blacks and greys, alive in their depths with vivid points of light. In the end, the trial had not done much to explain the overarching questions – what constituted a genuine 'work of art', how far a critic could legitimately go. Even professional artists like Burne-Jones, Frith and Moore seemed unable to agree on the rules governing their trade or what – since there had been much talk of guineas – represented value for money in that world. Now they could go back to their own modern lives: in *The Times*, there was news of British troops in Afghanistan and pollution levels in the Thames, and a letter about a recent invention called the telephone, meaning 'far sound', as most would remember from their schoolroom Greek. In January that year, at Osborne House on the Isle of Wight, Professor Alexander Graham Bell had placed a device like a miniature cannon on a table in front of Queen Victoria. He showed the monarch how to use his prototype receiver to put through trunk calls to an astonished courtier in London and then another in Southampton. Never before in Britain had the human voice travelled this far, this fast.

In the Westminster streets, the temperature had dropped. It was proper winter, much colder than this time yesterday. The horses' breath steamed. Around Parliament Square, down Whitehall, the gas lamps were being lit. By the river, all along the new Victoria Embankment, a necklace of luminous globes curved through the falling dusk towards Waterloo Bridge and the smoky old city beyond. Mirrored in the tidal water's inky heave and rush, the slippery white impressions left no imprint. They made this familiar scene – the cold, velvety sky, the lights along the shore – look like somewhere else. Like – what *was* that word?

2
Pushed by surroundings

Victoria Embankment, December 1878

Nocturne.

*The twilit Thames as Whistler painted it – drifting greys, midnight
blues, a waterman poling his punt as if sliding straight out of a print by
Hokusai – this species of dark, still London night is on borrowed time. In the
weeks following the libel trial, a team of workmen change half the lamps in
the glass globes along the Victoria Embankment. Out come the gas jets, in go
'Yablochkov candles' – pairs of carbon-rod electrodes that arc across a plaster
block, turning it white-hot. Earlier, on the evening of 12 November, crowds
surged along Regent Street, drawn like moths to the blaze of a single electric
light above a shop,* The Times *reporting that it had made the old gas lamps
look like 'nothing' and yet amazingly had 'no ill effects upon the eyes'. The
Victoria Embankment is the first London street to be lit by electricity from
end to end. Under the hard, even glare, strollers beside the Thames between
Westminster and Waterloo Bridge become natives of a new kind of sharp-
shadowed modern urban night. On many evenings, Walter Sickert, the
eighteen-year-old son of an artist, passes nearby on his way to the Lyceum
Theatre in Wellington Street, where the great tragic actor Henry Irving is
starring in a barnstorming Shakespeare season this Christmas.*

Electricity was the metaphor of the moment – 'electric' was a word
used to describe Irving's stage presence, Ruskin had complained about
'the hasty and electric enlightenment' that characterized the present
day – but in terms of practical technology, it was Paris not London that
was out in front. Through summer and autumn 1878, entire streets
in the French capital were bathed in Yablochkov arc lights for the
Universal Exposition. This vast world's fair was designed to position
France, seven years after humiliating defeat in the Franco-Prussian
War, as the global hub of the electric age. By the time the Exposition

closed in November, it had given some 16 million visitors an opulently packaged preview of how, very soon, it would feel to be modern – to listen to recorded voices on Thomas Edison's phonograph, make ice in Augustin Mouchot's solar-powered refrigerator or perhaps take a short, bumpy ride in a flying machine like Félix du Temple's 40-foot-wide monoplane (the balloon excursions over Paris were spectacular but nothing new). Another highlight was the chance to step inside a 17-foot-high copper female head designed by the sculptor Frédéric-Auguste Bartholdi – the first finished section of a colossal allegorical statue intended as a gift from the citizens of the French Third Republic to the vigorous young republic of the United States. Celebrating the victory of the anti-slavery cause in the American Civil War, *Liberty Enlightening the World* would eventually be installed on an island at the entrance of New York Harbor, complete with a torch of freedom and enlightenment, powered by electricity.

The unlit hall in which a leading intellectual had staked his reputation on his views about a small painting of a firework display already belonged to another world. Sickert had seen *Nocturne in Black and Gold* at the Grosvenor Gallery, where Whistler's paintings had come as 'a revelation' to a teenager trying to decide whether to become an artist himself or follow his gifts as an amateur actor: he felt he had witnessed the painterly 'finger of God'. The work that excited him most, however, wasn't the scene at Cremorne but Whistler's full-length portrait of Irving, svelte and poised against a deep nocturnal background, in costume in the role of Philip II of Spain. If he was stirred by Whistler's artistic impressions, he was starstruck by Irving.

The actor's big break had come in 1871, playing a tormented killer in *The Bells*, a melodrama translated by Leopold Lewis from a French original by the duo Erckmann-Chatrian. His stage charisma gained added frisson from what the Irish playwright and theatre critic George Bernard Shaw called 'glimpses of latent bestial dangerousness'. In December 1878, he took over the management of the Lyceum, where he headlined with Ellen Terry, who at sixteen had been briefly married to the Grosvenor artist George Frederic Watts, as his leading lady. He hired another Irish critic, Bram Stoker, as his personal assistant and business manager; Stoker later achieved fame of his own as the creator of Count Dracula, a fictional vampire modelled on his idolized boss. At the Lyceum, Irving transformed the Victorian stage. He conceived his productions as 'stage pictures', with

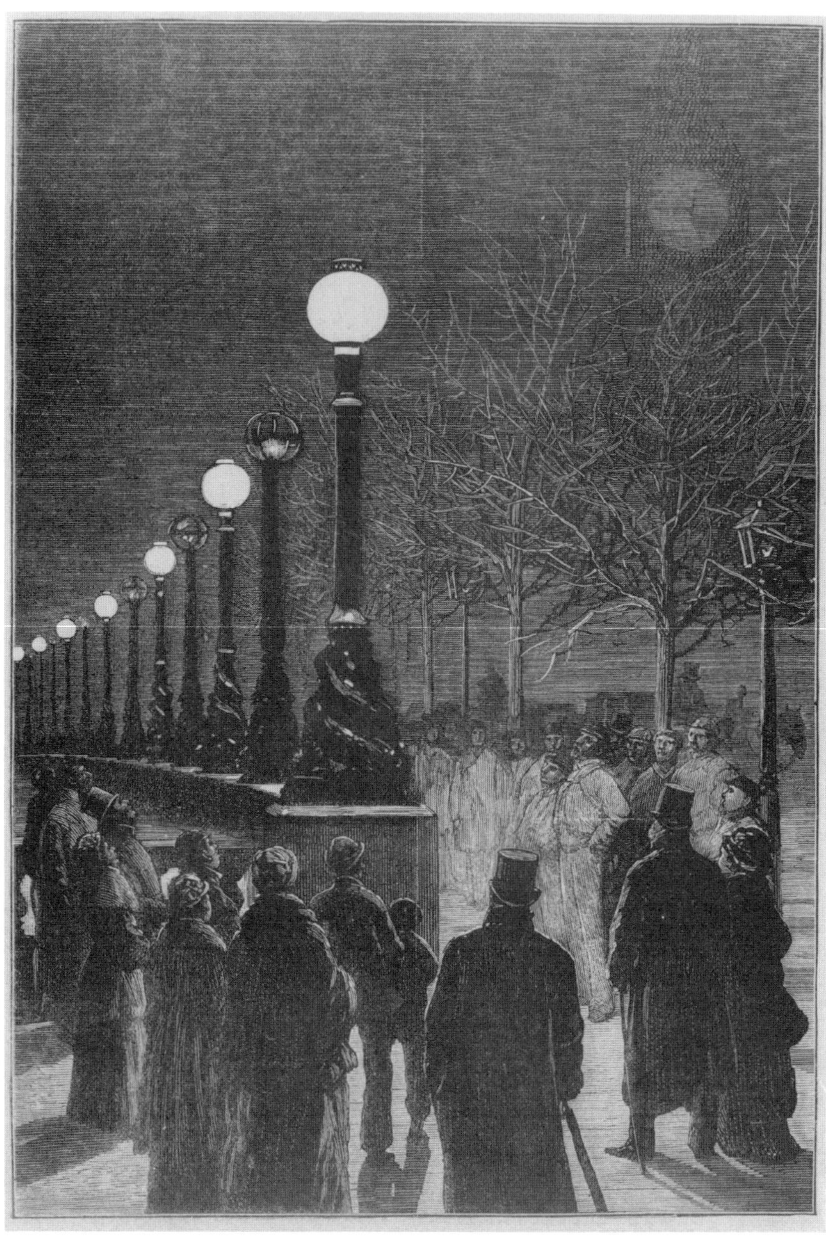

Newly installed 'Yablochkov candles' alternating with gas lamps on the Victoria Embankment, illustration in *The Graphic*, January 1879

specially commissioned music and much subtler lighting effects than London audiences were used to (he introduced the convention of darkening the auditorium before the curtain rose). Sickert hardly missed a night. Early in 1879, he came by an introduction to Irving and was hired as one of the 'Lyceum Young Men', a pool of extras regularly given walk-on parts and, if lucky, the odd line.

Until quite recently, acting had been a generally disreputable profession. Not that this would have deterred Sickert – he didn't have English middle-class expectations to contend with. Both his father, Oswald, and grandfather were artists from the German-speaking south of Denmark. His mother Eleanor, the illegitimate daughter of an Irish dancer and a Cambridge University astronomer, had been sent to school in Dieppe. Oswald Sickert trained in Paris in the 1850s and had fallen under realist painter Gustave Courbet's spell. When their first son, Walter, was born in 1868, Eleanor and Oswald were living in Munich. In the aftermath of the recent Austro-Prussian War, Oswald's native town of Altona had been annexed by Prussia. Concerned that this could make their sons liable to call-up for the Prussian army, the Sickerts emigrated to England (no passports or visas were needed at that time), settling first in Bedford, then London. Oswald continued to practise art, although, as a modestly gifted professional with family responsibilities (the Sickerts eventually had four children), his commitment to realism now went no further than prints commissioned as newspaper illustrations and workmanlike portraits. In English social terms, the Sickerts were hard to place. They were cultured and progressive in their educational views, encouraging their daughter Helena to enrol at Girton, Cambridge University's first college for women, but not well-heeled. Their Notting Hill home became a bohemian oasis in suburban west London, where family friends included Edward Burne-Jones and Oscar Wilde.

Sickert was sharing the stage with Irving and Terry but finding his own career slow to take off. The leading roles he had always enjoyed in amateur theatricals somehow failed to materialize. But there was always art. In October 1881, he signed up as a part-time student at the Slade School of Fine Art in Gower Street, which had opened ten years earlier, funded by a legacy from the same lawyer, Felix Slade, who had endowed Ruskin's professorship at Oxford. Part of University College London, the Slade introduced a new system of teaching, modelled on the way things were done in Parisian ateliers. Tutors were practising artists, who instructed by example rather than academic precept; for the first time in a British educational institution, women students were admitted on equal terms to men. The regime, however, still involved much patient copying of plaster casts and a certain vagueness about what an artist's training was ultimately for. Sickert found the drawing demonstrations provided by Alphonse Legros – one of Whistler's old Parisian *confrères*, appointed Slade Professor in 1876 – 'almost models of how not to do it', devoid of any 'philosophy of procedure' or understanding of 'the closely woven plexus between observation, drawing, composition and colour'. He was soon cutting class.

In the spring of 1879, Sickert bumped into Whistler – another regular at the Lyceum – in a tobacconist's shop. Could he call on him at his Chelsea studio, perhaps? Whistler, never averse to hero worship, agreed. When Sickert turned up at the White House – Whistler's purpose-designed, presidentially named and only recently completed studio-home in Tite Street – the place was almost bare. The libel trial had left him bankrupt; the house was up for sale, and most of his possessions, including his collection of Japanese prints, had gone. When, a couple of years later, Sickert was grumbling about the Slade, Whistler proposed that he should instead come and learn, disciple-style, from him. Early in 1882, Sickert became Whistler's pupil and volunteer studio assistant.

'It's not *what* you paint,' Whistler advised, 'it's *how* you paint.' An artist, as he had tried to explain to judge and jury, should regard the world as so much material from which to select and arrange, like musical notes to a composer (although Whistler himself had a tin ear). There had been a time, however, when he believed in subject matter as well as treatment. In his early days in Paris, he had aligned himself with Courbet and the younger realist painters, like Edouard Manet. He appears, dapper and self-assured, in Henri Fantin-Latour's group portrait of 1864, *Homage to Delacroix*, along with Manet and the poet-critic Charles Baudelaire. After moving to London, however, Whistler had disowned Courbet in characteristically blunt terms: his influence had been 'disgusting', he told Fantin-Latour – 'all that he represented was bad for me'. The flashpoint had been the older artist's infatuation with Whistler's then girlfriend, artist's model Joanna Hiffernan, subject of Whistler's full-length portrait *The White Girl* (1862; later retitled *Symphony in White, No. 1*), whom Courbet painted in 1865–66 as *Jo, the Beautiful Irish Girl* – that and his habit of referring to the touchy young American as his student.

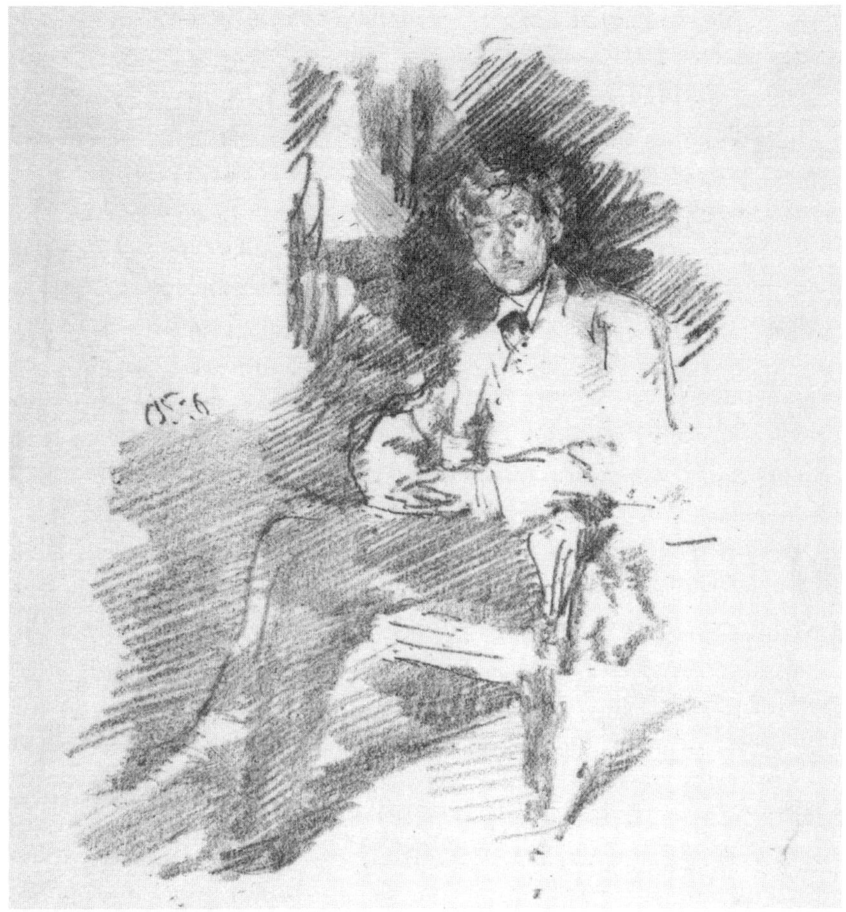

James Abbott McNeill Whistler, *Walter Sickert*, 1895, printed 1903. Transfer lithograph drawn on transfer paper, 27.9 × 20.2 cm (11 × 8 in.)

'Citizen Courbet' was scathing about 'the useless goal of *art for art's sake*'. He himself not only painted and pronounced: he was an activist, who had gone to prison for inciting the destruction of the Vendôme Column, symbol of 'the ideas of war and conquest of a past imperial dynasty', during the Paris Commune of 1871. If, in the 1880s, Whistler and his circle stayed out of politics (though not polemics), it wasn't so much that they were anti-realist as that they had a different take on what was *really* real. In Wilde's 1890 novel *The Picture of Dorian Gray*, the beautiful young Gray becomes ageless, while the painted figure in his portrait grows old. It is a classic parable of aestheticism, in which art becomes *more* real than life – it obeys the laws of time, it tells the truth. In his preface to *Dorian Gray*, Wilde defines the artist as 'the creator of beautiful things'. So far, so uncontentious, but when he goes on to claim, 'They are the elect to whom beautiful things mean only Beauty', the exclusivity of the art-for-art's-sake enterprise becomes clear.

For all his devotion to Whistler and his friendship with Wilde, who holidayed with the Sickerts in Dieppe in 1879, Sickert was more interested in how much, in terms of normal daily life, he could include in a painting than in deciding on the disagreeable or unaesthetic things that would need to be filtered out. Where Whistler loved being watched, Sickert liked watching people, no matter where they were or what they were doing. This was how an actor learned – and an artist too, who, Sickert believed, 'is guided and pushed by his surroundings, very much as an actor is'.

Easy to parody, liable to infuriate their elders, the aesthetes' faith in subjective impressions and the pursuit of beauty as a worthy life choice did find fertile ground in one potentially democratic arena: the modern home. Announcing a mission 'to diffuse beauty' throughout North America, Wilde sailed from Liverpool in December 1881 on what became a year-long tour of the United States and Canada. Crossing the continent, from New York to Cincinnati, to Colorado Springs, to Montreal, he delivered more than 140 lectures on art and literature. To vary the programme, Wilde shuffled a dozen or so titles, such as 'The House Beautiful', 'The Decorative Arts' and 'Dress'. Expounding the beauties of well-chosen wallpaper, door knobs and furniture, as well as Renaissance art and Irish poetry, he appeared at the lectern in 'a black velvet dress coat, knee breeches, silk stockings' and 'a profusion of lace...about his neck and wrists', prompting sniggers and adulation in equal measure. He addressed provincial townsfolk and university students, prison inmates in Nebraska, and Rocky Mountain miners, who, when Wilde had to explain that the sixteenth-century Italian artist Benvenuto Cellini was no longer alive, wanted to know 'Who shot him?' Journalists trailed him everywhere. At twenty-eight, he was indisputably the high-priest of aestheticism, a celebrity with a vocation – and among the first to recognize that while Europe might be the cradle of the Renaissance and all that had followed in art, America was where the audiences, the enthusiasm, the publicity and the money would increasingly be found.

After returning from his lecture tour, Wilde spent the first half of 1883 in Paris; it was here, in April, that Sickert caught up with him at the Hôtel du Quai Voltaire. He had been despatched by Whistler to accompany his 1871 painting *Portrait of the Artist's Mother: Arrangement in Grey and Black No. 1* on its journey to the annual state-sponsored Salon exhibition, where his work was still rated more highly than in London. Whistler also gave his pupil letters of introduction to Manet, his eminent but now rather distant former associate, and Degas, with whom he had maintained a competitive kind of friendship. Sickert had instructions to present each of them with a catalogue of Whistler's prints and to report, should they ask for news, that he was 'amazing'. In the event, Manet, too ill with syphilis to receive Sickert, delegated his brother, Eugène (husband of Berthe Morisot, one of the original impressionists), to show him round the studio.

On the easel was *A Bar at the Folies-Bergère*, a scene from the fashionable but déclassé cabaret theatre that Manet had painted the year before, in which a weary barmaid in a low-cut black dress leans against a counter amid an assortment of bottles – champagne, English Bass beer – and a cut-glass dish of glowing mandarins. Manet had mocked up the bar in his studio and persuaded one of the barmaids, Suzon, to pose. In the painting, she stands with her back to a large mirror, which reflects the crowd in the packed balcony and the venue's new electric globes. In Manet's rendering, their flat, unforgiving light makes her pale face and décolletage look flushed and exposed. Here, for the first time in a great painting, electric light has its unfriendly way with human flesh: not one of history's innumerable paintings of women's faces illuminated by daylight, fire glow or the flame of a candle, oil lamp or gas jet had registered a blush quite so recalcitrant and raw. So deep is the private reverie into which the barmaid slips away, as if by self-protective reflex, that her image in the mirror, turning to serve a top-hatted male customer, acts independently of her abstracted self.

Sickert moved on to Degas in Montmartre. He had admired his pastel drawing *The Curtain Falls* (c. 1880) at a small impressionist show in London. Bright in the footlights, ballerinas take their final curtsey, even as the curtain descends, shutting them from sight. Answering the door with his head bound in a scarf, Degas also claimed to be ill, but he ushered Sickert in and watched while Whistler's self-possessed young emissary took in his apartment, his paintings, his little wax sculptures of horses and dancers under their glass domes. The following day, Sickert called on him again, this time in his studio. It was obvious that, for Degas, *what* an artist painted mattered as much as how they laid on the paint. His pictures of racehorses at full stretch and pirouetting ballerinas, his pastel drawings of naked women crouching in tin baths, vigorously worked in layer on layer of colour, had an intensity and engagement beyond anything the phrase 'artistic impression' might suggest. Degas advised Sickert to go out and about, to observe, to draw, and then to bring this harvested material back to the studio and paint there – not set up his easel, impressionist style, in a field or a railway station like Claude Monet.

Drawing, for Degas, was the key to everything – the line that defines its own movement, like a galloping horse, like a dancer. He drew ballerinas on stage, in the wings, at the barre, eager, patient, exhausted – the intimate moments in the lives of young women whose public existence was pure display. This kind of intimacy was not a quality you would associate with Whistler, for all his sensitivity to atmosphere. In Degas's work, Sickert saw reflected his own attraction to backstage corners, everyday rooms where people were doing nothing extraordinary and yet were being themselves, 'as if you were looking through a keyhole', as Degas put it. But there was a certain haughty rigour and detachment to his gaze: he spoke of showing women 'stripped of their coquetry, in the state of animals cleansing themselves'. Sickert was, by nature, more participant than voyeur, and a London artist, he decided, rather than trying to paint like a Parisian, should 'seek to render on canvas a familiar and striking scene in the midst of the town in which he lives'.

In London's music halls, Sickert found what he was looking for. For some forty years, these theatres had flourished in working-class inner suburbs such as Islington (where the Sickert family now lived) and Camden Town. Often constructed on the sites of former public houses, they provided drink and food in the auditorium, while audiences were entertained with popular songs, comedy acts and magic shows, dancers and acrobats. People came in their work clothes, but the interiors were fitted out in gold and plush like an opera house. Theatregoers walked in off the street to find classical columns and friezes, mirror-lined foyers and swathes of red plush. The headline acts were working-class singers and dancers like Little Dot Hetherington and Minnie Cunningham, with whom Sickert briefly became infatuated, painting her portrait in

Whistleresque full-length on stage at the Tivoli, in the Strand, in 1892. He made her look too tall and thin, she complained. Sickert, in a rare, and perhaps his only, poem, wryly imagined the strain of being in love with an international star. What if she sailed away for a pantomime season in Melbourne? He would miss 'the fairy filigree/Of whirling lace', the 'dancing feet, the limelight's magic gleam'.

Pushing his way into the packed, fusty stalls near the stage, among the tobacco fug and onions, he drew the performers – Vesta Victoria with her mandolin, Dot Hetherington pointing into the limelight, towards the cheap seats in the Gods, 'The boy I love is up in the gallery…'. At Collins' Music Hall in Islington one night, Sickert found himself 'intensely impressed' not only 'by the pictorial beauty of the scene' but also by the way the performer and audience tuned in to each other:

> *A graceful girl leaning forward from the stage, to accentuate the refrain of one of the sentimental ballads so dear to the frequenters of the halls, evoked a spontaneous movement of sympathy and attention in the audience whose sombre tones threw into more brilliant relief the animated movement of the singer, bathed as she was in a ray of green limelight from the centre of the roof, and from below in the yellow radiance of the footlights.*

He understood how the singer felt, projecting her voice and presence into the auditorium, but increasingly it was the audience that held his attention.

Unlike Parisian café-cabarets in paintings by Manet, Degas, Renoir and Toulouse-Lautrec, which take the form of a party-themed demi-monde where social classes freely mix, Sickert's music halls are places where workaday drabness meets gilded fantasy. French artists homed in on individual figures and gestures, like the barmaid and customer in Manet's *A Bar at the Folies-Bergère*; Sickert saw the audience as an organism, alive in its 'spontaneous movement'. Earlier Victorian artists had painted contemporary crowds: William Frith's *The Derby Day* (1856–58) portrays a whole spectrum of social and moral types – the pickpocket, the prostitute, the acrobat family, beggars and toffs – but they are like characters in a novel. Sickert's audiences have a crowd dynamic, almost a sense of class solidarity, as in the uplit faces in *The Old Bedford* (pl. 2), painted about 1895, collectively transfixed by the same out-of-frame moment of stage magic. Partly this is Sickert's ability to put himself in their place, rather than, like Degas, coolly observing or, like Whistler, selecting his impressions on aesthetic grounds. Partly it reflects a social moment: during the 1880s and 1890s, the male franchise was extended to include many of the urban workers in those audiences, with the Independent Labour Party fielding its first parliamentary candidates in the 1895 general election. Where Ruskin's patrician socialism sought to create better conditions and 'higher' aspirations for the 'Workmen and Labourers of Great Britain', Sickert painted his working- and lower-middle-class subjects as if history, in the advance of mass culture and popular democracy, were on their side.

The Old Bedford was not the Folies-Bergère, but Britain could do with a therapeutic dose of impressionist-inspired modernity, Sickert and a group of fellow Francophiles decided. As an ideological antidote to the Royal Academy, and a platform for their own work, they founded the New English Art Club in 1886. They hired an exhibition room in the Egyptian Hall in Piccadilly, provocatively close to the Royal Academy, where relics from the Battle of Waterloo and watercolours by Turner had at one time been displayed but that was now best known as a venue for spiritualist lectures, seances and the long-running magical sketch *Arcana*, an 'ingenious interweaving of refined fun and profound mystery'. The club's first press controversy was provoked by Whistler's friend Théodore Roussel's innocuously titled *The Reading Girl*, painted in 1887. Hetty Pettigrew, a professional model and Roussel's mistress, relaxes naked in a folding chair reading a pamphlet, a silk kimono draped on the chair-back. Her crossed ankles and young breasts are almost direct quotations from Manet's *Olympia*, which had caused such uproar at the Paris Salon of 1865. But where Victorine Meurent in Manet's painting places her left hand decisively across her crotch, Roussel reveals a discreet shadow of pubic hair between Hetty Pettigrew's thighs.

This time, the critics' problem with the painting was not that it was a careless 'daub' but that it depicted, all too deliberately, something that should not be seen in public. It was 'the peak of abomination!' (*The Times*), 'a degradation of art' (*Spectator*), and so on. Even in 1887, female body hair was no secret; it was rumoured to have been the reason that Ruskin, accustomed to thinking of women as having marble pudenda like classical nudes, had been unable to bring himself to have sex with Effie Gray. As so often, journalistic huffing concealed class prejudice. The New English Art Club had an informal open-door policy – any artist could submit two paintings, providing a member put in a word for them, anyone could come to the exhibitions, but pictures of naked female bodies, frankly displayed and privately ogled, were considered to be luxuries, like good cigars, appropriate to the licensed freedoms of bourgeois males. Visible pubic hair was not, like flung paint-pots, an affront to honest working people but might, it was thought, have more the effect of an illicit treat, a kind of free visual alcohol that could lead to all kinds of immoral behaviour and implant the dangerous notion that social conventions could be breached.

For centuries, the human body depicted in art had been, with occasional exceptions, the body idealized. By the 1890s, photographs of actual naked bodies were widely available, often purporting to be artists' aids. In these circumstances, English squeamishness about public nudity was, in Sickert's view, an index of the hypocritical attitudes to art responsible for 'the obscene monster that has been evolved for public exhibition under the name of Nude'. In a suburban music hall one evening, he watched a 'living picture' act, a popular favourite titled 'The Wave'. A young woman in a pink knitted body stocking – 'a somewhat stiff little packet' – posed on the crest of a wooden 'billow': 'The audience, nourished for generations on the Academy...nudes, responded with enthusiasm, convinced that here was Art without what the papers call "vulgarity".' What was shocking in this display, suggested Sickert, was not the hinted nakedness but the ludicrous dishonesty of such coyness. 'Perhaps the chief source of pleasure in the aspect of the nude', he would later reflect, 'is that it is in the nature of a gleam – a gleam of light and warmth and life' – three words that equally apply to his music-hall scenes.

As the 'fast' or 'hasty' age deplored by Ruskin gathered momentum – as the sense of a world governed by movement, change and evolution instilled an altered consciousness of time – the production of 'living pictures' became a diverse and competitive business. Monet in the late 1870s, painting steam trains at the Gare Saint-Lazare in Paris, Degas at the ballet and the racecourse, Sickert catching the 'spontaneous movement' of a music-hall crowd – they were all trying to cast a visual spell over action, in which a picture contained but did not arrest the flow of time. Early cameras could only cope with immobile subjects, allowing impressionism to claim movement for painting. The impressionists, however, were about to lose their artistic monopoly on life in motion. In February 1895, the French brothers Auguste and Louis Lumière patented their cinématographe, a device that could turn photographic film into moving pictures; on 22 March, they gave a private screening of their first film, showing workers leaving the Lumière family's factory in Lyons.

Where the impressionists used myriad dabs and strokes of colour to build a painting that, within a single frame, held the flow of light, air and time, the Lumières (their very name meant 'light') translated this synchronous multiplicity of marks into linear, diachronic form. Ribbons of tiny images spooled in front of an electric light. Magnified by a lens, projected on to a flat, white screen, they left fleeting, rapid-fire retinal impressions in the audience's eyes. Processed by the brain, these thousands of separate, successive pictures coalesced, creating the illusion that the objects photographed (people, boats, horses, trains – subjects straight from the impressionist playbook) were actually moving. In February 1896, the Lumières brought their 'cinema extravaganza' to the Polytechnic Institute in Regent Street. The small audience watched, rapt, as a steam train pulled into a station and longshoremen loaded a barge in juddery black-and-white haste. Realist and then impressionist artists had painted innumerable scenes like these, yet no painting had ever made its viewers ask – as moving pictures did – 'What's going to happen *next?*'

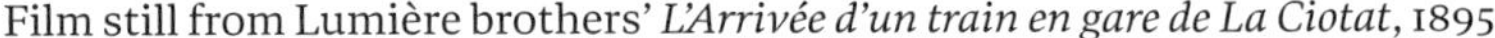

Film still from Lumière brothers' *L'Arrivée d'un train en gare de La Ciotat*, 1895

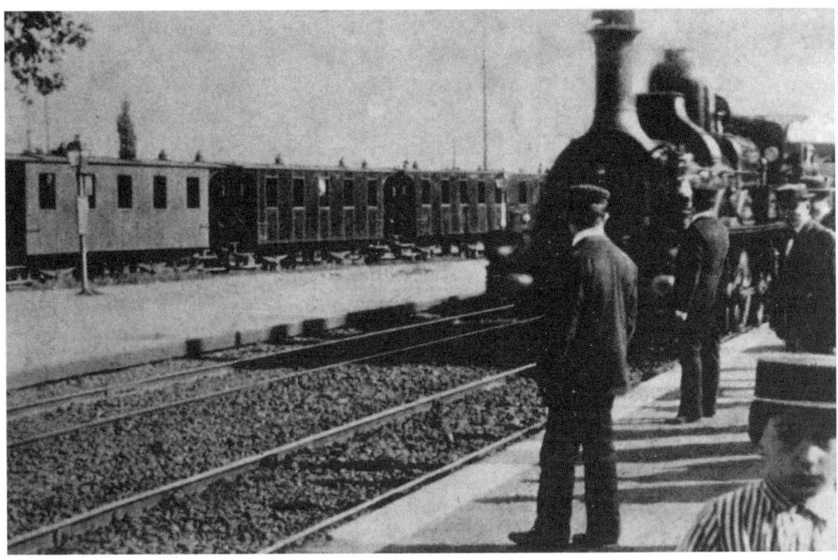

Late in 1895, and again the following year, Sickert went to Venice to paint. His marriage to Ellen and his long friendship with Whistler were both falling apart. He was shaken, although not surprised, by the London scandal of that year, the trial in April of Wilde on charges of 'gross indecency' (legal code for homosexuality), his imprisonment with a sentence of two years' hard labour, the breaking up of his family and home, in which bailiffs acting for the plaintiff, the Marquess of Queensberry, seized even his children's toys. In an effort to secure a regular income, Sickert was attempting, with mixed success, to establish himself as a portrait painter, but, pessimistic about his prospects in England, in the winter of 1898 he moved to Dieppe. He would spend the next seven years painting in France and Italy, exhibiting in Paris and in Munich, the town of his birth.

On returning to live in London in 1905, he found the old music halls being converted into 'picture palaces'. At the Mogul variety theatre in Drury Lane, he climbed up to the gallery for a showing of the ciné-matographe. It was standing room only. Down below, the stage was nothing like he remembered – no limelight or footlights, act drops, thunder runs, sloats, pulleys or flats, no scraping of feet on the boards, no Minnie Cunningham rousing the crowd to sing along to her lovely, smutty refrains. Instead, it was filled with a screen on which a huge head flickered in a wide-brimmed hat – an American cowboy, he understood. Back in his Camden Town studio, following Degas's routine, Sickert reconstructed the scene: the men craning forwards in ashtray-coloured clothes, the glaucous shimmer of the screen, the cowboy's hatted head – the cinema's tantalizing, colourless debut in paint.

3

Kimonos on the Clyde

Glasgow, August 1896

The old Panorama Building on Sauchiehall Street, with its grand domed rotunda like the Albert Hall, has been transformed into the Real Ice Skating Palace. This 'Triumph of the Age!' is equipped with electricity and a stage from which a 'magnificent orchestra' accompanies skaters on the indoor rink. Another innovation is the screen that sometimes fills the proscenium, on which, in May, a Scottish audience had its first sight of the cinématographe. Now, in August, the Skating Palace is hosting a gala evening, including another first, 'The Cinématographe with Local Pictures' – Scottish-made films of life in Scotland. Like the Lumière brothers' recent London extravaganza, these movies cast their black-and-white spell with brisk out-takes from everyday scenes: kilt-swinging Gordon Highlanders march out of Maryhill Barracks, people scurry through familiar Glasgow streets, the pleasure steamer Columba *docks at Rothesay, a seaside resort on the Isle of Bute. The rest of the programme consists of music-hall turns, headlined by 'the Great Modern Wonder', Harz the magician – a veteran of American vaudeville – and the Royal Yokohama Troupe of Jugglers, who perform their feats of knife-juggling and tightrope walking in an exotic flutter of silk tunics and painted parasols.*

———

Although panorama-viewing had had its day, it had been a popular entertainment throughout the nineteenth century. Inside Glasgow's Panorama Building, the German artist Philipp Fleischer's vast painting of the medieval battlefield of Bannockburn, 100 feet in diameter, was installed in such a way that it appeared to have no top or bottom edges, no beginning or end. Its epic scale and in-the-round format were immersive, placing the spectator at the hub of history's wheel. But the picture itself was static: in order to take in every detail, you had to turn your head or stroll around. Cinema worked in the opposite way: the audience sat still while the pictures moved. It was precisely the illusion of actual movement that made cinema both more magical and more modern than anything in Fleischer's panorama or Harz's well-travelled box of tricks.

More than twenty years had passed since the impressionists had realized that, where the visual world was concerned, to fix was to falsify – that movement, or its poetic equivalent, fleetingness, was an integral element in the contemporary reality they brought into their paintings, whether the play of sunlight on a woman's hat or a steam trail unfurling from a train. But not even the impressionists could overcome the fact that paintings inevitably drew you backwards in time, to the brushstroke-by-brushstroke process of their making, which usually displayed evidence of having lasted very much longer than the few minutes it took to appraise the result. The same was true of photography, a medium that, within living memory, had seemed almost supernatural but that was now as routine as pen-and-ink: photographs, like paintings, were pictures of time past, a snapshot immortalization of yesterday's news.

Cinema replaced retrospection with suspense, creating an uncannily lifelike frisson of anticipation – but better than real life, because real-life suspense is often disturbingly beyond control. Cinema framed and tamed it, as the theatre also did, of course, but the artifice and illusionism of the stage, the collaborative activity that led up to the 'what next?' moment – all this was part of the complex texture of the magic experienced by the audience, in a way that the wide, blank cinema screen was not. Because its ticking cascades of images were fused into a simulacrum of continuous motion in the audience's own brains, cinema's artifice was invisible. Unknowingly complicit, people forgot they were looking at art. They did not have to belong to a Whistlerian or Wildean beauty-loving elite to savour everything film could offer to the full, but nor were they participants, whose 'spontaneous movement of sympathy' became part of the performance itself, like the crowd at the Old Bedford. On the screen in the Skating Palace, Glaswegians watched people very like themselves silently puttering around in places they knew well. The absence of colour and sound, the staccato visual rhythm imposed by the passage of film through a machine – none of this spoiled the thrill of being as good as actually there, as the *Columba* backed away from Rothesay Pier and steamed into the Firth of Clyde.

Through these same waters every year passed thousands of ships, carrying millions of tons of cargo into and out of the Glasgow docks. In the 1890s, it is estimated that the shipyards along the River Clyde, between Helensburgh and Greenock, built half of the world's new shipping. If London was the British Empire's symbolic centre – its great administrative hub and trading floor – nineteenth-century Glasgow was the acknowledged 'second city of the Empire', with its own networks of international trade and cultural exchange. In the 1890s, some of the strongest of these links were with Japan. Scottish entrepreneurs had been quickly on the scene when, after a centuries-long policy of isolation from the West, Japan began to open up to trade. During the power struggle that led to civil war in 1868–69 and the restoration of imperial rule under Emperor Meiji, the Fraserburgh-born merchant Thomas Blake Glover, nicknamed the 'Scottish samurai', supplied ships, arms and ammunition, ultimately aligning himself with the victorious pro-Western faction. He established Japan's first industrial coal mine and encouraged modern-minded young samurai to study in Britain. With his airy residence, Lone Pine Tree, above Nagasaki harbour and his young Japanese consort, Tsuru Awajiya, Glover became a legendary figure in the East-meets-West mythology of the time, in which, although Awajiya was never a geisha, they were rumoured to have inspired Giacomo Puccini's 1904 opera *Madama Butterfly*.

Over the coming decades, Glasgow supplied much of the infrastructure and expertise for Japan's dizzyingly rapid industrialization. Ships departed the Clyde laden with industrial plant and railway parts; they returned bringing cargoes of pottery, lacquerware, metalwork, kimonos and ukiyo-e woodblock prints, along with high-caste engineering students like Yamao Yozo who would hone their skills in Glasgow's technical schools and shipyards. In a trade exchange of 1878, more than a thousand model specimens of Japanese artefacts arrived in Glasgow. These objects represented the perfection of essentially medieval skills, but to young artists, designers and architects, their newness appeared mysteriously modern. In 1884, the sixteen-year-old Charles Rennie Mackintosh became an articled pupil of John Hutchinson, a local architect. He had already started attending classes at Glasgow School of Art, next door to the Real Ice Skating Palace. In the family home in Dennistoun, a working-class suburb of east Glasgow, he pinned Japanese prints around his bed – a teenage statement that said 'art', 'new', and something else: 'simplicity'. Exactly what simplicity meant was hard to define, but this notion provided a connecting thread between art and the kind of life, different from that of previous generations, you might dream of leading one day. In the entire cultural production of nineteenth-century Britain – the paintings and buildings, the railway stations and public monuments – there was almost nothing to which the adjective 'simple' could be applied. In fact, you would have to return to the brutal dawn of the Stone Age to find simple objects of British manufacture. To conjure the spirit of simplicity in positive, modern, even – paradoxically – sophisticated terms, it was necessary to turn to Japan.

In 1882, the Glasgow-born designer Christopher Dresser published *Japan: Its Architecture, Art, and Art Manufactures*, the outcome of four months spent travelling the country in 1876–77 as a representative of the South Kensington Museum. Everywhere he looked in his 2,000-mile journey – in buildings, objects and attitudes to life – Dresser had encountered what he called 'simplicity'. His book is a lexicon of 'simple construction', 'simple purpose', 'simple character', 'simple form' and 'simple means': the word 'simple' occurs sixty-two times, 'simplicity' seventeen. Dresser also observed that in Japan there seemed to be no separation between different aspects of the visual environment. There was no special category of 'art', removed from a more general appreciation of 'simple' beauty. He invited his readers to picture the typical middle-class British home – a ridiculous spectacle in which art, in the form of framed pictures on the walls, was besieged by a jumble of 'incongruous and meretricious' objects – 'The vases on the chimney-piece, the epergne on the table, the nick-nacks in the cabinets.' Britain might be a world power, but in the art of living, Dresser was convinced, it had lessons to learn from the Japanese, who 'know the value of simplicity'.

In Western terms, simplicity was defined by what it was *not*. It was the absolute inverse of clutter – the twiddly medievalism and richly layered confections of historical and cultural allusion that had invaded British public spaces and homes in the past half-century. Simplicity meant replacing all this stuff with fewer, less ornamental things, and spaces that did not need to be filled with any things at all. This was not quite what its closest Japanese equivalent, the hard-to-translate concept of *wabi*, connoted: 'simple, austere natural beauty', 'quiet simplicity' – an aesthetic that expressed Zen Buddhist spiritual values in the context, especially, of the tea ceremony. In his admiration of all things Japanese,

Dresser was projecting as much as discovering 'the value of simplicity'. 'Simple', in common usage, also meant naive or backward: Dresser's characterization of the Japanese as 'simple and humorous people', who had 'a simplicity about their manners which has all the frankness of infancy', is shadowed by the old colonialist fantasy of the noble savage. And what value did the Japanese themselves place on simplicity in everyday life? Films of 'picturesque Japan' shot by Western cameramen around the time of the Russo-Japanese War of 1904–5 show a country readily adopting Western technology and dress, in which traditional events like religious processions appear as motley and arcane as any piece of Victorian pageantry.

The challenge for a Western designer was how to appropriate a simple style without loss of sophistication, without becoming a simpleton. Dresser's descriptions combine an ethical idea of purity with aesthetic qualities of clarity and brightness. He evokes the scene one afternoon outside a temple:

> *It is five o'clock; the rays of the sun pass brightly through the trees, and tip the distant hills with glory. The air is balmy and soft, and the sky is blue and bright. We soon reach a gateway; simple yet beautiful, formed of pure clean pine-wood and raised on two steps.*

Imagine a world, he seems to be saying, where objects and buildings do not obscure and obstruct but let you 'pass brightly through'. The two steps to the 'simple yet beautiful' gateway are there for anyone to ascend. The conjunction is 'yet', not 'and': his readers might still think of architectural beauty as something requiring a kind of ornamental fanfare. The Japanese gateway, like the natural beauty of which Ruskin wrote, is associated with atmospheric brightness and translucency. This kind of beauty, to do with opening your eyes and living in the moment, is – unlike the Whistlerian kind – democratic in essence.

The Western dream of a return to a 'simple yet beautiful' way of life went back to the utopian pastorals of ancient Greece and Rome, although the social and environmental ills that attended industrialization had given it the new urgency voiced not only by Ruskin but also by William Morris, writer, designer and leading spirit of the late nineteenth-century arts and crafts movement. From 1861, when he founded the decorating company Morris, Marshall, Faulkner & Co., Morris had sought through

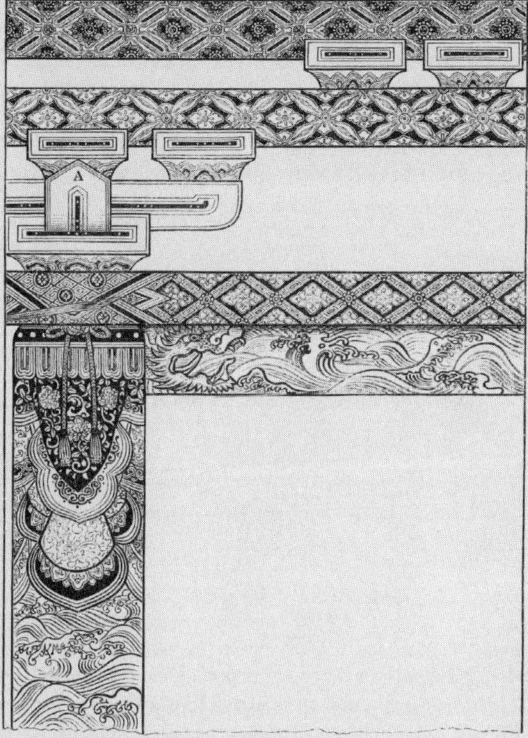

'Column and tie-beams' from Christopher Dresser's *Japan: Its Architecture, Art, and Art Manufactures*, 1882

various initiatives to bring the beauty of hand-crafted objects and furnishings into the industrial-era home, particularly, as his socialism became more radical in middle age, the worker's home. Whereas Morris had focused on the virtue of making – the traditional skills of the weaver or woodcarver – Dresser was more interested in the visual ensemble: the view as well as the portal. Morris, like Ruskin, whose writings had revealed to him 'a new road on which the world should travel', had turned his idealizing gaze towards medieval England. Dresser looked east: present-day Japan was, in fact, a unique case in the West's long search for 'simple' cultures on which to remodel its own. India, China and the kingdoms of South-East Asia had all to a greater or lesser extent been subject to Western military and political intervention, if not formal colonial rule. But not Japan. Here was an imperial state whose culture and institutions were magnificently Other yet remained unconquered. This was part of the reason why artists like Whistler, who were determined to prove their superiority in difference from traditional academic art, felt such a strong affinity with Japan.

From the revelatory first outings of Japanese art and cultural artefacts in Europe, initially in small curiosity shops and then larger outlets like La Porte Chinoise in Paris, japonisme became chic. With projects like the Peacock Room, the cosmopolitan Whistler positioned himself as London's go-to japoniste, signing his paintings and prints with a butterfly monogram. This kind of japonisme, which had an eye to surface motifs rather than underlying structures, often barely went beyond the skin-deep appropriation of a style or manner. It happily coexisted with the eclectic opulence and music-hall plush at either end of the Victorian social scale. Like many other 'oriental' commodities, the Royal Yokohama Troupe, who pulled crowds on both sides of the Atlantic, belied their name: they were in fact a yellowface ensemble from Edwin Bale's lucrative British-born stable of circus acts. The relationship of Glasgow, whose resident Japanese population was second only to London's in Britain, to the real Japan went far beyond the modish affectation of japoniste fantasy.

Although the much-travelled Whistler never made the journey, several of his contemporaries felt the need for direct experience of Japan. They included Walter Sickert's fellow pupil–assistant Mortimer Menpes, who in 1896 went to gather ideas for a house in Chelsea he was planning to build, and, in 1893, two young Glasgow artists, Edward

Atkinson Hornel and George Henry, both followers of Whistler. On his return eighteen months later, Hornel immediately painted *Geisha Girls*, an impressionistic bouquet of kimonos, fans and beehive hairdos resembling a Japanese-themed party at a Renoir café-cabaret. It is bright and painterly in a now-familiar Parisian way, but it lacks that elusive modern quality: simplicity.

The poster for the exhibition at which Hornel showed *Geisha Girls*, on the other hand, was a model of clean, pure linearity, simple to the point of austerity yet lyrical, too. It made Hornel's impressionist-inspired attempt to notate atmosphere and movement look yesterdayish, overdone. Three students from Glasgow School of Art – Margaret and Frances Macdonald, and James Herbert McNair – had collaborated on the design, as they had already been doing on projects such as clocks, chairs and other domestic objects. The single symmetrical figure of a standing woman, her stylized hair flaring to each side like the canopy of an elegant tree, her oval face a mask with downcast eyes, suggesting both innocence and world-weariness, was not the sociable kind of female beauty that the impressionists – Renoir certainly, and even the more disciplined Degas – had painted.

The young Scottish designers were soon joined by their Glasgow School of Art contemporary Mackintosh, becoming known as The Four. In 1896, Mackintosh drew Margaret Macdonald, with her hair up, geisha-style, dressed in a kimono and standing tall – a woman of the linear, soulful but independent kind. The upper half of the image is a portrait, simple in the Japanese sense, in which drawn contours feel as if they have been incised with a sharp blade in wood; the lower half is an airy cage of lines – Mackintosh called his design *Part Seen, Part Imagined*. When Catherine Cranston, proprietor of a chain of fashionable tea rooms, invited Macdonald and Mackintosh to decorate her Buchanan Street premises – the idea being to introduce a modish note of Japanese ceremonial into bourgeois Glasgow social life – Mackintosh proposed a mural based on the picture of Macdonald. The Four shared a belief in the kind of approach to making that Dresser admired in Japanese culture – a seamless continuity between all the elements that went into creating an inhabited space, including the colour of the walls and the size of the windows, as well as the qualities of individual objects. Japanese-inspired simplification changed the nature of boundaries: walls and picture frames would no longer serve as the four sides of a treasure chest but as the defining edges of a space – more cinema screen than stage set, in effect.

At the age of twenty-five and a draughtsman with the leading Glasgow architectural practice of Honeyman and Keppie – an up-and-coming starched-collar professional – Mackintosh had himself photographed wearing the slouch jacket and floppy silk necktie of a *fin de siècle* bohemian. Why shouldn't he be both architect and artist? Three years later, in 1896, Honeyman and Keppie worked up a submission for a competition to design a new building for Glasgow School of Art on Renfrew Street, on a site previously occupied by the offices of the Real Ice Skating Palace Ltd. Mackintosh, still a junior member of the team, was responsible for much of the entry. He adapted ideas from drawings he had made of castles in the Scottish baronial style – massive, unornamented walls, corner towers and small rectangular windows, like postage stamps on a sheet of grey paper – but not in the historicist spirit in which Victorian architects had typically worked. The point of the strong, plain exterior was less to make a stylistic statement than to frame the spaces inside. Mackintosh conceived the art school's library and the studios not as containers to fill with things but as places in which to make or read or think, or perhaps 'simply' be.

Mackintosh befriended a German architect and diplomat, Hermann Muthesius, who had spent three years in Japan. The wooden Evangelical church he had designed in Tokyo was, naturally enough, in gothic revival style, but he had had plenty of opportunity to observe Japanese architectural methods and principles in action. It is likely that, for Mackintosh's benefit, Muthesius was able to put a practical gloss on the numerous descriptions of these things that had been published in the West. When Macdonald and Mackintosh married in August 1900, he gave them two *surimono* prints as a wedding gift. These fine woodblock prints, carved with poetic texts as well as images, were, Mackintosh enthused, 'among the most valuable things we possess'.

Miss Cranston's tea rooms were doing well. In the context of teetotal Presbyterianism, they offered a popular alternative to the public house, specifically a social space outside the home where educated middle-class women could meet. Japan again provided inspiration, in the form of the tea ceremony described by Dresser and other travellers, at which discussions about philosophy or poetry took place in a wooden hut floored with bamboo matting, with ceramic cups and utensils crafted to

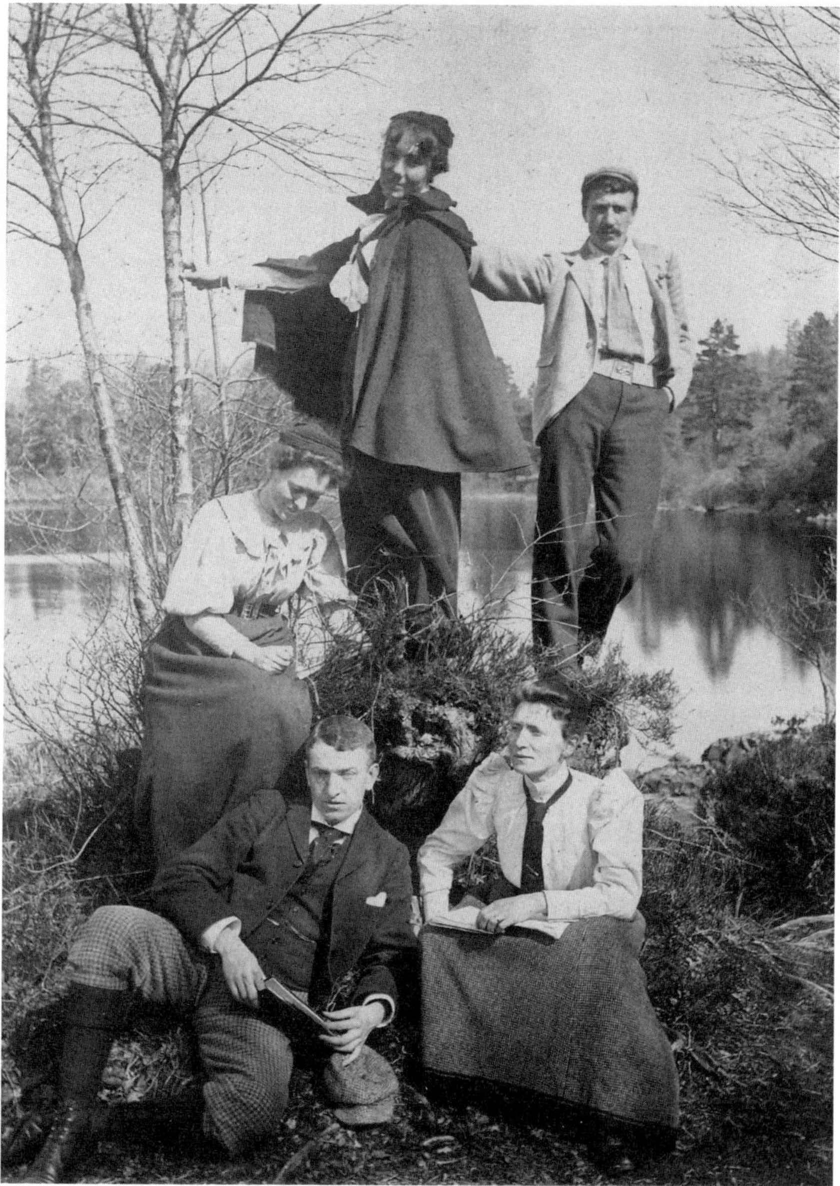

Margaret Macdonald (top) with (clockwise) Charles Rennie Mackintosh,
Jessie Keppie, James Herbert McNair and Frances Macdonald, *c.* 1890

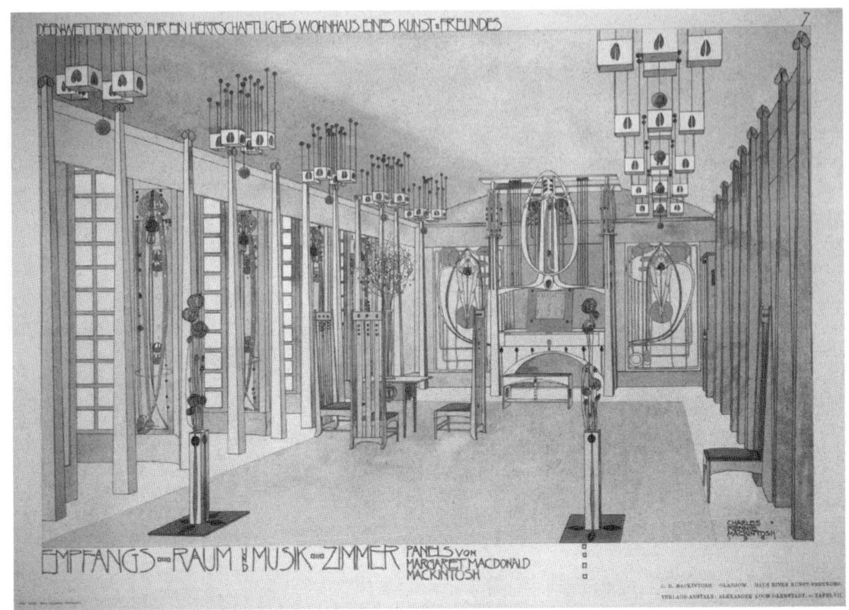

Margaret Macdonald, decorative panels in House for an Art Lover, competition design produced in collaboration with Charles Rennie Mackintosh, 1901

reflect the *wabi* aesthetic of 'quiet simplicity'. After their work on her tea rooms in Ingram Street and Buchanan Street, Cranston commissioned Mackintosh and Macdonald to design an entire building in Sauchiehall Street – the Willow Tea Rooms. Here, they introduced features such as white plaster panels articulated by a wooden grid that resembled the criss-cross frames of Japanese paper screens. In the eighteenth and nineteenth centuries, Western artists and poets who extolled the 'simple life' were invariably thinking of a rural idyll. For Mackintosh and Macdonald, by contrast, simplicity was entirely compatible with the modern city, in which, as German literary critic and philosopher Walter Benjamin would put it, in the context of early nineteenth-century Paris, 'The street becomes the room and the room becomes the street.' Customers in the Willow Tea Rooms joked about the 'spooky' black-and-white decor but felt thoroughly contemporary eating their cake.

Mackintosh and Macdonald turned their Glasgow home at 120 Mains Street into another total environment. In a standard tenement apartment, they painted the walls dove grey and white, divided horizontally by the rail at window height, with muslin curtains to diffuse the light. On a white table in the middle of the drawing room floor they placed a single round vase containing an arrangement of bare twigs with a scatter of pale blossom – an authentic *wabi* note. For them, as for Morris, the arena in which art touched life most vividly was the home. 'Have nothing in your houses', he had famously prescribed, 'that you do not know to be useful or believe to be beautiful.' These useful, beautiful yet somehow inevitably unaffordable objects would have to be individually produced by a craftsman (almost always a man). The difference now, at the turn of the century, was that, through the spare linearity and crisply defined shapes employed by artist-designers like Macdonald and Mackintosh, useful beauty of a simplified modern kind potentially found a more viable fit than ever before with industrial production. In future, you would not have to be or employ an artist to make your surroundings *artistic* or to express yourself through aesthetic choices. In its practical application in domestic product design, simplicity would open a new chapter in the relationship between art and its public.

In 1900, an invitation came to Mackintosh and 'Mr' Macdonald to show in the eighth Secession exhibition in Vienna. This group of artists and designers was the Austrian incarnation of a Europe-wide movement that had emerged in the 1880s, known in Germany as Jugendstil, in Italy as Stile Liberty (named for the London department store) and in Barcelona as Modernisme català. But the term most widely recognized, especially after the Paris Universal Exposition of 1900, where the new style set the tone, was Art Nouveau – 'New Art'. Its defining features – seen in building facades and teapots, haute couture and cheap costume jewelry – were sinuous lines enclosing clearly defined shapes, with a top note of erotic reverie, in which the curves and motions of young female bodies and growing plants echoed each other in a kind of mutual visual ventriloquism. In the form of consumer goods and consumer spaces, like the new Parisian department stores, Art Nouveau proved that industry need not always be – as Ruskin and Morris had believed – art's nemesis: the modern city and its commercial products could be both industrially manufactured *and* beautiful. While Mackintosh and Macdonald's designs were generally one-off creations, not intended for industrial production, they belonged to a moment when Art Nouveau was changing the public realm. In Paris, architect and designer Hector Guimard designed entrances for the Métro – curving stalk-and-tendril, seed-and-flower forms in cast iron and glass. In the wake of the 1888 World's Fair, central Barcelona had been transformed by the swelling roofs and curving bay windows, punctuated by fairy-tale gothic features. If the female figure in *Part Seen, Part Imagined* suggests the japoniste dream of a kimono-wearing geisha, she is also a poster-girl for Art Nouveau, whose air of romantic abstraction is slimly contoured, brisk and modern.

After a delay of several years, in 1906 funding at last became available to complete the west wing of Glasgow School of Art according to Mackintosh's designs. For the library interior he employed a version of Japanese post-and-lintel wood-frame construction of the kind that Dresser had observed – 'simple yet beautiful, formed of pure clean pine-wood' – and Muthesius described in functional detail. Mackintosh's direct quotation from ancient Japanese temple architecture struck a paradoxical note of Art Nouveau modernity in its minimal, anti-gravitational framing of space. His wider contribution to Glasgow's urban fabric, rivalling the Art Nouveau ensembles of Barcelona and Budapest, supported the city's claim at the turn of the century to be more forward-looking than London. In 1902, *The Times* had declared Glasgow to be 'more responsible than any other town or city in the UK for the spread of various forms of municipal progress'.

The nature of art's potential contribution to the cause of social progress was a question that had preoccupied Ruskin and Morris. Their loathing for industrial capitalism went far beyond aesthetics: the ugliness of industry, for them, directly expressed the way it degraded the worker. Lecturing at Oxford in November 1883 on 'Art under Plutocracy', with Ruskin as chair, Morris declared that,

> *the chief accusation I have to bring against the modern state of society is that it is founded on the art-lacking or unhappy labour of the greater part of men; and all that external degradation of the face of the country of which I have spoken is hateful to me not only because it is a cause of unhappiness to some few of us who still love art, but also and chiefly because it is a token of the unhappy life forced on the great mass of the population by the system of competitive commerce.*

In January 1883, he had joined the revolutionary Democratic Federation and turned his energies to radical socialist activism. This led to regular confrontations with the police (on one occasion he was charged with assaulting a policeman) and being placed under surveillance. In April 1887, Morris was in Northumberland, addressing a six-thousand-strong crowd of striking miners; on 13 November, he participated in 'bloody Sunday', a mass protest in Trafalgar Square against political oppression in Ireland in which violent clashes with police and soldiers resulted in four hundred arrests.

It was Morris's earlier, gentler utopianism, rather than his adoption of direct political action, that inspired urban planner Ebenezer Howard to conceive a scheme for building a new type of settlement in which the advantages of industrial modernity could be effectively combined with the benefits of rural life. Imagine, Morris had mused in 1874, that 'people lived in little communities among gardens and green fields', with few possessions but time to study 'the (difficult) arts of enjoying life'. In *To-morrow: A Peaceful Path to Real Reform*, published in 1898 and reprinted in 1902 as *Garden Cities of To-morrow*, Howard made his case for what he called the 'town-country' or 'garden city'. The logic of capitalism, which was responsible for the concentration of low-paid workers and their families in slums, had deformed society itself. Almost everyone, he claimed, agreed 'that it is deeply to be deplored that the people should continue to stream into the already overcrowded cities, and should thus further deplete the country districts'.

Howard presented his concept in the form of a geometric diagram of 'The Three Magnets': 'The People' are surrounded by three horse-shoe magnets – 'Town', 'Country' and 'Town-Country'. Both 'Town' and 'Country' had fundamental pros and cons: 'Closing out of nature' in Town was balanced by 'Social opportunity'; 'Beauty of nature' in Country was offset by 'Long-hours-low-wages'. Town-Country combined the best in both. Here, 'Pure air and water' could be enjoyed alongside 'High wages' and other benefits of industrially generated prosperity. According to Howard, a population of 32,000 could be housed in a city of 1,000 acres, set in 5,000 acres of countryside, including allotments, brickfields, asylums for the blind and deaf, and a 'farm for epileptics'. The city would be circular in plan, built in alternating rings of housing and boulevards around a central park, with a local railway running around its outer periphery, linked to the main line. Rent control, pension provision and investment in community services were all part of the scheme. The steps needed to make this ideal but apparently achievable future a reality were illustrated by mandala-like patterns.

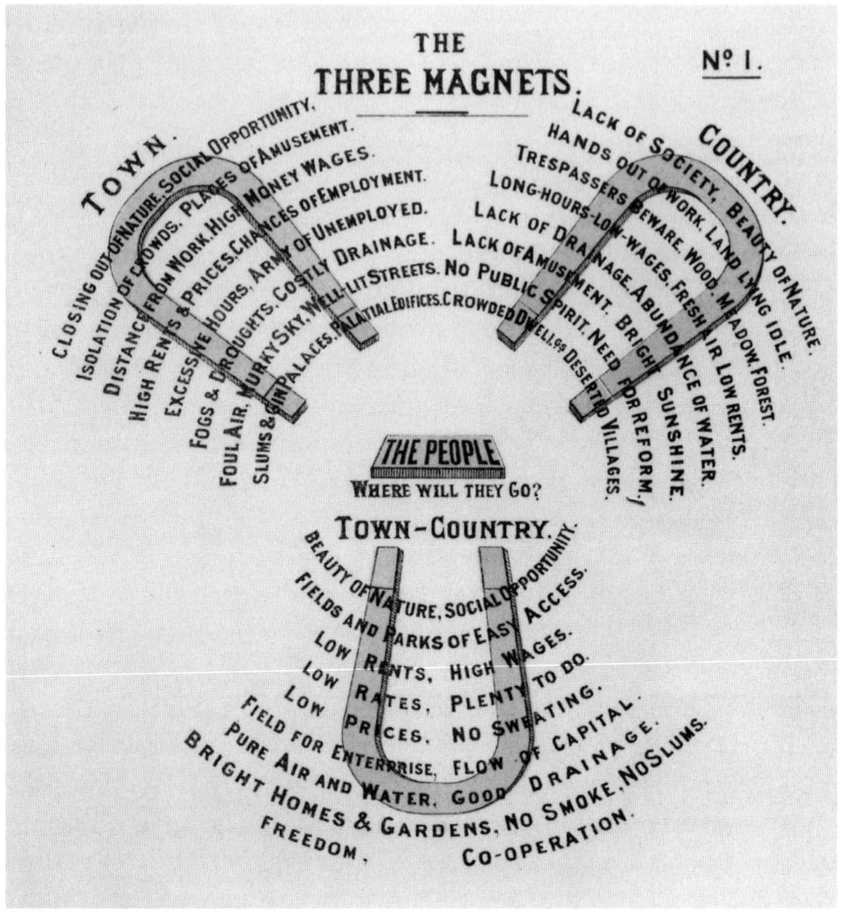

Ebenezer Howard, 'The Three Magnets', *Garden Cities of To-morrow*, 1902

The first of the new towns on Howard's model to be constructed was Letchworth in Hertfordshire. The competition held in 1903 to design this ambitious project on a 4,000-acre site was won by the architectural partnership of Raymond Unwin and Barry Parker. In 1901, Parker and Unwin had published their own vision, *The Art of Building a Home*, offering both theory and templates for the different kinds of buildings that garden cities required. In his chapter 'Art and Simplicity', Unwin described 'looking over some Japanese coloured prints'. Like others before him, he had been 'much impressed by the extreme simplicity which characterizes the interiors of Japanese houses.... Print after print shows us a room almost bare, the walls in some delicate brown or grey tint, with the wood framing exposed' – very much the Mackintosh–Macdonald look. But a scheme of interior decoration that had, for them, been essentially a personal statement was for Unwin a blueprint for social change. In the garden city of the future, there would be many modest houses in which 'the mere form of a chair, the contour of a mould, the shape of a bracket, a scheme of colour' would have the power to affect its occupants 'in just the same way music does'. Unwin wanted everyone involved in the project – architects, carpenters, plumbers, painters and decorators – to make their music from the same page. Each craftsman and tradesman needed to be 'deeply impressed with the dignity this places on him, and the responsibilities it brings with it'.

Japanese-style simplicity expressed the functional beauty of the home; it also shut the door on bourgeois ornament and clutter, eclectic ostentation and elephantine upholstery, all of which went hand in hand with social injustice. 'If the love of art did really result in making more and more elaborate collections of beautiful things necessary to us,' Unwin proposed, 'then indeed it would be the enemy not alone of simplicity but of liberty also.' The modern room should not be merely somewhere to eat or sit or socialize: it should be 'a place in which to think of other things', a place, in other words, of individual freedom and self-realization. In July 1904, when Letchworth's first new houses were ready to move into, the pioneer residents of the garden city movement had the chance to discover what this might mean.

In the four years since Macdonald and Mackintosh had married and moved into their Mains Street flat, the room – drawing room, tea room, library, studio, whatever function it happened to serve – had become an arena of change. A room's layout, appearance and atmosphere – 'the choice of some delicate brown or grey tint' – could be a personal statement. One effect of this focus on domestic interiors was to bring women's traditional relationship to these spaces to the fore. Even at its most extreme, the Victorian patriarchy had allowed the home – the room – to be the domain of women, although only on condition that all their energies were devoted to looking after other people in it. But rooms of this communal, family kind, devoid of privacy, were not the way forward. If a room was to become 'a place in which to think of other things', what a woman needed, as the novelist Virginia Woolf would categorically insist, was 'a room with a lock on the door'.

4
Shadows in my room

Montparnasse, Paris, 1907

White curtains. Sifting through lace or muslin, the pulse of midsummer – or, just possibly, the bloom of snow. But the posy in a glass of water on the table says a warm day, its colours gathered in. A sign. No one is visible, but this quiet room is inhabited, clearly. Whoever lives here seems to be observing her own life ('her' feels more likely than 'his') from a vantage point not quite inside it, as if to keep the space uncluttered by events. The wicker chair with its spotted cotton cushion – a provisional item of furniture that can move between outdoors and in, under sun or ceiling – looks content to be not sat in. A folded parasol (another note of spring or summer) leans against one arm, next to a blue wrap. Left there, or waiting to be picked up – either way, these objects (the table too, its small drawer shut tight) have arranged themselves with no urgent concern for being useful. Behind the bridal-veil drapes, the hulking outline of a building opposite dissolves. Outside, unseen, a courtyard, a tree.

———

This small painting, *A Corner of the Artist's Room in Paris* (pl. 3), depicts the latest in a series of rooms that began when Gwen John put up at the Hôtel du Mont Blanc in February 1904. Living alone in Paris was her choice. Her attic in the rue du Cherche-Midi in Montparnasse, to which she moved in 1907, was nothing like the rooms in her childhood home in the seaside town of Tenby, on the south coast of Wales. She was eight, her brother Augustus six, when their mother, an amateur artist, died, after what Augustus later imagined to have been 'I fear, a very tearful existence'. Their widowed solicitor father was austere and distant, obsessed by his social status. She and Augustus escaped the loveless propriety of Victoria House by running down to the promenade and swimming out into Carmarthen Bay. Art, too, became their shared refuge. In 1895, aged twenty-two and eager to escape her mother's fate, Gwen made her bid for freedom. Augustus had already left for London and the Slade. He encouraged Gwen to follow him, and persuaded their father to let her go.

The teaching regime developed at the Slade by its second principal, Frederick Brown, and his assistant, the surgeon-turned-artist Henry Tonks, owed more to Parisian studio practice than other British art schools. Students were still required to perfect their skills in drawing plaster casts of classical sculptures, but life drawing was more central to the programme, and – unusual for the time – there was a focus on nurturing students' individual gifts. They quickly learned, however, that Tonks's sensitivity to impressionist light and colour did not imply the slightest scope for vagueness. In the practice of observational drawing, his professional knowledge of anatomy made him an uncompromising master, and drawing was regarded as the foundation stone of art, almost, it could sometimes seem, to the exclusion of painting. At the same time, the experience of art school could be socially extraordinarily liberating. Since the Slade admitted female and male students on the same terms, it offered young women of Gwen John's generation and class a rare glimpse of the real possibility of independence. The idea of living and studying in London, away from the family home, with no thought – yet – of marriage and children would have been all but inconceivable for their mothers.

Beyond art school, however, what lay ahead? How could a female artist make room for herself – literally and figuratively – in a profession whose institutions were run entirely by men and in which the highest accolade was to be hailed as that quintessentially masculine phenomenon, the *genius*? There was, it was true, the well-established role model of the Lady Artist, and even a Society of Lady Artists, whose membership included professional painters, although its genteelly gendered name gave it an air of dilettantism (a Society of Gentlemen Artists would have announced itself as a club for wealthy amateurs). Sickert, for one, was not impressed: reviewing the Society of Lady Artists' 1889 spring show in the Egyptian Hall in Piccadilly, he found it as dull as 'the usual mixed exhibition', with 'the same mass of frames closely packed one above the other, surrounding the same strips of canvas or paper painted by people who ought never to paint'. Not an inspiring prospect.

In London, Gwen and Augustus shared lodgings, where they lived 'like monkeys, on a diet of fruit and nuts'. Before the start of his third

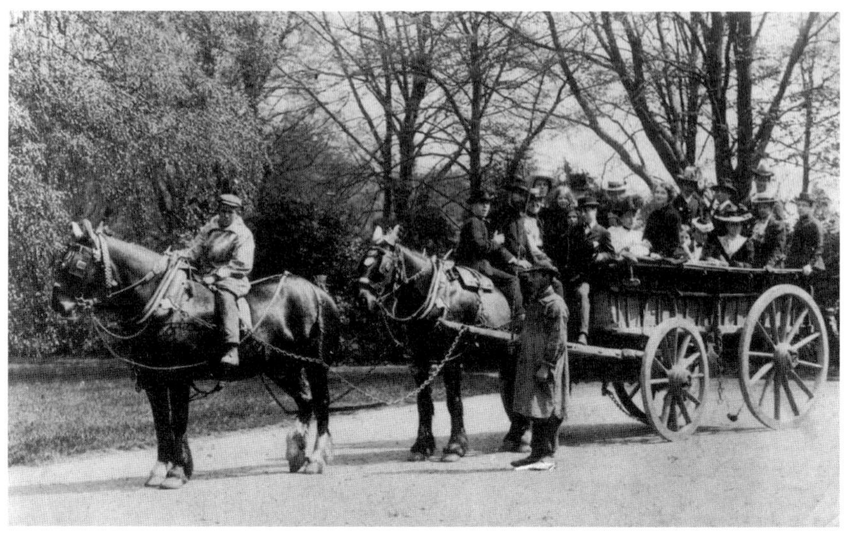

Slade School country picnic, with Augustus John (in beard and hat on first horse) and Gwen John (second to the right of him), 1899

year at the Slade, the shy and studious Augustus received a bad head injury diving into the sea; he returned, months later, a changed man. He had become – no one knew how, but it was strikingly evident in his new extrovert manner and the virtuosic drawings he was now producing – a 'bloody genius'. He won prizes, began to exhibit commercially and to sell, and became a celebrity bohemian. His fame as a polyamorous *homme fatal*, irresistible (or by some accounts doggedly ardent) in beard and felt sombrero, would soon rival his reputation as an artist. A woman might paint, might see her work hung in an art gallery, but there was no equivalent, even in bohemian circles, of the Augustus John phenomenon. After art school, women were neither expected nor encouraged to become professional artists but to retain, in charmingly passive form, their artistic tastes and qualities, which would be deployed in supporting their male artist partners, creating artistic homes and bearing artistic children.

Gwen's first move, after finishing at the Slade in the summer of 1898, was to leave for Paris with her student friends Ida Nettleship and Gwen Salmond. For five months, she attended the Académie Carmen, a private art school opened by Whistler's model Carmen Rossi. Whistler, who had been living in Paris since 1892, gave classes there to a clientele of predominantly female students, many of them American. An erratic teacher, he 'airily picked his way amongst the easels', devoting his attention to favourites, blithely ignoring others. His precepts had not changed much since the libel trial: 'Art is the science of beauty' was still his watchword. He did, however, get pupils working immediately with oil paint on canvas, introducing them into impressionist colour theory and how to organize tones on the palette – a freeing experience in itself after Tonks's exacting drawing classes at the Slade.

There had been English painters who thought in paint – in colour, texture, depth – rather than as draughtsmen. Turner, most obviously, Constable too, and watercolourists like John Sell Cotman handled the material substance of paint as if it *gave* them ideas, as distinct from being a medium for pictures they had already conceived. But English painters' relationship with colour was never quite shot through with the theoretical fire that the work of the French chemist Michel-Eugène Chevreul had injected into the divisionist (or pointillist) experiments of Georges Seurat and, via Seurat, Vincent van Gogh – the belief in the pure agency of colour, as if different tones were like chords in music, each with a unique emotional timbre. Although Whistler had spoken of the artist's vocation in comparable terms at the trial, it was clear that, in giving the verdict against Ruskin, the jury had in no sense endorsed Whistler's view. In Britain in the 1890s, painters were still generally seen as practitioners of a particular set of skills, like surgeons or bricklayers. Whistler might be repeating himself to his acolytes at the Académie Carmen, but he introduced them to a feeling for the stuff of paint and the music of colour that they had not found at the Slade. His old enthusiasm for Japan must also have chimed with Gwen's instinct for keeping things simple, and her intuition, in which she could not have been more different from Augustus, about the need to be still and quiet in order to work. 'We have a very excellent flat,' Nettleship reported from Paris to a friend. 'Gwen John is sitting before a mirror carefully posing herself – She has been at it for half an hour – It is for an "interior".'

On their return to London, Gwen became a recluse, moving between 'dungeon-like' basements in Bloomsbury and Bayswater. She worked slowly, exhibiting little and socializing as seldom as possible. 'I am like a shadow to people', she said, but that was how she wanted it. In March 1903, she showed three small paintings alongside dozens by Augustus at the Carfax Gallery in London, yet he told the well-connected artist William Rothenstein, who had arranged the show for them, that Gwen 'has the honours, or *should* have' – her 'little pictures to me are almost painfully charged with feeling'.

That autumn, she was back in France, for a walking and drawing expedition with another Slade contemporary, Dorelia McNeill. For two women to undertake a long-distance walk through foreign countries was, like going to art school, an expression of independence of a kind that had previously been a male domain. Walking, according to the redoubtable hiker, essayist and editor Sir Leslie Stephen (writing admittedly with 'great men' in mind), was 'favourable to the equable and abundant flow of tranquil and half-conscious meditation' – very much the state of mind Gwen John often spoke of seeking. In 1902, the writer Hilaire Belloc had published *The Path to Rome*, an account of walking through France and Italy in which sightseeing and self-discovery unfold together at a steady andante pace. John and McNeill had a similar plan: they would sail to Bordeaux, then set off east along the Garonne Valley, before turning south for the Alps, Italy and Rome. This trip would be an education in art history: since colour photographs of artworks were not available (they remained a rarity well into the second half of the twentieth century), travel was the only way to experience the great Renaissance fresco cycles and the art treasures in French and Italian collections in full colour.

By November 1903, they had reached Toulouse, where they stayed for the winter and where John painted three portraits of McNeill. In *The Student*, McNeill stands in the corner of a room, between the wall and the edge of a table, on which lie two books. She holds a third, closed, beside her. Her face, with downcast eyes, and her simple white-and-grey plaid dress are lit by a single electric light, which – as in Manet's *A Bar at the Folies-Bergère* – accentuates the atmosphere of introspection: while she poses for John, McNeill is clearly elsewhere. This kind of far-awayness in a sitter infuriated many portraitists, including Whistler, but where John was concerned it was fine. *Not* being available to the artist's gaze was, in fact, the very aspect of McNeill she wanted to paint. Another of the Toulouse portraits, *Dorelia in a Black Dress*, has a Whistleresque japonisme about the standing figure in velvety black, with suave highlights of glossy pink ribbon and white collar at her neck, although this young woman, whose gaze is patient but restless, distrait but stubborn (as if, at moments, she was seeing the brother in the sister's face), looks as if her big, capable hands would swat away Whistler-words like 'arrangement' or 'harmony' should anyone try to label her with them.

John and McNeill gave up on the idea of walking to Rome in February 1904, instead turning back north. 'What a surprise to hear from you in Paris,' Augustus replied to a letter from Gwen that spring. Whistler had died the previous July, but Augustus gave his sister the names of other art world contacts. 'And why not call on Rodin,' he suggested, 'he loves English young ladies.' He asked what she had seen by Gustave Courbet and Théodore Géricault: Paris was still, in Augustus's mind, the city of the last century rather than the new one, where, in October 1903, the inaugural Salon d'Automne had been held in the basement of the Palais des Beaux-Arts. Featuring work by Pierre Bonnard, Albert Marquet and Henri Matisse, and a posthumous tribute to Paul Gauguin, its 'boldness and youthfulness' struck the art collector André Level as 'a revelation': 'I saw canvases there which seemed to me, without the slightest shadow of a doubt, to be the authentic art of our own age, and of the immediate future.' Gwen and Dorelia were more preoccupied by making ends meet; after putting up at the Hôtel du Mont Blanc, they found lodgings nearby in Montparnasse and work as artists' models. 'I trust you are careful to pose only for good young artists,' Augustus advised. Within weeks, McNeill had left, finally turning up in Bruges in Belgium, where she was pursued (successfully) by Augustus, who was now married to Ida Nettleship. Gwen stayed on.

In her London basement days, Gwen had struck friends as worryingly self-marginalized. Paris, she told Augustus, was where she had to be: 'There are people like plants who cannot flourish in the cold, and I want to flourish.' The difference in cultural temperature between the two cities was real enough. Artists in turn-of-the-century London, complained Sickert, were 'citizens...of a country where painting forms no living part of national life' but was 'kept alive, a dim little flickering flame, by tiny groups of devoted fanatics mostly under the age of thirty'. For young artists who attempted to live on sales of their work, 'The national taste either breaks these fanatics, or compels them to toe the line.' In Paris, John found that she could paint alone in her room and at the same time feel part of national life, balancing solitude with a sense of connection in a way that she found impossible in London. She enjoyed the foreigner's privilege of being free to participate but not obliged to belong, and could just about pay her way by modelling for what Sickert would have called Lady Artists. She did not mind being looked at, sitting quietly, staring at the walls or the window, because no response was required. It was less demanding than being the one who did the looking and who then had to decide what to make of what she saw. Sometimes she unbuttoned her blouse and felt the air on her shoulders and breasts while the artist scribbled or dabbed. She wondered whether they would ever like to look at the rest of her, but they never asked. Then, in a sculptor's studio, she was introduced to Auguste Rodin, who did ask.

Rodin, the most eminent sculptor in Europe, had just returned from London, where he had been invited to succeed Whistler as president of the International Society of Sculptors, Painters and Gravers. His election was followed by a commission to create a monument to Whistler, to be sited on the Chelsea Embankment, near the artist's former London homes. Rodin's idea was to sculpt a young woman, representing Whistler's muse, or perhaps the goddess Venus, climbing the 'Mountain of Fame'. Would John pose for this figure? She would be naked to the waist, or completely naked, leaning forwards, her right leg straight, her left leg raised high, her foot planted on the allegorical rock of fame. In the room where she was now living, in the rue Saint-Placide, Rodin visited in the early evenings, after he had finished in the studio. Now in his sixties, he appears to have found that the regular after-work sex with John taxed his legendary powers, or at any rate he began to object that he needed to conserve his energy for work. In any case, she liked her solitude, her things, her tortoiseshell cat Edgar – alter ego and exemplary sitter. 'My room is very neat,' she wrote to Rodin. 'I like it very much in the evening when there are shadows in my room.' And again, 'I like days like these, when I don't talk to other people.'

Someone she did talk to was a young German-speaking poet from Prague, Rainer Maria Rilke. Between September 1905 and May 1906, Rilke was with Rodin much of the time, acting as his personal assistant and tracing a path from besotted hero worship ('his greatness mounts up before one like a tower') to bitter contretemps ('I shall not see you again'). On an earlier visit to Paris in August 1902, to work on a book about Rodin, he had lodged at 11 rue Toullier, off the busy boulevard Saint-Michel near the Sorbonne, where he had been unable to find solitude or quiet. Every night – in his later fictionalization of these unsettled weeks – he was tormented by the cacophonous anti-nocturne of the modern city: 'A door slams. Somewhere a windowpane shatters', while at other moments, 'Electric trolleys speed clattering through my room. Cars drive over me.' These sounds had barely existed when Rilke and John, a year his junior, were children. It was only in 1889 that Parisians had witnessed their first motor car, with German engineer Gottlieb Daimler at the wheel; by 1903, French factories were producing 30,000 cars a year – about half the world's total.

Where John's room in Paris was calm and self-contained, Rilke's was jangling and broken-into, but they shared an understanding of things (*die Dinge*) – how an object, such as a book or a flower or a chair, can radiate a palpable otherness, living a mysterious life that only partly intersects with our own. 'Things,' Rilke advised a young correspondent, 'are not all so comprehensible and utterable as people would mostly have us believe.' For an artist like Rodin, the things he made became his reality: 'he lived in it as in a wood', Rilke told his wife, the German artist Clara Westhoff, 'for what he himself planted has become a tall forest', where

Auguste Rodin, *Gwen John (Study for a Muse)*, probably modelled *c.* 1904. Cast plaster, height 10.2 cm (4⅛ in.)

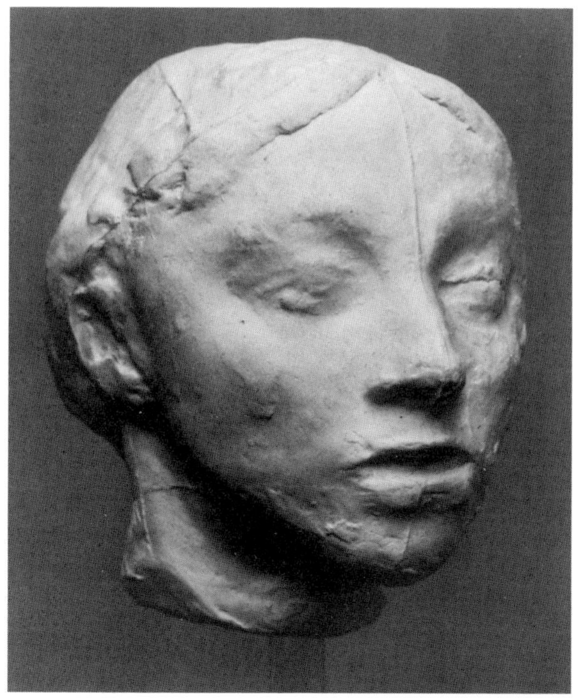

'you can hear the vast murmur and the mighty course of the river that refuses to divide into two branches'. Rilke watched Rodin at work, he talked with John and with Clara. It all convinced him that 'most events are unutterable, consummating themselves in a sphere where word has never trod, and more unutterable than them all are works of art'.

Rodin's personal forest of things largely consisted of sculptures of naked young bodies, both men and women, although he specialized in asking his female models to assume extreme, often frankly erotic poses. Rodin described an especially agile female model as 'utterly primeval, the way people were in prehistoric times.... Look at those slim legs, look at those clever feet. With these she could have climbed and lived in trees.' Rilke tried to explain to Rodin that modern relationships between women and men could be more equal than those about which the old sculptor complained. Rodin saw the woman as 'the snare, the man-trap on those roads which are the loneliest and serenest'; or, in more lyrical mood, he mused that a woman was 'like nourishment for the man, like a drink which courses through him...like wine'. Rilke, a generation younger, saw in Rodin's figure of *Eve* from *The Gates of Hell*, a woman 'leaning forward as if to listen', not to a man but 'to her own body, in which an unknown future begins to stir'. Yet this future was not so unfamiliar (except to the male poet): it consisted in the woman's being drawn 'away from the distractions of life down into the deep, humble service of motherhood'.

This was not a service to which Gwen John felt personally summoned. In the early 1900s, the gap between what she must have felt, as Rodin told her to lift her leg higher or hold still while her back ached, and what Rodin himself saw as he stared at her body, had become a politically charged space. In 1886, the German psychologist Richard von Krafft-Ebing had declared that, for women, 'voluntary subjection to the opposite sex is a physiological phenomenon'; ten years later, the 'New Woman' was seen as having upended this position. New Women, in the sense in which Henry James helped to popularize the phrase, were independent-minded, often with independent careers or financial means, refusing to think, behave or dress in ways traditionally expected of them by men. In cartoons and joke family photos, they smoked and read the newspaper while their menfolk slaved over a washtub or rocked the cradle, as if nothing were more demeaning to male pride than having to care for your child. 'I'm off to the Feminist Congress!'

a bicycle-riding, knickerbocker-wearing *femme nouvelle* admonishes her harassed husband on the cover of the satirical journal *Le Grelot* in April 1896. 'You're going to have dinner ready for eight o'clock sharp, you hear?' In Britain, women were organizing to shape a future of their own, not men's, choosing. In October 1903, a group of women gathered in the middle-class home of Emmeline Pankhurst, in the Manchester suburb of Moss Side, to establish a women-only group to campaign for the right to vote in general elections. Members of the Women's Social and Political Union would do plenty of climbing – on to the steps of government offices and buildings, over railings and fences – but there would be no return to the primeval trees.

In 1911, John painted a self-portrait, *Girl Reading at a Window*, in which she adopted the same pose as for the Whistler monument but this time clothed, like Dorelia, in a long black dress. She stood by the window, one foot Cinderella-style on the spotty cushion of her wicker chair, a book in her hand. The act of reading is the outward sign of an inner life: the book on which her gaze rests is like a door, which will open fully when she finishes or closes it. Rodin was world-famous as a sculptor of sex – of young bodies torqued in ecstatic consciousness of their physicality – but John's kind of intimacy, replete with thought and selfhood ('unutterable', as Rilke might have said) lay outside his range. A couple of years before, she had drawn *Self-portrait, Naked, Sitting on a Bed*, in which she looks down, as if again reading, although whatever she is gazing at, lost in reverie, is hidden behind the bedhead. She brushed gouache colour on to her face and hair – her breasts and sides too, although more faintly – as if her consciousness rested in those parts of her body. Rodin, from whom she had learned to draw with a quick, fluid line and light touches and washes of colour, would have got her to pull her knees up, push them apart, grasp her ankles, arch her back, as if acting the primeval woman in the least intimate space imaginable.

John usually took months to complete a small painting. Almost all her subjects were women. Often, they sit reading or musing, hands folded in their laps, quietly lit against the walls of anonymous rooms – *Girl in a Blue Dress*, *Girl Holding a Book*, *Woman Holding a Rose*, *The Convalescent*, *The Seated Woman* (all *c.* 1910–1920s). The softly mottled walls are not of the fashionable Macintosh–Macdonald kind, crisp and smart, but suggest the nuanced calm and safety John craved. In her notebook, she listed her 'Rules to keep the world away': 'Do not look at people

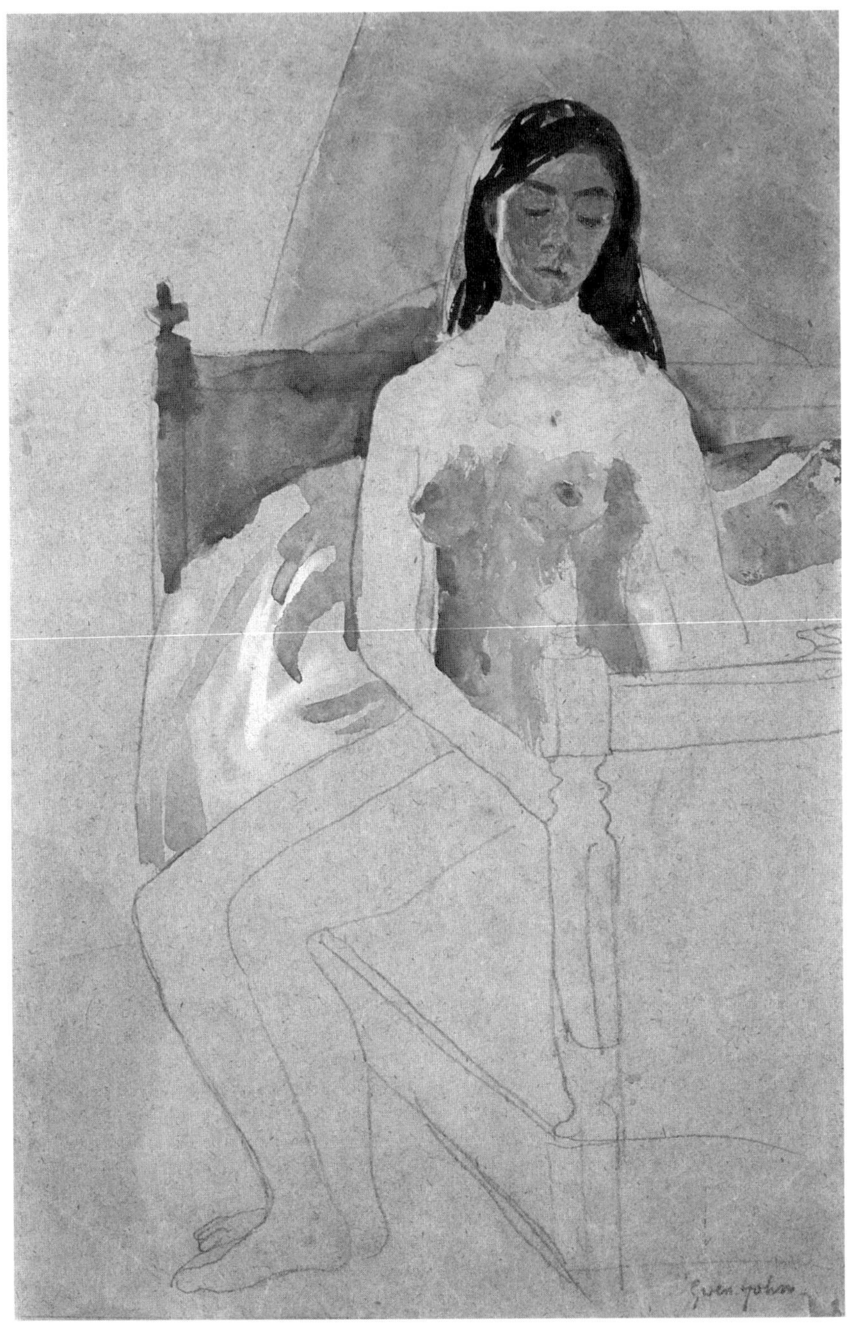

Gwen John, *Self-portrait, Naked, Sitting on a Bed*. Pencil and gouache on paper, probably 1909

(more than is necessary)', 'do not look in shop windows…'. She made almost no effort to get her work shown, although Augustus occasionally pulled strings on her behalf. In 1910, he persuaded one of his own patrons, the New York financial lawyer and Democrat politico John Quinn, to commission a painting from Gwen. In the economic context of the time, Quinn's focus as a collector had a political edge. Among the foreign goods on which the Republican-sponsored Payne–Aldrich Tariff Act of 1909 levied duties were works of art less than twenty years old, which included anything by younger British painters like Gwen John. Quinn's patronage offered John the first chance she'd had to earn anything substantial from her work – but she was not going to be pressurized. 'I am afraid you must wonder why the picture you ordered has not arrived,' she wrote, courteously but unapologetically to Quinn in July. 'I am,' she promised vaguely, 'doing one which will be more agreeable.' 'I don't often get a picture done,' she told a friend around this time; 'that requires, for me, a very long time of a quiet mind, and never to think of exhibitions.' Quinn – convinced and patient – eventually bought *Girl Reading at a Window*.

John's women are often accompanied by reading matter: there is a book on the table and a bookshelf on the wall in *Girl Reading*, books in *The Student*, a letter in *The Convalescent*. The encouragement of girls and young women to read widely and seriously was one of the ways in which enlightened male relatives – usually well-educated middle-class fathers – gave the green light to other thoughts of independence. Art school, university, novel-writing, Paris…. The Victorian literary grandee and proselytizer for creative walking Sir Leslie Stephen believed that his two daughters should nurture intellectual aspirations, although boarding school and university were still reserved for the boys. Vanessa Stephen and her younger sister, Virginia, were homeschooled in the grand townhouse at Hyde Park Gate in London, with its library and literary soirées. From as early as they could remember, Vanessa felt destined to be an artist, Virginia a writer. After their mother Julia died in 1895, Vanessa became the de facto lady of the house, but the following year she managed to enrol at a small private art school nearby, then in 1901, aged twenty-two, she started at the Royal Academy Schools.

The Stephen family occupied a much higher social rung than the Johns of Tenby, but a spell at art school had become an acceptable form of 'finishing' (rather than launching) for young women like Vanessa; it was not expected, when the time came, to get in the way of a suitable marriage. Although this was not perhaps how Leslie Stephen thought of it, art school conveniently framed the admissable aspirations for daughters of the enlightened late nineteenth-century bourgoisie, combining a freedom judiciously bestowed with a woman's traditional role in beautifying the home, not least with her own decorative presence, a task to which an art school training would allow her to add the grace of self-expression. At the Royal Academy Schools, which were considered more respectable and less Frenchified than the Slade, Vanessa received encouragement from the society portraitist John Singer Sargent – like Whistler, an expatriate American and well-travelled Europhile, although of a less theoretical, combative temperament. What rescued her from the weight of social expectation, however, was not training or talent but her father's death in 1904.

Soon afterwards, Vanessa, Virginia and their two brothers left Hyde Park Gate and moved east across London to Bloomsbury, a district of imposing but unfashionable eighteenth-century squares north of the British Museum. This was Slade territory – not quite Montparnasse but more of a *faubourg* than a suburb, and thankfully off the map as far as London high society was concerned. Where Gwen John yearned to 'keep the world at bay', Vanessa Stephen liked the world to come to her drawing room at 46 Gordon Square, in the form of new ideas delivered by highly educated, convention-despising men. Here she founded a salon, the Friday Club, at which Clive Bell, a Cambridge friend of her brother Thoby, held forth on art. He fell for Vanessa and, in 1907, on his second attempt, persuaded her to marry him. The following year, her first child, Julian, was born. Watching him, she became an artist over again, filling sketchbooks, painting *Julian Asleep*. This small, tender picture is evidence enough that art and 'the humble service of motherhood' could, after all, coexist. It also suggests that Bell had absorbed the London version of impressionism, aligning herself with the New English Art Club crowd with whom she had begun to exhibit. Bloomsbury society wasn't quite bohemia, however: it functioned as an alternative power base for a group who rejected the social norms of the ruling class but not the prerogative (which they considered themselves to have inherited or earned) of ruling. In Bloomsbury, the yardstick of talent was not art but brains, and the ability to demonstrate your brainpower in well-informed and witty conversation, which gave a distinctly academic tone to even practical talk about painting. In *Art*, a short book he published in 1913, Bell modestly claimed to present 'a complete theory of visual art...in the light of which the history of art from paleolithic days to the present becomes intelligible'. So much for art's 'unutterable' mysteries.

Bell explained that his theories had been 'tempered and burnished' by conversations with Roger Fry, who had appeared on the Bloomsbury scene in June 1910. Fry had exhibited his paintings with the New English Art Club since 1898 and served on their jury, but he was better known as a writer on art, who had helped to launch the scholarly *Burlington Magazine* and reviewed for *The Nation*. He had a reputation as a charismatic lecturer, whose sonorous voice, according to George Bernard Shaw, held listeners spellbound irrespective of whatever he was saying. Fry came from a distinguished Quaker dynasty, which traced its roots back to seventeenth-century Wiltshire. His father, Sir Edward Fry, was a senior lawyer, appointed Lord Justice of Appeal in 1883, while his millionaire uncle Joseph ran the Bristol-based family business, J. S. Fry & Sons, which produced Fry's Chocolate Cream, Fry's Turkish Delight and other sweetshop staples, employing a workforce of three thousand. Roger Fry had spent much time in Italy and in 1899 published a book on the Venetian Renaissance painter Giovanni Bellini. The artists he wanted to talk about with Vanessa, Clive and Virginia, however, were Paul Cézanne, Paul Gauguin and Vincent van Gogh, whose names were starting to be mentioned in Britain, although few people had seen their work.

Fry was forty-four but looked older. His efforts to create a happy, beautiful home with his artist wife, Helen, for whom he designed a large, sunny house on the outskirts of Guildford, had not prevented her schizophrenic episodes from taking an increasingly violent turn. Fry was cheered, however, by a new project: the Grafton Galleries, in Grafton Street near Berkeley Square, had invited him to organize an exhibition of modern French art. 'His excitement transmitted itself,' Virginia felt. 'Everybody must see what he saw in those pictures – must share his sense of revelation.' When she dropped into the Grafton during the exhibition installation, the canvases were propped on chairs, 'bold, bright, impudent almost'. And there was Fry, 'gazing at them, plunging his eyes into them as if he were a humming-bird hawk-moth hanging over a flower, quivering yet still'.

5

Who's afraid of the avant-garde?

Mayfair, November 1910

What will Fry call his exhibition? What do the 250 or so works he has managed to round up by Cézanne, Gauguin and Van Gogh, Georges Seurat, Henri Matisse, Pablo Picasso, André Derain, Maurice de Vlaminck, Odilon Redon, Georges Rouault and a dozen others have in common? Kicking around possible titles with Desmond MacCarthy, a friend from his Cambridge days who accompanied him to Paris to negotiate loans, Fry lost patience. 'Oh', he sighed, 'let's just call them post-impressionists; at any rate, they come after the impressionists.' So 'Manet and the Post-Impressionists' it is. In the first room at the Grafton Galleries, they hang Manet's great painting, A Bar at the Folies Bergère *– the painting Walter Sickert saw in the artist's studio in 1883, hardly new. But in London, Manet's name still says 'modern art', of the kind that people will happily pay their shilling (catalogue included) to see. Nearby is a Cézanne still life and his statuesque* Madame Cézanne in a Striped Skirt, *the soft blues and greens of her jacket framed against a deep-red armchair. Fry prides himself in hanging pictures so that their forms and colours resonate with each other. Altogether, there are twenty-one Cézannes, even more works by Gauguin, whose paintings of Tahitian women fill the largest room – the luminous earthy flesh, the red and indigo robes, the landscape pink, yellow, green – and Van Gogh. The artist's sister-in-law Johanna van Gogh-Bonger has lent a large group of paintings, including his* Vase with Irises, *all radiant yellow and writhing blue, and* Self-portrait in Front of the Easel *– blue jacket, straw-coloured hair and beard, the palette with its vivid stabs of colour. About the few paintings in the show that are actually recent, Fry is not so sure, but Matisse's* The Girl with Green Eyes *is growing on him. Her red Chinese dress, the pale plaster sculpture behind her, the green, ochre, violet, yellow, black – there is 'novelty, frankness and bravery' in the way Matisse succeeds in harmonizing these strong tones. What the British press will make of it all when the exhibition opens is anyone's guess.*

If things had gone to plan for Fry, he would not have been devoting his energies to 'Manet and the Post-Impressionists' but scouting for Old Masters to ship to the United States. In January 1905, he had been headhunted for the directorship of the Metropolitan Museum of Art. It was his reputation as an expert on historic European art, rather than the liveliness of his ideas, that attracted the Met's trustees – that and his art-market nous. The museum's collection was growing fast, and the trustees needed someone in charge who could challenge a rip-off or spot a fake. As guest of the millionaire art collector and president of trustees John Pierpont Morgan ('the most repulsively ugly man… with a great strawberry nose', reported Fry), he rocked through the snowbound East Coast landscape in a private railroad carriage and dined with President Theodore Roosevelt. 'There's glory for you!', he bragged wryly to Helen. Art had never worked this way for Fry in England, where his career was stymied by an inconvenient readiness to hold the British cultural establishment to account, for instance berating the Royal Academy for misuse of legacy funds. He knew that this was the reason he was rejected for the Slade professorship at Oxford (Ruskin's old post), despite being the best-qualified candidate. The approach by the Met felt providential. 'I think it's rattling good pay,' he told his wife, 'and it's a big job worthy of any ambitions we may have. It's a place where one will have power to influence and where one will be recognized.'

In his late thirties, the son of Sir Edward and Lady Mariabella Fry was still troubled by a sense that his achievements so far as an artist and writer on art ('art historian' did not yet exist as a profession) were recognized by neither his parents nor the world at large. After studying natural sciences at Cambridge University, Fry had become convinced that his true calling was art. His lawyer father took some persuading, although he eventually stumped up the funds. Fry took lessons from Francis Bate, an able but uninspired admirer of Whistler, then toured Italy for the traditional gentleman's education in art. In 1892, he spent two months at the Académie Julian, one of the largest Parisian teaching ateliers, which was thronged with American and English students, eager to escape their puritan roots. Fry struck his contemporaries as 'shy and uneasy at first in the free atmosphere'. Back in London, he attended Sickert's evening class in Chelsea, learning the arts of visual memory passed on to Sickert by Whistler and Degas, and an understanding of

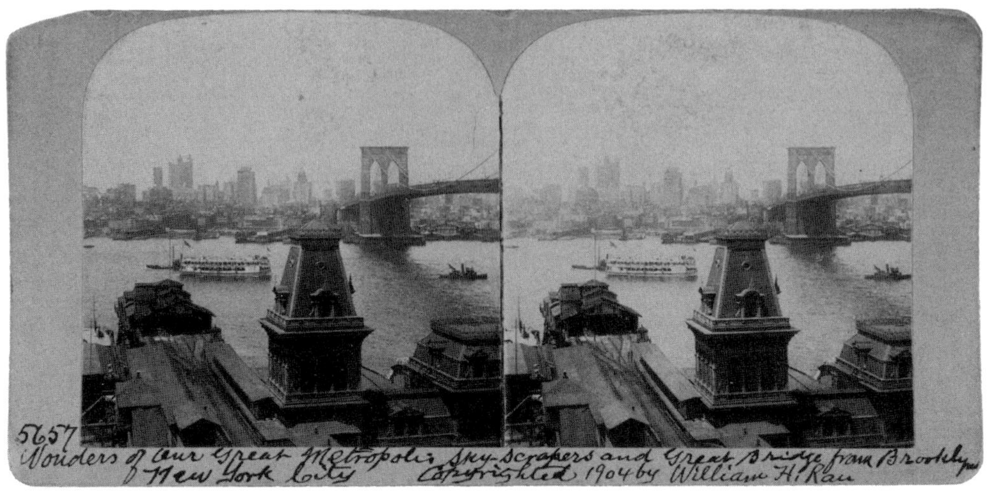

Brooklyn Bridge and the New York skyline, stereoscope slide with photograph by William Herman Rau, *c.* 1904

drawing and painting not as distinct disciplines but as interrelated skills. He was unexcited by modern art, however: French impressionism was a let-down, with its 'lack of structural design', and the British impressionists of the New English Art Club were equally misguided. Fry felt much more drawn to 'the Old Masters and, in particular, those of the Italian Renaissance', from whom he hoped to discover 'the secret of that architectonic idea which I missed so badly in the work of my contemporaries'.

Fry made further extended visits to Italy in the late 1890s, during which he researched his monograph on Giovanni Bellini, published in 1899, and befriended Bernard Berenson, a young American connoisseur and scholar, who had already published four books on Italian Renaissance painting. Well versed in Ruskin's writings, Fry struggled with his conflation of the love of art with love of God: where, if you took God out of the equation, did that leave art? 'What makes ART so dangerous,' he confided to a Cambridge friend, 'is that it has got separated from religion and life; by religion it could hang on to life, without it it can't, and so one has to make it a religion by itself, to the great detriment of both or rather of all three.' By autumn 1902, Fry felt more assured in his role as an interpreter, as well as a practitioner, of art: consulting on the establishment of Britain's first art history periodical, the *Burlington Magazine*, he looked forward to contributing to 'an expression of authoritative opinion' on the subject. The *Burlington*, however, ran on a shoestring, 'with absolutely no business method'. When, in December 1904, the telegram came from the Met, Fry was under the impression that he was being invited to court sponsors for the ailing magazine, making the prospect of a winter crossing just about bearable. His storm-tossed week on RMS *Teutonic* was a 'feverish nightmare': nauseous and sleepless, he found the Atlantic Ocean 'simply disgusting', he told Helen, while New York itself held little appeal. Writing to the artist William Rothenstein – a fellow student from Sickert's evening class – he predicted, 'I shan't stay long.'

New York, at the time of Fry's arrival in January 1905, was a boom city in the process of rapid and visible change. In 1900, its population of 3.4 million was approximately half that of London. During the next ten years, it grew by almost 40 per cent, much of the increase fuelled by immigration from Russia, Poland and Italy. By 1910, three-quarters of New York's population were either immigrants or their American-born children. The city's appearance was also undergoing a metamorphosis. At the harbour entrance, finally installed in October 1886, stood Frédéric-Auguste Bartholdi's *Liberty*. What kept this 150-foot copper colossus erect was an ingenious system of internal supports designed by the great French engineer Gustave Eiffel, whose wrought-iron lattice tower had been the centrepiece of the 1889 World's Fair and would symbolize Paris in general consciousness for the rest of time. *Liberty* and the Eiffel Tower validated the vision of the 1878 World's Fair – that, while industry might determine the wealth of nations, it was the arts and industry in tandem that shaped the fortunes of a modern city.

Eiffel's pioneering application of curtain-wall construction in Bartholdi's statue was the method now being employed for New York's own distinctive contribution to the modern cityscape, the burgeoning crop of outlandishly tall buildings serviced by elevators that American gossip journalists nicknamed 'sky-scrapers'. Returning in 1904 for the first time in more than twenty years, Henry James found the low-rise Atlantic seaport of his youth transformed by 'multitudinous sky-scrapers standing up to the view, from the water, like extravagant pins in a cushion already overplanted'. Set beside Europe's tallest buildings (he thought wistfully of Giotto's Florentine campanile), 'these giants of the mere market' struck him as belonging to an alternative temporal universe,

'Crowned not only with no history, but with no credible possibility of time for history, and consecrated to no uses save the commercial at any cost.' Life without history had an unsettling fast new rhythm, mirroring the jagged skyline: 'the whole community crams into...the desperate cars of the Subway or the vast elevators of the tall buildings'. James especially loathed riding the 'packed and hoisted basket' – it was 'an almost intolerable symbol of the herded and driven state'.

Fry, whose visual sensibility had been shaped by Italian Renaissance art, felt much the same: 'wonderful as the front view of New York is, it seems a fierce and cruel place, monstrous and inhumane'. Yet there was 'far more enthusiasm for art in America...than in England', and – once the extraordinary job offer was on the table – the money was hard to turn down. He felt confident in his ability to handle the American plutocracy, which he was now observing for the first time in its natural habitat: there was 'precious little distinction or cachet about the whole lot', he informed Helen, and in any case 'they've not got anything but money to intimidate you with'. After a year of on–off negotiations, however, he agreed to become curator of European painting, a more junior post that would allow him to spend much of his time in London, where Helen's health was a constant anxiety.

On both sides of the Atlantic, wealthy industrialists had embarked on a campaign of competitive cultural philanthropy and collection-building. New money was eager to re-baptise itself in the font of culture, and world-class art of the kind for which Fry would soon be negotiating on the Met's behalf was a commodity like no other – both an index of unimaginable wealth and an asset whose value transcended any merely financial measure. In London, the sugar magnate Henry Tate bankrolled the construction of a neo-Palladian gallery by the Thames, to which he gave his name and a more or less distinguished consignment of pre-Raphaelite paintings – still regarded, along with Turner, as Britain's trump card when it came to modern art. In Glasgow, profits from an international trade fair in 1888 were ploughed into an enormous Spanish-baroque-style Palace of Fine Arts in Kelvingrove Park. The dream-child of a group of Americans in Paris in 1866, the Met had been one of the first of these temples of capitalist largesse, opening its doors on Fifth Avenue in 1870. Its founding mission – to bring art to the American people – needed no further justification, in light of Ruskin's widely accepted creed that art opened people's eyes to nature's beauty, which in turn revealed the mind of God ('the Laws of Nature and of Nature's God' were, after all, the bedrock of the United States Declaration of Independence).

Donations flowed. In 1880, the Met relocated to a larger Fifth Avenue site, where James discovered that the museum he recalled from its modest early days in a patrician townhouse now occupied 'a palace of art, truly, that sits there on the edge of the Park, rearing itself with a radiance, yet offering you expanses to tread'. Even as he trod the marble acres of the new Great Hall, however (more duomo than palace with its cavernous arches and domes), James smelled 'money in the air, ever so much money'. 'Acquisition' was what the new Met embodied above all else, 'if need be on the highest terms.' As a novelist, James was closely attuned to these nuances: he had explored what it means to desire and acquire – artworks and precious objects, histories and people – in his 1904 novel *The Golden Bowl*, which features a Morganesque American art collector, Adam Verver. The greatest catch of Verver's European acquisition spree is an Italian prince reputedly descended from Amerigo Vespucci, the Renaissance-era adventurer for whom America itself was named, who marries and betrays Verver's daughter.

The United States in the early 1900s was heavily protectionist in its international relations and had not yet overtaken Britain as the dominant global trading power, but its economy had outstripped Britain's in the late nineteenth century. Vast fortunes were being made in steel, oil, electrification, railroads, finance and shipping. When Morgan and rival millionaires like Henry Clay Frick and Nelson Rockefeller began to buy art and sponsor museums, the sums involved were – as Fry immediately realized – in a completely different league from the those of British tycoons. Henry Tate put £80,000 into founding the Tate Gallery; while employed by the Met and acting privately for American collectors, Fry would spend this kind of money on a handful of prize acquisitions. Around the time he met Vanessa Bell and Virginia Stephen, he travelled to Poland on a commission for Frick to buy Rembrandt's *Polish Rider* (*c.* 1655) for £60,000. Most of his dealings, however, were with Morgan, whose empire at various times included stakes in twenty-one railroad companies, US Steel, General Electric, the London Underground and the White Star shipping line, soon to launch two mega-liners, the *Olympic* and *Titanic*, constructed in the Harland & Wolff shipyard in Belfast.

As America's most influential financial player, Morgan had twice been instrumental in averting a national banking crisis.

Although Fry discovered a natural gift for sealing five-figure deals, he disdained the bullish new economy of acquisition, casting himself, in stories involving Morgan, as the straight player in a farce. Recounting a buying trip to Italy in May 1907, he painted Morgan as a caricature megalomanic, indiscriminately wielding his wealth to hoover up art and bully his way through every transaction, while the sycophantic, cash-strapped Italian nobility swarmed around him, desperate 'to catch some of the golden shower'. As Morgan's limousine bowled through the Marche, 'Oxen dragging loads of hay plunged wildly into ditches and up the opposite bank, fowls, dogs and children rushed screaming away.' In entertaining his friends with slapstick tales of lucre and art (recalled here by Virginia in terms evoking Toad's madcap antics in Kenneth Grahame's *Wind in the Willows*), Fry was being much wittier than Ruskin but also less forthright. The problem of art's relationship to money had not gone away. However out of touch with the de facto economics of the art world Ruskin had been, he had at least taken a stand, believing that money-value should apply to the artist's labour, not to whatever result – sublimity or rubbish – it produced.

A year or so later, another speeding car ran riot on Italian roads. The young poet Filippo Tommaso Marinetti had spent a heady evening in Milan with poet friends, 'filling up masses of paper with our frenetic writings'. Suddenly, they felt that they had reached the outer limits of their art, 'like guards in forward positions, facing an enemy of hostile stars'. They had become, in other words, the new poetic avant-garde, standing shoulder to shoulder with the workers who fuelled the furnaces of modernity, 'the stokers working feverishly at the infernal fires of great liners…the black spectres through the red-hot bellies of locomotives, hurtling along at breakneck speed'. Since being *of* their time meant being ahead of it, there wasn't a moment to lose. In this hyped-up state, they leaped into their cars and set off 'along roads as deep and plunging as the beds of torrents… squashing beneath our scorching tyres the snarling guard dogs on the doorsteps of their houses'. By his own account, Marinetti was barrelling down the wrong side of the road when two cyclists appeared, 'dithering about in front of me like two lines of thought'. He braked, skidded and 'flew into a ditch'. Clambering out of the 'strength-giving sludge', he experienced an epiphany. While he waited in a garage, 'all bruised and bandaged', for his car to be repaired, Marinetti 'dictated our foremost desires to all men on Earth who are truly alive'.

On 20 February 1909, the 'Futurist Manifesto' was splashed across the front page of France's *Le Figaro*. Taking his cue from Karl Marx and Friedrich Engels's 1848 *Communist Manifesto*, Marinetti demanded nothing less than a revolution, in which the entire existing cultural order, including everything on the walls of museums and galleries, must be torn down. The future's new relationship to the past would be the inverse of the evolutionary connection between historical eras in which Fry believed. For futurists, as young artists throughout Europe soon began to identify themselves, the past was no longer a living basis for development but a dead object to be destroyed. 'We believe that this wonderful world has been further enriched by a new beauty, the beauty of speed,' announced Marinetti, firing off a series of call-to-arms aphorisms:

> *A racing car, its bonnet decked with exhaust pipes like serpents with galvanic breath...a roaring motor car, which seems to race like machine-gun fire, is more beautiful than the Winged Victory of Samothrace....*
>
> *There is no longer any beauty except the struggle....*
>
> *We wish to glorify war – the sole cleanser of the world...*

By the summer of 1909, translations of the *Futurist Manifesto* were circulating in leaflet form in most of the main European languages.

This was also the year in which Fry parted company from the Met. In June 1909, acting for the museum, he offered a Parisian dealer £10,000 for a *Virgin and Child* attributed (wrongly) to Fra Angelico, from the collection of the Belgian king Leopold II, whose quasi-genocidal reign of terror in the Congo had just come to an end. Morgan paid, then claimed the painting for his personal hoard. Politely but firmly, Fry rebuked him. Morgan did not have the right to dismiss Fry from his curatorship, but sacked he was. The following year, when Fry made his entrance in Bloomsbury drawing rooms, he was looking for sources of income to replace his American earnings (to cover, among other things, Helen's medical expenses), even perhaps a senior post at a British art gallery. In organizing 'Manet and the Post-Impressionists' – a large, ambitious exhibition containing many striking paintings that had never been seen in London – Fry could hope to exercise the 'power to influence' of which America had given him a taste.

'Manet and the Post-Impressionists' opened to the press on 5 November 1910 and to the public three days later, unleashing what Fry, feeling both shaken and vindicated, described as 'a wild hurricane of newspaper abuse'. *The Times* blasted the show as 'the rejection of all that civilisation has done', comparing it to 'anarchism in politics'. 'Don't go in,' a young visitor was warned. 'The pictures are evil.' Virginia Stephen witnessed, or at any rate heard about, visitors convulsed in 'paroxysms of rage and laughter'. She saw her new friend Fry as self-lessly attempting to enlighten the lumpen British public, then, all too predictably, encountering ridicule and resistance of the kind that ulti-mately confirmed the Bloomsbury view that the intellectual elite could expect to be understood only by their social equals. Sickert, who had seen innumerable exhibitions and heard every shade of misjudgment applied to art, paid little attention to the fuss: 'None of us, not straight out of the egg, take the leaders or the "tendentious" arrangements of news in the daily papers seriously.' On the contrary, Fry had 'earned the gratitude of all painters, students, and lovers of art in this country', precisely because his exhibition 'has caused a rumpus. The rumpus has collected a crowd, and the crowd is quite ready to listen to reason and to learn.'

Sickert, a seasoned teacher himself, was right: Fry was the only person in Britain in 1910 who could have delivered a lesson of this kind on modern art. With the attention 'Manet and the Post-Impressionists' received, both in the press and in the shape of 25,000 visitors, Fry began to assume a place in twentieth-century national cultural life comparable to that occupied in the previous century by Ruskin. He was, Sickert shrewdly observed, 'nothing if not an educationist and an *impresario*'. Yet, unlike Ruskin, for whom an autodidact factory worker was far more admirable than a paint-flinger like Whistler, Fry viewed the 'average man' with a certain involuntary distaste, even as he framed his ideas in ways he felt the public would respond to. It was around this time that 'form' began to crystallize in his thinking as the key to the meaning of art. In 1913, Clive Bell's book *Art* would popularize the phrase 'significant form', but the concept itself owed much to Fry. As Bell defined it, 'the one quality common to all works of visual art' was the ability of formal combinations of lines, colours and shapes to 'stir our aesthetic emotions'. What more was there to say? Art had definitively slipped its moorings from religion. But it would be Fry – painter, writer, theorist, connoisseur, communicator, and, for all his social limitations, much closer to the complex pulse of art than Bell – who would preach the gospel of Form.

While Fry and Bell were deep in conversation, others were listening. If 'significant form' could be analysed and demonstrated, in Picasso's cubism and the windows of Chartres Cathedral equally, it could surely be learned. A true understanding of form, to look at it another way, might make it possible to enjoy a thoroughly bourgeois life *and* become an avant-garde artist – like Gauguin, but without slumming it in Tahiti, or Van Gogh, but without the madness and self-harm. In September 1911, the Bells rented a house at Studland Bay on the Dorset coast; Fry, with whom Vanessa had fallen in love, and his sister Joan stayed nearby. In *Bathers* (pl. 6), Bell has ditched her earlier New English Art Club manner and become a post-impressionist. The scene itself still lies within the impressionist social arena of middle-class rural leisure, but the Dorset sand is a yolky sunflower yellow, the sky a glowing violet-blue, like Van Gogh's Arles canvases. Among the eleven figures in Bell's painting are a naked woman whose body is enclosed in a Cézanne-esque broken contour line, and the figure of Virginia, stretched out on the beach, languorous as one of Gauguin's Tahitian girls and sporting a Vincent-style straw hat. 'I've been trying this morning on the beach to paint your subject,' she told Fry.

'Post-impressionism' – Fry's label quickly caught on – might have burst on London like an anarchist bomb, but many of the most talked-about works in the Grafton exhibition were more than twenty years old. Did they really point the way forwards for art in 1911? Not for Marinetti. He was categorical: 'Any work of art that lacks a sense of aggression can never be a masterpiece.' In futurist terms, Fry's beloved Italy was 'a marketplace for junk dealers', its museums 'cemeteries of wasted effort', conspiring to stifle the 'violent outbursts of creation and action' demanded by the machine age. Marinetti's first manifesto had soon won artist recruits. In February 1910, Italian painters Umberto Boccioni, Carlo Carrà and Luigi Russolo launched their own *Manifesto of Futurist Painters*, vowing to 'Destroy the cult of the past.' From now on, artists must 'Support and glory in our day-to-day world, a world which is going to be continually and splendidly transformed by victorious Science.' Two months later, Marinetti and a group of fellow futurists climbed to the top of the fifteenth-century Clock Tower in the Piazza San Marco in

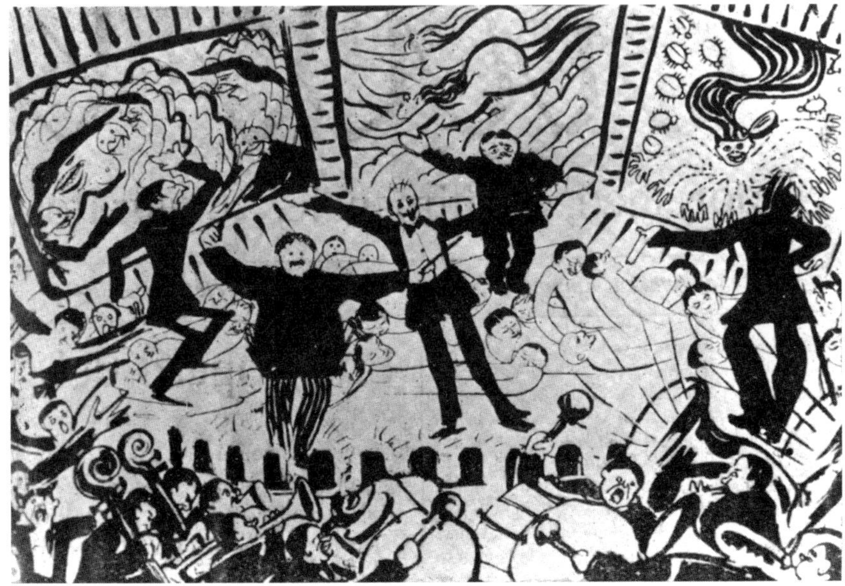

Umberto Boccioni, *A Futurist Soirée*, 1911 (left to right: Boccioni, Francesco Balilla Pratella (conducting), Filippo Tommaso Marinetti, Carlo Carrà and Luigi Russolo)

Venice, from where they hurled fistfuls of leaflets, calling for the entire historic city, 'this immense sewer of traditionalism', to be razed. In its place would rise 'an industrial and military Venice', liberated from 'the whorish moonlight of its furnished bedrooms'. Fluttering past the statues of the Lion of St Mark and the Virgin Mary, the manifesto blizzard settled in the square, its message to the bemused citizens: 'Let the reign of Electric Light begin.'

In Marinetti's view, however, 'the most futurist city in Europe' wasn't Venice or Milan or even Paris but London – not because British writers and artists were any more futuristic than others, but because Britain was still by a wide margin the world's most heavily industrialized and mechanized nation and London the most populous city, the cosmopolitan nexus of a global trading empire. The London public was also well known for its eclectic tastes in entertainment and its appetite for the new and controversial, although even its post-impressionist-inspired paroxysms were less stagey than the traditional Parisian first-night brouhaha. In the winter of 1910, Marinetti made the first in a series of London visits to promote his futurist agenda in person. His attempts to engage the British press, mailing out manifestos and leaflets, had flopped.

In France, Spain and Germany, futurism was taken seriously; in Britain, it seemed to be a joke. There was 'no future for the Future', opined the satirist Max Beerbohm, 'in the universe of silly Signor Marinetti'.

Marinetti chose his first London audience with care, lecturing to a gathering of suffragettes at the Lyceum Club on 13 December. He was taking a risk: his original manifesto, glorifying speed, war and youth, had also promoted 'scorn for women'. Many campaigners for women's rights shared his conviction that conventions of marriage and domesticity belonged to the scrapheap-ready baggage of the past, but what of his vision of a future shaped by aggressive men? According to his own version of events, Marinetti succeeded in injecting futurist fire into the increasingly politicized arena of gender relations, provoking a 'violent riot'. The *Evening Post*'s reporter simply observed that 'The ladies of the Lyceum Club sat very still [and] smiled at the most daring utterances of this young Italian philosopher, and actually applauded some of his most violent phrases.'

In June 1911, another of modern art's most inspired publicists and impresarios, Sergei Diaghilev, arrived from St Petersburg via Monte Carlo and Rome with his touring ballet company, the Ballets Russes. Their first London season, at the Royal Opera House, would be part of the coronation celebrations for George V, who had succeeded his father, Edward VII, the previous year. Ballet was already big business in London, with venues like the Alhambra Theatre in Leicester Square staging cast-of-hundreds spectaculars in which – as in Degas's Paris – the workhorse corps de ballet were local girls hired to create an entrancing froth of leg-lifting and twirls, with visiting European stars dancing solos. Some of Diaghilev's top talent – the ballerinas Anna Pavlova and Tamara Karsavina – had danced as guest artists in London before the 1911 season. But this was music-hall entertainment for a largely working-class crowd (a 'miscellaneous audience', sniffed Fry). Diaghilev's programme at the Royal Opera House included *Le Spectre de la rose* (The Genie of the Rose), a *pas de deux* danced by Karsavina and the charismatic Vaslav Nijinsky (Diaghilev's lover), whose flame-like athleticism was unlike anything the London stage had seen. Nijinsky's skin-tight silk-elastic costume was designed by Russian artist Léon Bakst, whose colour-burst peasant-oriental-style costumes for Igor Stravinsky's *The Firebird* (1910), brought to London by Diaghilev in summer 1912, triggered a wave of Russophile chic in interior design and high-society fancy dress. London, Diaghilev found, was the most successful stop on his company's successive European tours, in terms of both box office takings and the enthusiastic response to all things connected to the Ballets Russes.

For similar reasons, Marinetti kept coming back. In March 1912, the London Futurist Exhibition opened at the Sackville Gallery on the second leg of a two-year European tour. Futurism had already evolved from a poet's manifesto into a fully fledged movement, represented by thirty-five works by Boccioni, Carrà, Russolo and Gino Severini, and a catalogue of futurist tracts. In Russolo's *The Revolt* (1911), a dense V-formation crowd of arm-waving, red protesters pierces and topples the blue ranks of blank-faced city apartment blocks. The cubist-style fracturing of planes and high graphic colour announce a futurist moment, when youth and energy, like a wedge, will break up the staid old world. Once again, the London public was receptive and anything but riotous. Sickert was 'surprised to find the tiny galleries in Sackville Street, off Piccadilly, packed with an orderly crowd, consisting mostly of the mothers of England', while here and there 'a grandfather of distinguished appearance was pointing out to a delicious grand-daughter the obvious beauties of the pictures, and the sound reasoning of the accompanying tracts'. Futurism, he decided, was 'Austere, bracing, patriotic, nationalist, positive, anti-archaistic, anti-sentimental, anti-feminist', and something 'from which we in England have much to learn'.

On a wet March evening, after visitors to the Sackville Gallery had been 'circulating slowly, and verifying with reverence the statements in the descriptive catalogue', streets throughout the West End rang to a series of small, bright explosions – the unmistakable sound of breaking glass. This was the second such action organized by Emmeline Pankhurst's Women's Social and Political Union, which, after promises and inaction from the male political establishment, had adopted the slogan 'Deeds not Words'. The 'Great Militant Protest' of 4 March was to involve 150 volunteers in synchronized window-smashing in central London. Details of the 'secret attack' were, however, leaked to the police, who trailed suspects through shops and cafés, making 126 arrests. Protesters inscribed messages on their projectiles: 'Better broken windows than broken promises,' wrote suffragette Lillian Ball on her hammer.

Although Fry stayed out of politics, he had, by introducing Gauguin and Van Gogh, Matisse and Picasso to London, given radicals of all persuasions a sense of how a new social order would look, as well as be, very different from the old. 'In politics the only movements worth considering are Woman Suffrage and Socialism,' the poet Christina Walshe bluntly stated. 'They are both post-impressionist in their desire to scrap old decaying forms and find for themselves a new working ideal.' In this version of suffragist thinking, both Marinetti's and Fry's preoccupations – regenerative destruction and post-impressionism – merge in a wider ideology of protest. Fry's own programme of reform held its course, maintaining its focus on colours and shapes. The furore that attended the 1910 exhibition had pretty much died down. The press response to 'An Exhibition of Pictures by Paul Cézanne and Paul Gauguin' at the Stafford Gallery in Mayfair in November 1911 was positive to the point of adulation. Gauguin was praised for his 'genius for decoration', his 'strong and sensitive gift for drawing'; Cézanne for his 'fine feeling for structural composition'. A year after Fry had been accused of hastening the end of civilization, British collectors like the academic educationalist and Ruskin devotee Michael Sadler, recently appointed vice-chancellor of Leeds University, were snapping up post-impressionists.

In October 1912, Fry staged the Second Post-Impressionist Exhibition, in which he included young British artists like Stanley Spencer and Percy Wyndham Lewis, in a bid to draw contemporary British art into the slipstream of radical Europe. For the artists themselves, Fry's two exhibitions provided what was often their first direct contact with works by the European avant-garde (a term that had recently appeared in print for the first time in Britain). Fry had also taught London's social elite how to make a splash with modern art – that is, how to deactivate avant-garde art's radical thrust while retaining its convention-flouting cachet. Shouting out for Matisse and Picasso joined skinny-dipping and love triangles as the badge of an exclusive bohemian tribe, for whom the traditional attributes of pennilessness and social marginality were strictly relative.

Across the Atlantic, New York had woken up to modern art, and on a scale that once again dwarfed the resources that Fry had been able to marshal in London. In February 1913, New York City's 69th Regiment Armory hosted an exhibition of some thirteen hundred works by three hundred artists (known as the Armory Show). For its organizers, the Association of American Painters and Sculptors, this was a bid 'to lead the public taste in art, rather than follow it'. The range of artistic idioms

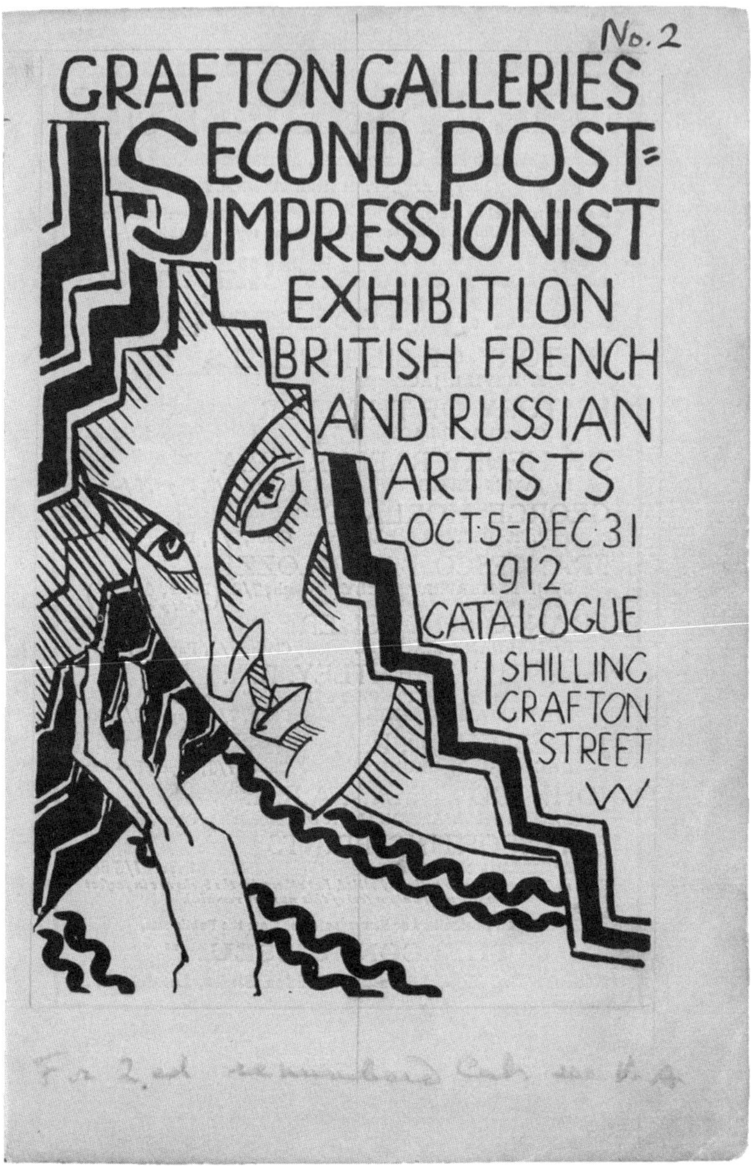

Vanessa Bell, Roger Fry and Duncan Grant, poster for the Second
Post-Impressionist Exhibition, Grafton Galleries, London, 1912

and artists' nationalities was accordingly inclusive: there were impressionists and post-impressionists, cubists and post-cubists, like the maverick Frenchman Marcel Duchamp, who showed *Nude Descending a Staircase*. The show also featured work by some fifty women, including Gwen John's *Girl Reading at a Window*, bought from her by John Quinn. The United States at this moment was in open-door mode – and not only culturally. Between 1900 and 1910, some nine million immigrants had arrived from Europe, among them a fair proportion of the talent in the Armory Show.

A fortnight after the exhibition closed, news came of John Pierpont Morgan's death in Rome. He'd had a lucky escape the previous year, having abruptly cancelled his suite on the maiden voyage of his White Star Line's stupendous new liner, SS *Titanic*. In its April 1913 issue, the Met's *Bulletin* saluted Morgan as a 'Great Citizen', who had given art real prominence in public life – and more. Morgan and his money had made it plausible to claim that 'art is necessary to upholding the ideals of a nation'. In America or in France, perhaps, but – Fry might have reflected – certainly not yet in Britain. There was still work to be done before people would stop comparing Picasso's 'jig-saw puzzles' to the 'incoherent ravings of a lunatic'.

6
Primitive mercenaries

Spitalfields, winter 1913

*On Friday, after work, the men come here, to the Russian Vapour Baths,
86 Brick Lane, where a shilling will buy 'relief from all your troubles' and,
more to the point, you can clean up before Sabbath prayers in the Machzike
Hadath Synagogue across the road. This is London's immigrant heartland,
where Huguenot weavers chased out of Catholic France in the seventeenth
century set up their looms. Now, the decrepit terraces are home to a large
community of Ashkenazim from eastern Europe. Thousands of Jews fleeing
persecution in the Russian Empire have settled in London, rather than – as
many originally dreamed of doing – making the crossing to America.
Since 1881, when Tsar Alexander II was killed by an anarchist bomb, they
have suffered wave after wave of pogroms. Each time the bloodlust has
got worse; in autumn 1905, the year of the abortive Russian Revolution,*
pogromshchiki, *the pogrom-mobs, murdered and raped their way through
660 towns and villages. Among the two million refugees who have sought
safety in the West, there are revolutionaries, like Leon Trotsky, but most
of those disembarking at the London docks bring only their families and
trades – costermongers from Lodz, bagel-bakers and sweatshop tailors from
Minsk, cigarette-makers from Vitebsk. These are the men who congregate
on Friday evenings in the Vapour Baths – the most popular of Rabbi
Benjamin Schewzik's slumland community schemes. Shaking off their work
clothes, they crouch in the steam room, relishing the undreamed-of blended
joys of shtetl banter and modern plumbing. David Bomberg, twenty-three
and son of a Warsaw leatherworker, comes here too.*

Vas tustu? What are you doing?, *they ask.*
Zeykhenung. Drawing.

————

Apprenticed to a lithographer at the age of fifteen, Bomberg began
taking evening art classes at the City and Guilds Institute run by Walter

Bayes, Roger Fry's successor as art critic of *The Athenaeum.* By seventeen, he knew he wanted to be an artist. After attending Walter Sickert's evening class in Westminster and the revelation of 'Manet and the Post-Impressionists', in April 1911 he started at the Slade. Two years later, Bomberg was expelled – a star student who'd become too big for his boots, too eager to 'theorise and analyse', who insisted on working 'upon lines of his own which were not at all in accord with those laid down by the authorities'. The Jewish Education Aid Society, which was so successful in getting East End talent into art school (including Bomberg's friend Mark Gertler), stopped his grant, so he continued his work in a room next to his large family's cramped flat in Tenter Buildings, Whitechapel. During 1913, a strange new painting, more than 6 feet high and 7 feet wide, was taking shape. It resembled a twisted kaleidoscope or multiplying shards of splintered mirror – blue, brown, pink, grey, black. Bomberg called it *In the Hold*: behind and within those sharp geometric shapes it was just possible to make out the movement of people, swarming in a ship's hold as they prepare to step ashore. A man lifts a child high, a pair of hands rises from the depths.

In Whitechapel tenements like Tenter Buildings, along Brick Lane, down Commercial Road and Brushfield Street, refugees shared and stowed away their trauma – the Russian atrocities, the filthy ships, the arrival in a city where you could not make yourself understood and didn't know where or how you would live, the being demonized in newspapers and jeered at in the street. At the Slade, on the other hand, drawing the biceps of a Greek statue under the surgical gaze of Henry Tonks, such things did not seem real. This is perhaps one reason why Bomberg stopped drawing like his hero Michelangelo, even though his Michelangelesque *Head of a Poet* had won him the Henry Tonks Prize. If he'd wanted to paint like Van Gogh, or even the young, pre-cubist Picasso, as Gertler did, he might have been left alone. But to his teachers, Bomberg appeared to have been swept up in the cubist madness, questioning everything, drawing human figures as if the body were constructed from parallel lines, angles, crosses, blocky brick-and-girder shapes. Free of the Slade, he made drawings in chalk and wash of bodies stretching and twisting in the Vapour Baths, as if the place had been commandeered by his dancer friends from the Ballets Russes. *Vos idyotish bilder!* he heard his father's comrades tease him.

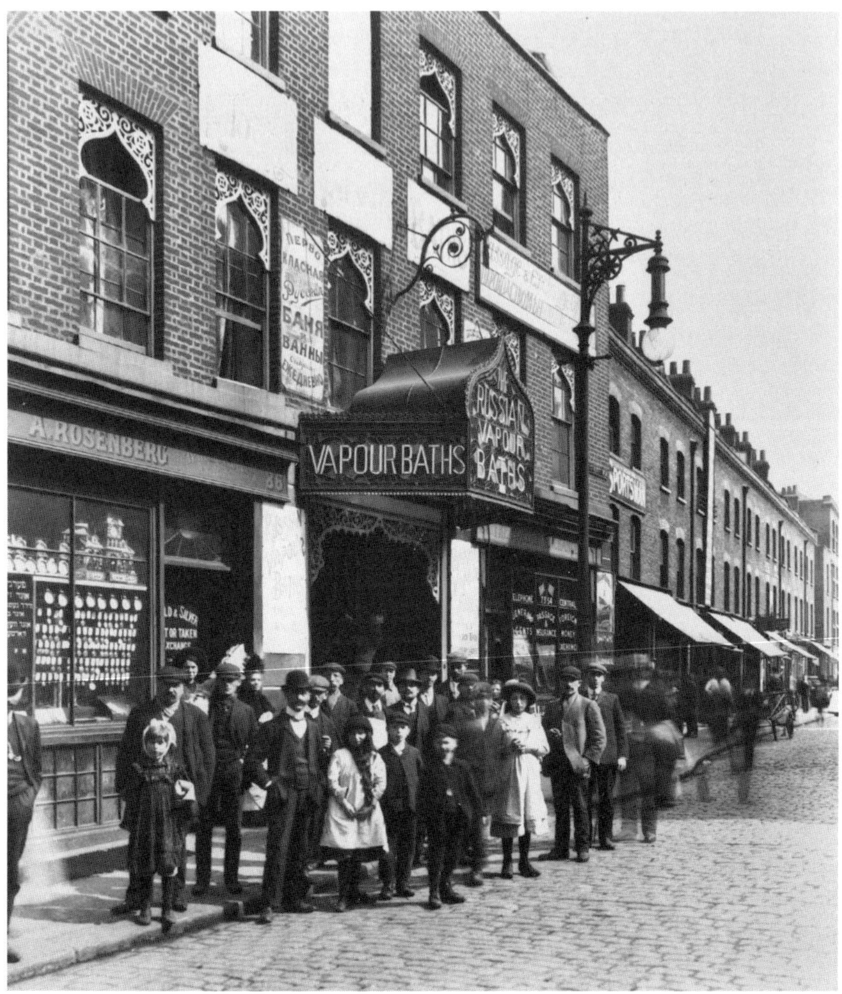

The Russian Vapour Baths, Brick Lane, London, 1904

Even in Spitalfields, people knew about the futurists. However Marinetti originally defined it, the word was now in common use to mean any kind of image that looked incomprehensible, machine-like, explosive, assertively modern. When a reporter for the *Jewish Chronicle* interviewed the East End's precocious 'Jewish Futurist', Bomberg had to explain that, strictly speaking, he wasn't one, because 'the Futurist school is so largely destructive'. In any case, what could be *less* machine-gun-like than his latest theme – the slow, steamy dance of naked men plastering each other with therapeutic mud? Bomberg rejected Marinetti's 'condemnation of old art' but insisted instead that 'We must build our new art life of today upon the ruins of the dead art life of yesterday.' If, after all, he had to be labelled a futurist, he was only being loyal to his roots, he joked, because 'Futurism is in accordance with Jewish law, for its art resembles nothing in heaven above, the earth beneath, nor the waters under the earth.' More seriously, Bomberg described how he painted *In the Hold* in a 'cubist' spirit, superimposing 'a scheme of sixty-four squares, whereby the subject itself is resolved into its constituent forms which henceforth are all that matter.'

This was the kind of talk that helped get him expelled from the Slade – the doctrine that, in art, form is primary, subject matter and observational detail secondary. In this age of manifestos, a radical young artist needed to wield radical language; revealingly, though, the terms Bomberg chose weren't Marinetti's but Clive Bell's and Roger Fry's. Sure enough, when Fry reviewed the London Group's inaugural exhibition in March 1914, he singled out Bomberg's *In the Hold* for praise: 'In his colossal patchwork design, there glimmers through a dazzling veil of black squares and triangles the suggestion of volumes and movements.' There were other cubist–futurist newcomers to the group – Percy Wyndham Lewis, Edward Wadsworth (a Slade contemporary of Bomberg's) and London's most enthusiastic disciple of Marinetti, C. R. W. (Richard) Nevinson – but it was Bomberg in whom Fry detected 'the ambition, the energy and brain power to strike out a line on his own'. Design, squares, triangles, volumes: Fry, who may have got wind of what was said about Bomberg at the Slade, evidently saw him as a promising new recruit to his school of form, although personally the two men had already fallen out over Fry's latest project, the Omega Workshops.

Sometime in 1911 or early 1912, Fry had been sitting in a railway refreshment room, drafting his contribution to *The Great State*, a collection of political essays edited by H. G. Wells, and mulling over the fact that, although he would declare 'I am not a Socialist', he believed that the experience of art should be part of daily life. Looking up, he noted that 'The space my eye travels over is a small one, but I am appalled by the amount of "art" that it harbours.' He saw gothic-style stained-glass windows, covered by lace curtains 'with patterns taken from at least four centuries and as many countries', embossed wallpaper, machine-cut Greco-Roman style mouldings, and café tables, each one adorned by 'a large pot in which every beautiful quality in the material and

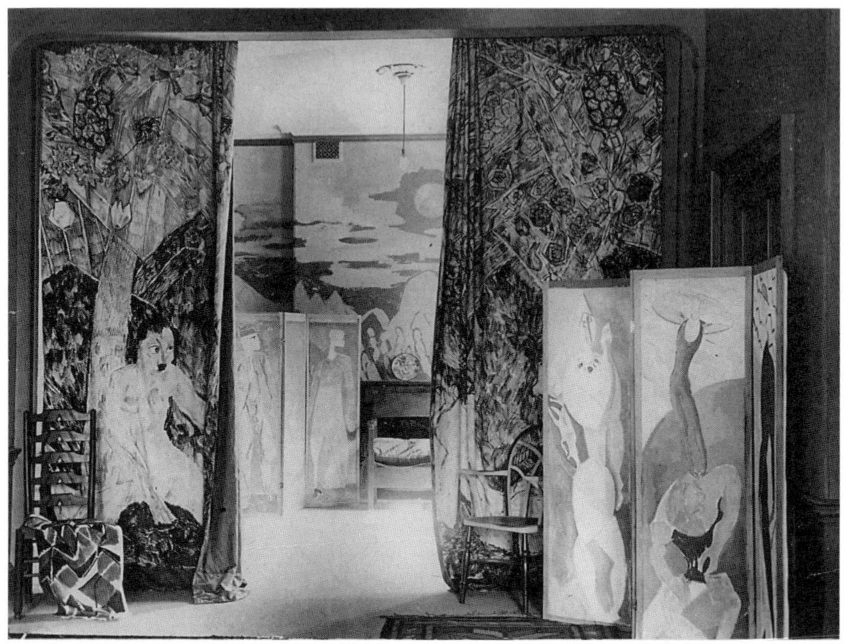

Room at the Omega Workshops, 33 Fitzroy Square, London, 1913

making of pots has been carefully obliterated by methods each of which implies profound scientific knowledge and great inventive talent'. The twentieth century was wearing on, but it seemed that efforts by Ruskin and Morris to democratize the experience of good art, or by Macdonald and Mackintosh to instil a spirit of simplicity in the modern room, had met with, at best, only patchy success.

In December 1912, Fry began drumming up sponsorship for 'a workshop for decorative and applied art'. He needed to raise about £2,000, he told George Bernard Shaw, to enable him to start commissioning 'young artists whose painting shows strong decorative feeling, who will be glad to use their talents on applied art'. They would be paid 30 shillings a week (above the average manual wage), and there would be no danger of artistic compromise. Post-impressionism, after all, was 'definitively decorative in its methods'. The Omega Workshops opened in Fitzroy Square on 8 July 1913, buoyed by Fry's recent large inheritance from his chocolate-magnate uncle Joseph. The Matisse-style curtain fabrics and desks adorned with cubist-inspired designs proved useful, if sporadic, earners for young artists with Bloomsbury connections, but everyday objects they weren't. Just as the theory of 'significant form' suggested that avant-garde art could be as learnable as piano scales, the Omega Workshops tamed its hard-won strangeness and immediacy, adapting its wildest gestures to the medium of soft furnishings. Marinetti, all the while, was trumpeting avant-gardism as a terrorist campaign against the cultural status quo. No young artist could face both ways. When, in autumn 1913, Fry invited Bomberg to design something for Omega, he must have been tempted by this evidence of recognition and the prospect of paid employment, but negotiations ended in a row.

Although Bomberg was much too 'blasty' – as a friend described him at this age – for Bloomsbury, he had become familiar with the eighteenth-century terraces and squares of this part of town. Three miles west of the Whitechapel tenement where he'd grown up with ten siblings, no bathroom, not a single picture on the walls, his art student's London was another world. In the grand classical courtyard of University College, the Slade looked more like a pocket palace than a studio block. Bomberg walked there every day, saving the London Underground fare to buy materials. Most of his fellow students did not have to make these calculations, but Bomberg appears to have held his own. Photographed with Nevinson, Wadsworth and other well-heeled young men at the 1912 Slade summer picnic, he sports the same kind of felt sombrero tipped over his brows, the classless headgear of the British bohemian. From the Slade, the West End opened out. A half-hour walk downhill was the National Gallery, already a favourite haunt. Standing in front of Botticelli's *Venus and Mars* (*c.* 1485) or Nicolas Poussin's *Bacchanalian Revel before a Term* (1632–33), Bomberg learned how a complex image can be formed from shapes described by human limbs – flexed, flung, quietly and yearningly observed. His dancer girlfriend Alice Mayes recalled being hurried through the galleries to Michelangelo's *The Entombment* (*c.* 1500–1), where Bomberg pointed out 'the wonderful composition of the picture and the marvellous proportions of the figures', explaining 'that the modern pictures that were such a revelation to me, had their beginning with the Old Masters'.

From the great portico of the National Gallery, they looked down on Trafalgar Square, where Marinetti's vision of modernity embodied in 'a roaring motor car' was on its way to becoming reality, in the shape of B-type motor buses rattling through the horse-drawn throng at 12 miles per hour. Beyond, in the Strand, stood more naked artistic bodies – notorious modern ones this time. Installed in 1908, the fourteen statues on the facade of the headquarters of the British Medical Association (BMA) by the American-born sculptor Jacob Epstein had ignited one of the new century's first art scandals. Representing *Maternity*, *The Newborn*, *Matter*, *Primal Energy* and other allegorical subjects of medical attention, the nude figures stood in niches so high above the street that their anatomical details couldn't be made out by passers-by, but the press and the National Vigilance Association (whose office windows unluckily faced the BMA's) kicked up a storm: stiff nipples, life-size scrotums 'laid bare to the gaze of all classes, young and old'. Epstein was made to feel 'like a prisoner in the dock' – not actually on trial but subject to accusations of perverted wrongdoing into which hostility to modern art was mixed with strong doses of prudery and anti-Semitism. After a pushback from assorted respected experts on art, including Fry, who 'failed to find anything approaching "suggestiveness"' in Epstein's figures, the statues were allowed to stay.

The BMA furore highlighted the peculiar charge that nakedness, as fact and idea, still carried in the dawn of the machine age. A kind of sensual equivalent to the spatial and formal ideal of simplicity, it was somehow both the glory of the Old Masters, in its literal, fleshy sense, and at the same time a metaphor for the modern, the stripped-to-essentials, the honestly revealed. Charles Holden, architect of the BMA building who commissioned Epstein, had been making his pitch as a modern spirit when he claimed, 'it is in the frank confession of our nakedness that our regeneration lies'. Confusingly, futurism itself had an ambivalent attitude to the body, with is bully-boy fixation on the eroticized yet dehumanizing piston rhythm of 'broad-breasted loco-motives', its aggressive glorification of 'the slap and the punching fist'. The manifesto that accompanied the Futurist Exhibition of March 1912 called for 'the total suppression of the nude in painting'. How this was to be achieved was left, like every prescription for the future in every futurist tract, extremely vague.

Not so vague were the actions of Canadian suffragette Mary Richardson, who on 10 March 1914 strode through the National Gallery with a meat cleaver tucked inside her coat. She paused to sketch the face of a Renaissance Madonna, then made her way to *The Rokeby Venus*, a celebrated painting by the seventeenth-century Spanish court artist Diego Velázquez, which shows the back view of a naked woman reclining on a slew of crimson silk while she contemplates her reflection in a mirror. This was one of very few naked women that Londoners could stare at in public with a presumption of worthy self-improvement rather than guilty depravity. Richardson swung her cleaver at the glass. The gallery attendant looked up, mistaking the sound for a smashed skylight, as Richardson hacked the canvas seven times. Her protest underscored the irony – lost on the gallery staff who finally managed to restrain her – that the British state would use force to protect a valuable painting of a woman's body while using even greater force to destroy the bodies of real women. Richardson had been one of the first of many women to be arrested, force-fed while on hunger strike in Holloway Prison, then released to recover and immediately reimprisoned under the 'Cat-and-Mouse' Act of 1913. The health of the much older Emmeline Pankhurst was being all but broken by such treatment. 'I am a suffragette,' Richardson shouted as police arrived to arrest her. 'You can get another picture, but you cannot get a life, as they are killing Mrs Pankhurst.'

Art as 'aggression', poetry as 'violent assault'. Who was this futurist rhetoric actually aimed at? What achievements, in the five years since Marinetti's first manifesto, could it lay claim to, other than cliquey quarrels, firecracker performances and exhibitions that somehow never quite lived up to the hype? Did Picasso or Braque ever approach a canvas, thinking 'I am a cubist. Let me show you how a cubist paints'? But with the Italian futurists, art sprang from rhetoric, not the other way round. By 1914, their British fellow travellers had begun to realize that the results could underwhelm. 'AUTOMOBILISM (Marinettism) bores us,' announced Percy Wyndham Lewis. 'We don't want to go about making a hullo-bulloo about motor cars, anymore than about knives and forks, elephants or gas-pipes.' Futurism's macho misogyny was also out of step with the fact that it was women, not anarchists or artists, who were detonating the real bombs in Britain, and who had given reasons clearer than anything in the *Futurist Manifesto* for their course of action. Christabel Pankhurst, Emmeline's daughter and companion-in-arms, argued:

> *If men use explosives and bombs for their own purpose they call it war, and the throwing of a bomb that destroys other people is then described as a glorious and heroic deed. Why should a woman not make use of the same weapons as men. It is not only war we have declared. We are fighting for a revolution!*

Acts of suffragist terrorism had become the subject of weekly news-paper round-ups. In 1913, postboxes were booby-trapped in Dundee, telegraph wires cut in Dumbarton, and there were arson attacks on a series of targets, including Saunderton and Croxley Green railway sta-tions, the tea house in Kew Gardens and the home of the chancellor of the exchequer, David Lloyd George.

London's art skirmishes bristled with war cries but had few concrete results beyond self-promotion – or so Gertler seems to have felt in 1912, when, demoralized one autumn evening by the sight of his own paint-ings in the sinking light, he decamped to the Café Royal in Piccadilly. It was full of artists 'talking art, Ancient art, Modern art, Impressionism, Post-Impressionism, Neo-Impressionism, Cubists, Spottists, Futurists, Cave-dwelling, Wyndham Lewis...Roger Fry!' Far from finding cama-raderie or stimulation, he 'walked home disgusted with them *all*'. For years the Café Royal had been London's only approximation to the louche liminality of Parisian artists' cafés, but by the time of Gertler's visit, it had become a parody of itself. Around the corner in Heddon Street, there was a livelier scene at the Cave of the Golden Calf – at least until February 1914, when it folded. This was the subterranean inner sanctum of the Cabaret Theatre Club, founded and bankrolled in June 1912 by Austrian writer Frida Strindberg, the charismatic but flaky ex-wife of the Swedish playwright August Strindberg. The Cave was London's first proper nightclub – according to the American poet Ezra Pound, the only club 'impovrished artists cd/get into'. In the wake of the London seasons of the Ballets Russes, Fry's post-impressionist shows and the gossip from cubist Paris and Secessionist Vienna (Strindberg's hometown), her recipe for success became obvious: the Cabaret Theatre Club would celebrate 'intuition and simplicity', with American ragtime music, gypsy dancers and 'futurist' wall hangings of wild beasts and naked revellers.

The experience of being stalked by Madame Strindberg 'unnerved' even Augustus John, but he was persuaded to help round up artists to design her *mise-en-scène*. Erotic sculptures were commissioned from Epstein and Eric Gill, a wall hanging, stage curtain and publicity materi-als from Lewis. After finishing at the Slade in 1901, Lewis had travelled in Europe, spending several years in Paris, unable to decide whether to concentrate on writing or art. *Kermesse*, his mural for the Cave, depicted bacchanalian folk dancing at a village fair in Brittany – Paul Gauguin

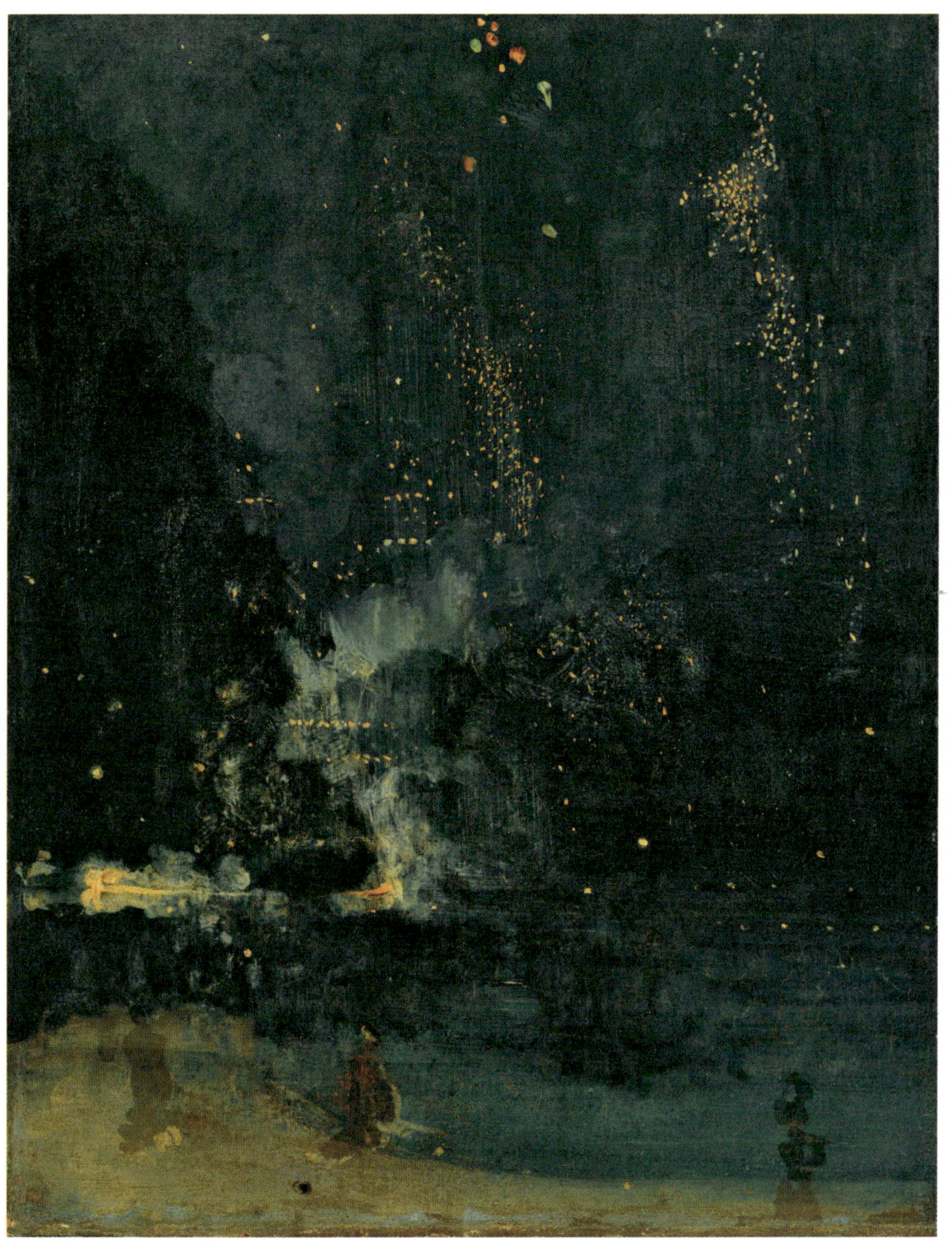

1 James Abbott McNeill Whistler, *Nocturne in Black and Gold, the Falling Rocket*, 1875.
Oil on panel, 60.3 × 46.7 cm (23¾ × 18½ in.)

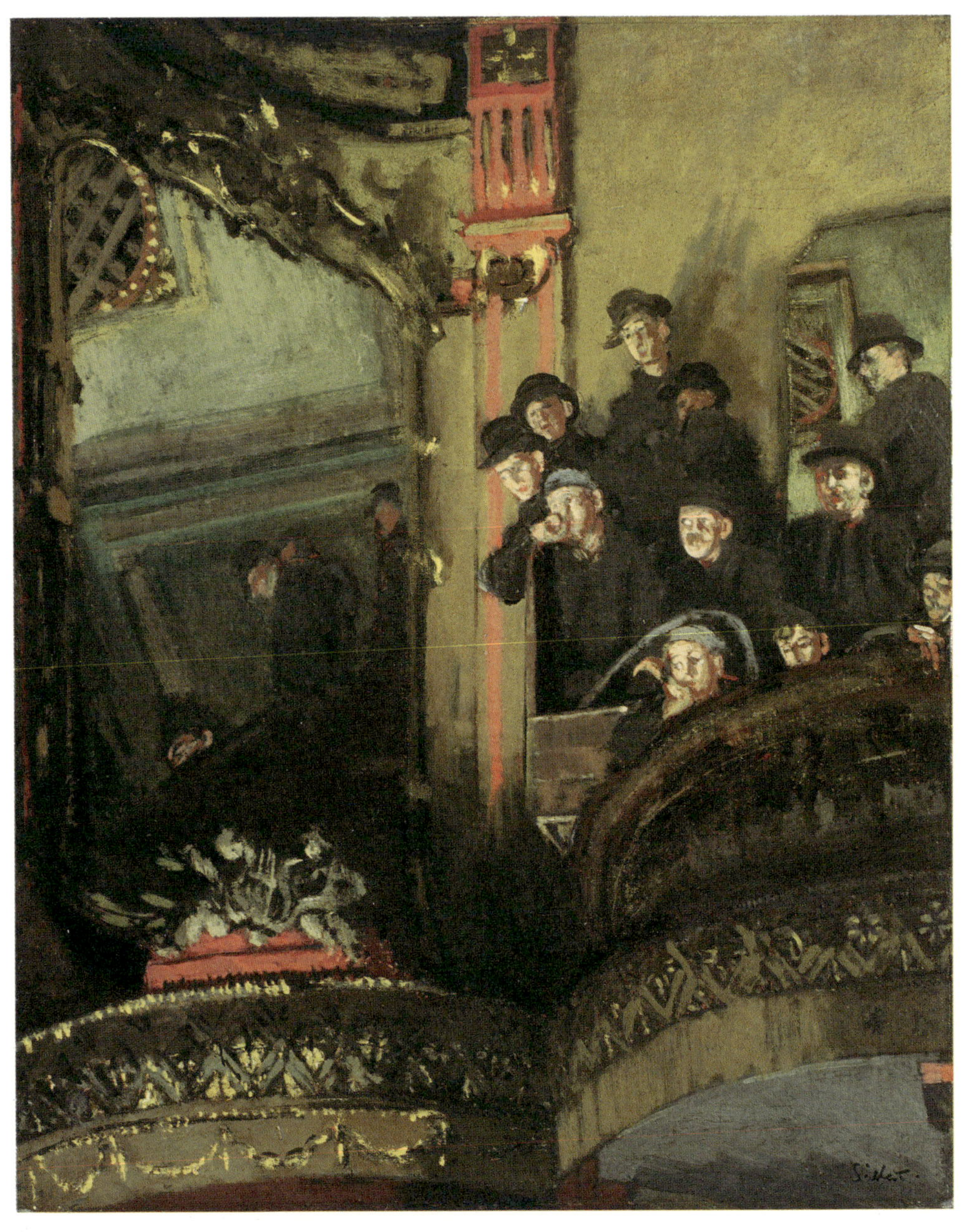

2 Walter Richard Sickert, *The Old Bedford*, *c.* 1895.
Oil on canvas, 76.3 × 60.5 cm (30⅛ × 23⅞ in.)

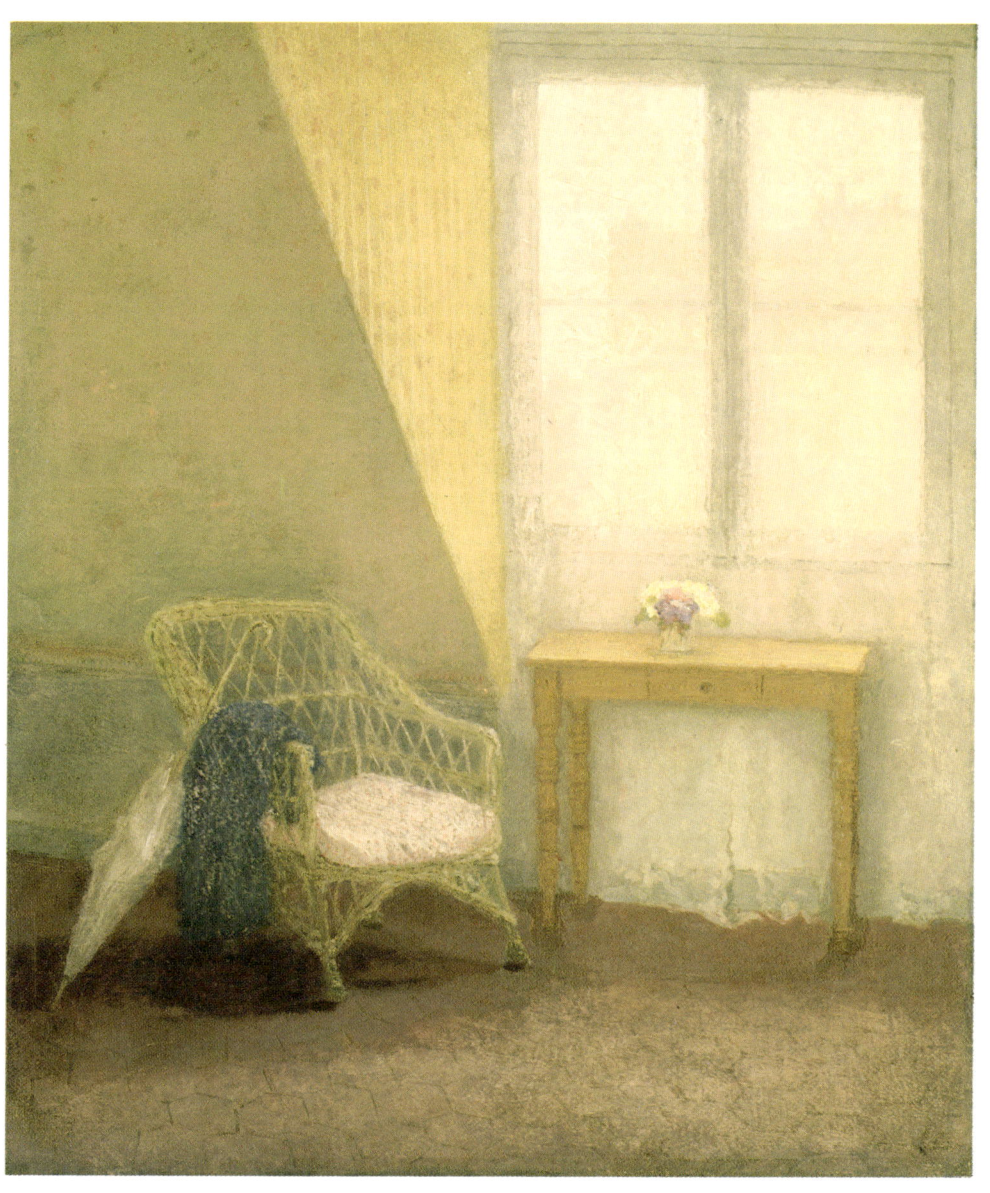

3 Gwen John, *A Corner of the Artist's Room in Paris*, 1907–9.
Oil on canvas, 31.7 × 26.7 cm (12½ × 10⅝ in.)

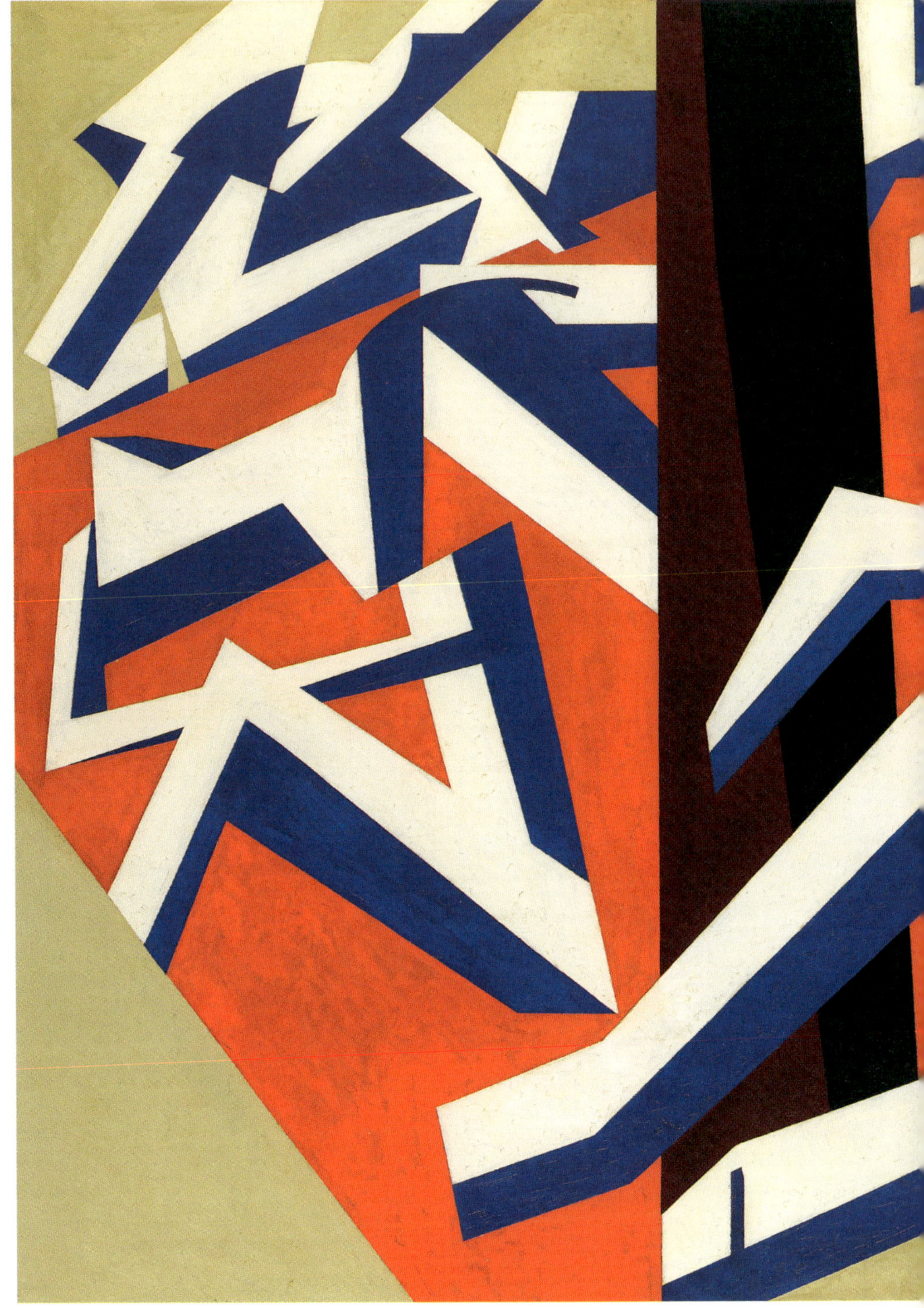

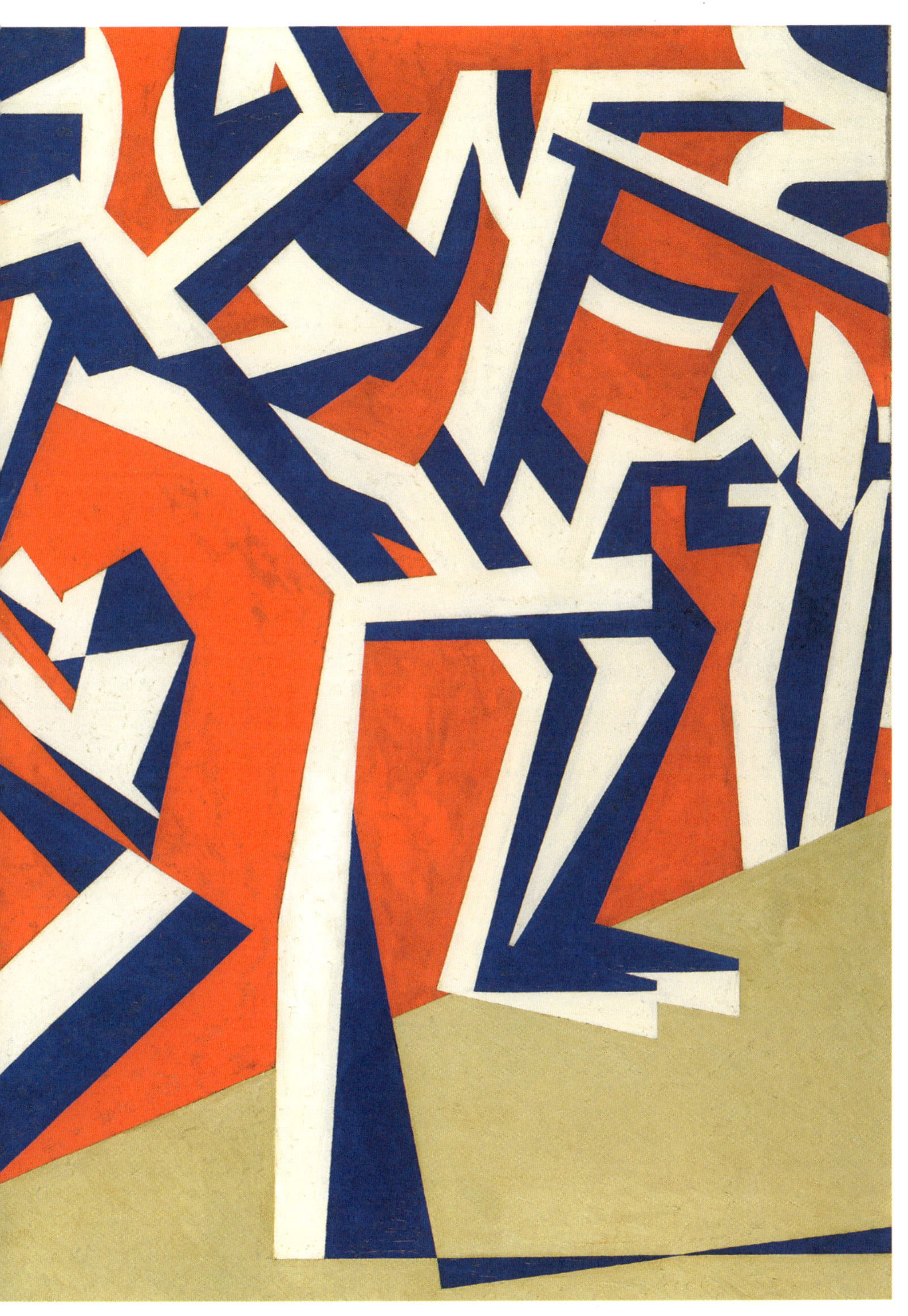

4 David Bomberg, *The Mud Bath*, 1914. Oil on canvas, 152.4 × 224.2 cm (60 × 88⅜ in.)

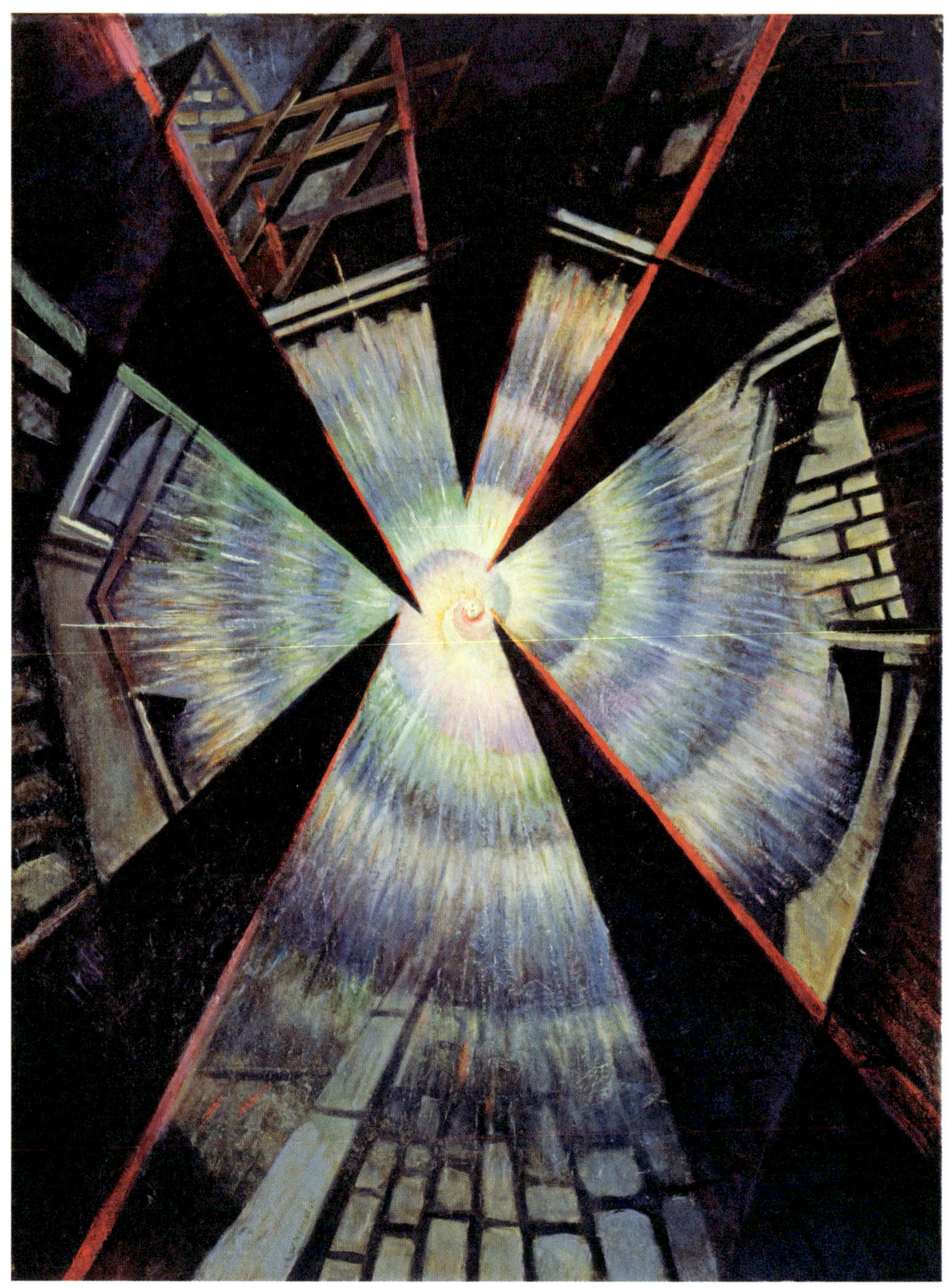

5 Christopher Richard Wynne Nevinson, *Bursting Shell*, 1915.
Oil on canvas, 76 × 56 cm (30 × 22⅛ in.)

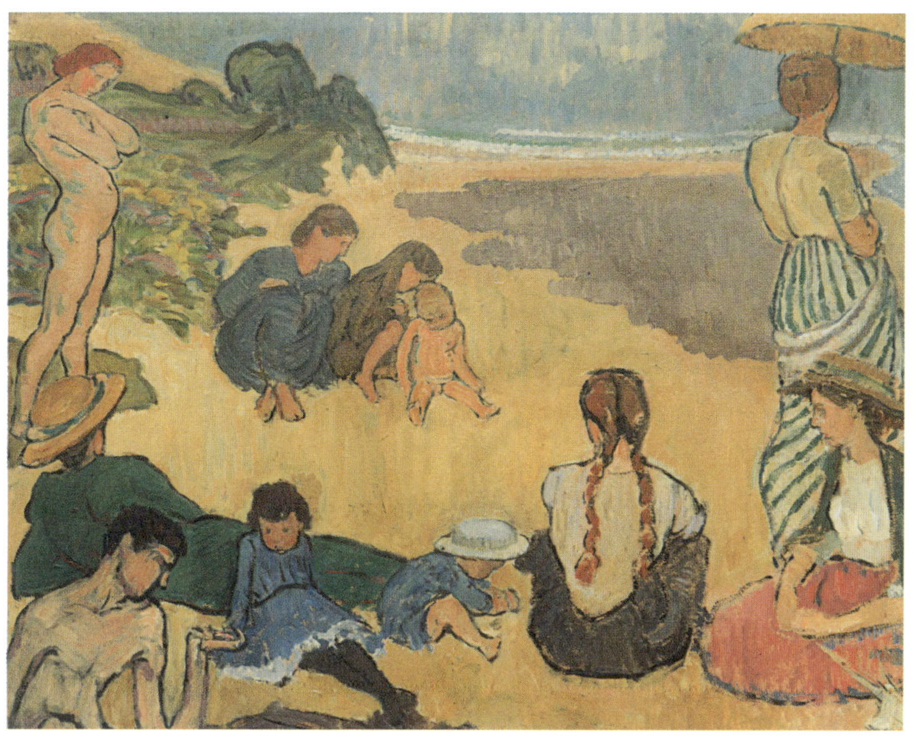

6 Vanessa Bell, *Bathers*, 1911. Oil on canvas, 76.2 × 101.2 cm (30 × 39⅞ in.)

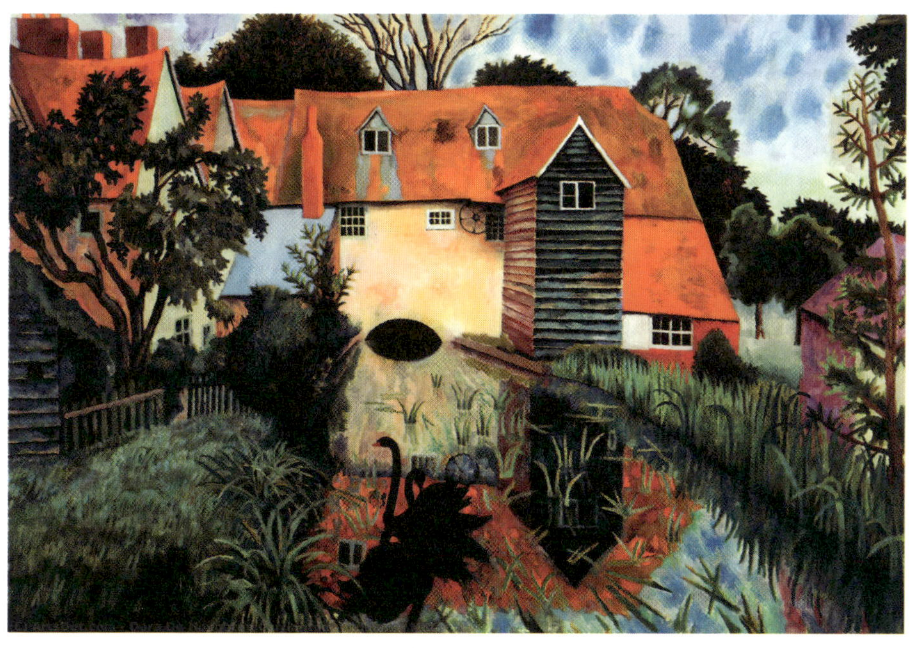

7 Dora Carrington, *The Mill at Tidmarsh, Berkshire*, 1918.
Oil on canvas, 71.1 × 101.6 cm (28 × 40 in.)

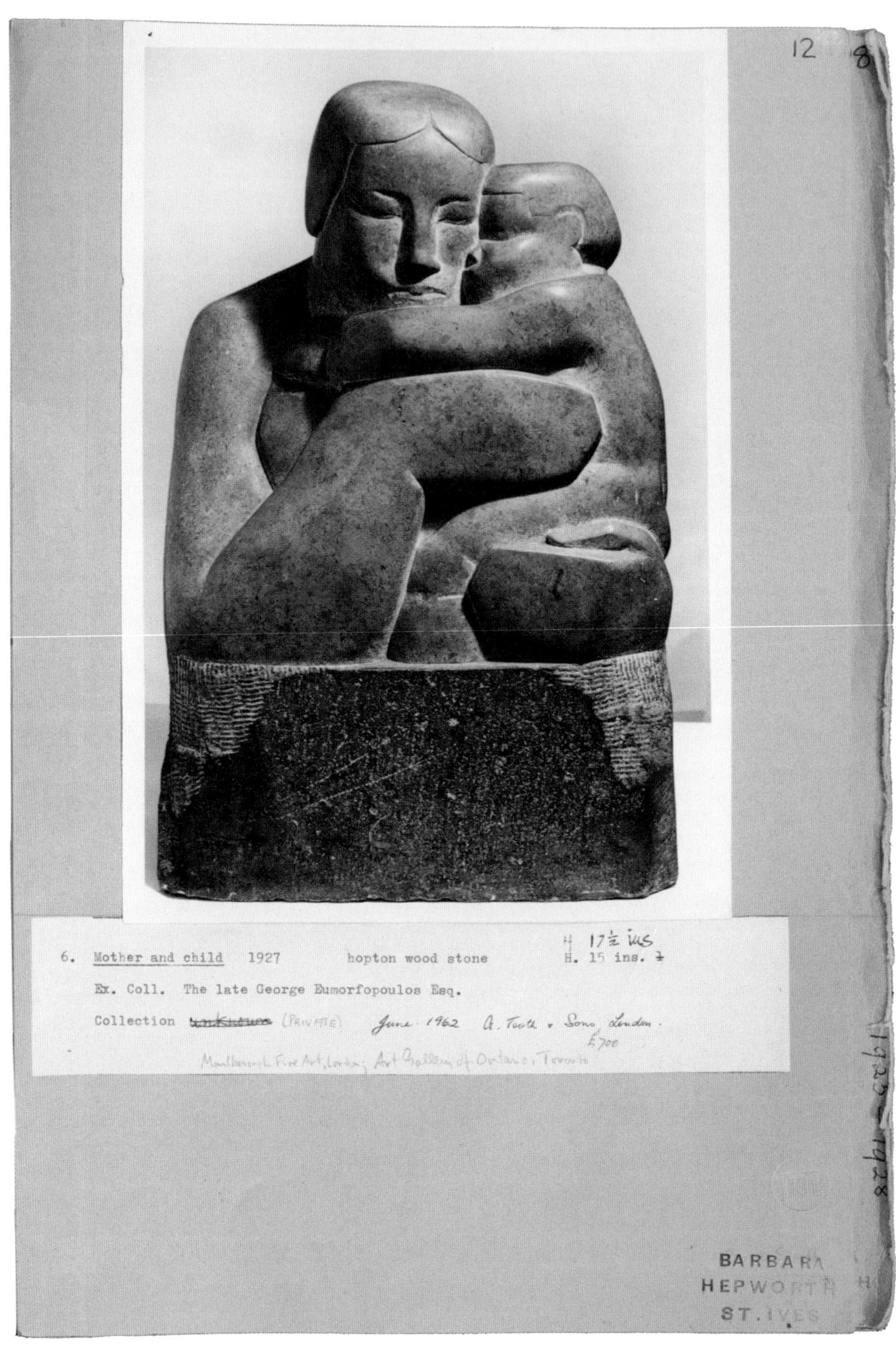

8 Barbara Hepworth, volume of sculpture records, page 12,
with reproduction of a photograph of *Mother and Child* (1927), 1925–28

country, which Lewis, too, had explored. For this, his first big piece of work, he produced a scissory cubo-futurist melange in blue, white and black – slant lines and poking curves, from which snarling or hieratic faces sprang like the knobs on African war clubs. He adroitly combined the energy of the Ballets Russes with the brutal masks in Picasso's 1907 *Demoiselles d'Avignon*, which he had seen in Paris, thanks to a tip-off from John. *Kermesse* was exactly the primitivist–contemporary mix Strindberg was after: it struck partygoers as the very spirit of the Cave. Recalling 'super-heated' good times there, writer Osbert Sitwell imagined Lewis's mural come to life, an orgy of 'gesticulating figures, dancing and talking while the rhythm of the primitive forms of ragtime throbbed through the whole room'.

Working-class male students at the Slade like Bomberg and Gertler felt awkward socializing because, although accepted for themselves and their talent, they were unable to reciprocate hospitality. 'By my ambitions I am cut off from my own family and class,' complained Gertler, 'and by them I have been raised to be equal to a class I hate! They do not understand me nor I them. So I am an outcast.' The Café Royal and the Cave of the Golden Calf – a short walk after an hour or two with Michelangelo and Botticelli in the National Gallery – were places where the usual social rules and hierarchies did not apply. At the Cave's communal round table, Bomberg 'wined & dined to contentment' in company with Lewis, Nevinson and guest of honour Marinetti, but clearly struck Lewis as something of an enigma. One wintry night, while working on *Kermesse*, he tracked Bomberg down to Whitechapel. Hearing a 'peremptory knuckle on the door', Bomberg was disconcerted to find Lewis on the threshold. It was surely 'an inconvenient hour to tramp through the snow and mount three flights of stairs with the gas-jets off – anyhow, how did you know I lived up here?' To which the reply came: 'Nothing is impossible for Wyndham Lewis – Bomberg! I have come to see what you are doing.' Bomberg laid aside the drawing he was finishing of performers at the nearby Yiddish theatre. Lewis stayed until dawn, by which time, Bomberg would recall, 'we had talked ourselves silly'.

After the Cave mural, Lewis conceived a venture of his own – a clubhouse or headquarters for the London avant-garde, to be funded largely by his rich artist girlfriend, Kate Lechmere. Its aim would be to counter the Italian takeover of the avant-garde agenda – the ubiquitous Marinetti's 'Futurist Evenings' at the Poetry Bookshop in Bloomsbury, his twelve 'noise-making' gigs at the London Coliseum and Albert Hall. In April 1914, the Rebel Art Centre opened in Great Ormond Street, Bloomsbury; its founding members included Bomberg, Wadsworth, Nevinson (whom Lewis hoped to wean away from Marinetti), Lechmere and Jessica Dismorr, a suffragette and recent convert from sunny fauvist landscapes to London-coloured futurism. The oldest 'Rebel' was the thirty-three-year-old Epstein, who was renting a garage-studio in nearby Lamb's Conduit Street.

Calling round to see Epstein there in December 1913, Bomberg found him working on a strange new sculpture – a plaster figure poised astride a miners' pneumatic rock drill, which Epstein had picked up in a junk shop. There was a tall steel tripod, with a seat on which the driller sat, the bit pointing down between his legs, like a machine gun directed at the rock face, or a futuristic steel penis (Epstein was said to be 'mad about sex'). The figure operating the drill was not a miner but more like a machine-age centaur, with caliper legs and a taut, scooped-out torso – part-strongman, part-skeleton. Skewed forwards and staring, instead of a face it had a helmet-beak, shaped to both wound and protect. All that was missing was the hammering shudder of the drill itself – movement and noise – although every shape in Epstein's 'robot' seemed tensed in a silent yell.

The Italian futurist painters had already claimed to be able to give form to sound. Painting had once been 'a silent art', announced Carlo Carrà, but not any more. The futurists' 'love of modern life in its essential dynamism' embraced 'its sounds, noises and smells'. Where 'silent' painters dipped their brushes in mere colours, futurists wielded 'Reds, rrrrrreds, the rrrrreddest rrrrrrreds that shouuuuuuut.... Greens, that can never be greener, greeeeeeeeeeeener that screeeeeeeam...'. In the 'mechanical and sporting world', explained Carrà, 'sounds, noises and smells are predominantly red'. In restaurants, they were 'silver, yellow and violet', while 'those of a woman are green, blue and violet'. The futurists were the first artists to make noise a specific part of their platform, and London in 1914 was the epicentre of futurist noise. Futurist paintings might in reality be as silent as 'the serene, the hieratic and the mummified' Old Masters mocked by Carrà, but they looked as if – were you able to hear them – they would emit percussive, whooshing, rhythmic sounds. 'You must paint,' commanded Carrà, 'as drunkards sing and vomit, sounds, noises and smells!'

When Nevinson painted the crowd in a nightclub, he could have had Carrà's 1913 manifesto ringing in his ears. In *Dance Hall Scene* (*c.* 1913–14), the revellers surge towards the viewer as if futurism were a recreational drug they had all dropped, a silent rave of faces and tuxedoed torsos. In April 1914 – undiplomatically timed to coincide with the inauguration of Lewis's Rebel Art Centre – Nevinson collaborated with Marinetti in *Zang Tumb Tumb*, a futurist performance at the Doré Gallery. This was Marinetti's party piece, a sonic re-enactment of the 1912–13 siege of the Turkish city of Adrianople (Edirne) by Serbian forces in the First Balkan War, which he had covered as a correspondent for the French newspaper *L'intransigeant*. Marinetti stood behind a table, on which were arranged a telephone – a noise-transmitting gadget still only to be found in elite households and offices, and on battlefields – as well as 'some boards, and the right sort of hammers so that I could act out the orders of the Turkish general and the sounds of rifle and machine-gun fire':

> *At three different points in the room, three blackboards had been set up, and these I approached, each in its turn, either walking or running, so as to make rapid chalk sketches…. In a room some distance away, two great drums were set, and with these the painter Nevinson, who was assisting me, produced the thunder of cannon, when I telephoned him to do so.*

It was as if machine guns and bombardments had become such well-worn futurist tropes that their sensationalism had to be ratcheted up anew each time, like cranking the handle on a telephone. Yet as metaphors, they still embodied the 'blasty' energy of this avant-garde moment in London, as well as the uncanny mutual mirroring between art and politics. The opening of the Rebel Art Centre and the performance *Zang Tumb Tumb* coincided almost to the day with the destruction of the Great Yarmouth Pier (luckily deserted at the time) by a suffragist bomb, adding to the Women's Social and Political Union's recent tally of cultural scalps, such as the Empire Theatre in Kingston-upon-Thames and a cinema in Penzance, Cornwall.

The fitting-out of the Rebel Art Centre was in full swing, with Nevinson designing futurist screens and Lewis painting murals, when, on 7 June, another manifesto appeared. 'Vital English Art' was published in *The Observer*, to which it had been delivered on Rebel Art Centre notepaper, apparently signed by the entire membership, although this was the first they'd heard of it. Worse still, it had clearly been authored by Marinetti,

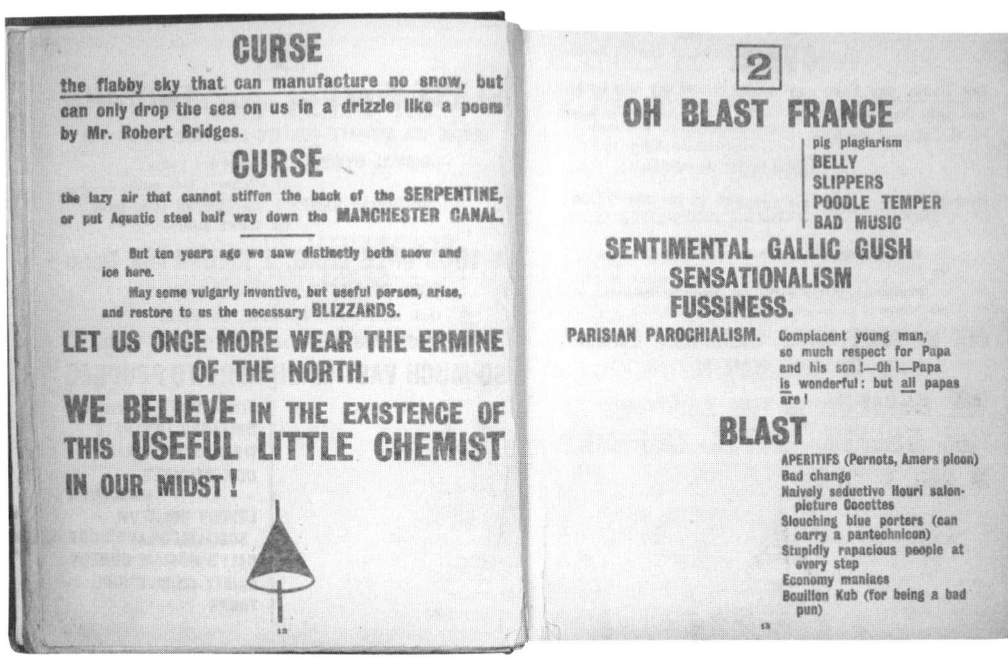

Percy Wyndham Lewis, page from *BLAST*, no. 1, July 1914

abetted by Nevinson. Only one thing, it proclaimed, could save English art from 'certain death', namely 'a great Futurist avant-garde'. Softening the nihilistic chutzpah of Marinetti's 1909 manifesto, it played on the idea of radical art as life-saving therapy for a soul-sick world, listing twelve fatal symptoms. These covered the 'commercial obsession' of English painters, the public's 'pessimistic, sceptical, and nostalgic tastes', and the 'English perception of art as an idle pastime'. Oddly enough, the healing power of futurism was not expected to work on the people who needed it most, the 'false revolutionaries of the New English Art Club' and the 'sub-Rossettis with long hair beneath their sombreros'. Lewis and the sharp-eyed wordsmith Pound saw 'Vital English Art' exactly for what it was: a piece of nightclub burlesque posing as that most attention-grabbing genre of the moment, the manifesto. Within days they were drafting their response, a magazine-manifesto to which they gave the title *BLAST*.

BLAST was at the printers when, on 29 June 1914, news came of a terrorist incident the previous day – not in Yarmouth or Penzance, but in faraway Sarajevo, in Bosnia and Herzegovina. Archduke Franz

Ferdinand, heir to the throne of Austria-Hungary, and his wife had been assassinated by Gavrilo Princip, a Bosnian Serb student and member of The Black Hand, an underground organization dedicated to the creation of a South Slav state. Austria immediately declared war on Serbia. Few in Britain took much notice: this was the kind of thing you might expect to happen in the Balkans, the land of *Zang Tumb Tumb*. On 2 July, *BLAST: Review of the Great English Vortex* appeared. The title was a stroke of genius: 'blast' meant an explosion – louder than any noise a noisy futurist could make – but it was also a storm-wind, a lightning bolt and a typically English imprecation. Conflate all these meanings and *BLAST* signified pure energy, channelled by a new weapon in the manifesto wars – the vortex. This word, and the term 'Vorticism', were Pound's contribution: he defined the vortex, as in 'a textbook of Mechanics', as 'the point of maximum energy'. Translated into visual art, the vortex took the form of zigzags and V-shapes – much like futurism, except that Vorticism was not inspired by wheels and propellers but instead by the stern structures of the modern 'steel city'.

'Vital English Art' mocked England as an anti-avant-gardist land of 'Garden Cities, maypoles, Morris dances, Fairy stories, aestheticism, Oscar Wilde'. The Vorticists, as they styled themselves (there was even a 'Vortographer', Alvin Langdon Coburn), would fight back, deploying English humour 'like a bomb'. *BLAST* affirmed that England's worst shortcomings – 'the *idée fixe* of Class', the 'heavy stagnant pools of Saxon blood, incapable of anything but the song of the frog' – paradoxically accounted for the fact that (unlike modern Italy, it was implied) 'England produces such good artists'. In England, Lewis affirmed, 'a movement towards art and imagination could burst up...with more force than anywhere else', because industrial England was the birthplace of 'Machinery, trains, steamships, all that distinguishes externally our time'. It was English 'mechanical inventiveness', not 'Futuristic gush over machines, aeroplanes, etc.', that had 'brought all the hemispheres' of world culture here, now, to London.

Despite its call-to-arms typography, *BLAST* read more like a long, rambling poem than a manifesto. And the Vorticists, characterized by Lewis as 'Primitive Mercenaries in the Modern World', were in effect another club that – despite Lewis's insistent invitations – Bomberg declined to join. His summer of 1914 was busy enough, the kind of time that comes only once in a young artist's life. On 8 May, 'Twentieth

Century Art: A Review of Modern Movements' opened at Whitechapel Art Gallery. Bomberg and Gertler were well represented in the large Jewish section, for which Bomberg and Epstein had selected work on a trip to Paris in 1913. Among the 133 artists, there were 34 women. Press coverage since 'Manet and the Post-Impressionists' had made the public aware of modern art's proliferating groups and subgroups, the Darwinian evolutionary tree of related and rival species that was almost its most distinctive feature when compared with earlier eras. In the *Daily Express*, Paul Konody wondered how East End people would cope with the 'whole flood of the various isms let loose like a catalyst' by 'Twentieth Century Art'. The exhibition presented 'a complete résumé of the whole rapid evolution, beginning with a revolt against liberal realism and ending in utterly unintelligible abstraction'. *What did we expect?*, Bomberg must have thought.

In July, he had his first solo exhibition at the Chenil Galleries in Chelsea. Inside the gallery hung fifty-four works; outside, on the street, stood his latest big painting, *The Mud Bath* (pl. 4), over 7 feet long. It is an even bolder statement than *In the Hold*: in place of 'cubist' fragmentation, Bomberg painted big, clean shapes, a tumbling semaphore of geometrical gestures, in blue and white, on a red background. A dark shaft, like a pillar, divides two sides of what looks like an indoor space, where figures – if those shapes are human figures – sit or lie or dance. The rhythm is physically contagious, not machine-like: you want to join in with them, but you can't – they are being human in their way, not in yours. Around the canvas, Bomberg stuck Union Jacks. It amused him to see the horses drawing the number 29 bus shy at the flags as they rounded the corner of the King's Road. This was Bomberg's humour-bomb for England – each Union Jack a Vorticist picture (the V-shapes of energy focused at the core) adorning his image of a Jewish bathhouse in patriotic red, white and blue.

Before the exhibition ended, there were plenty of Union Jacks on the streets. War. It had happened so quickly. No one had expected Russia to mobilize its entire army in support of Serbia (which had managed to keep the Austrians at bay) or that, within two days, Germany would launch all-out war on Russia and declare war on France, or that the following day, 320,000 German troops would march on neutral Belgium. Britain finally stepped into the ring, declaring war on Germany on 4 August. By mid-August, the Belgian city of Liège was under siege, its civilian population bombed from the air by Zeppelins, shelled from 10 miles' distance by a gigantic howitzer that needed a thousand men to assemble it from parts brought to the battle lines by train. Many people still believed it would be a fast war. Belgium was overrun and Paris nearly seized by the Germans, then the German army fell back to the River Aisne, all within a month.

Lines on the map of Europe, familiar from the school atlas, took on the queasy ambiguity of a cubist painting. To make sure that spies and fifth-columnists were prevented from crossing them, the government introduced photographic passports. Foreigners, from now on, would be officially, bureaucratically foreign. In mid-September, the opposing German and Anglo-French armies dug the first lines of trenches in northern France, and it began to dawn that this war, in which machines set the pace and scale of the killing, was snarled in stalemate, spelling the muddy end of futurism's dream of speed. War was no longer a manifesto-writer's metaphor but a present reality that would stress-test every precept of the avant-garde.

7
Chamber of horrors

Cape Town, July 1914

'Art is now, as it were, a volcano. Eruptions are continual, and immense cities of culture at its foot are shaken and shivered.' Isaac Rosenberg, a short, slightly built young artist from London, with large, rather mournful eyes, surveys the all-female audience that artist and pianist Madge Cook has invited to hear him lecture in her Cape Town studio. 'The roots of a dead universe are torn up by hands,' he continues, 'feverish and consuming with an exuberant vitality – and amid dynamic threatenings we watch the hastening of corroding doom.' Rosenberg grew up in Whitechapel, the son of Jewish immigrants. Like his friend David Bomberg, he studied at the Slade, producing sensitive drawings in an accomplished Slade manner, and portraits of himself and members of his proud but penurious family, some of which were shown in May at 'Twentieth Century Art' at Whitechapel Art Gallery. The following month, on medical advice, he sailed for Cape Town, to stay with relatives, to give his weak chest respite from London pollution and stress. He now tells his audience that, although the only sensation a futurist picture has ever given him 'is that of a house falling', futurism has changed the game: it has 'introduced urgency – energy into Art, and striven to connect it more with life'. This kind of life, he implies, is not intimate or domestic, like the life observed by Gwen John or even Van Gogh. Despite his pacifist instincts, Rosenberg has been stirred by the futurists' summons to set about art with a martial 'energy in destroying'. 'Art is not a plaything,' he informed Mrs Cohen, who sponsored his place at the Slade, 'It is blood and tears.'

———

War – 'the sole cleanser of the world' in Marinetti's words. According to the bestselling German military author General Friedrich von Bernhardi, war was a Darwinian 'biological necessity' and every man's 'moral obligation'. Bernhardi was a nationalist extremist, whose victory formula in *Germany and the Next War* (published in English in 1912) included a strong libertarian strand. In a healthy society that gave free rein to 'the fullest development of all individual forces and capacities, of all spiritual, scientific, and artistic aims', war could be seen as *the* transcendent expression of creative energy. This was not quite as fanatical as it seems. Since the Franco-Prussian War of 1871, Europe had enjoyed an unprecedented four decades of freedom from large-scale conflict. Even among war enthusiasts like Heinrich von Treitschke – another German ultra-nationalist – there was a belief that mechanization and 'the progress of culture' would make wars more focused, 'rarer and shorter', although also 'far more sanguinary' than in the Napoleonic or early modern past. War theory, like art, had developed its own avant-garde ideology of invigorating violence in the cause of human advancement.

Generals and futuristically minded artists were far from alone in their fixation on a phantasmagorical drama in which Western civilization, imagined as a moribund body, received life-giving 'cleansing' (*igiene* was Marinetti's term) through the agency of war – 'medicine for mankind diseased', as Treitschke put it. How the soul of Europe had become sick and dirty in the first place was unclear. Ruskin would have blamed industrialization and capitalist greed; Bernhardi identified the cause as a degenerate addiction to peace. Instead of taking advantage of peace to prepare for war, governments had allowed 'the misery produced by weakness' to take root. In the early weeks of actual conflict, Virginia Stephen's heartthrob Cambridge friend Rupert Brooke, fresh from travels in America, Canada and Tahiti and newly commissioned into the Royal Naval Reserve (his commanding officer, Winston Churchill, had taken a liking to Brooke's verse), wrote a poem celebrating the demise of peace. As a raw volunteer, Brooke had watched the people of Antwerp fleeing their pulverized city after German bombardment by 160 heavy guns, but his tone in 'Peace' is jubilant, as if war will deliver rebirth rather than its opposite.

> *Now, God be thanked who has matched us with this hour*
> *And caught our youth, and wakened us from sleeping!*

The time had come,

> *To turn as swimmers into cleanness leaping,*
> *Glad from a world grown old and cold and weary.*

With its megaphonic posturing, the *Futurist Manifesto* of 1909 had been the least Bloomsburyish document imaginable. Roger Fry even-handedly allowed that there were 'positive elements in the creed', although the futurists' 'love of speed and mechanism' personally left him cold. Reviewing their 1912 exhibition, he decided that the futurists had 'failed to produce that lyrical intensity of mood which might alone enable the spectator to share their feelings'. The realization that Brooke's 'Peace' reads at times like a pastoral iteration of the futurist creed reveals the depth at which fantasies of transformative annihilation had leached into youthful consciousness in the years before 1914. Rosenberg was talking art, not geopolitics, in his lecture for 'the Cultured Woman' of South Africa when he conjured the futurist energy of 'Violence and perpetual struggle'.

He was sceptical about art's ability to realize this vision (those futurist 'falling bricks'), but he spoke as if, like a Bible story, the apocalyptic vision itself were entirely capable of realization – which of course it was, although in armaments factories and battlefields, not artists' studios. In 1912, just three years after Marinetti sang 'The lissom flight of the aeroplane, whose propeller flutters like a flag in the wind', the Royal Flying Corps was established. The first squadrons of Avro 504 biplanes fluttered into action with the British Expeditionary Force in August 1914, with mixed but promisingly speedy results. Futurism's 'ravening motor cars' would play their part, too, in the slaughter grounds of northern France, together with new British devices like the long-serving Mills bomb and Lewis automatic machine gun, the 2-inch trench mortar and the Mark I tank. Britain might not, yet, have reached white heat as a crucible of modern art, but by the end of the war the deadly logic of invention and investment would equip it with the world's most machine-heavy army.

For whatever reasons – adventure or resignation, money worries or a desire to participate in the defining experience of their generation – few of the male students in soft sombreros in the 1912 Slade picnic photograph resisted the call to war. Well before March 1916, when national conscription of men between the ages of eighteen and forty-one came into force after the passing of the Military Service Act, Bomberg, Rosenberg, Richard Nevinson, Stanley Spencer and Edward Wadsworth were all in khaki, along with Augustus John and Percy Wyndham Lewis. Tasked with fighting for a cause much harder to frame than the defence of the nation's own borders and population, they and many recruits to

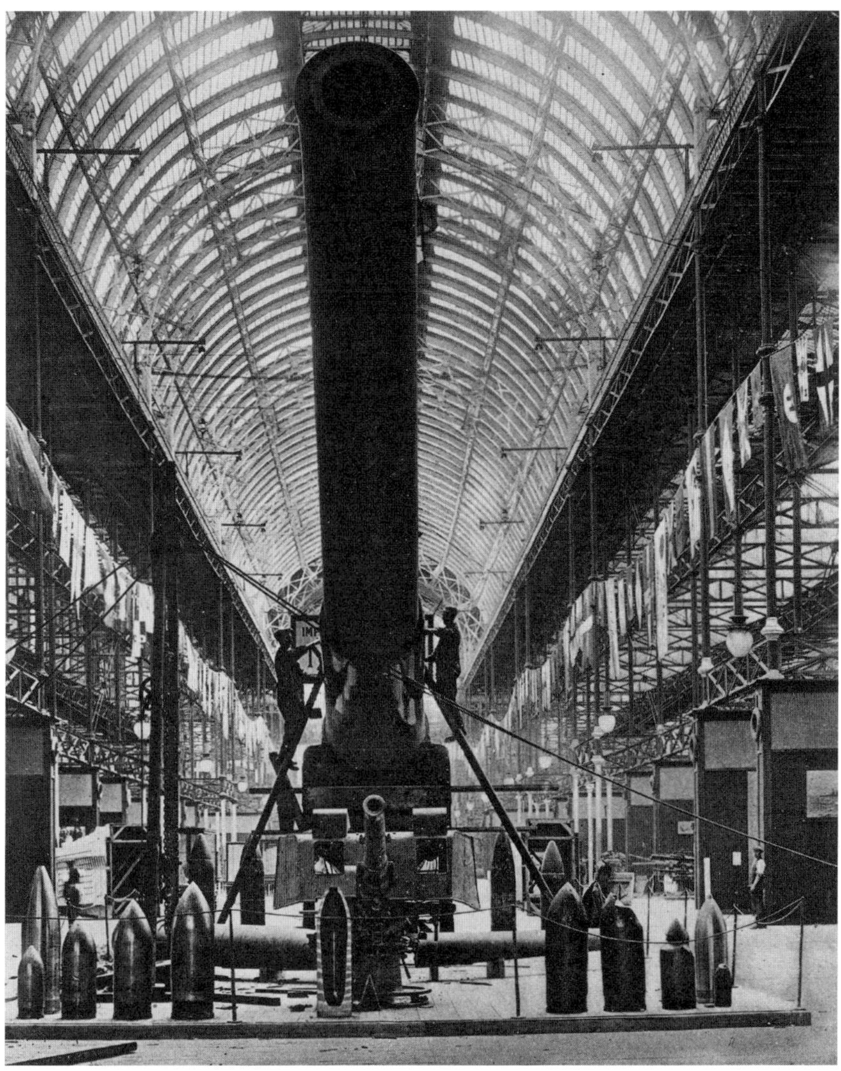

Full-size model of the largest (18 in.) type of British gun used in the First World War, on display at the Imperial War Museum, Crystal Palace, London, 1920

Britain's volunteer army would have heard, and perhaps believed, the new narrative of modern war, which defined their job not as warriors but as peacemakers. In September 1914, Prime Minister H. H. Asquith announced that going into battle in support of Belgium was essential for 'the repudiation of militarism as the governing factor in the relations of states and in the future moulding of the European world'. The fruits of victory would be 'a real European partnership based on recognition of equal rights and established and enforced by a common will'. In other words, the route to lasting peace lay through war. The future-focused idealism on which this paradox rested was perfectly pitched to disarm democratic opposition. Emmeline Pankhurst and the Women's Social and Political Union put aside their bomb-making kits and fell in behind the war effort. 'It's a fearful nuisance, this war,' Rosenberg wrote to the literary editor Edward Marsh; and yet, 'I think the safest place is at the front – we'll starve or die of suspense, anywhere else.'

Suspense, that essential ingredient of pre-1914 modernity – the what-next? of cinema and the fast-breaking waves of artistic 'isms' – had become the property of war. Yet Rosenberg still hoped that, as an artist, he could contribute to the long-term project of international peace. While Europe 'stepped into its bath of blood,' he wrote from Cape Town, 'I will be waiting with beautiful drying towels of painted canvas, and precious ointments to smear and heal the soul.... I really hope to have a nice lot of pictures and poems by the time all is settled again; and Europe is repenting of her savageries.' In September 1914, as Allied and German forces faced off in deepening stalemate along the River Aisne, the Western Front was still for artists a largely imagined 'point of maximum energy', with a certain fierce glamour. The contagiously performative nature of the avant-garde in its various manifestations in London in the past four years – Sergei Diaghilev's Ballets Russes, Marinetti's futurist cabarets, Bomberg's *Mud Bath* hedgehogged with horse-scaring Union Jacks – all of this associated modern art with action. And avant-garde, after all, literally meant being out in front of the front line. Now, suddenly, the Front was France, which for young British artists had traditionally represented the kinds of art they were drawn to, the life they dreamed of leading.

After returning to England in the spring of 1915, Rosenberg agonized about the best course of action. Should he volunteer? Perhaps the Royal Army Medical Corps would have him: 'the idea of killing upsets me a bit', he confessed. By October, he had decided not to, because 'more men means more war – besides the immorality of joining with no patriotic convictions'. A week or so later, Private Rosenberg was in training with the Bantam Battalion (he was too short for a regular unit) at Bury St Edmunds. The prospect of regular pay had been a deciding factor – he hoped that half his wages could be paid to his mother – but the squalor and anti-Semitism at boot camp were 'unbearable'. He had packed hurriedly and had only a handkerchief to wash with – there would be no more 'beautiful drying towels of painted canvas'. This was a life stripped of art, literature and basic personal freedoms: 'There is not a book or paper here; we are not allowed to stir from the gate…and are utterly wretched.' In June 1916, his regiment was posted to France, where 'we made straight for the trenches'. In the poem 'From France', he juxtaposed his pre-war fantasy of artists' Paris – 'The spirit drank the café lights;/All the hot life that glittered there' – with the wartime reality:

> *Heaped stones and a charred signboard shows*
> *With grass between and dead folk under,*
> *And some birds sing, while the spirit takes wing.*
> *And this is Life in France.*

Nevinson had been the first of his Slade cohort to cross the Channel for active service, as a medical orderly in the Friends Ambulance Unit. Arriving in Dunkirk in November 1914, he was immediately put to work, unskilled and unprepared, in a railway shed hastily repurposed as a clearing station for three thousand wounded French soldiers. The task of hygiene and cleansing became a grimly practical business of wound-dressing and bedpan-emptying, in the course of which Nevinson grew inured to 'sights so revolting that man seldom conceives them'. A few months earlier, he and Marinetti had roused a gallery audience to quasi-orgasmic rapture with 'onomatopoeic artillery' – 'their bodies alight with emotion at the violent effects of battle'. In France, he slogged through days and nights amid 'shrieks, pus, gangrene and the disembowelled'.

Stricken by rheumatism, Nevinson was shipped back to London, where his residual loyalty to futurism led him to cobble together a revisionist version of the 'creed', 'A Futurist's View of War':

> *All artists should go to the front to strengthen their art by a worship of*
> *physical and moral courage and a fearless desire of adventure, risk and*
> *daring and free themselves from the canker of archaeologists, cicerones,*
> *antiquaries and beauty worshippers.*

The pain and squalor he witnessed in Dunkirk are weirdly absent from this grandstanding appeal to courage and adventure, which reads as if the terminology of the futurist–Vorticist art war, when put to the test, was too brittle to stretch around the brute facts of conflict. In his

1915 painting *Bursting Shell* (pl. 5), Nevinson attempted to synthesize futurist form with battlefield realism: the aerial explosion is a rainbow-coloured Catherine wheel of futuristic energy sliced by knife-like black Vorticist V-shapes – savage, yes, but more redolent of Whistler's *Falling Rocket* than night in no-man's land. In another painting from 1915, *La Mitrailleuse*, a sleek French machine-gun crew with Vorticized faces and helmets have an air of auditioning for the cover of *BLAST*.

In July 1915, Lewis edited a special – and final – 'War Number' of *BLAST*, but his tone throughout is that of a stand-up pressing on with his act in the face of audience drift. Will the war change art? No, because 'All art that matters is already so far ahead that it is beyond the sphere of these disturbances.' War might provide artists with new imagery ('The huge German siege guns, for instance, are a stimulus to visions of power'), but will, it seems likely, mainly affect them through the collapse of sales: 'I will put it to some people,' Lewis airily proposed, 'that, could a few hundred pounds be divided up amongst those artists who in ordinary times find difficulty in selling their work, and now must be penniless, it would be a noble action.'

A more disturbing picture of the situation for combatant artists comes from a contribution by the sculptor Henri Gaudier-Brzeska, a Vorticist associate who had returned from London to his native France to enlist. After two months at the Front, Gaudier-Brzeska still clung to the notion of war as a cleansing agent, even a form of population control – a 'MECHANISM, WHICH SERVES AS A PURGE TO OVER-NUMEROUS HUMANITY', asserting that 'MY VIEWS ON SCULPTURE REMAIN ABSOLUTELY THE SAME'. He cited an 'experiment' he had undertaken in the trenches near Arras:

> *Two days ago I pinched from an enemy a mauser rifle. Its heavy unwieldly shape swamped me with a powerful IMAGE of brutality.*
>
> *I was in doubt for a long time whether it pleased or displeased me.*
> *I found that I did not like it.*
> *I broke the butt off and with my knife I carved in it a design, through which I tried to express a gentler order of feeling, which I preferred.*
> *BUT I WILL EMPHASIZE that MY DESIGN got its effect (just as the gun had) FROM A VERY SIMPLE COMPOSITION OF LINES AND PLANES.*

Gaudier-Brzeska died a Vorticist. His piece in *BLAST* is followed by a black-edged notice announcing that, a month before publication, he had been killed in combat at Neuville Saint-Vaast. Vorticism's most impressive appearance in the theatre of war, however, may have been due to Wadsworth, who managed to design a few Vorticist woodcuts while serving with the navy on Lemnos in the eastern Mediterranean. It is possible that he shared these with his brother officer and artist Norman Wilkinson, who persuaded the Admiralty to adopt a new method of camouflaging ships with abstract 'dazzle' patterns of bold stripes, slashes and zigzags, making it difficult for observers in enemy submarines to fix their speed and position. Wadsworth later supervised the dazzle-painting process in naval dockyards in Bristol and Plymouth.

Lewis managed to get a commission as an artillery officer. At a howitzer battery outside Bailleul, near the Belgian border, he received his 'baptism of fire', spending the night under bombardment in a cramped 'earthen igloo', protected by 'a few shovelfuls of earth and a log or two', in the company of a terrified fellow officer. Recounting the experience in his 1937 war memoir *Blasting and Bombardiering*, Lewis adds another dimension, and a retrospective humour, to the semantics of *BLAST*.

> *As the shell descended – with its strange parabolic whooping onrush – an anal whistle answered it, from the neighbouring bed.... And at each successive shell-swoop it was repeated. He raised himself slightly; and he answered the frightening onrush of the cylinder of metal with his humble gaseous discharge. He did not seem to mind at all my seeing this.*

Since artists were sharing both the most mundane and extreme moments of their lives with men for whom modern art meant nothing, the war fundamentally recast the relationship between artist and public. No aesthetic strangeness or shockingness could match the ordinary soldier's experience. Rosenberg sketched with pencil stubs on the backs of envelopes, wrote poetry on any scrap of paper he could pocket. It was not only that the conditions for painting – time, space, materials – had disappeared, but also that painting requires and creates relationship with external objects, of the kind that is quickly extinguished when real 'energy in destroying' defines the situation. Lyric poetry, on the other hand – as the Russian poet Marina Tsvetaeva would frame it in comparably extreme circumstances – 'is the sheer condition of going through something, suffering something through, and in the intervals...it is a condition of infinite poverty'.

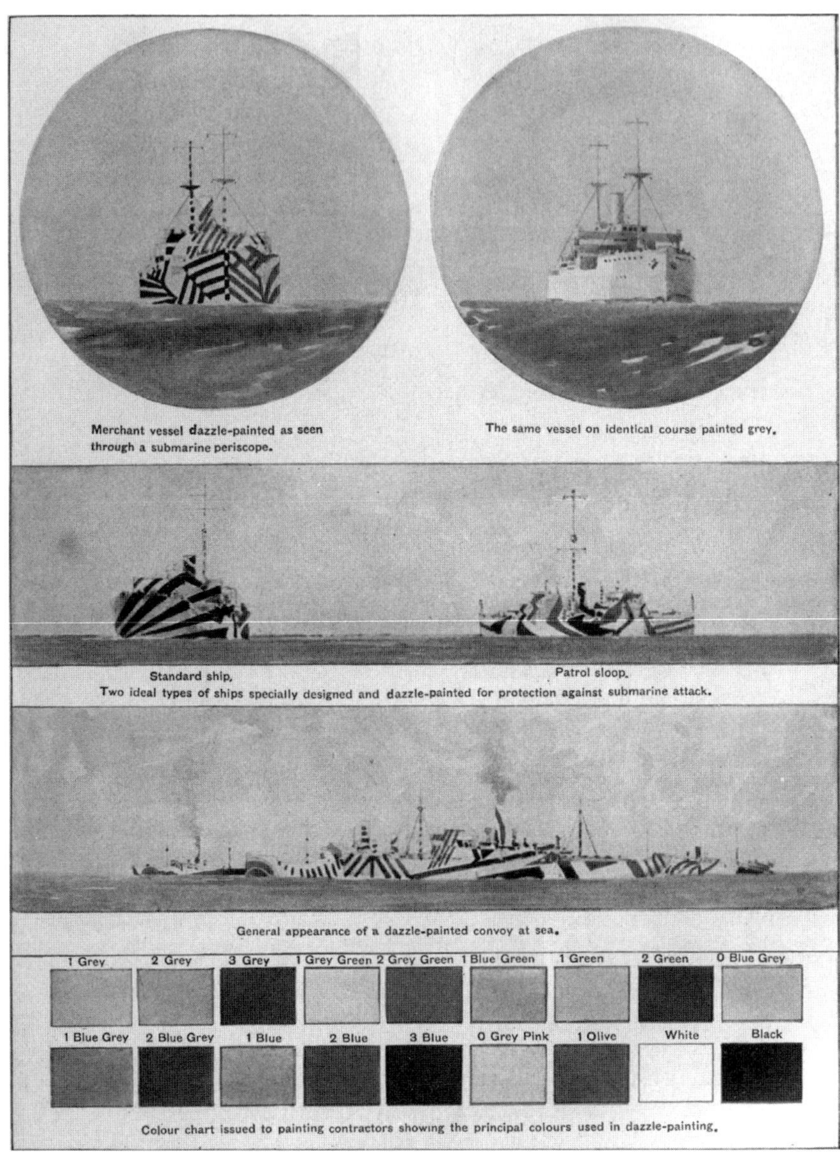

Norman Wilkinson, plate illustrating the 'dazzle painting'
method of camouflaging ships, 1922

In Bloomsbury, an embattled island of pacifism held out. Clive Bell dashed off a pamphlet, *Peace at Once* (1915), spelling out the pointlessness of war with the same brainy lucidity with which he had earlier explained the point of art. Was the effort to 'crush Germany', which had, out of nowhere, become the rallying cry and *raison d'être* of the entire British Empire, really worth 'killing and maiming half the serviceable male population of Europe, starving to death a quarter of the world, and ruining the hopes of the next three generations'? If anyone had imagined that the machine age connoted a triumph of rational thought, it was already clear that the machinery of official censorship and propaganda – more effective in achieving its lobotomizing ends than any actual weapon – had all but closed down the spaces in public discourse where such questions could be asked, let alone answered. *Peace at Once* was swiftly suppressed by order of the Lord Mayor of London.

To counter the flow of German propaganda in 1914, the Liberal chancellor David Lloyd George set up the War Propaganda Bureau under journalist and politician Charles Masterman. This was the latest extension of what Christabel Pankhurst presciently described in 1908 as 'the new kind of politics, [which] means, as it never has before, interference with us all in our daily lives'. It was the British government's first foray into state-funded, systematically crafted and widely disseminated mass deception. Its initial aim was to spin a story that would bring the United States into the war, but as the fighting dragged on into 1915 and stalemate combined with high mortality on the Western Front stirred public disillusionment, there was a parallel imperative to convince the home audience that the picture of purposeless bloodletting they were piecing together from letters home, menfolk on leave and the swingeing daily tithe of bereavements was somehow not the whole truth. The government was reluctant to let photographers loose anywhere near wounds and corpses, but what sense could worried people make of *Punch* cartoons in which a helmeted Britannia chastised a madly moustachioed kaiser, or a British 'tommy', in the heat of a bayonet charge, turned to his mate shouting 'Look out, Bill. Your bootlace is undone!'?

In May 1916, Masterman's team despatched its first official war artist, the Scottish printmaker Muirhead Bone, to France to provide illustrations for suitably censored reports. In Bone's sketches, the Front resembles a dystopian landscape in a children's story – ruined buildings to hide in, tents and camp fires, a dead forest of broken trees where witches might nest. But it was a start. In February 1917, the War Propaganda Bureau became part of the Department of Information, with a wider remit. The British government was learning how images and words, nicely produced publications and art exhibitions could serve its turn. Britain was the only combatant nation to employ official artists in the service of state messaging throughout and after the war. The public were hungry for almost any reasonably authentic images of soldiers' lives, although there were strict controls on what could be shown. At a 1918 exhibition of propagandistic paintings at London's Leicester Galleries, titled 'War', official war artist Nevinson wanted to show his 1917 painting *Paths of Glory* (he was now working in a straightforward academic realist manner), in which the bodies of two British soldiers sprawl face-down in the mud of no-man's land. Ordered to withdraw the painting, he hung it anyway, with a brown paper strip reading 'CENSORED' covering the corpses.

Even propaganda had its socially progressive side: women artists were recognized with official commissions to record women's involvement behind the lines or on the home front. There is a sense in the quick, informal watercolours and drawings of Olive Mudie-Cooke, art student turned ambulance driver, of clear-eyed witness of a kind that eluded male artists almost entirely. The unremitting stress placed on stereotypical manhood by the war – ideas of courage and service, loyalty and fortitude – along with the rigours and terrors of front-line life, made it hard even for artists to retain a sense of personal identity and continuity with the life they had led before.

For the generation who were in their teens during the war, the battlefield came before any possibility of art school. Henry Moore, an eighteen-year-old Yorkshire miner's son, volunteered for the Civil Service Rifles. At the 1917 Battle of Cambrai, he was caught up in the newest forms of machine killing, as his unit advanced with cover from tanks and planes to be met by poison gas. Moore survived to be posted to Wimbledon as a bayonet instructor. Recruits practised on suspended straw-filled bags painted with white circles. These represented body parts – heart, kidneys, stomach – which they were exhorted to spear with one decisive thrust. Moore's role was to teach them 'how to do it, viciously and violently'. Under his direction, young men unused to games of imagination screamed and lunged at abstract shapes as if they were living flesh.

Futurism had, in its way, been an extreme manifestation of youth. Its fortunes were tied to a vision of time in which the present hurtles into the future: *we want to, we shall, we intend, insist, desire* run the key statements in Marinetti's first manifesto. 'Time and Space died yesterday', not because they had come to a halt, but because 'we have already created infinite, omnipresent speed'. The war not only put an end to this machine-dream, it altered the very texture of time, bringing life to a futureless standstill. In this sense, the frozen stasis that pervades Nevinson's last futurist fling as a painter – the machine-gunners in *La Mitrailleuse* whose belt of bullets looks as if it has been carved from stone; the fizzing flatness of *Bursting Shell* – conveys a counter-intuitive truth, as in the weirdly paused duration of traumatic accidents. These images have none of the heightened sensations associated, at a distance, with war – neither fear, pain, panic and confusion, nor courage and heroic elation. Brooke, who died in April 1915 – not in battle but of septicaemia caused by a mosquito bite en route to the Dardanelles – had some poems in a copy of *Poetry Review* that was posted to Rosenberg in the trenches. 'I do not like Rupert Brooke's begloried sonnets,' he responded. The experience of war should, he felt, 'be approached in a colder way, more abstract, with less of the million feelings everybody feels; or all these should be concentrated in one distinguished [i.e. clearly perceptible] emotion'. But Brooke, in what became his most often-quoted line – 'Now, God be thanked...' – had grasped one essential fact. In 'this hour', time's trajectory had shifted, both in common, shared perception, in which the four and a half years of trench warfare would feel many times longer than any other equivalent spell of time, and in artists' work.

Bomberg volunteered for the army soon after war was declared but was initially rejected – 'perhaps because of his foreign sounding name and beard', thought Alice Mayes. In November 1915, he succeeded in enlisting in the Royal Engineers, transferring to the 18th King's Royal Rifles. He and Alice married in March 1916; by June, he was at the Front. 'I am glad Bomberg has done something definite at last', Rosenberg empathized from his own dugout, as the Somme offensive, which had delivered a record 57,000 British casualties on its first day, entered its fourth blood-soaked week. 'I do hope nothing will happen to him out here.' Bomberg, too, began writing poetry: the imagery in his 'Winter Night' echoes the dynamic geometries of pre-war paintings ('six wiring-stakes driven into the ground') but also testifies to the time-stopped world of the Western Front, which feels both claustrophobic and exposed: 'Hemmed in. The bolted ceiling of the night rests / on our heads, like vaulted roofs of iron huts.' 'What's left of the soldier man, killed on / patrol some months back?' another poem asks. The answer, 'sun-burnt bones, a hard / tanned hairy hide, and rags'. In 1917, he had a breakdown, and, as Alice recalled, 'deliberately put the gun to his foot and pulled the trigger'. Bomberg narrowly escaped the firing squad for 'depriving his Majesty of the services of a sworn member of his Forces'.

Henry Tonks, *Portrait of a Wounded Soldier before Treatment*, 1917. Pastel on paper

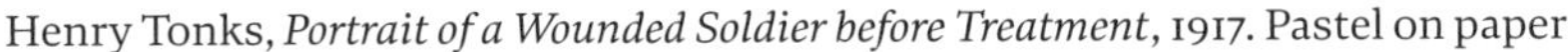

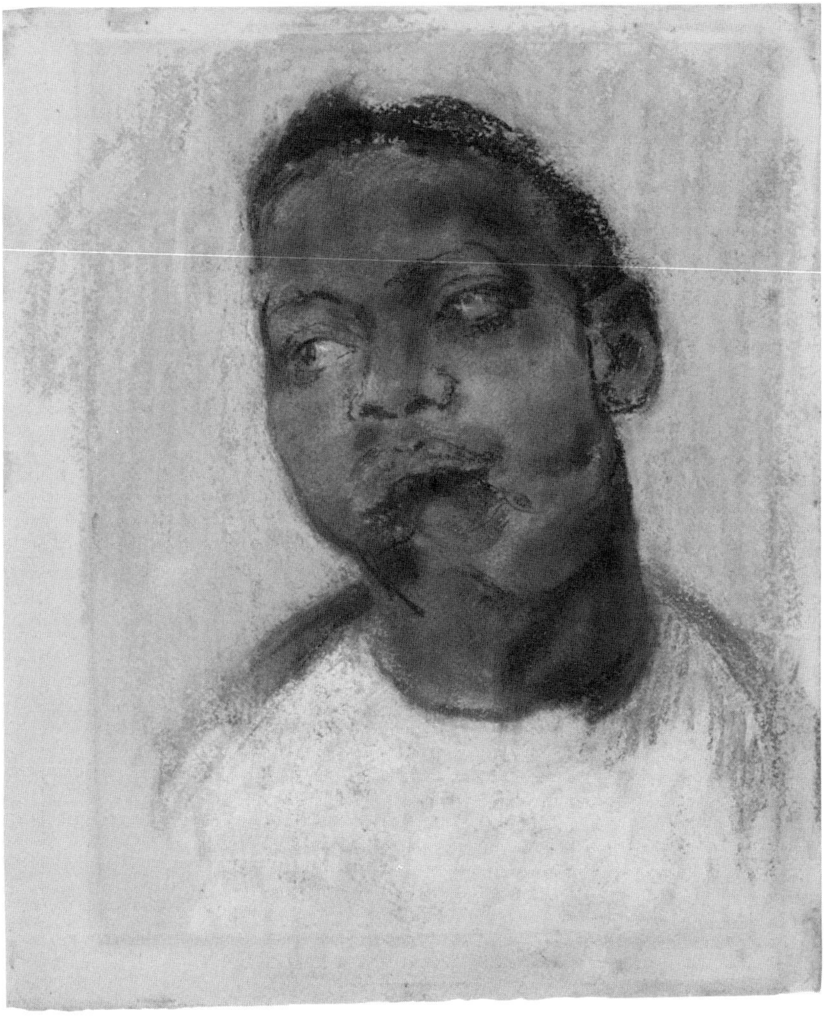

In December 1917, out of the blue, Bomberg received a commission to produce a large painting for the Canadian War Memorials Fund. The critic Paul Konody, who had been so disparaging about 'Twentieth Century Art' at the Whitechapel in 1914, had kept tabs on the young soldier-artists Bomberg, Wadsworth, Lewis and Nevinson. The well-funded Canadian project would ostensibly represent 'the most momentous epoch of the world's history' with paintings by 'every school and group, from the most academic and traditional to the most revolutionary and advanced', but Bomberg was warned that, in treating his allotted subject – the destruction of a German observation post at St Eloi by mines laid by Canadian sappers after eight months of tunnelling – 'cubist work would be inadmissible'.

Cubism, futurism – all Bomberg wanted now was 'the relief – and the sublimation of creating forms of war not in the dank, death-smelling underground mine – like a coal pit – but in the open-air, bathed in sunlight'. Released from front-line service, he sent Konody what Alice thought were 'the most wonderful drawings' of the painting he proposed, on which he worked in earnest on returning to London after the armistice of November 1918. On a bigger scale than *In the Hold* and *Mud Bath*, at 10 feet high and 8 feet wide, *Sappers at Work* (1919) reprises the theme of close-packed figures in a boxed-in space, structured by the energetic movements of the many bodies it barely contains. A pulley and pit-props braced against the sides of the tunnel echo *Mud Bath*'s geometries; the colours – blues, whites, airy greys – breathe the sunlit relief of the artist (how could he help it?) rather than the sappers' subterranean danger. The men are recognizable, non-cubist soldiers, with pockets and creases in their uniforms and every finger visible in their clenched hands. When he delivered the painting to Burlington House, however, Konody flatly rejected 'this futurist abortion'.

Out of all the pre-war Slade cohort, it was Professor Henry Tonks – impatient, uncompromising mentor and humdrum impressionistic painter – whose art had the most life-changing effect on individual soldiers. Tonks had put aside his brushes and returned to medicine in 1915, tending German prisoners of war in Dorset. 'Modern war is so horrible,' he told writer and Bloomsbury hostess Mary Hutchinson, 'owing to the artillery fire that it simply shatters people.' He had dusted off his surgical skills of twenty-five years ago, but the injuries he was now dealing with – many inoperable, all of them septic – were beyond him. In 1916, after serving with ambulance units in France and Italy, he transferred to a hospital in Cambridge, a 'chamber of horrors', where New Zealand-born surgeon Harold Gillies was pioneering facial reconstructive surgery on shrapnel victims. He operated successfully on men who had lost jaws, noses, ears, tongues – extreme disfigurements that made even their families and the nursing staff drop their gaze and shy away. Tonks sat down with them, and, working along lines that he and Walter Sickert had honed in their early New English Art Club days, patiently observing unbeautified facts, he drew their portraits in coloured pastels as attentively as if they were rosy-cheeked Edwardian brides: thick curly hair, fresh skin, clear eyes, lower jaw blown away. These drawings were Gillies's reference points for the new branch of surgery that restored not only the men's faces but their sense of self. He called it 'aesthetics'.

8
A new space to be in

Prestbury, Gloucestershire, 31 October 1918

'I hate coming home.'

Days before a ceasefire with Germany takes effect, Dora Carrington is stay-ing with her parents in the Cotswold village of Prestbury. At ten in the even-ing, ambushed by grief, she writes to the biographer Lytton Strachey – her gay friend, housemate and occasional lover – about the loss of her younger brother. Teddy went missing in action in the first battle of the Somme; his body was never found. 'You know it was just two years ago this October. At the very place where they are shooting now.' Everywhere in the house, 'I see his things and in my rooms all his school books, the queer boxes, and his carved things he made, old chemistry jars, boats, and in the drawers his note books, drawings of engines, and frigates.' Reeling off this small, raw litany, she pic-tures him on his last home leave, 'lying fast asleep on the sofa, curled up. His dark brown face, and broad neck, the thick black shiny hair and the modelling of his face, like some chiselled bronze head'. She feels 'so heavy inside'.

———

Before the First World War, Carrington – from the age of eighteen always known by her surname – had been one of the Slade 'cropheads', a coterie of bob-cut, well-born women students, whose jodhpur-clad androgyny gave them an air of all-purpose radicalism as well as in-group social and sexual cachet. Carrington was chased after by Paul Nash, Richard Nevinson and especially Mark Gertler, whose anguished campaign to get her into bed finally climaxed in December 1916 in defeat by contraception ('really I did try that thing. Only it was much too big, and wouldn't go inside no matter what way I used it!'). By then, she had been welcomed as a promising newcomer by the Bloomsbury crowd. Carrington wasn't initially overawed. Invited by 'the Clive Bells' to a house party at Asheham House in Sussex, Virginia and her husband Leonard Woolf's rural retreat near Lewes, in December 1915, she observed the guests' self-satisfied inability to perform basic domestic tasks usually delegated to servants. 'What poseurs they are really,' she told her Slade friend Christine Kühlenthal, after watching painter Duncan Grant 'putting remnants of milk pudding into the stock pot!' and being herself hailed as a wonder 'because I knew what part of the leek to cook!' The flamboyant Strachey particularly repelled her, 'with his yellow face & beard, ugh!' Three years later, Carrington herself was a Bloomsbury insider, relaying news and gossip in voluble, often illustrated letters to Vanessa Bell, Virginia Woolf, the society hostess Ottoline Morrell and the Cambridge economist John Maynard Keynes. In October 1917, she and Strachey settled into an ambiguous ménage in a 'romantic and lovely' old Berkshire watermill, with 'Vast big rooms… very good garden and a shady grass lawn/with river running through it.'

Carrington's grief for her brother and her elation at launching into an independent, unprescribed life of her own at the Mill House flowed into and out of each other within the same few weeks around the armistice of November 1918. 'The sky is blue and the sun shines,' she was writing to Gertler in December. 'It's like the ballet with an orchestra…one must dance to the tune they play.' While the war blundered on, women had had to hug and conceal their inner heaviness as best they could. There had effectively been a four-year embargo on the subversive passions – anger, desire, even grief in its natural uncontrolled state – while factitious public emotion was relentlessly beamed on to figments of militaristic male valour and heroic male suffering, away from anything that could be remotely construed as female or feminine. There was no escape from this heart-numbing mindset: propaganda and censorship had done their work. In her letter to Strachey, Carrington summons an image of her brother, innocent and unharmed, in the form of a 'chiselled bronze head' – an imaginary sculpture, which she can contemplate with at least some sense of consoling calm and detachment. Art, or the dream of art, provides a salve for loss – which is more or less what happened, on a national scale, in the five or six years after the Great War. The construction of bearable memory became an all-consuming project: not only were soldier-artists able to hand in their guns and return to their studios, they were given materials and public money for making art.

Of the Slade class of 1912, David Bomberg, Richard Nevinson, Edward Wadsworth and Stanley Spencer had survived. Isaac Rosenberg had been killed while on night patrol during the Battle of Arras, as dawn broke on 1 April 1918. He had 'managed to do a bit of sketching' the previous week: 'I don't think I have forgotten my art after all', he wrote to the editor Edward Marsh. Discharged and back in London in November 1918, Bomberg confessed to being 'so excited' by his commission for *Sappers at Work*, 'that I did not go out once to take part in the Armistice celebrations'. The Canadian project inspired a similar British scheme, a Hall of Remembrance that was to be lined with scenes of 'fighting subjects, home subjects and the war at sea and in the air'. These monumental paintings, for which artists who had seen active service were enlisted a second time by the state, would memorialize the spirit rather than record the actual face of war. There would be no examples of front-line photo reportage or even stills from the propaganda film *The Battle of the Somme*, a feature-length documentary shot on location in summer 1916, heavily censored to remove footage of British dead and wounded, and watched by an estimated 20 million people in 2,000 cinemas within weeks of opening in London that August. For the projected Hall of Remembrance, the Ministry of Information deliberately commissioned younger artists, known or suspected of having post-impressionist, futurist or other modern sympathies, as well as safe-bet traditionalists. The generous scale of these works (72 × 125 inches) was based on a famous panel in the National Gallery by the Florentine Renaissance artist Paolo Uccello, in which a brutal cavalry engagement at the 1432 Battle of San Romano takes place in impeccable linear perspective.

The official co-option of modern art to work of collective memory ensured that, should any future-focused energy still survive from the radical pre-war years, it was channelled into the imaging not of the new but of the lost. As far as artists in Britain were concerned, any feelings of rage or rebellion, like those that had boiled over into the first anarchic Dada cabarets in Zurich in 1916, were sublimated into the equally emotive but profoundly conservative project of memorialization. There would be no equivalent of German artist George Grosz's bestial caricatures of German fat-cat war profiteers – the 'Swamp Flowers of Capitalism' – and the disabled veterans who had been forced to dance to their tune. It wasn't impossible to resolve traumatic memory with the desire to live again – the two primal instincts that Sigmund Freud identified in 1920 in *Beyond the Pleasure Principle* as *thanatos* (destruction, death) and *eros* (sex, love) – but visual art would not provide the medium. In his long poem *The Waste Land*, published two years later, the American poet T. S. Eliot, who had spent the war as a bank clerk in London, used a cinematic technique of verbal montage, 'mixing/Memory and desire', to evoke a fractured landscape in which death and decay cohabit with hope and sexuality, and past and present flow seamlessly if disturbingly into each other. 'These fragments', the poem draws to its calm-after-storm conclusion, 'I have shored against my ruins'.

No such subtlety would be possible in the Hall of Remembrance. In Percy Wyndham Lewis's contribution, *A Battery Shelled* (1919), mantis-like infantrymen stalk through a maze of gluey grey furrows like sightseers on an alien planet, while the larger figures of three officers loiter on the fringes as if waiting for a bus. *This is what became of the future*, Lewis seems to be saying, *but do I care?* He was detaching himself from his former role as avant-garde culture warrior (an attempt in 1919 to reboot Vorticism as Group X came to nothing), and was about to embark on a series of science-fiction novels and a parallel career as a society portraitist, a cubist-savvy version of his former mentor Augustus John. Paul Nash, who had studied with Lewis under Henry Tonks at the Slade, slightly before Carrington and Bomberg's time, painted a cratered landscape through which two British soldiers find their uncertain way, like a tin-hatted Adam and Eve. Concrete blocks and corrugated iron from smashed defences resemble the husks of futurist paintings scarred on entry into the real world – itself a phantasmagoria of shattered trees, set against an apocalyptic broth of far-off explosions and pewter storm clouds, pierced by searchlight rays of sunshine.

Nash described *The Menin Road*, completed in February 1919, as 'a tract of country near Gheluvelt village in the sinister district of "Tower Hamlets", perhaps the most dreaded and disastrous locality of any area in any of the theatres of War'. The Gheluvelt Plateau, blitzed to a man-eating soup of mud by artillery bombardment and unrelenting rain, was the site of the Third Battle of Ypres in summer 1917. Serving in this area earlier that year, Nash had tumbled into a trench, breaking a rib. While he was recovering in hospital in London, his unit was all but wiped out. When he returned to the Western Front that November, it was as an official war artist, with a car, a chauffeur and a burgeoning anger that, as he moved in and out of the firing line, had time to grow. He wrote to his wife, the suffragette and social campaigner Margaret Odeh,

No pen or drawing can convey this country.... Sunset and sunrise are blasphemous, they are mockeries to man, only the black rain out of the bruised and swollen clouds all through the bitter black night is fit atmosphere in such a land. The rain drives on, the stinking mud becomes more evilly yellow, the shell holes fill up with green-white water, the roads and tracks are covered in inches of slime.... I am no longer an artist interested and curious. I am a messenger who will bring back word from the men who are fighting to those who want the war to go on for ever.

In 1919, the war over, the angry messenger had to rediscover what it meant to be a curious artist. 'Struggles of a war artist without a war', was how he summarized the situation in an autobiographical note. This is the landscape Nash revisits in *The Menin Road*, inflected (as he noted to Margaret) by his reading of Dante's *Inferno* and the horror tales of Edgar Allan Poe. Often cited as a great work of front-line witness, the painting is in reality Nash's symbolic translation of his experience into dystopian pastoral. All the fighting, the death, the suffering, the disfigurements and disembowellings have been to do with defending the memory of a lost Eden – even perhaps nurturing a delusion that Eden can be regained.

The Hall of Remembrance was never built; the Ministry of Information's commissions were transferred to the newly established Imperial War Museum, which opened in June 1920 in the Crystal Palace in Sydenham, south-east London. Since the summer of 1917, there had been a museum team at the Western Front, with a brief to collect material that would speak for ordinary people's experience of war and commemorate the barbaric violence they had been forced to endure, to which the word 'sacrifice' lent a smoothing gloss of religiously inspired, ennobling passivity. Sacrificial nail-studded home-made clubs for trench raids, gruesome samples of barbed wire, captured enemy helmets, flags, uniforms and guns were squirrelled away in a store at Hesdin, behind the lines near Abbeville. This was the first war for which the museum displays and exhibition script were being devised eighteen months before the fighting was over, a measure of how crucial and increasingly sophisticated public communications were becoming for the modern state. Women's involvement in the war, as nurses, munitions workers and in many other support and semi-menial roles, was belatedly acknowledged in 1919–20 by commissions to about a dozen women artists by the Women's Work Sub-Committee of the Imperial War Museum, chaired by the suffragette and MP's wife Lady Priscilla Norman. The photographer Olive Edis visited military sites still in operation in northern France and Belgium in March 1919; challenged by the official censor, she explained that 'a woman photographer, living among the girls in their camp, was likely to achieve more intimate pictures, more descriptive of their everyday life, than a man press photographer.'

Once the military hospitals no longer needed their services, and wartime munitions factories closed, women were expected to return to their pre-war domestic lives, as if that were possible. In the visual record produced by women artists – in contrast to Lewis or Nash's images – war appears as work like any other, without pathos or heroics, and in that sense part of a living continuum. In a church in the East End of London, the art student Winifred Roberts, granddaughter of the Earl of Carlisle, painted a watercolour of the 'War Corner'. On the church wall, under a stained-glass window, is a photograph gallery consisting of blurry grey figures of dead or missing fathers. In front, in brighter colours, attentive, informal, a group of young children, for whom the atmosphere inside the church is no more than a solemn little tunnel through which their day is passing. Roberts's small, bright picture expresses more interest in the children than in the photos and what they stand for – a rare affirmation of future peace and growth that had been all but lost sight of.

The state-sponsored memorialization of the war and the religio-civic cult of sacrifice launched a sculptural programme on a bigger scale and with a wider social reach than anything since the great architectural ensembles of the Middle Ages. Communities and institutions across Britain set about commissioning their public war memorials, in the form of obelisks, statues, friezes, plaques, and sometimes entire buildings like village halls. During the actual hostilities, the death toll had been released as neutral data – lists of small-print names in newspapers. Now the dead could take their place in the world they were meant to have been fighting for: they were 'the fallen', as if the denial of will and agency obeyed some natural law, like autumn leaves. As tokens of the 1.1 million men no longer standing, tens of thousands of monuments were constructed in stone and bronze, some of them, like the naval memorials in Portsmouth, Plymouth and Southampton, on a gargantuan scale.

Whatever their form, these memorials tended to share an emphatic plainness, vaguely echoing Greek and Roman tombs and altars, and the

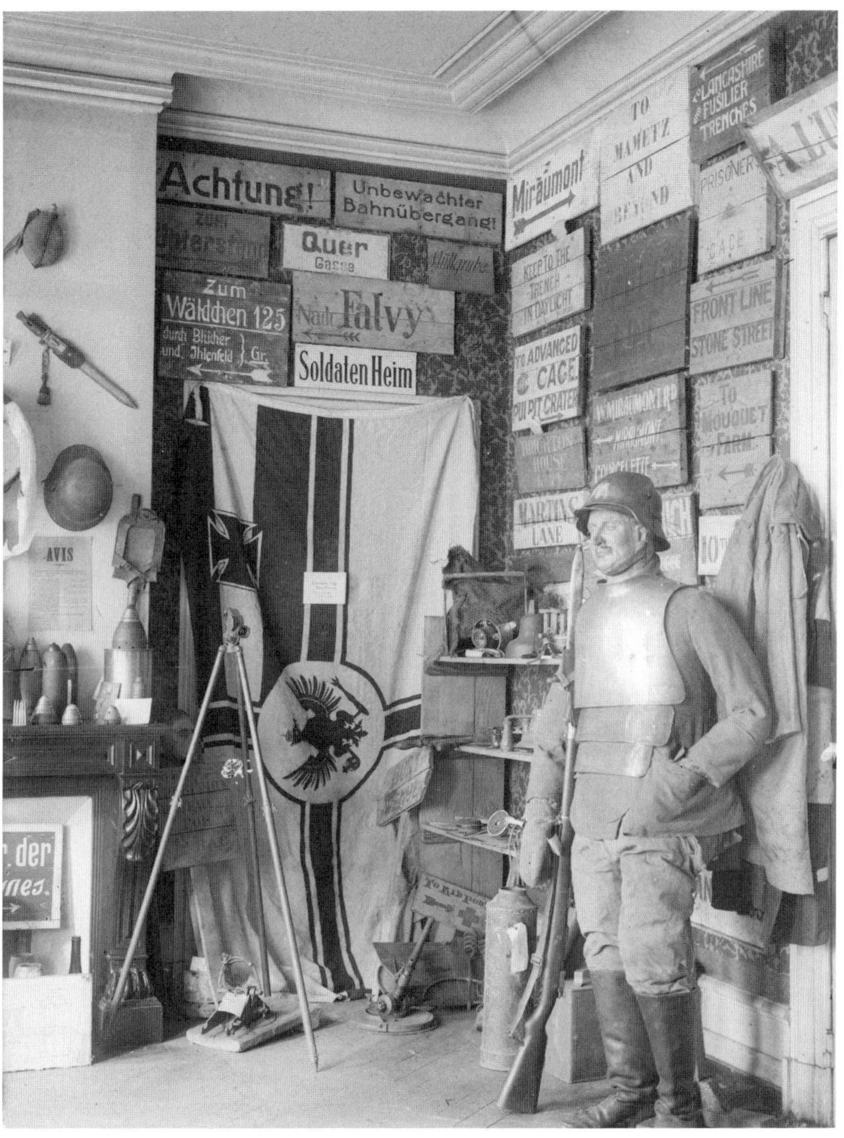

National War Museum Store at Hesdin, northern France, September 1917

ideals of do-or-die patriotism and sexless virility long associated with these ancient cultures in British schoolrooms. This was the concept behind the architect Edwin Lutyens's London Cenotaph, a foursquare wooden tower hastily designed and knocked up as a saluting-point for the victory parade along Whitehall in July 1919, then immediately given permanent form in Portland stone as a 'national tomb'. 'Simple' was a word often used in praise of the Cenotaph – the same word that artists, architects and designers had been using since the 1890s to express ideals of one kind or another (to do with surfaces or arrangements or ways of life) that felt integral to the project of being modern. In Lutyens's Cenotaph the virtues of simplicity suddenly appeared obvious to everyone: this simple structure – a tapering, blank-faced rectangular block on a stepped base – was somehow able to focus and absorb the entire nation's post-traumatic groundswell of survivor's guilt and mass bereavement. Less, at long last and after so much lost, was more.

The war memorial programme not only testified to the decimation of the working-age male population but also laid bare British sculpture's minuscule pool of serious talent, compared to painting. No wonder: it was many centuries since sculptors had been given much to do except portraits of monarchs and assorted heroes of empire, and architectural ornament. Designed in the first years of the twentieth century, Thomas Brock's Victoria Memorial, in front of Buckingham Palace, and George Frampton's and Albert Toft's equivalents, in St Helens and Leamington Spa respectively, were typical in their tight-laced stolidity, representing the elderly queen-empress as a grim-faced tea-cosy, gripping her orb like a hand grenade. There were now, of course, a few sculptors who did things very differently, such as Jacob Epstein and Eric Gill. After conscription in autumn 1917 as a private in the Jewish battalion of the Royal Fusiliers, but before leaving for France, Epstein had a breakdown; in any case, the scandal of the British Medical Association sculptures and his rumoured Bolshevism would likely have put him out of the running. Gill was commissioned by Michael Sadler to carve a frieze for Leeds University's war memorial. His choice of subject – Jesus whipping the money-changers out of the temple, with the money-men shown in modern dress – outraged local businessmen, sensitive to implication that they were the profiteer 'swamp flowers' of northern capitalism. In general, the work went to well-behaved Royal Academicians like Toft, who received a string of commissions. But where, after all his experience in sculpting catatonic worthies, could he turn for a model of an ordinary young male body engaged in vigorous action? There was really only Auguste Rodin, whose *Burghers of Calais*, installed next to the Houses of Parliament in 1911, seemed to anticipate, in the sombre passion of its body language, the task he now faced. For his memorial at Oldham, Toft produced three life-size bronze infantrymen scaling a rock. They stretch and clamber like figures seconded from Rodin's *The Gates of Hell*, kitted out with uniforms and rifles, bayonets fixed for the occasion.

Among British memorial sculptors, the best and most in-demand was Charles Sargeant Jagger, a Yorkshire colliery manager's son and former skilled metal engraver. After evening classes at Sheffield School of Art, he studied at the Royal College of Art, then enlisted in the Artists' Rifles in 1914; he was gassed and wounded repeatedly, and awarded the Military Cross. Jagger's gift as a sculptor was to imbue his sad bronze warriors – again much indebted to Rodin – with an air of reflective stoicism rather than melodramatic valour. His Great Western Railway War Memorial, commissioned in 1920, on Platform 1 at Paddington Station, takes the form of *Tommy*, an over-life-size everyman–soldier in helmet and greatcoat, who stands squarely, head bent, reading a letter – a token of inwardness – not brandishing a weapon. His woollen scarf, heavy boots and other accoutrements manage to be both monumental attributes and intimately observed. For his Royal Artillery Memorial at Hyde Park Corner, Jagger enlisted a whole spectrum of sculptural techniques – a carved full-scale howitzer sits on a 'simple' plinth the size of a pocket mausoleum, faced by relief sculptures of gunners at work and fronted on all four sides by life-size bronze figures. It would be a long time before sculpture on this kind of scale, with a comparable assurance in its ability to address the public, would again appear in Britain.

War memorials' appeal to popular sentiment, their 'vague idea of holiness and patriotism combined', devalued art, in Roger Fry's opinion. Fair criticism, but it shows how beside-the-point Fry's view of art through the exclusive prism of formal values could be. In the first half of the 1920s, memorials claimed the lion's share of materials, money, energy and sculptural competence, as well as public awareness and emotional investment, available for art of any kind. Whatever their limitations, they had, psychologically, a genuinely liminal function, providing a passage – however obscure or confused – between the material and

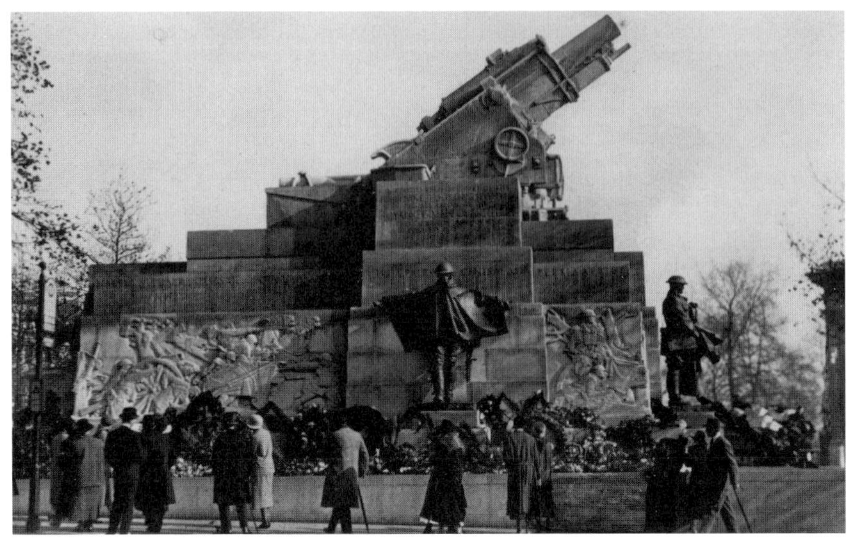

Charles Sargeant Jagger, Royal Artillery Memorial, Hyde Park, London, 1925

metaphysical realms. Everywhere – in beds, at family tables, on pavements and factory floors – the ghosts stirred. Something had to be made for them to cling to, at least for the time being. The multiplying memorials were also, by their nature, a naked political raid on private emotion, dragging attention away from the questions that had occupied so many people before the war – not just futurists and suffragettes – of how and where to begin anew.

There was enormous official resistance to the idea that the war had fundamentally changed life in Britain: it had supposedly been fought, after all, to protect the cherished values of the peace it had destroyed. But change there had been: after the window-smashing and the bombs, the arrests and force-feeding, the rallying to the war effort, and the sheer numbers of women of all classes involved in the campaign, in February 1918, women over the age of thirty finally gained the right to vote in general elections. This was nowhere near the end of the struggle for representation and equality ('The walls of Jericho have not fallen at the first blast of our trumpet,' the veteran campaigner Millicent Fawcett observed), but the women's movement's pre-war campaign of radical protest would not be repeated for fifty years. Sylvia Pankhurst, Christabel's sister, became a founder member of the Communist Party of Great Britain; her mother became a vocal opponent of Bolshevism and promoter of British imperialism. 'Slasher Mary' Richardson, who vandalized the Rokeby *Venus* in protest at the government's torture of suffragettes, proclaiming those who criticized her actions to be guilty of 'artistic as well as moral and political humbug and hypocrisy', would become a senior figure in the British Union of Fascists.

In contrast to the situation in Germany, where the Kaiser abdicated, and Russia, where the revolution of October 1917 had been followed by a civil war fought along ideological fault lines, the pressure for social and political change was successfully managed by the British authorities. In 1919, the government responded to a strike by Clyde shipyard workers in support of ex-soldiers unable to find work by reading the riot act and deploying tanks, last seen in action on the Somme, on the streets of Glasgow. Trade union membership had grown steadily since 1900; the 1920s would be a time of widespread industrial unrest, but not of common cause between workers and women. In a social history of the period, published in 1940, the poet and Western Front veteran Robert Graves and historian Alan Hodge summed up the attitude to working women:

> *The women who only a year or so earlier had been acclaimed as patriots... were now represented as vampires who deprived men of their rightful jobs. By Trade Union pressure they were dismissed from engineering, printing, and transport work...and from factories where they had worked on munitions.*

Unable to see the slightest sign that the British establishment and public had learned anything from the war, the young novelist D. H. Lawrence, who had been rejected for army service but nearly killed by the Spanish Flu epidemic of 1918–19, left for Italy. In 1920, he would publish a novel he had written in Cornwall and London during the war, *Women in Love*. Its lead characters are the two twenty-something Brangwen sisters – Gudrun, an artist, and Ursula, a primary school teacher. The novel seems to be set before the war, which is not directly mentioned, but intimations of a world reborn, where human relationships will be different – more honest and more fulfilling – drive the story. At one point, Ursula and Gudrun speculate about what life will be like, in this new world:

> *Ursula was silent, trying to imagine.*
> *'I think,' she said at length..., 'one wants a new space to be in, and one falls away from the old.'*

Gudrun watched her sister with impassive face and steady eyes.

'One wants a new space to be in, I quite agree.... But I think that a new world is a development from this world, and that to isolate oneself with one other person isn't to find a new world at all, but only to secure oneself in one's illusions.'

A new space, a shared space, different from the old. The urge to remake the basis of both social and emotional life stood directly counter to the memorialization mania, with its rhetoric of sacrifice and remembrance, which was in full swing when *Women in Love* was published.

As both woman and artist, Gudrun is one voice among many others of an endeavour to live differently in the aftermath of war. New ways of living would typically centre on small, non-hierarchical groups rather than regiments or crowds. They would focus on beginnings – children and childhood, skills not yet learned, or the learning of familiar things afresh – and involve a rejection of established consensus on both the traditional and the early twentieth-century avant-garde wings of art. This would be a different kind of new from the 'new vortex' of 1914 that 'plunges to the heart of the Present'. There would – at least, for now, in Britain – be no more *Zang Tumb Tumb* and shouty art wars. All the chatter about 'primitive' and 'savage' art, the blossoming British enthusiasm for Cézanne and Gauguin, had left their legacy. But the idea of 'savage' energy was softened to something closer to its original meaning – natural, non-civilized, *sauvage* – while 'primitive' gradu-ally lost its sensationalist aura of nightclub jungle drums and (among thoughtful artists, anyhow) came to signify origins rather than orgies, often with the sense that the roots of the immediate present lay in the deepest strata of primordial time.

The sites artists chose for new spaces where that future might take shape would no longer be in the 'steel city' where Bomberg had once, opti-mistically, located his quest *'for an Intenser* expression'. Some – although not all – of these experiments in art and living would be underwrit-ten by inherited money. Self-funded alternatives to the mainstream were nothing new – Cézanne's banker father's fortune had freed him from any real anxiety about sales, and Marinetti had used his private wealth to maintain a futurist hub of operations in Milan. The 1920s saw resources of this kind being deployed by women in a rather different spirit, more communitarian than exclusively or politically personal.

Winifred Roberts would look back on this decade, during which she lived and worked in a series of remote spots in the Swiss–Italian alps, in Cumbria and the western tip of Cornwall, as a time when 'To say that a thing was Modern was to say that it was "good".' In the 'new world' she dreamed of, there would be 'no slums...no false ornament – but clarity, white walls, simplicity – complete and satisfying.'

Steeliness and machinery were out. Halfway through the war, in summer 1916, Virginia Woolf had drawn her sister's attention to a large old house in Firle, near Lewes. By now separated, more or less amicably, from husband Clive, Bell was in a relationship with Grant (who was still seeing his lover, the editor David 'Bunny' Garnett), hoping they would have a child together. Charleston farmhouse struck her as a place where they could escape the war and be themselves. It had everything needed for a self-sustaining rural life in which work and family and friends could coexist in a cocoon of like-mindedness and freedom from material anxieties: 'A large lake, an orchard, trees all round the back of the house & farm buildings.... The rooms (according to today's impression) are very large & light & numerous. There are huge cupboards, innumerable larders – a dairy – cellars – all sorts of out-houses – lots of room for hens.' No matter that Grant couldn't tell a pudding from a stew, at Charleston he became, nominally at least, a farm labourer, which helped him to plead lawful exemption from war service. In July 1919, Virginia and Leonard would buy a new place of their own nearby, Monk's House, beside the River Ouse, outside the village of Rodmell.

Tidmarsh Mill in Berkshire, discovered by Carrington the following year, shared many features with Charleston. In 1918, she painted the Mill House (pl. 7), reflected in the weedy mirror of its pond, as a storybook refuge. Part quotation from early Renaissance art, part vernacular inn-sign, it promises an infantile heaven of freedom, safety and agelessness. The dominant red planes of the roof protect and enchant the shared life inside, symbolized by two black swans – imaginary birds representing herself and Strachey. Tiles, limewash, shingle boards, a mackerel sky, all mirrored in the millpond with an effect that you can almost hear Ruskin describing ('Go to the edge of a pond in a perfectly calm day, at some place where there is duckweed floating...'). In Carrington's letters from this time, she explores her own new but not yet clearly articulated space as both artist and woman. 'One cannot be a female creator of works of art and have children,' she decides. 'That is the real reason why so few women have reached any high plane of creators.' Marriage itself was problematic: 'I dislike merging into a person, which marriage involves.... I hate those little self-centred worlds which married people live in.' Or, as Lawrence has Gudrun exclaim, 'It's just impossible. The man makes it impossible.'

This is not the voice of turn-of-the-century sombrero-sporting bohemianism, in which male artists like Augustus John practised 'free love' entirely on their own terms: namely, anything that happened after fertilization was understood by both partners to be the woman's responsibility (as Ida John lay dying of puerperal fever in March 1907, she did her best to distract an anxious Augustus by sending him shopping for peppermints). Carrington's reflections on female creativity are closer to the rethinking of gender roles and social relationships that had been a feature, from the first, of the suffragette political project but that now felt more possible, and more urgent, in relation to this young artist's vision of her future. More reliable contraception would play its

Ben and Winifred Nicholson, early 1920s

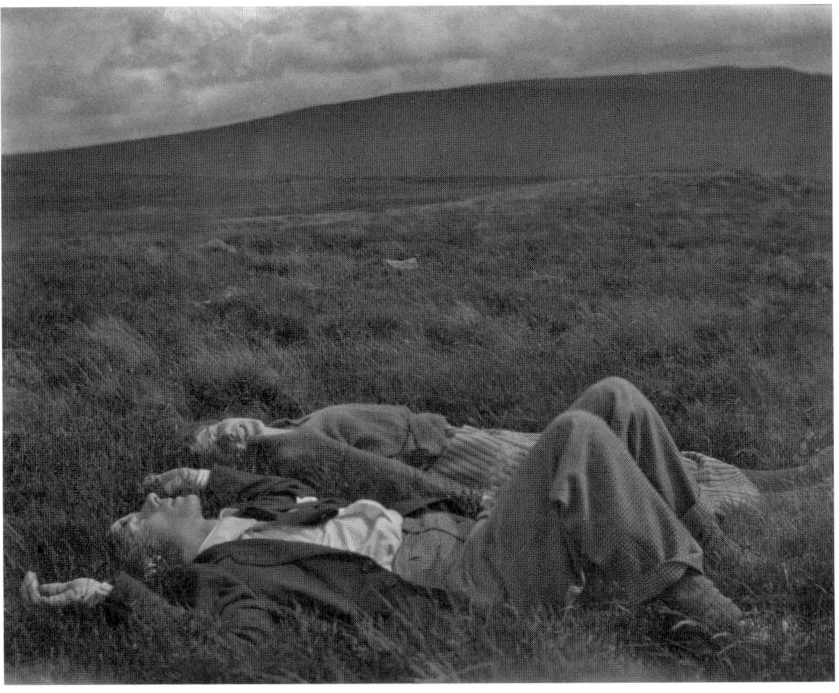

part: in March 1918, Marie Stopes published her trailblazing guide to sex and birth control *Married Love*, in which she asserted, 'The future is full of hope. Already one sees beginning to grow up a new relationship between the units composing society.'

In November 1920, Winifred Roberts married 'a painter man', Ben Nicholson, wearing 'a long brown woollen dress chosen by him, like a monk'. This sounds more like a shared joke than controlling behaviour – a rejection of sacramental (or sacrificial) white. Winifred and Ben took off for a rural retreat on the shores of Lake Lugano in Switzerland (in a villa bought for the newly-weds by Winifred's aristocratic grandfather), where they became 'utter paint fiends. We have cobalt green with our coffee for breakfast, lunch at 4, and rose madder for supper, and all our clothes smell of turpentine.' Life – food, clothes – and art had become, as Winifred hoped they would, indistinguishable. Her word for herself and Ben in their honeymoon creative ecstasy, 'fiends', is one that was also used of mischievous, unruly children: this is painting very much as adult play. In 1922, they invited David and Alice Bomberg, who had themselves quit London for a Hampshire farm, to join them at Castagnola, where they would paint the landscape together. Alice recalled the trip as 'a great fiasco': 'David hated being hauled out in the snow on painting expeditions, expected to play the maestro and teach them how to paint. Finally there was a show-down and they paid our fares home to get rid of us!'

The Nicholsons then settled on another new place, a cottage at Banks Head, on Hadrian's Wall, in Winifred's ancestral homeland in Cumbria. Here she painted the maze of drystone field walls, stubby trees, the soft, churned greys of winter skies – more friendly than threatening – and a black iron pan on a glowing grate. She and Ben admired the work of the self-taught old customs official Henri 'Le Douanier' Rousseau, but they could not themselves pretend to be unsophisticated or untaught – they had looked long at Giotto and at Picasso, and had a full set of cultural bearings in Paris and London. Still, if there was one word that summed up what they were searching for, it was (again) 'simplicity'. And, as for Carrington in her 'communal nest for breakers of the law' at Tidmarsh Mill, this search had an instinctively regressive element – not prettily 'childlike' but more determinedly quasi-infantile – in its attempt to re-experience the rapt earnestness that children bring to play, with their delight in sand and soil, pots and buckets, water and fire. Or like learning a foreign language and using only the words provided in the first few pages of the primer.

The summer of 1928 found the Nicholsons on holiday in Cornwall with a friend from Paris, Christopher (Kit) Wood. There had been much talk of 'beginning again in painting', but if they were serious about this, it left them with the problem of locating the true ground zero. At this point, an unlikely role model appeared in the form of the retired St Ives scrap dealer and sometime mariner Alfred Wallis. Poorly educated, antisocial, fixated on the Bible and on his late-flowering obsessional pastime of painting, Wallis seemed to provide the key to making art that was at the same time simple *and* real. It had to do with the materials he used – torn-up cardboard boxes and house paint into which bits of sand and pipe tobacco found their way – and the exotic life of working-class grind and seafaring risk he'd lived. Wallis's painting, mused Ben, contained 'an intensity and depth of experience which makes it much more than merely childlike'. But how? There had to be another word than 'childlike' with which to express Wallis's freshness of perception and innocence of academic painterly tricks – which did not suggest an actual child's inexperience or lack of skill. 'I don't think a good Wallis is representational,' Ben tried again, in a letter to fellow Wallis fan and collector Jim Ede, 'it is simply REAL?' 'Real' as in convincing but not 'realistic', a record of experience that was also a dreamworld manifestation, an image that had become a thing, or was it the other way round? The canny, cantankerous Wallis appeared to solve the mystery: how to paint without having to ask yourself these questions.

Rural Devon was the setting for another type of new beginning. In 1925 the American multiple heiress Dorothy Elmhirst and her agronomist husband Leonard bought a medieval manorial enclave outside the village of Dartington as a centre for their 'Dartington Experiment' – a community inspired by the ashram headed by Indian poet Rabindranath Tagore, for whom Leonard had worked in West Bengal. The Elmhirsts' idea, in this period of economic insecurity, was to introduce enlightened practices in land management and domestic life, with an American-style demonstration kitchen, combined with creative arts and crafts. In 1926, they established a progressive co-educational boarding school, where there would be 'no punishment at all; no prefects; no uniforms... no compulsory religion or compulsory anything else...no competition; no jingoism'.

Not all of the family-scale creative and educational communities that seeded themselves around Britain in the 1920s were led by women. In 1923, after teaching at the progressive Neue Schule in Dresden and attempting to set up his own 'free school', run on less austere, more child-centred lines in a mountaintop Austrian castle, A. S. Neill moved to Lyme Regis in Dorset, where he founded Summerhill, beginning with just five pupils. Neill too believed that there should be no imposition of rules, no hierarchies, none of the public-school training and values that had sustained the Great War: 'I see that all outside compulsion is wrong,' he wrote, 'inner compulsion is the only value.' At Capel y Ffin, a remote former monastery in the Brecon Beacons in Wales, the artist and former soldier David Jones joined the sculptor Eric Gill in another attempt to 'begin again' in art. Stanley Spencer, veteran of the pre-war Slade, the Second Post-Impressionist Exhibition and the army medical corps in western Greece, turned semi-recluse, forming a community of one in the Berkshire village of Cookham.

If the women's movement of the 1900s had concentrated on political progress, the focus in the 1920s, as variously represented by Carrington, Winifred Nicholson and Dorothy Elmhirst, was on a broader revisioning of social and gender relationships, and what this meant in terms of education, and personal and creative fulfilment. Around 1925, as the mammoth artistic programme of war memorialization was winding down, new places were being discovered and established where the dream of a society reborn through 'childlike' creative endeavour could be pursued. Memory – this time individual rather than national or historical – played a part here too. In 1926, the child psychoanalyst Melanie Klein, leaving behind a failed marriage and endemic anti-Semitism in Budapest, moved to London. After analysis with Hungarian psychoanalyst Sándor Ferenczi, Klein – a mother of two – had begun to develop her 'play technique' in which, in notable contrast to Sigmund Freud, she directly observed and interpreted the behaviour of young children. In a lecture Klein gave to the British Psycho-Analytical Society on 15 May 1929, she explored the sources of children's destructive impulses in Oedipal Freudian terms – that is, the theory that every infant has a repressed desire to destroy the parent of the same sex in order to possess the other parent entirely. She ended with a theory of her own, citing the case history of an artist, Ruth Kjär, who had felt a compulsive desire to paint portraits of her mother. 'It is obvious,' Klein concluded, 'that the desire to make reparation, to make good the injury psychologically done to the mother and also to restore herself was at the bottom of the compelling urge to paint these portraits.' Klein's theory of reparation, the attempt to remake a psychological object that has been Oedipally destroyed, locates a fundamental creative impulse in every human psyche.

Ten years after the conclusion of a mass frenzy of destruction, evidence was emerging that everyone – not only artists – possessed an instinctive urge to create. Something like a consensus would take shape among progressive thinkers of all kinds and a growing popular audience that human creativity might be the key not just to finding a personal 'new space to be in' but to reconstructing the wider world.

9
Deep Britain

West Yorkshire, 1920

It is ten in the evening, very often, before Barbara Hepworth gets back to Wakefield from Leeds School of Art. Much of her long day has been spent drawing – plaster casts of ancient sculptures, buildings, bodies, the traditional academic routine, although to this seventeen-year-old daughter of a local civil engineer, fresh from Wakefield Girls' High School, it is all a brave new world. As the train steams home, the dark landscape glows here and there with colliery lights. Rothwell, Beeston, Middleton Broom, Lofthouse, East Ardsley – there are dozens of collieries in this part of Yorkshire, thousands of men underground. In Wakefield itself – an old market and cathedral city turned sooty powerhouse – there are textile mills, engineering, brick and glass works, and boatyards on the River Calder. In Hepworth's childhood memories, the town is 'dominated by the structure of the mills, works' yards, mines, slag heaps, warehouses, noise, dirt and smell'. But she remembers, too, being perched up beside her father in his high old car, when his work took him out towards Ilkley and the Yorkshire Dales. While he muttered quietly about 'the stresses and strains of roads and bridges', she looked out across the landscape – the scoured ridges and long, broad valleys slung with nets of drystone walls. 'From the deep indigo and blacks and scarlets of the industrial heart we sailed through unimaginable beauty of unspoiled countryside.'

All her life, the Yorkshire of her girlhood would remain for Hepworth the 'deep true landscape – the real source of man's energy'. Not that these are terms she would have chosen, or concepts she can have formulated, at the time. This is the voice of the most famous female artist in Britain, if not the world, who was asked to pen a few words about her early life for a monograph published in 1952. And yet, 'Perhaps what one wants to say is formed in childhood and the rest of one's life is spent trying to say it.' Formed, or laid down at depth, like the thick seams in the Yorkshire coalfields, to be drawn up as fuel for adult creative life, in which Hepworth would repeatedly return to her search for an 'underlying principle', a 'piercing of the superficial surfaces of material existence'. In her memories of the 'producer country' of childhood, 'Every hill and valley became a sculpture in my eyes, and each landscape was intrinsic in the astonishing "architecture" of the industrial Pennines which spread east, north and south of us.'

In the mines of the early 1920s, a collier might hew 3 or 4 tons of coal per day, sometimes more. It was still largely pick-and-shovel work, although machine cutting was coming in, rising from 6 per cent of coal production in 1914 to 60 per cent in 1938. Yet the Nottinghamshire miner's son D. H. Lawrence recalled how his father 'loved the pit, as men in the war loved the intense male comradeship of the dark days'. In this 'intimate community', the miners

> *knew each other practically naked...and the darkness and the underground remoteness of the pit 'stall', and the continual presence of danger, made the physical, instinctive, and intuitional contact between men very highly developed.... When the men came up into the light, they blinked.*

Above ground, women toiled, pushing the laden tubs and grading the lumps of coal. Everywhere the greasy smell of coal, the bituminous smoke. When Lawrence pictured his childhood, 'it is always as if there was a lustrous sort of inner darkness, like the gloss of coal, in which we moved and had our real being'. He remembered, too, the 'extremely beautiful countryside' around the pits, 'between the red sandstone and the oak trees of Nottingham, and the cold limestone, the ash-trees, the stone fences of Derbyshire'.

British mines in 1920 produced 233 million tons of coal, with output beginning its steep, steady decline only in the late 1950s. Factories, trains and ships were fuelled with coal; it heated public buildings, offices, schools and homes. But it was never the 'real source of man's energy', as Hepworth came to see it: 'Power is not man power or physical capacity – it is an inner force and energy.' It was as if, to address the needs of society in the post-war world, the artist would have to reformulate industrial definitions of productivity and power in human terms. The question of human energy – whatever it was that drove people to want to live and do and make things, after so much power had been expended in killing them during Hepworth's girlhood – also surfaces in Lawrence's 1920 novel *Women in Love*. One of his main male characters, Gerald Crich, is a mine-owner's son and former soldier, now bullishly mechanizing his family's pits. He is 'good-looking, healthy, with a great reserve of energy' – a charismatic personification of 'physical capacity', or '*go*' – but he fatally lacks what Hepworth would have called 'vitality' or 'spiritual inner life'. 'The unfortunate thing,' Gudrun Brangwen observes of Gerald, to whom she is strongly sexually attracted, 'is, where does his *go* go to, what becomes of it?' 'I suppose,' Gerald will limply concede, when pushed, 'I live because I am living.' Survival might have been success enough for any man at the war's end, but could the mere fact of survival propel him into the future? In their different ways, Hepworth and Lawrence shared a preoccupation with energy, vitality, power, life force, psychic drive, libido, *go,* and how this quality – whatever you chose to call it – manifested itself in a world that had devoted phenomenal ingenuity to its destruction. Where, and how deep, did the 'real source' of 'real being' lie?

In Adel Woods, on the outskirts of Leeds, a looming outcrop thrusts through the leaf mould like a gritstone submarine. This 'big, bleak lump of stone set in the landscape and surrounded by marvellous gnarled prehistoric trees' is known as the Sphinx of Adel Crag. Growing up in the pit town of Castleford, just east of Wakefield, Henry Moore had visited this local beauty spot from childhood; as a fellow student of Hepworth's at Leeds School of Art between 1919 and 1921, he came with friends to picnic and draw. Adel Crag 'influenced me quite a bit,' said Moore. 'It had no feature of recognition, no element of copying of naturalism, just a bleak, powerful form.' The feeling for this 'prehistoric' landscape as a place where sculptural shapes were born stayed with Moore. Like Hepworth's 'intrinsic' landscape, its primitiveness was temporal rather than cultural, very different from the pre-war craze for 'primitive ragtime' at the Cave of the Golden Calf, or the orgiastic pagan tribes in the Ballets Russes's production of Igor Stravinsky's *The Rite of Spring*. In place of sensual abandon, this kind of primitiveness connoted something much more austere, to do with geological and environmental process. 'Perfectly beautiful – full of primitive passion,' the condescending socialite Hermione Roddice rhapsodizes about Gudrun's wood-carvings in *Women in Love*. You get the sense that, for Moore, this kind of art chat would have smacked of the modish enthusiasms of yesterday's debutante. 'I do not much like the application of the word "primitive" to art,' he curtly observed.

What made Moore want to carve, however, undoubtedly had its primitive component in terms of his intuition of deep time and unconscious process. 'Pebbles and rocks,' he explained, 'show nature's way of working stone. Smooth, sea-worn pebbles show the wearing away, rubbed treatment of stone and principles of asymmetry.' Exposed rocks, like Adel Crag, 'show the hacked, hewn treatment of stone, and have a jagged nervous block rhythm.' Natural forces, in these analogies, operate like an artist, 'working' and 'treating' their material, only with the advantage of having countless eons in which to perform their task. Moore described the kind of sculpture 'which moves me most' as having 'a life of its own': it was 'strong and vital, giving out something of the energy and power of great mountains'. These comments were made by a mature sculptor – they are not an apprentice's manifesto – when Moore and Hepworth had often exchanged ideas about the shaping power of natural processes, although both insisted that they had, separately, been convinced from the outset that vitality in sculpture was connected to something deep within the very substance of wood or stone.

Moore, like Lawrence, was a miner's son. His father had started work on a Lincolnshire farm aged nine, then, as a young man, had hacked and hewn the jagged coalface, taught himself maths, engineering and the violin, read the complete works of Shakespeare, and qualified for a manager's job. Raymond Moore exhorted his eight children to study hard, to avoid 'the suffering, the drawbacks and the restricted life he'd had'. Moore's teacher at Castleford Secondary School, Alice Gostick, belonged to the Art Teachers Guild, which published papers on subjects like 'The True Place of Art in Education'. Through magazines such as *Studio*, she introduced him to modern European art and encouraged his idea – apparently sparked by a Sunday School talk on Michelangelo – that he might one day become a sculptor. On leaving school, however, Moore became a pupil teacher ('the most miserable period of my life'), the first menial step towards a teaching career, and then, in February 1917, a soldier. In September 1919, an ex-serviceman's grant gave him the opportunity, almost unknown to his father's generation, of vocational training without the immediate pressure of earning a living: he enrolled on the drawing course at Leeds. When, with the new demand for monumental sculptors, a separate sculpture department opened the following year, Moore became its first and, for a while its only, student.

Leeds University's vice-chancellor, Michael Sadler, had started his modern art collection with Paul Gauguin's *Vision After the Sermon* shortly after seeing Roger Fry's first post-impressionist show in 1910. Fry, in turn, applauded Sadler's readiness to share his collection and enthusiasm. 'He had civilised a whole population. The entire spirit had changed from a rather sullen suspicion of ideas to a genuine enthusiastic intellectual and spiritual life. He showed what *can* be done, but rarely is, by education.' This was overstating the case, but it was true that Leeds in the 1920s, with its art school, gallery, university and philanthropic local industrialists, was a city with a robust sense of independence from, and rivalry with, London. Invited to Sadler's home, Moore at last saw actual works of modern art – Gauguins, Cézannes, Van Goghs and work by artists still little known in Britain, like the Russian Wassily Kandinsky. His art school experience had so far involved the kinds of drawing and clay-modelling tasks that would qualify him for teaching or a trade. In these circumstances, Moore's first sight of *Vision After the Sermon* must have felt like a real-life encounter with a semi-mythical species. In a Breton farmland setting, the biblical figures of Jacob and an angel wrestle in a rich red field bisected slantwise by an arching tree trunk that, in the manner of a Japanese print, is both an elegant graphic motif and potent physical presence, strong and compact. In the foreground, women look on with rapt devotion or stolid impassivity. Their big white Breton bonnets assume hard-to-read shapes, like bleached crustaceans. The ambiguous, compelling energy of this painting – the biblical rough-and-tumble, the vivid monolithic watchers – lay in some source far outside the art school curriculum.

Sometime in early 1921, Moore made 'the most lucky discovery'. He picked up a copy of Fry's latest book, *Vision and Design*, published in 1920. In this collection of essays and articles from the past ten years, Fry applied his theory of form to many kinds of art, including Paul Cézanne's paintings, the Florentine Renaissance, and African and Mesoamerican sculpture. Most of these articles had appeared in small-circulation journals, but *Vision and Design* became a bestseller. It hit the moment when artists – and not only artists – were seeking 'a new space to be in', an alternative to the mausoleum that state-sponsored art was attempting to erect in public consciousness. 'Once you'd read Roger Fry,' said

Moore, 'the whole thing was there.' He responded in a direct, practical way to Fry's belief that art communicates primarily through form, not subject matter or narrative. Through his feeling for wood and stone as materials with their own intrinsic vitality, Moore translated Fry's essentially analytical idea of form into sculptural practice. 'Complete sculptural expression,' he would succinctly state in 1934, 'is form in its full spatial reality.'

Vision and Design almost read like a manifesto for a new beginning in art. Fry wrote of the 'whole well-ordered system' of Greek and Roman art being 'blown away', leaving present-day culture 'bare to the blast' of change. His chapter 'Negro Sculpture' described an exhibition of African carvings he'd seen at the Chelsea Book Club shortly before *Vision and Design* went to press: he pronounced it 'great sculpture – greater, I think, than anything we produced even in the Middle Ages'. 'Without ever attaining anything like representational accuracy,' African sculptors had 'complete freedom', said Fry, creating their figures through 'an extraordinarily emphatic and impressive sequence of planes'. They underlined 'the three-dimensionalness' of forms, which gave their carvings 'disconcerting vitality' and 'an inner life of their own'. On the next the page, Fry upended the Western narrative of cultural superiority, describing the 'wanton destruction of the ancient civilisations of America'; he encouraged his readers to look at the 'magnificent collection of Mexican antiquities' in the British Museum.

When, later that year, a scholarship to the Royal College of Art (RCA) took Moore to London, he eagerly followed Fry's advice, going often to the British Museum. He ignored the Elgin Marbles – the revered fountainhead of Western figure sculpture – and instead studied every other example of stone-carving in the labyrinthine halls: African, Assyrian, Etruscan, Cycladic, Egyptian, Native American, and especially Mesoamerican, whose 'three-dimensionalness' he interrogated with the mental stamina of the true-born autodidact. 'Mexican sculpture, as soon as I found it,' he recalled, 'seemed to me true and right.' In 1924, after three years at the RCA, he went to Italy on a travelling scholarship but was confused to the point of 'violent conflict' by the Renaissance masterpieces he saw there. In a German magazine, he found an illustration of a thousand-year-old sculpture from the Toltec-Mayan site of Chichén Itzá. A male warrior figure, known as a *chacmool*, reclines on its back, head erect, knees raised, hands on stomach, holding a bowl that would have contained the blood of sacrificial victims. The tree-trunk limbs and boulder knees gave this stone thing something of the obdurate presence and strangeness of Adel Crag. What Moore saw in pre-Columbian Mexican sculpture, and what he felt about how and why it had been made, had apparently not been seen or felt by anyone before.

However excited Moore was by *Vision and Design*, Fry had not, in fact, delivered 'the whole thing' on a plate for him. As an interpreter of art, Fry was more subtly attuned to visual patterns and structures than to historical causation. His idea of form essentially existed in the present moment – very much the arena of the pre-war 'primitive mercenaries in the modern world' – to which objects from any place or time could be summoned for comparison. 'Almost any turn of the kaleidoscope of nature,' Fry wrote, could stimulate in the artist a 'detached and impassioned vision', in which 'forms and colours begin to crystallise into a harmony'. This focus on forms and colours, as distinct from the materials and processes by which they are created, appeals to the experience of the viewer more than the maker.

It did not, at any rate, reflect Moore's feeling for time as an element in his art. In 1924–25, he carved a *Mother and Child* in greenish-brown limestone from the quarries at Hornton in Oxfordshire. He chose a theme that resonated through Egyptian, Renaissance, African and other artistic traditions, which could also be observed any day in the real-life 'kaleidoscope of nature'. The mother figure is a torso, head and shoulders, balancing the child behind her neck; it echoes Fry's description of 'negro sculpture', in which 'the neck and torso are conceived as cylinders', heads 'as a single whole'. Moore's conjoined figures speak more strongly, however, on a metaphysical than on a formal plane – as embodiments of deep-rooted, life-giving 'generation' rather than satisfyingly balanced cylinders and cubes.

Moore's stocky mother figure, with thick arms raised and bent to support her naked child, has the flat-nosed, mask-like face of a *chacmool*. But while the mother-and-child theme felt ageless, his treatment of the female form was new. When British sculptors had produced female figures in the past century or so, these had generally been either notables or nymphs, either stolidly sexless or smoothly erotic. There were exceptions, but even Jacob Epstein's 1907–8 *Maternity* was still, despite her milk-heavy breasts and erect nipples, recognizable as a relative of the academic nude. For Epstein, the carving of the Portland limestone was a process of executing a design; for Moore, the sculptor and his chisel were a medium through which the stone itself could speak. 'Every material,' he believed, 'has its own individual qualities. It is only when the sculptor works direct, when there is an active relationship with his material, that the material can take part in the shaping of an idea.' This 'active relationship' between sculptor and material was a complete reversal of the role of the sculptor in the service of the state – almost the only service in which professional sculptors could have been observed at work during Moore's student years: stones cannot 'take part' in sculpting war memorials.

In 1927, Hepworth carved a *Mother and Child* (pl. 8), in a manner that at first looks very close to Moore's. In her sculpture, too, the mother's thick torso almost appears contained by the envelope of the original block of stone. Like Moore, she practised and proselytized about 'direct carving':

> *I like the resistance of the hard material and feel happier working that way...also, there are all the beauties of several hundreds of different stones and woods, and the idea [for a sculpture] must be in harmony with the qualities of each one carved.*

Hepworth, like Moore, had followed her studies at the RCA with travel to Italy in autumn 1924, on a West Riding Scholarship. 'There had been something lacking in my childhood in Yorkshire, and that was light'; in Italy, she experienced 'light which transforms and reveals, which intensifies the subtleties of form and contours'. In Florence, she discovered the romanesque carvings in early medieval church buildings. In Rome, she met a young British sculptor, John Skeaping; they moved on to Siena, married in Florence and returned to Rome, where Hepworth learned – and learned to love – the art of chiselling Carrara or 'Luna' marble, a cloud-white, sparkling crystalline limestone, the opposite in every sense of carboniferous Yorkshire coal. By November 1926, they were back in London, where Moore, too, had recently settled, teaching at Chelsea School of Art and starting to exhibit.

From this point on, both Hepworth and Moore began to describe the practice of sculpture as if it were less an art form than a way of relating to the world. They shared and developed their metaphors: 'If a pebble or an egg can be enjoyed for the sake of its shape only,' wrote Hepworth, 'it is one step towards a true appreciation of sculpture. A tree trunk, with its changing axis, swellings and varied sections, fully

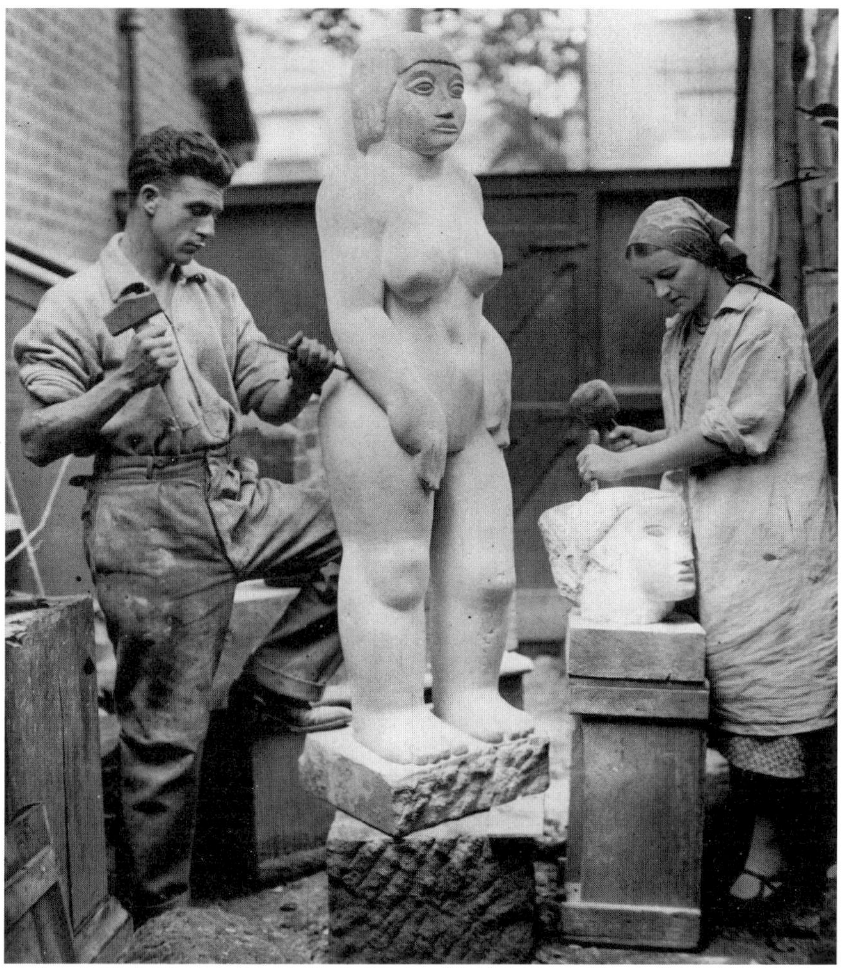

Barbara Hepworth and John Skeaping carving, the Mall Studios, Hampstead, 1930

understood, takes us a step further.' The pebble connotes environmental process, the egg birth, the tree growth: together they mark out a path to 'appreciation of sculpture', in which, unlike the thousands of tons of fresh-cut stone standing around in town centres and on village greens, it signifies not death but life.

Life with a subtly different emphasis, in Hepworth's case. Instead of carrying the child on her shoulders, Hepworth's stone mother hugs her baby close, their limbs interlock. Where Moore's figures suggest the biological growth of one form out of another, Hepworth's stress relationship and balance – two forms becoming one, rather than one becoming two. In August 1929, Hepworth gave birth to a son, Paul. Other female artists had discovered that – whatever the accepted wisdom and the many examples of talented artists whose careers had been torpedoed by pregnancy – the roles of artist and mother were not necessarily mutually exclusive. Advances in contraception in the past twenty years and a more liberal attitude to birth control, once considered 'a sort of secret vice', noted Robert Graves and Alan Hodge in *The Long Week-End*, but now regarded as having 'hygienic advantages over the old leave-it-to-chance system', had introduced a more reliable element of personal choice. Hepworth was one of the first women artists to embark on a determined attempt to make a success of both sculpture and motherhood. Paul was six months old when she wrote her 'pebble, egg and tree' statement for *The Architectural Association Journal* in April 1930. The steps towards understanding sculpture, Hepworth explained, finally led to a realization 'that abstract form, the relation of masses and planes, is that which gives sculptural life', which in turn 'admits that a piece of sculpture can be purely abstract or non-representational'. This is her earliest expression of the connection between 'sculptural life' and 'purely abstract' form, which she imagined as the latest iteration of a long continuum: 'Tradition is no longer a day-dream and things that have been made seem like the unfolding and development of one idea, the growth of some great tree.'

Where 'speed' had been the futurist watchword, the whole thrust of Hepworth and Moore's sculptural practice and their public statements was to slow and still. They emphasized permanence and gravity, vertical instead of horizontal time, in which the present moment was linked via the thread of the artist's consciousness to primordial human experience and pre-human nature. Hepworth described how 'The sounds of unseen birds and droning aeroplanes in the sky' were connected, through the sculptor herself, to 'the earth revealing its shape to the feet and eye'. 'Abstract' would become one of art's most imprecise, ideologically loaded labels, with a baffling range of connotations from purity to formal angularity to ludicrous incomprehensibility. As Hepworth employed it to describe the 'relation of masses and planes' in the sculptures she was carving in the late 1920s, it can be understood in poetic terms, in the sense in which configurations of ordinary words (the raw material of language) like 'unseen birdsong' or 'droning aeroplanes' conjure a reality more vividly than prosaic descriptions of these phenomena.

Among Hepworth and Moore's contemporaries at the RCA was a group of painting and design students who sat at a different table in the canteen. They did not – either then or later – share the Yorkshire contingent's interest in nature's means of sculptural self-expression through pebbles and trees, the mysterious synergy between artist and material, or the essential purity and vitality of abstract art. In 1928, William Rothenstein, artist friend of Augustus John, now principal of the RCA, proposed members of this group for a public mural commission, brightening up the dingy refreshment room in Morley Memorial College for Working Men and Women, next door to the Old Vic Theatre in Waterloo, with 'subjects from Shakespeare'. Over the next sixteen months, Edward Bawden and Eric Ravilious collaborated on this project. Bawden's sections included *Scenes from the Tempest*, which featured a toy-like theatre consisting of three stages stacked one above the other against a backdrop of sea and sky. Ravilious inserted an un-Shakespearean modern scene, *Life in a Boarding House*, in which the facade of a London townhouse was cut away like a Victorian dolls' house to reveal the rooms and their occupants, floor by floor. Nature, in both Bawden's *Tempest* and Ravilious's *Boarding House*, is a backdrop to an ordered, enclosed arena of human action, taking the form of placid skies across which float playful clouds, friendly as wallpaper.

Where Hepworth and Moore produced smooth, self-contained, generic shapes, Bawden and Ravilious's scenes were vivid with illustrative detail, but there were two elements their murals (destroyed in 1940) shared, strangely enough, with the sculptors' contemporaneous work. First, was their sense of time as a vertical shaft, sunk down through the present. Where the sculptors' time-shafts reached all the way from aeroplanes to bedrock, however, Bawden and Ravilious treated the Jacobean past and present-day London as elevations, layered with distinct strata. Second, was a deep sense of stillness and poise. In the company of Hepworth's 1927 *Mother and Child* or Bawden's *Scenes from the Tempest*, it was hard to remember that 'the beauty of speed' had ever been extolled as the defining spirit of modern art.

Bawden moved in the spring of 1931 to Great Bardfield, a sleepy market town in Essex. In the main street, built wide for stagecoaches and market stalls, there was little sign, apart from the occasional car, that the Industrial Revolution had happened, let alone the machine age. Brick House became the latest incarnation of the rural, family-scale artist communities that had sprung up throughout the 1920s. Double-fronted, three-storeyed, supplied by well water with no electricity and a river running at the back, it had the picturesque bulk and calm seclusion of Dora Carrington and Lytton Strachey's Tidmarsh Mill. Here Bawden, together with Ravilious, his girlfriend Tirzah Garwood, and a changing cast of like-minded visitors including Helen Binyon and John Nash (Paul Nash's brother), set about reviving the art of wood engraving, emulating the eighteenth-century master Thomas Bewick, and hoping to make a living from commissions for small-press illustrated books (another revivalist niche). The figures in their drawings, prints and watercolours wear modern clothes but inhabit pre-industrial scenes. In Bawden's illustration for the month of May in Ambrose Heath's seasonal recipe book *Good Food* (1932), four friends gather round a lunch table. The overarching, leaf-laden branch of a venerable tree is not there to take us 'one step further' towards the realization of abstract form but to symbolize the order, peace and safety of the *hortus conclusus* or enclosed garden. Securely fenced, hedged or walled gardens often appear: in Bawden's *June*, where friends crouch this time under strawberry nets in a vegetable patch; in Ravilious's watercolour *Two Women in a Garden* (1933), where the great tree again shades and shelters. Often people are absent, letting the tilled soil or a kettle on the kitchen range express a sense of halcyon domesticity and old-school rural skills.

As distinct from Moore's sense of connection across eons with 'prehistoric trees', the Great Bardfield pastoral version of Deep Britain is a place in which time both stands still and loops forever in a seasonal round, anaesthetizing all anxiety about the future. Trees in Bawden's and Ravilious's pictures do not hint at primal sculptural forms but at the generations of patient husbandry that have shaped gardens, fields, woods and orchards, ringed safely with walls and fences, cut into patterns by empty roads. There's also much evidence of actual digging into the soil – here a spade propped against a greenhouse door, there a chalk figure cut into Wiltshire downland turf, a motif that particularly fascinated Ravilious. Occasionally, 'droning aeroplanes', steam trains or cars traverse this time-bound Britain, but they appear as incidental figures in the vista, not forces of change. Apart from the weather, all sources of unpredictability and disturbance are banished from these landscapes.

There was trouble, however, in the world beyond the walled garden. In the early 1930s, economic depression and industrial unrest – particularly acute in coal-mining districts, affected by falling demand for export coal – brought a series of strikes, lockouts and hunger marches. In the autumn of 1932, with unemployment edging towards three million, the Great National Hunger March from Scotland, Wales and northern England reached London on 27 October. About 100,000 protesters were confronted by 70,000 police in the British state's most violent engagement since the Clydeside strikes of 1919. In Germany, political volatility exacerbated by the Depression was playing into the hands of the National Socialist Party, which had been dismissed at the time of the abortive Beer Hall Putsch of 1923 as a marginal mob of right-wing extremist troublemakers. In Italy, a long-time fan of Marinetti's, the former journalist Benito Mussolini had staged a successful coup in October 1922 and already been in power for a decade.

None of this registered in the work of Bawden or Ravilious, Hepworth or Moore – or at least, not directly. In 1931, Hepworth experimented by carving a hole right through a piece of alabaster, which became *Pierced Form*. She felt 'intense pleasure in piercing the stone in order to make an abstract form and space'. The breakthrough here, which was to be much developed and repeated by Hepworth, Moore and others, was to allow space – in effect, the outside world – to flow through, not round, a sculpture. Form itself had, up to this point, been a kind of walled garden, with an inside and an out-there. By making an aperture in the stone, Hepworth created a point of interpenetration and interaction between sculpture and environment. Local, personal and abstract though this experiment might have seemed, it was in its way an acknowledgment of the sculpture's presence in place and time, and the sculptor's connection with the wider world and her responsibility towards it.

The effects of the Great Depression in Britain, especially in the south, were neither as general nor as devastating as in the USA. They coincided with the nation's transformation into a mobile, suburban society. A house-building boom resulted in the construction of some 2.5 million half-timbered, bay-windowed semi-detached family houses – comfort architecture for these post-traumatic years. 'Ribbon-building', as Graves and Hodge explained in *The Long Week-End*, 'meant stringing houses along main roads instead of building them in compact village-like masses', so that the occupants 'had direct access to the road' and at the same time 'an uninterrupted country view from their back windows'. It was the private car – symbol of cultural revolution in 1909, *sine qua non* of outer-suburb living in 1929 – that dictated this arrangement, in which the semi-detached home, Janus-like, looked two ways: towards the road and the connected modern world, and, at the back, towards an enclosed and arrested version of the rural past. Although the maniacal futurist had been replaced at the wheel by the sporty young executive or pipe-smoking paterfamilias, the car still retained something of its radical glamour. Graves and Hodge reported that:

> *Country people grew to hate cars, for their noise, smell, danger, and the unconcerned bearing of their drivers, and often encouraged children to pelt them with stones and line the road with glass and upturned tacks…. A new division of Britain took place: Motorists and Pedestrians.*

In the hands of the 'weekend motorist', the car became a mode of time travel. Launched with the poet John Betjeman's guide to Cornwall in 1934, the Shell County Guides targeted the new demographic of leisure motorists, for whom their cars were conceived as vehicles for 'seeing' Britain. In this process, driving through the present-day

Frank Dobson, *The Giant, Cerne Abbas*, 1931. Shell advertising poster, 76.2 × 114.3 cm (30 × 45 in.)

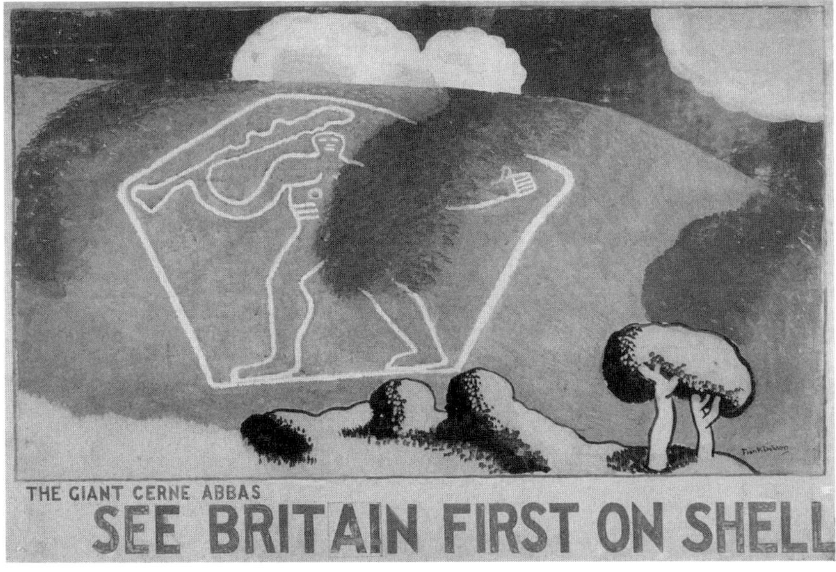

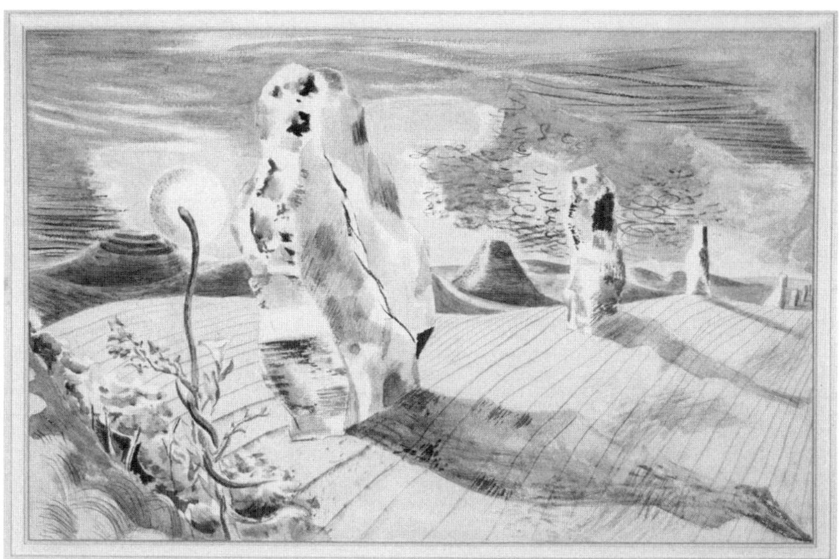

Paul Nash, *Landscape of the Megaliths*, 1937. Watercolour on paper,
50.2 × 75.6 cm (19⅞ × 29⅞ in.)

landscape could simultaneously become a journey into the deep past.
In the Cornish village of Zennor, Betjeman noted how 'Nature and pre-
history in this treeless parish strewn with granite boulders among the
heather, make the efforts of modern man even five hundred years ago,
seem small and futile.' In a more elemental manner than Bawden and
Ravilious's Essex vegetable plot, this ancient landscape limited modernity's reach: there was solace, Betjeman suggests, rather than terror in
seeing the 'efforts of modern man' as 'small and futile'.

As the Shell Guides' general editor, Betjeman commissioned painters
such as the former war artist Paul Nash (*Dorset*, 1936) and John Piper
(*Oxfordshire*, 1938) to give the series a contemporary feel: modernity meets
beauty spot. Piper and his girlfriend, the writer Myfanwy Evans, had
been undertaking explorations of their own, touring Dorset churches and
villages, photographing Norman carvings and rustic gravestones – the
local, lichen-covered visage of the past. After his interest in surrealism
was awakened by the dreamlike cityscapes of the Italian painter Giorgio
de Chirico – strange, silent theatres of nocturnal incident – Nash
made several visits to the famous Neolithic stone circles at Avebury in
Wiltshire. In *Equivalents for Megaliths* (1935), cylindrical and rectangular

abstract forms stand like ancient stones amid the harvested wheatfields, with the earthen ramparts of an Iron Age hillfort in the distance. His later watercolour *Landscape of the Megaliths*, by contrast, interprets the Avebury henge through more romantically surrealist-tinted glasses. In 1938, Nash came across a field in Gloucestershire in which the shattered, desiccated trunks and branches of fallen trees irresistibly suggested dinosaurs or mythical dragons. His photographs of the 'Monster Field' present a case study in the surrealists' Freudian conviction that what an artist perceives in the external world is in fact a projection of images from his or her unconscious.

Sigmund Freud's theory of the unconscious, radical in the 1900s, had by the 1930s become mainstream. English translations of Freud's works sat on many British bookshelves alongside Betjeman's *Cornwall* and other popular titles. Freudian concepts, reported Graves and Hodge, including the inferiority complex, sadism, masochism, ego, libido and id, were 'bandied across the tea cups', while the British stiff upper lip was challenged by the new wisdom that a healthy approach to life involved 'letting the bottled-up emotions have free vent'. 'We are all psychoanalysts now,' the *Daily News* announced as early as 1922, although readers were advised to avoid taking 'a morbid interest in their primal instincts'.

On holiday with a group of friends in the village of Happisburgh in summer 1931, Moore and Hepworth had been gathering pebbles on the Norfolk coast, when Ben Nicholson, who had left Winifred at home with their children, joined the party. He and Hepworth fell for each other. Within a year, their first marriages over, they were sharing a life in Hampstead, north London, making regular trips to Paris, where they met Piet Mondrian, Pablo Picasso, Constantin Brancusi and Jean (Hans) Arp and – this had not happened in any serious and sustained way for twenty years – bringing home to London something of the energy and ambition, the belief in modern art as an ideology of social progress, that they discovered in Europe. In June 1933, Nash – a Hampstead neighbour of Hepworth, Nicholson and Moore – wrote a letter to *The Times*, in which he announced the formation of Unit One, dedicated to 'the expression of a truly contemporary spirit' in art, in other words abstraction or surrealism. The following year, the group staged a touring show, which opened at London's Mayor Gallery, featuring work by Hepworth, Moore, seven painters (including Nicholson) and two architects, all united in the aim of 'putting new life into a force we all believed in'.

Moore's catalogue statement for this exhibition summarizes his project of the past decade. In language whose directness and clarity probably owe much to a helping hand from another Hampstead neighbour, fellow Yorkshireman and Western Front veteran, the writer Herbert Read, he expounds his pursuit of 'truth to material', his search for 'dynamic tension', 'vitality of life' and 'pent-up energy' through art. The survivor of the Battle of Cambrai, in which gas, machine guns and strafing from the air had cut down seven in every eight men in his regiment, explains that, for him, sculpture is 'an expression of the significance of life, a stimulation to greater effort in living'.

At which point, following Nazi success in the German elections of March 1933 and Adolf Hitler's declaration in July that Germany was now a one-party state, geopolitics once again brought pent-up energy and dynamic tension of a different kind to bear on artists' visions of the future.

10
Storm and ashes

Hampstead, November 1936

> Above the tempests of our weekdays,
> Across the ashes and cindered homes of the past,
> Before the gates of the vacant future...

As things have turned out, this is the shape Naum Gabo's future has taken: Hampstead. He walks along Lawn Road, past dull London houses, white-capped maids and stately black perambulators. When he wrote those words, he was a young man in Moscow, in the anything-is-possible years just after the revolution. He had foreseen 'The blossoming of a new culture and a new civilisation with their unprecedented-in-history surge of the masses towards the possession of the riches of Nature.' Today, despite the talk of another war and news of atrocities in Spain, it seems unlikely that anyone he passes on the pavement will have the faintest clue what revolution means. In Hampstead, where the intelligentsia of London – now including himself – are distributed in surprising numbers among the leafy, uneventful streets, the word itself feels almost abstract. But 'Life does not wait and the growth of generations does not stop.' After weeks of discussions, he and artist Ben Nicholson and their architect friend Leslie Martin have decided on a title for their journal. Rejecting the mystical-sounding 'Cosmos and Synthesis', they have chosen Circle. *The circle is a shape with which Gabo has endlessly played in designs for constructions of many kinds – sculptures, buildings, and projects that might end up being neither, either or both. As a title, 'Circle' satisfyingly evokes the compass-drawn enactment of a new idea, fresh on the drawing board, as well as the universe of space and time, 'the only forms on which life is built'.*

———

Gabo was born Nehemiah Pevzner, the son of a Jewish foundry owner in backwoods Bryansk, western Russia, and brother of Noton, later Antoine, Pevzner. His first vocation was poetry, but in 1910 he went to the University of Munich to study medicine, switched to natural sciences and then, in 1912, an engineering course at the Technische Hochschule. By 1913, he was in Paris with Antoine, who had become a painter. Gabo read Wassily Kandinsky's book *Concerning the Spiritual in Art* (1911), a meditation on the metaphysical significance of forms and colours, and a rejection of the kinds of figurative art that serve and reproduce the 'nightmare of materialism'. 'The life of the spirit,' wrote Kandinsky, is represented by 'a large acute-angled triangle...moving slowly, almost invisibly forwards and upwards. Where the apex is today, the second segment is tomorrow.' The triangle was a clear mathematical shape – but imagine it moving in space. Imagine watching squares and rectangles, cones and cylinders, curves and straight lines, all moving in relation to each other.

In the art Gabo saw in Paris and the artists he met, he recognized an attempt to get away from the old idea of the static, flat or solid work of art – in the cubist fracturings and collagings of Pablo Picasso and Georges Braque, or in the Romanian sculptor Constantin Brancusi's idea of a bird in space, to which he gave form in smooth spindle shapes, carved in marble or cast in bronze. But Gabo felt that none of these artists had grasped what space and movement really meant. In Norway during the First World War to evade conscription into the Russian army, he realized that all his studies in different disciplines were leading him towards a path that perhaps no one had taken before. The terms 'artist' or 'sculptor' did not quite describe it. It was around this time that he invented his new name.

Gabo and Pevzner returned to Russia after the October Revolution of 1917. In August 1920, they staged a small exhibition in the bandstand on Moscow's Tverskoi Boulevard. It included examples of the new 'stereometric' type of sculpture Gabo had devised – three-dimensional forms like a human head constructed out of flat, interlocking panels cut from wood or cardboard. Walls and fences all over the city were a collage of slogans, like poster artist Dmitri Moor's summons to join the Red Army, in which a bug-eyed soldier jabbed his finger: *Ty zapisalsia dobrovol'tsem?* ('Have *you* volunteered?'). Gabo and Pevzner pasted up their own call to arms, the *Realistic Manifesto*, jointly signed but authored by Gabo. 'Space and time are re-born to us today', they announced, echoing Lenin's prophecy that revolution would transform everyone's relationship to space and time – *prostranstvo i vremya* – so that human experience and perception would inevitably adapt 'more and more to *objective* space and time, and *reflect* them ever more correctly and profoundly'.

For Gabo, even contemporary artists whose work was still considered avant-garde held false and outdated notions of space and time. 'The distracted world of the Cubists, broken in shreds by their logical anarchy, cannot satisfy us who have already accomplished the Revolution.' The futurists' 'pompous slogan of "Speed"' was laughable: 'ask any Futurist how does he imagine "speed" and there will emerge a whole arsenal of frenzied automobiles, rattling railway depots, snarled wires, the clank and the noise and the clang of carouselling streets.' 'Look at a ray of sun,' Gabo exhorted his readers on the Moscow streets: 'the stillest of still forces, it speeds more than 300[000] kilometres in a second... behold our starry firmament...who hears it...and yet what are our depots to those depots of the Universe? What are our earthly trains to those hurrying trains of the galaxies?' Static sculptural mass was a legacy of a 'thousand-year-old delusion in art', in place of which the *Realistic Manifesto* affirmed 'a new element the kinetic rhythms as the basic forms of our perception of real time'. Gabo had already put this theory into practice, constructing a small kinetic sculpture: he inserted a thin vertical steel rod into a motor that made it oscillate, producing the optical illusion of a three-dimensional vase-shaped solid.

After arriving in Berlin in early 1922 to help organize the First Russian Art Exhibition, Gabo stayed on. While Soviet officialdom grew increasingly hostile to non-representational artists, progressives and transgressives of all kinds thrived in Berlin under the Weimar Republic of 1919–33. Comrade Gabo of the *Realistic Manifesto* became a transnational artist, exhibiting in New York in 1924 and, the same year, being approached by Sergei Diaghilev to design a production for the Ballets Russes. Gabo and Pevzner collaborated on the set and costumes for *La Chatte*, the tale of a cat transformed into a woman, choreographed by George Balanchine, which opened in Monte Carlo in April 1927. In shimmering transparent plastic skirts, the dancers moved like quicksilver abstract shapes within the framing geometries of the set. Gabo was invited to lecture at the Bauhaus in Dessau, Germany, Europe's leading experimental school of art, architecture and design; in 1930, he had a solo exhibition in Hanover, featuring what he now termed 'constructive' sculptures. The following year, he submitted a visionary (though unrealized) design for a projected Palace of the Soviets in central Moscow, in which the floor, walls and roof would form a single continuous concrete membrane. By the time he moved to Paris in 1932, Gabo was at the centre of an international creative network united by a conviction that abstraction, in one form or another, was the universal visual language of the future.

If the Bauhaus led the field in abstraction applied to architecture and industrial design, Paris was still the capital of avant-garde painting and sculpture. Along with the Dutch painter Piet Mondrian, the American artist Alexander Calder and the British couple Barbara Hepworth and Ben Nicholson, Gabo became a member of Abstraction–Création, an association formed in 1931 as a counterpoise to the well-organized surrealist movement and its figurative dream-fantasies. He also met

Naum Gabo, *Construction on a Line*, 1935–37. Perspex, 45.1 × 43.2 × 8.9 cm (17⅞ × 17⅛ × 3⅝ in.)

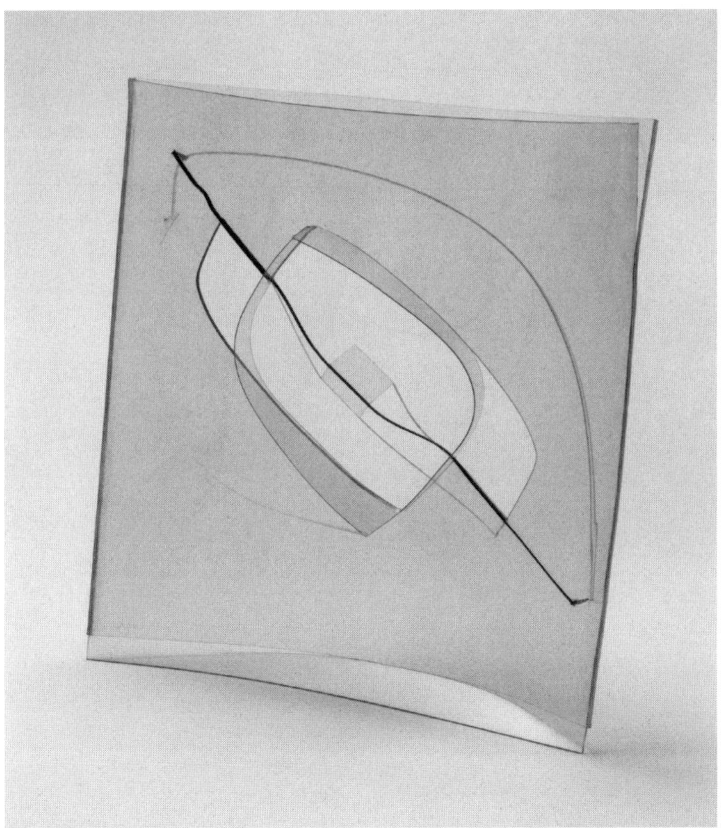

Nicholson's ex-wife Winifred, now living in Paris with their children, and a close friend of Mondrian. In 1935, Abstraction–Création's British contingent, buoyed by the confidence around abstract art in France, set about planning a show, inviting Gabo to contribute. In March 1936, a month after 'Abstract and Concrete' opened in Oxford, Gabo arrived in London.

All things considered, London, where Hepworth and Nicholson immediately offered to find him a studio, seemed a good move. In the Soviet Union under Stalin, socialist realism was the only officially sanctioned art. After 1933, there was no future for a Jewish artist in Hitler's Germany. Added to these factors, Gabo had fallen in love with Miriam Franklin, a married American-Jewish artist to whom a friend in Berlin had given him an introduction as a potentially useful London patron. In an effort to obtain official permission for Gabo to remain in Britain, his art world contacts procured a letter to the Ministry of Labour from 'Tate galerie', as he reported to Miriam, explaining that he 'was such an artist whose work can not be done by any other English artist'. It was, he complained, 'even neccessary to lunch in the Hous of Common and to be introduced to some mighty people. All difficulties are arisen from

Opening day at the Isokon Building, Hampstead, 9 July 1934, photograph by Edith Tudor-Hart

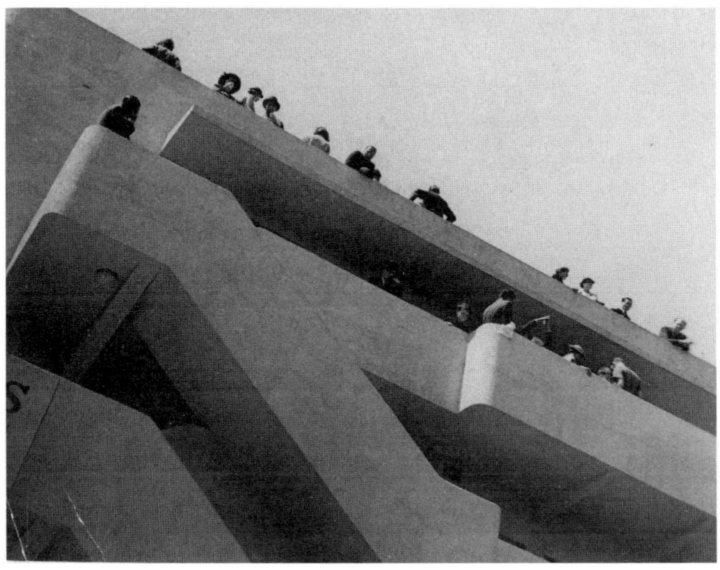

the fact that I am Soviet-citizen.' In September, he had his constructions, mostly in the form of small-scale models, shipped from Paris; in November 1936, he was informed he could stay for one year.

Reason to celebrate – and even in Hampstead, there were signs that the 'new civilization' was being born. Almost opposite his flat on Lawn Road were the blank white walls and long white ramps of the Isokon Building, the first modernist apartment block in Britain, designed by a Canadian architect, Wells Coates. In the mid-1930s, the little box-like apartments had become a kind of pigeon loft for former colleagues from the Bauhaus, who, like Gabo, had found their way to London. The Dessau school was closed by the Nazis in 1931; the Bauhaus's short-lived move to Berlin effectively ended when, on 11 April 1933, the secret police or Gestapo locked teachers and students out of the building. In the Isobar café on the ground floor of the Isokon Building, Gabo might meet his neighbours Henry and Irina Moore, Hepworth and Nicholson, German architect Walter Gropius or Hungarian designer Marcel Breuer. Further on, past the bus-stop and the green, was the row of cottages that the Hungarian architect Ernő Goldfinger planned to demolish to build his own modern house, with long horizontal windows, a flat roof and thin cylindrical columns, or pilotis, Le Corbusier-style.

In Germany, the purge of 'non-Aryan' state employees, from university professors to teachers and post office workers, began in earnest with the Restoration of the Professional Civil Service Act of April 1933, leading many to attempt to emigrate to Britain and the United States. Numbers actually arriving remained small, however; there were long waiting lists for visas and vocal opposition to skilled immigration from professional bodies like the British Medical Association and British Dental Association (between 1935, the year of the Nuremberg Race Laws, and 1937, only 183 refugee doctors and 78 dentists were allowed entry). Among the Isokon's ex-Bauhaus residents, Gropius had fled to London in 1934; he was not Jewish but, as former director of the Bauhaus, *persona non grata* in Nazi Germany. Prompted by Gropius, Breuer arrived in 1935, along with Hungarian artist, photographer and designer László Moholy-Nagy; both found work designing furniture for the Isokon company, including moulded plywood chairs for the apartments and café. The social vision that informed the Bauhaus project and was shared by the contributors to *Circle* – the belief that artists had both an inspirational and a practical role in designing for modern life – was succinctly expressed by the Swiss-French architect Le Corbusier's idea of the modern house as a *machine-à-habiter* ('machine for living in').

The conceptual energy that Gabo and the Bauhaus émigrés brought to north London was contagious. Thanking Gabo for helping her to 'see things differently and clearer', Winifred Nicholson observed that 'by the way the people that I met were talking in London you had given them the same'. In her essay in *Circle*, Hepworth described her sculptural vision in social terms: 'The language of colour and form is universal and not one for a special class...it is a thought which gives the same life, the same expansion, the same universal freedom to everyone.' The collective feeling grew that there was a natural association between abstract art and combating fascism: British artists and thinkers would join forces with the exiled European avant-garde to build a better world. In the 1936 science fiction film *Things to Come*, scripted by H. G. Wells, world war breaks out in 1940 and lasts for twenty years. Peace finally comes to Everytown in the shape of sleeping-gas bombs; the population awakes to 'a new life for mankind' under the rule of a pacifist brotherhood, Wings Over the World, whose leader, John Cabal, was modelled on Hepworth's friend the Irish crystallographer and *Circle* contributor J. D. (Desmond) Bernal.

Hampstead was also a London base for abstract–constructivism's rival tendency, surrealism. In Downshire Hill, a short walk from the Isokon flats and from Hepworth, Nicholson and Moore's studios in Parkhill Road, lived Roland Penrose, wealthy artist, collector and friend of Picasso and the German surrealist Max Ernst. In 1936, Penrose had thrown himself into organizing the International Surrealist Exhibition, which opened at the Burlington Galleries on 11 June, when André Breton, author of the original 1924 *Surrealist Manifesto* and the movement's acknowledged 'pope', had addressed a two-thousand-strong crowd. This was the first big London survey of modern European art since Roger Fry's Second Post-Impressionist Exhibition in 1912. During its three-week run, it attracted 33,000 visitors, generating press coverage on a scale of which north London's abstract–constructivists could only dream. After seeing the exhibition together, Hepworth, Nicholson and Gabo adjourned to a nearby ABC teashop to plot their response. It was time, they agreed, to spell out their alternative vision for an art that was not built on dreams but on clear concepts – constructive in every sense. Gabo, whom Nicholson admiringly noted was very much 'in touch with Today', was the obvious choice as lead author. Writing to Gabo from her Cumberland cottage, Winifred Nicholson had high hopes of this new venture: he understood 'all the different human beings so well that they all become especially constructive, like flowers under sunlight', she rhapsodized; 'really if you and Ben work together with your vital fire, things will begin to move in London.'

Circle: An International Survey of Constructive Art was published in July 1937, with contributions from some seventy painters, sculptors, architects, designers and writers, from France, Germany, the Netherlands, Finland, America and Britain. Mondrian wrote about 'Plastic Art and Pure Plastic Art', Moholy-Nagy on photography, or 'Light Painting', Le Corbusier on 'The Quarrel with Realism' and Bernal on 'Art and the Scientist'. Alongside these visionary tracts, Ben Nicholson and Moore provided brief, generalizing statements. 'I dislike the idea that contemporary art is an escape from life,' opined Moore. '"Painting" and "religious experience" are the same thing,' asserted Nicholson, not quite hitting the high notes of Kandinskian afflatus: 'You cannot ask an explorer to explain what a country is like which he is about to explore for the first time.' The 'constructive moment is a living force', he concluded, 'life gives birth to life'– notes from a British artist gamely trying to absorb the slightly indigestible theoretics of the European avant-garde.

Whether or not *Circle* won any converts to 'the constructive idea', it injected an unusual intensity of intellectual fervour into the London art scene. 'Since the beginning of Time man has been occupied with nothing less but the perfecting of his world,' announced Gabo. Art would not now be directed towards 'an immediate construction of material values in life' but would bring about 'a state of mind which will be able only to construct, coordinate and perfect instead of to destroy, disintegrate and deteriorate'. Although a European war felt increasingly imminent, Gabo saw beyond the coming conflagration, confident that 'in the realm of ideas we are now entering on the period of reconstruction.'

A fortnight after the International Surrealist Exhibition closed on 4 July 1936, General Francisco Franco declared a right-wing rebellion against Spain's Republican government, sparking almost three years of civil war. In Britain, left-wingers younger than the *Circle* crowd responded to the call of the Comintern (Communist International) to join the International Brigades, supporting Republican forces against Franco's Nationalist insurgency. Volunteers came from all backgrounds and social classes – bus conductors, bricklayers and doctors, and a higher proportion of artists than in the general population. The poet and pacifist Julian Bell, son of Clive and Vanessa, whom she had painted in his crib in 1908, enlisted as an ambulance driver and a month later, in July 1937, was killed by shrapnel at the Battle of Brunete. Throughout this year, the Nationalists gained ground, with military support from the Fascist regimes in Germany and Italy. On 26 April, German ground-attack aircraft of the Condor Legion subjected Guernica, a Republican-held town in the Basque region, to its new strategy of carpet-bombing, dropping a mixture of heavy, anti-personnel and incendiary explosives. Civilians had been targeted during the First World War by siege artillery and cumbersome Zeppelins with a limited payload. Guernica took the terror to an unprecedented level: for two and a half hours, three squadrons of Junkers 52 aircraft bombed the town in twenty-minute relays. People and farm animals were burned alive with white phosphorus, strafed in the fields. Guernica was razed. News broke in Britain the following day in a *Times* report by George Steer.

In central Paris, the national pavilions for the International Exposition of Arts and Techniques in Modern Life – the 1937 World's Fair – were almost ready for the opening ceremonies on 24 May. On the north bank of the Seine, opposite the Eiffel Tower, the Soviet and German pavilions – bombastic totalitarian barns, each fronted by an eerily similar tower – faced off across the central avenue. Crowning the German pavilion, designed by architect Albert Speer, an eagle gripped a swastika-filled wreath; atop the Soviet tower stood Vera Mukhina's 78-foot-high sculpture of a male worker flourishing a hammer, while a female farmworker swung her sickle, striding east as if to fell the swastika. The totalitarian towers dwarfed the Catalan architect Josep Lluís Sert's nearby pavilion of the Spanish Republic – three light-filled storeys, white-walled and wide-windowed in the most optimistic Le Corbusian manner, but displaying photographs of murdered children in the streets of Guernica, and Picasso's mural-scale howl of protest, painted in just one month between the massacre and the opening. For thirty-three-year-old British art historian Kenneth Clark, a Leonardo expert and the National Gallery's youngest ever director, *Guernica* 'filled me with all those sensations of horror and pity and indignation which Picasso intended', although he found the cubistic distortions of the figures 'puzzling'.

Across the Seine stood Oliver Hill's British pavilion, an uninspired white box faced with a painted frieze by Hepworth's ex-husband John Skeaping. To *Circle*'s Leslie Martin, it represented – like Hill's Midland Hotel in Morecambe – a *'modernistic'* pastiche whose reliance on 'the spurious appeal of surface decoration' he judged to be 'a positive danger'. It evidently had not occurred to British officialdom that, in the jittery political context of appeasement, it might make diplomatic sense to cut a serious figure at the Paris fair. Whereas totalitarian regimes excelled in 'the aestheticisation of politics' (in Walter Benjamin's phrase), British cultural diplomacy was irresolute and underpowered. In 1934, in response to Hitler's withdrawal from the League of Nations and the Geneva Conference, the Foreign Office had established the British Committee for Relations with Other Countries (soon renamed the British Council), with a brief to foster 'friendly knowledge and understanding of the people of this country, of their philosophy and way of life'. This would, it was hoped, be naturally conducive to 'a sympathetic appreciation of British foreign policy, whatever for the moment that policy may be'.

The artwork inside Hill's pavilion was commissioned by Frank Pick, chair of the Council for Art and Industry, whose chosen theme was 'elements in the current civilisation of Western Europe which have been contributed mainly by Great Britain'. These were to be identified by English words that had been adopted by the French, such as *le Sport, le tennis, le football, le golf* and, of course, *le week-end*. The first thing visitors encountered was a cut-out figure of Prime Minister Neville Chamberlain engaged in fly fishing. Further on was a set of panels by Eric Ravilious, depicting cricketers and tennis players, long-legged and carefree on tree-fringed lawns. They gave the impression, his on–off girlfriend artist Helen Binyon tartly observed, 'of an England largely rural and inhabited by comfortably off sportsmen'. It was all 'misleadingly out-of-date and trivial', though 'pretty enough'.

In London, artists of all persuasions put aside their differences in demonstrations of solidarity with the European refugees, especially after the notorious Nazi-sponsored exhibition 'Degenerate Art' had toured the Reich in 1937, pairing the work of avant-garde, or simply unconventional, artists with that produced by mental asylum inmates and 'savage' peoples. In spring 1937, the left-wing Artists' International Association staged the exhibition 'Unity of Artists for Peace, Democracy and Cultural Development'; in July the next year, the New Burlington

Galleries hosted 'Twentieth Century German Art', followed by Picasso's *Guernica* in October. In November, Penrose, along with members of the New English Art Club and other groups, set up the Artists' Refugee Committee. Even at this late stage, there was still hope that peace could be secured by force of reason. But how? Virginia Woolf mulled over the problem in her essay *Three Guineas*, published in June 1938. Why – since it was men, not women, who made war – did women's education, which had taken great strides since 1919, not concentrate its energies on the case against war, instead of attempting to copy the model of male university studies as an induction into the social and political status quo? She quoted the soldier-poet Wilfred Owen, who had died on the Western Front in November 1918, 'Suffer dishonour and disgrace, but never resort to arms. Be bullied, be outraged, be killed; but do not kill.' How was it happening again?

After the German invasion of Poland in September 1939 triggered Britain's declaration of war, Gabo's Hampstead circle rapidly dispersed. Hepworth and Nicholson, along with their cook, nanny and four-year-old triplets, decided to stay on in Carbis Bay in Cornwall where they had been holidaying in August as guests of former Hampstead neighbours, the artist Margaret Mellis and writer Adrian Stokes. In October, Gabo and Miriam accepted their eager invitation to join them, setting up home in 'Faerystone', a cliffside, sea-view bungalow in Carbis Bay. Gabo's adult life had been spent in capital cities – Moscow, Berlin, Paris, London. Now he woke every day to sea sounds, sea smells, the wind, seagulls, jackdaws, but at least Cornwall promised safety and fellowship. A young artist, Peter Lanyon, who enrolled as a mechanic in the Royal Air Force, lent him a studio in St Ives. It contained a 'Baby Belling' oven, in which Gabo could heat the sheets of Perspex from which he had started to construct his work. John Sisson, chair of Imperial Chemical Industries, had first supplied him with this new synthetic polymer product three years earlier. Perspex was transparent but, unlike glass, could easily be bent and shaped when warm, formed into curves as well as planes. You could look at, into or through a plastic sculpture: it resolved a conundrum that had preoccupied Gabo since the days of the *Realistic Manifesto* – how to define space without obstructing it.

In June 1940 came the fall of France; in September, the Battle of Britain. The German invasion did not happen, after all, but the bombs finally fell on London. Henry and Irina Moore moved out to Perry Green in the Hertfordshire countryside; Mondrian, who in autumn 1938 had left Paris for Hampstead, sailed for New York. In May 1941, Miriam gave birth to a daughter, Nina Serafina. In June, the Germans invaded Russia, the largest military operation in history. Hitler declared it a *Vernichtungskrieg* – a war of annihilation – against Jews, communists, Slavs, the vast category of the *Untermensch* ('sub-humans') to which the Russian-Jewish Gabo, all of his family and many of his friends and fellow artists found themselves consigned. He followed the press reports of Soviet defeats: Murmansk fell, then Kiev and Smolensk; by late August, German tanks had almost reached Bryansk in their push to Moscow. Gabo feared that everyone he knew in Russia and everything he remembered would be destroyed. Leningrad was surrounded and besieged, its entire population would, announced Hitler, be starved to death. In summer 1942, Nina turned one. They scrambled down the cliff path from 'Faerystone', with Snieshka ('Snowy'), the big white dog. There were tangles of barbed wire all along the beach. Barefoot, they paddled and dug.

Gabo's 'Constructive philosophy', he explained to Herbert Read in 1944, 'recognizes only one stream in our existence – life.... Any thing or action which enhances life, propels it and adds to it something in the direction of growth, expansion and development is Constructive.' In January that year, the siege of Leningrad was lifted after 842 days; two million of its citizens had died, perhaps more. Thinking constantly of his homeland, and the guilt of being 'physically...incapable of doing anything', Gabo created a new construction to 'dedicate to Leningrad'. 'I will try with all my might to make this work the best of my best,' he confided in his diary. He fashioned a rectangular Perspex frame with an oval aperture in the middle, strung with nylon monofilament. Where the clear threads crossed, tensile yet tenuous, close to the curved edge of the hole, they formed a kind of ethereal lip, two mirrored curves. It resembled 'a heavenly instrument', a collector told him; Gabo kept 'the secret of its meaning' to himself. As with the title of Dmitri Shostakovich's Symphony No. 7, premiered during the siege, Gabo's title, *Linear Construction in Space No. 1*, is an abstract descriptor, making no direct reference to the impassioned 'stream in our existence' that flows through the work. Gabo discovered his forms, he told Read, in many places:

in a steamy trail of smoke from a passing train...in the bends of waves on the sea between the open-work of foaming crests.... I can tell you more (poetic though it may sound, it is nevertheless plain reality): sometimes a falling star, cleaving the dark, traces the breath of night on my window glass, and in that instantaneous flash I might see the very line for which I searched in vain for months and months.

To describe his constructions, or indeed any art, as abstract made 'no sense', Gabo insisted, 'since a materialized form is already concrete', and 'any work of art, even those representing natural forms, is, in itself, an act of abstraction, as no material form and no natural event can be re-realized'.

Obvious though this was to Gabo, 'the use of the weapon "abstract" against our art' continued to be practised, not least by the most influential figure in the British art world during the Second World War. Kenneth Clark had set out his views in 'The Future of Painting' in October 1935:

Abstract art, in anything like its pure form, has the fatal defect of purity. Without a pinch of earth, the artist soon contracts spiritual beri-beri and dies of exhaustion. The whole cubist movement has revealed the poverty of human invention when forced to spin a web from its own guts.

The 'super-realists' (as he pointedly anglicized surrealists), including 'all artists who are exploiting the unconscious mind', were equally deficient. Although Freud's theories had 'influenced the lives and habits of thought of every educated person' during the past twenty years, this didn't justify the 'odd, unprecedented images' that the surrealists 'forced themselves to produce'. What most irked Clark, however, was the claim he felt that both abstract art and surrealism were making to be 'the painting of the future...linked up with the evolution of a new social and economic system':

Whatever shape society is going to take it is not going to be ruled by people who like cubist and super-realist painting. Perhaps we are going to be ruled by bands of hired toughs, perhaps by the proletariat.... Neither like modern painting...ask your taxi driver next time he sets you down in front of a gallery of modern art, and you will find that he is half shocked that such monsters should be displayed and half amused that there are idiots who are willing to pay for them.

During the First World War, when there had been no serious possibility of invasion, the British government had done little constructive thinking about what form a future peacetime nation might take. This time, despite justifiable fears that Britain might end up under Nazi rule or be forced to sue for peace with a Nazified Europe, thoughts were focused almost from the outset on a changed post-war polity. In November 1942, the social economist William Beveridge published a report, *Social Insurance and Allied Services*, in which he proposed a comprehensive overhaul of the citizen's relationship to the state, 'from the cradle to the grave' – a blueprint for what became the welfare state. Clark had been busy since the autumn of 1939 with his own practical initiatives to secure the future of art in Britain. His first priority was to safeguard the National Gallery's contents from bombing. Instructed by wartime prime minister Winston Churchill that 'not one picture shall leave this island', Clark arranged for the whole collection to be stored in specially constructed brick 'bungalows' deep in a disused slate mine near Blaenau Ffestiniog. He served briefly as head of the film unit at the Ministry of Information, and persuaded the government to set up a commissioning body for official art, the War Artists Advisory Committee (WAAC), with himself in charge. Like its predecessor scheme, WAAC would employ artists to produce domestic propaganda and record the conflict. It would also, he hoped, save talented artists from being killed. By 1943, Clark was convinced that WAAC offered a new model for the unwritten contract between artist and public, in which he believed as passionately as had Ruskin: state patronage of the arts.

At WAAC, Clark's personal taste ruled. He liked what came to be termed neo-romantic art, which gave a quirky modern twist to the landscape idioms of Turner and Samuel Palmer. War art, he felt, should soothe rather than stimulate public anxieties. He exhorted friends to look out for 'old inn signs which were good primitive works of art', suggesting to the Ministry of Information pundit Sir Ronald Storrs that war records should ideally be 'a little dull and naïve'. With the art market shut down for the duration, artists who did not fit Clark's bill had few other sources of professional income. The four hundred or so artists commissioned by WAAC, who between them produced some 5,500 works, were mostly deployed on the home front, rather than on or near the battlefield, where – as Clark would eventually, reluctantly acknowledge – the increased speed and mobility of warfare made film and photography far more viable media than the stained sketchbooks of the trench artists.

The plan was to commission 'images encouraging to ourselves but depressing to the enemy', although in practice much of the output was humdrum: watercolours of barrage balloons, convoys rumbling through the night. Graham Sutherland was despatched to record coal mines in Wales; John Piper painted bombed-out historic buildings. Paul Nash, who managed to combine his allegiance to Englishness in art with his engagement with surrealism, painted a moonlit graveyard of shot-down German planes he titled *Totes Meer* (Dead Sea; 1940–41). 'The thing looked to me,' he recalled, 'like a great inundating sea...the breakers rearing up and crashing on the plain.' It was a Turneresque tempest for the 'fight them on the beaches' age.

Henry Moore spent nights on the platforms of London Underground stations, in which the local population sought refuge from air raids. In the drawings he made and annotated on the spot, the figures of men, women and children resemble Moore's sculptures. They perch on bunks or sleep side by side along the platform, arms flung out or wrapped around each other, blankets ridged like hills. Moore shared Gabo's conviction that art should reflect the 'real laws of Life', but his laws were to do with time (the passage of eye or hand over a living contour) rather than space (a taut filament spanning a void). Resembling ancient Pompeians, fossilized in their last refuges by volcanic ash, Moore's archetypal shelterers look nothing like the offbeat photographs of lively, stoical Londoners commissioned from Bill Brandt. Both were shown in 'Britain at War' at the Museum of Modern Art, New York, in May 1941: combining reportage (Brandt) with timeless images of human endurance (Moore) was an astute pairing in this propaganda exercise, seven months before America entered the war.

For most people on the home front, the defining images of the war came from cinema newsreels and photojournalism in magazines like *Picture Post*. Because everyone had some emotional investment or personal involvement in the war, photography's ability to present an apparently objective record of events while encoding profoundly symbolic messages had a powerful effect. High-grade hand-held cameras like the Rolleiflex and Leica enabled battlefield photographers to travel lighter and shoot very much faster and more prolifically than their predecessors in the First World War. Among thousands of memorable

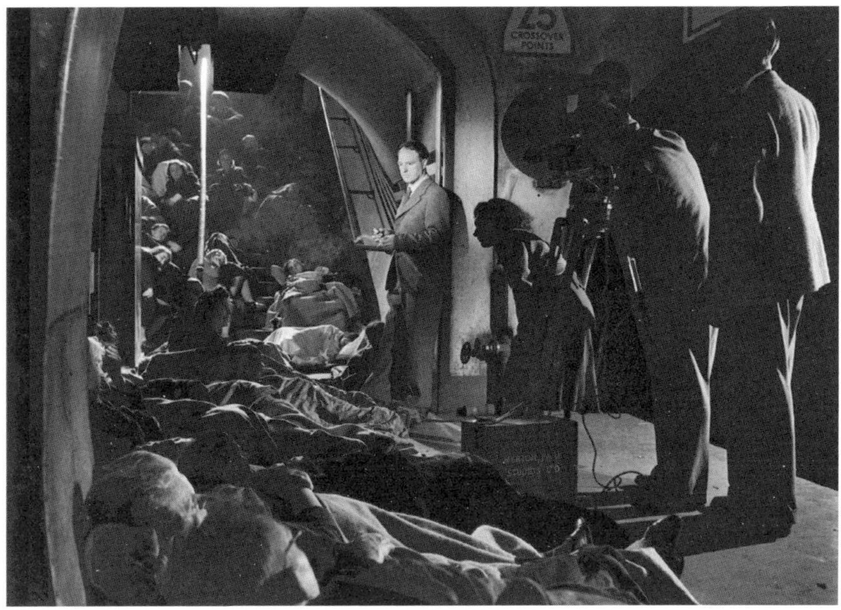

Henry Moore during the filming of *Out of Chaos*, Holborn Underground Station, 1943

images – more memorable and complete in their way than any of the epic war paintings designed for the 1919 Hall of Remembrance – some quickly took on the aura of icons, like *Daily Mail* photographer Herbert Mason's photograph of the dome of St Paul's Cathedral intact amid the conflagration of the Blitz.

In September 1944, the American photographer and surrealist muse Lee Miller, who had been living with Penrose in Hampstead since 1939, became the first woman photographer to report from the Allied lines in Normandy, with a piece on a field hospital. The following month, British *Vogue* splashed her shots of liberated Paris in a montage of avant-garde chic, in which Picasso poses with Miller by his studio window and fashion models disport themselves in the bullet-pocked streets. Then she was in Saint-Malo: from her hotel balcony, Miller captured the dense cauliflower-shaped clouds raised by the Allied bombardment of the German garrison, apparently an early use of napalm. In the spring of 1945, in the wake of the US Third Army's advance through Germany, she filed shots from Buchenwald, liberated by the 6th Armored Division on 11 April. Her piece in *Vogue* juxtaposes photos of peaceful rural German towns with a full-page pile of skeletal bodies, semi-clothed, intimately entangled – striped jackets, naked legs, slumped or tilted heads. An upside-down male face stares straight to camera, as if alive.

In the face of such sights, for which no words could be found, the photograph became the primary act of shared witness – perhaps, as the American photographer Margaret Bourke-White confessed to feeling, the only one possible. On assignment at Buchenwald for *Life* magazine, she kept telling herself 'that I would believe the indescribably horrible sight in the courtyard before me, only when I had a chance to look at my own photographs. Using the camera was almost a relief.' As successive camps were liberated, beginning in July 1944 with Majdanek near Lublin in Poland, British and American army and press photographers, and a few servicemen with cameras, recorded what they found. 'It is the desire of the Theater Commander', General Omar Bradley announced in April 1945, 'that both still and moving pictures be utilized to the fullest extent practicable as exhibits in reports of investigations of war crimes committed by the Nazis.'

Since these images of inhuman brutality and suffering were initially demanded and circulated primarily as evidence of German war guilt, it was irrelevant that, as the German-born American philosopher Hannah Arendt pointed out, the pictures of mass starvation and rampant disease portrayed the collapse of the Nazi extermination machine in the war's chaotic closing stages rather than its systematic operation. Once concentration camp photographs entered general circulation, however, with newsreels of death pits and ovens shown in British cinemas and schoolrooms after the war, it became difficult to seal their meaning within the good-versus-evil narrative of Allied propaganda. Perhaps for the first time in the history of image-making, a kind of collective shock occurred. 'When I looked at those photographs, something broke,' the American writer Susan Sontag recalled of her first sight, as a child in the mid-1940s, of images from Bergen-Belsen and Dachau. She felt 'irrevocably grieved', and worse: 'a part of my feelings started to tighten; something went dead'. You might emerge from a shock of this nature through various routes, from denial to horrified self-scrutiny; for Sontag, it came to be 'plausible to me to divide my life into two parts, before I saw those photographs (I was twelve) and after'. In some absolute and widely shared sense, it was easier to imagine a time before such things had happened than a future unhaunted by those scenes.

11
Curious liberty

Hamburg, April 1939

Hoping that things would not get worse, they almost left it too late. Charlotte Auerbach, a former art student, and her husband Max, a patent lawyer and decorated war veteran, wave goodbye to their only son, Frank, on the quayside at Hamburg. Then they return to their apartment in Güntzelstrasse, central Berlin, where – in another life, it already seems – Charlotte packed her son's suitcase, folding clothes into which he can grow, also slipping in sheets and tablecloths for his eventual adult home. A fortnight shy of his eighth birthday, Frank shares a cabin on SS Washington, *an American luxury liner bound for New York, with the two Altenberg children and their nanny. The little group disembarks at Southampton, then travels by train to Victoria Station in London, where arrangements have been made, thanks to the intervention of an expatriate Anglo-American writer, Iris Origo, with whom the Auerbachs have a family connection of sorts. There is a school near Faversham in Kent, run by a German-Jewish teacher, Anna Essinger, who will give these refugee children a home.*

On 31 March, four days before the *Washington* sailed from Hamburg, Germany invaded Czechoslovakia. By the time it docked at Southampton, the British government was hastily negotiating a military alliance to support Poland in the event of attack by a 'European country'. Frank Auerbach settled quickly at New Herrlingen School, better known as Bunce Court, after the eighteenth-century red-brick manor house to which Essinger had relocated the progressive school she had originally established in Germany, along with its predominantly Jewish pupils. Another move came with the Battle of Britain in 1940, when the school was evacuated to Shropshire.

Auerbach would spend eight years at Bunce Court, where he and his refugee classmates 'were encouraged to be part of a community'; they 'were enrolled as Wolf Cubs or Brownies and did country dancing in the hall', and so, he recalled, 'without any conscious effort we were anglicized'. His separation from his parents turned out to be final. He later learned that in March 1943 they had been deported on the *Osttransport* to Auschwitz, where they were murdered. 'I think I did this thing which psychiatrists frown on,' Auerbach would later reflect. 'I am in total denial. To be quite honest I came to England and went to a marvellous school, and it was a truly happy time. There's just never been a point in my life when I felt I wish I had parents.' 'Denial' makes it sound as if there had been an alternative: in effect, the severance of his Berlin childhood from the life he went on to lead in Britain – schoolboy, young actor, art student, artist – was all but absolute. The country-dancing Englishness into which he was initiated during the war, as if invited into an Eric Ravilious mural, contained no coordinates by which his parents' parallel journey could be mapped.

Between 1933 and 1945, the experience of this young refugee was echoed, with varying degrees of trauma, in millions of lives. If there was a distinct generational awareness of growing up and being young in Europe in these years, it had to be very different from the youth of the parental generation thirty years earlier. Despite the common denominator – war – the breadth and scale of destruction and displacement, the disruption of human attachment and continuity in every conceivable way, were incalculably greater this time than in 1914–18, although it was another story in uninvaded Britain, where some 80,000 refugees arrived during the Nazi era. Throughout this period, official, professional and public nervousness about refugees persisted. Children were required to have financial guarantors, adults the offer of a job, typically of a menial nature (British dentistry was a crude affair, but the far better trained German-Jewish dentists were debarred from practice).

In the summer of 1940, as France and the Netherlands fell and fears of invasion grew, around 29,000 'enemy aliens' – British residents of German, Austrian or Italian birth as well as people fleeing persecution – were interned in makeshift camps. In Douglas on the Isle of Man, entire streets of seaside boarding houses were ringed in barbed wire. Inmates of Hutchinson Camp, or the 'the artists' camp', included Kurt Schwitters, one of the original Dada subversives and inventor of *Merz*. This personal variant of Dada involved collaging and assembling pictures, and constructing room-sized 'grottos' (*Merzbau*) in his house in

Hanover from ephemera and rubbish. In January 1937, Schwitters had fled to Norway, then, with the German invasion in spring 1940, escaped on an icebreaker to Scotland, where he was interned in Midlothian, the first of a series a camps to which he was transferred, ending up on the Isle of Man in July. Here he pursued his experiments in scavenging undeterred. With time on their hands, the polyglot community of artist-internees improvised art materials from whatever they could find, making lino-cuts from old floor tiles and paint thinner from sardine oil. Schwitters boiled up an extra-stodgy porridge from which he modelled 'statues'. His fellow enemy alien Fred Uhlman, a writer and self-taught painter interned between June and December 1940, observed how Schwitters's sculptures underwent steady spontaneous transformation, becoming 'covered in greenish hair and bluish excrements of an unknown type of bacteria'. In Germany, Uhlman had been a lawyer; threatened with imprisonment for defending anti-Nazis, he had escaped to Paris in March 1933, finding his way, via war-torn Spain and marriage to Diana Croft, daughter of a Tory grandee, to Downshire Hill, Hampstead, where the Croft fortune helped to launch the Free German League of Culture and the Artists' Refugee Committee.

Refugees made significant contributions to the Allied war effort in many fields. Had the Nazis not forced Jewish physicists like Hungarian Leo Szilard into exile, for example, Germany would quite possibly have won the race to develop the first atomic bomb. Yet the British myth of the heroic island nation allowed few places for them in its hall of fame: it is the Scot Alexander Fleming, rather than the German-Jewish Ernst Chain, whose name is associated with the Nobel Prize they shared in 1945 for research into the therapeutic use of penicillin. The divergence between the insular view and the ways in which the war years were experienced in Europe could become extreme. In an interview in the 1980s, the Italian poet and chemist Primo Levi recalled his time in Auschwitz in his early twenties. 'It *is* a little paradoxical,' he confessed, 'that I feel a certain nostalgia for Auschwitz of course. But the *Lager* coincided with my youth, and it is for my youth, and for the few people with whom I made friends at Auschwitz, that I feel nostalgia.' *Nostalgia*? The note of pain and yearning Levi strikes is of a very different order from the vein of patriotic nostalgia that Kenneth Clark thought could be usefully tapped by his War Artists Advisory Committee (WAAC) artists in the stirring form of traditional pub signs.

Lucie Freud and her architect husband Ernst (son of Sigmund Freud), another bourgeois Jewish couple in Berlin, had been quicker than the Auerbachs to gauge the existential threat of Nazism. In September 1933, when it was still possible for Jews to take substantial capital and possessions out of Germany, Ernst moved his family to England. He enrolled his three sons at Dartington School, which had become a fashionable alternative to conventional English public schools, impishly described by John Betjeman in his 1935 *Shell Guide to Devon* as a place 'to which modern authors and intellectuals send their sons'. Pupils in the 1930s included the children of Barbara Hepworth and Ben Nicholson, the writer Aldous Huxley and philosopher Bertrand Russell. As at A. S. Neill's Summerhill, rules were negotiable and attendance at lessons optional. *Ich gehe jeden tag an die farm* ('I go to the farm every day'), the Freuds' son Lucian, born in Berlin in 1922, announced to his father.

In appearance, Dartington was archetypally English – a medieval great hall with high gothic windows, flanked by ancient residential wings that had a semi-fortified, fairy-story air. There was a sunken lawn on which knights were said to have jousted, wide acres of park and soft folds of Devon farmland. In its social make-up, however, it was turning into a rustic version of refugee Hampstead, where Dorothy and Leonard Elmhirst offered shelter and some form of employment to artists and other creatives, such as the Austrian-Jewish sculptor Willi Soukop and German choreographer Kurt Jooss, who had had to leave Germany in 1933 after refusing to dismiss Jewish dancers from his company. As in Hampstead, there were direct links to the Bauhaus: Walter Gropius remodelled a barn to serve as a theatre, and introduced the goldsmith and Bauhaus professor Naum Slutzky to the Elmhirsts, who gave him a job teaching metalwork. In common with other progressive schools like Bunce Court, there was an ethos of equality between pupils and staff, but where Auerbach's memory of his anglicization suggests a benign programme of cultural indoctrination, Lucian Freud's accounts of his Dartington schooldays conjure a semi-feral existence of sleeping in stables and bareback riding, more like the bohemian gypsydom of Augustus John and his tribe. These were two distinct faces of rural England – on the one hand, a cradle of tradition and belonging, on the other a place of adventure in which to run wild – but both held out the promise of security, unlike the situation for children almost anywhere in mainland Europe at this time. Although in their adult lives Auerbach and Freud would be seen as quintessentially urban artists, steeped in London, their induction into Englishness began among farmhouses and fields.

The Freud family spent their holidays at Walberswick, a small town on the Suffolk coast. Like Dartington, it was 'very much a slightly artistic place', Lucian recalled, with 'ladies with amber beads doing watercolours on the green and Leach pots in the crafts shop'. It sounds as if, by the mid-1930s, the radical dream of 'beginning again in art' in some innocent coastal location – the dream that a few years earlier had drawn Winifred and Ben Nicholson to Cumbria and then St Ives – had already evolved its genteel suburbanized incarnation. Or maybe the young Freud was simply picking up on the element of class privilege in the naïf new wave of the 1920s – its licence to pursue the artistic life irrespective of earnings, its social confidence, the fuzzy boundaries between joyous experimentation and leisured freedoms. One lifelong effect of Freud's boyhood anglicization, which included the absence of formal hierarchies at Dartington, was his almost anthropological curiosity about British social strata, especially in the uppermost and lower registers of the scale, the aristos and the crooks. But you had to start somewhere: by the age of fourteen, Freud, too was wielding brushes in Walberswick, although he was painting his beloved horses rather than landscapes and sea views.

Deciding that he needed to 'de-Dartingtonise' his wayward son, Freud's father sent him instead to Bryanston, a Dorset public school, from where he was expelled, apparently for a trouser-dropping prank in Bournemouth. Next came two terms at Central School of Arts and Crafts in London; he was taught sculpture by Hepworth's ex-husband John Skeaping ('charming, encouraging, glamorous'), carving an alabaster frog, which he gave to his psychoanalyst grandfather, but was generally bored by the course – although not by London. In the spring of 1939, he enrolled 'on impulse' at the East Anglian School of Painting and Drawing in the Essex village of Dedham, run by the artists Cedric Morris and Arthur Lett-Haines. Morris had slightly preceded the Nicholsons in west Cornwall, where he'd been nicknamed 'the Cézanne of Newlyn'. He, too, was well born and well-connected, and had set about making a reputation for modern painterly simplicity of a whimsical British kind. Morris and Lett-Haines's hospitable style of rural bohemianism had less to do with progressive educational theory than with the reality that, for a gay couple living in the country, the pursuit of art was licence enough for almost any kind of perceived unconventionality.

As at Dartington, the East Anglian School provided refuge for assorted moneyed misfits and plenty of personal freedom for students, who could hang out in barns and drink at the communal dining table. On the evening of 27 July 1942, smoking outside, Freud flicked a glowing stub into the dark. That same night, the art school caught fire and burned down. Whether or not the two events were connected (Freud was convinced he'd ignited a pile of oily rags), Morris appeared not to blame him and soon found new premises nearby. Pupil and teacher painted each other's portraits: Freud's Morris (1940), in browns, greys and flesh tones, is a faintly sinister, pipe-smoking mask, one eye fixed on the viewer, the other blacked out; Morris's Freud has wavy swirls of hair, sulky lips, a rumpled, dull cerise work shirt and hypnotic stare.

The story of the art school fire had – as accidents often do – its symbolic aspect. Freud would become notorious among his social circle, and eventually in the press, for injecting into any situation a palpable allure of danger. The conflagration fed by paint rags fits with his scorn for artsy rusticity. 'The Constable country was rather sickening,' he complained of the East Anglian landscape. 'Ghastly women went there and did watercolours of the Stour and I thought it was [Morris's] fault.' Morris referred to London as 'that evil place'; for Freud, it would be the place where he achieved and explored the kinds of freedoms that artists and educators between the wars had sought in the embrace of Deep Britain – at Tidmarsh, Charleston, Dartington, St Ives and Capel y Ffin. And London didn't need burning down: during the summer of 1944, when the twenty-one-year-old Freud moved to Paddington, a decayed and dodgy area by the Regent's Canal, two thousand German V-1 flying bombs fell on the city. One foggy day, he was working on *The Painter's Room* – a surrealistic interior, furnished with a battered sofa and yucca palm, into which a red and yellow zebra thrusts its outsized head through the window – when he left his flat to buy art materials. On his way back, a bomb fell: 'I saw a red thing moving towards me in the fog. I put out my hand and it was wet, covered in blood...just walking a few steps and then it was gone. Dead. No face. Completely gone.'

That same year, Freud approached Erica Brausen, an émigré German art dealer then working at the Redfern Gallery in Cork Street, about arranging an exhibition. Born in Düsseldorf, Brausen had lived in Weimar-era

Berlin and could summon up for Freud the legendary excesses of the city of his early childhood, like her story of a nightclub in which 'this huge snake in the ceiling...would piss all over us'. Brausen wasn't Jewish, but as a lesbian she, too, was a target for Nazi violence. Leaving Germany around 1930 for Mallorca, she then moved on to Paris and by 1937 was in London. While Brausen 'hummed and haahed' about Freud's request, in November 1944, the Lefevre Gallery offered him his first show. 'All my relatives turned up and shamed me by buying things'; his lover Lorna Wishart paid 50 guineas for the most expensive work, *The Painter's Room*. Brausen had plans of her own: in late 1947 she opened the Hanover Gallery, near Berkeley Square, where she intended to show young artists that no one had heard of – there had, after all, been almost no way of getting started professionally during the war – alongside artists she had befriended in Europe before the war, such as the Swiss sculptor and painter Alberto Giacometti and Spanish-Catalan painter Joan Miró.

This kind of formula was being introduced in other new galleries established by émigré dealers, which refreshed an introverted London art scene further damped down by import controls on foreign artworks. There was Gimpel Fils, run by Ernest (known by his Resistance code-name Charles) and Peter Gimpel, sons of the eminent Parisian gallerist René Gimpel, friend of Proust and dealer in Monet, Renoir and Picasso, who had died in Neuengamme concentration camp near Hamburg. Marlborough Fine Art was founded in 1946 by Austrian-Jewish refugees Heinrich Fischer and Franz Levi; they chose the name because 'everything in England seemed to be named Marlborough'. Anglicizing themselves as Harry Fischer and Frank Lloyd, they appointed David Somerset, future Duke of Beaufort, as chairman, to bring 'some class, some atmosphere' to the business, along with an 'entrée into the British aristocracy'. These dealers adopted a more commercial approach to contemporary art than had been the norm in the hushed, plush world of West End galleries, offering contracts to artists and paying professional rates. But this was still a tiny, exclusive world that barely impacted on public awareness. West End exhibitions were usually anonymously reviewed in short, unillustrated newspaper columns. If the public had a mental image of a famous modern British artist, it bore the avuncular face of Henry Moore.

The central European cultural diaspora was also seeding a change to the way art as a subject, its whole nature and history, were talked and thought about in Britain. A few weeks after Hitler's appointment as chancellor, the Warburg Institute's entire library – six thousand books and innumerable photographs and transparencies of works of art – was shipped for safety from Hamburg to London. At the Warburg, art was a subject for intellectual enquiry on a level with philosophy, literature or science, in sharp contrast to the British tradition of amateur connoisseurship, in which paintings and sculptures were appreciated, like fine wine, rather than analysed. Over the next few years, Jewish lecturers followed, among them the architectural historian Nikolaus Pevsner, whose pro-Nazi sympathies meant nothing in light of the race laws, and who would make his mark in the forty-six-volume *Buildings of England* (1951–74), and a young Viennese academic, Ernst Gombrich, with a doctorate on the Renaissance painter and architect Giulio Romano. Gombrich had grown up in a sophisticated high-bourgeois milieu – composers Johannes Brahms, Gustav Mahler and Arnold Schoenberg were among his pianist mother's friends. His first book – intended for schoolchildren and titled *A Little History of the World* – had been deemed subversively pacifist by the Nazis and banned. He had conceived the idea for it after the Viennese publisher Walter Neurath sent him an English children's book to translate for a projected series, *Wissenschaft für Kinder* ('Knowledge for Children'). 'It's absolute rubbish,' thought Gombrich; he decided that 'rather than translating that book, I'd write one myself'.

Working in London during the war as a monitor of foreign broadcasts, Gombrich met the Hungarian publisher Béla Horovitz, who had saved his company, Phaidon-Verlag, from Nazi takeover by selling it to a British firm. When Gombrich mentioned that, before leaving Vienna, he had started writing a second history for young people, this time about art, Horovitz responded, 'Give it to me. I'll show it to my daughter.' There was an appetite for popular books about serious subjects – Penguin paperbacks, launched by publisher Allen Lane in 1935, sold 28.5 million copies in their first four years. At the National Gallery and WAAC, Kenneth Clark had done much to push art on to the political agenda and into public awareness; in director Jill Craigie's documentary *Out of Chaos* (1944), which makes a persuasive case for art as a positive force in the nation's psyche, Clark speaks with studied nonchalance from his desk about artists' ability to 'convey the feel of the war to posterity far more vividly than a photographic record could do'.

After receiving then trying to return a £50 advance from Horovitz, explaining that his monitoring work left him no time, Gombrich dictated the book, largely from memory and at speed. He had noticed 'the hunger of ex-servicemen for learning'; he was speaking not to his academic peers but to 'all who feel in need of some first orientation in a strange and fascinating field'. Art was for 'All of us', who 'when we see a painting, are bound to be reminded of a hundred-and-one things which influence our likes and dislikes'. Published in 1950, *The Story of Art* would sell many millions of copies and remain continuously in print. The same year, Neurath – who had reached England in June 1938 after narrowly evading arrest by the Gestapo, been interned on the Isle of Man and, in 1949, ploughed all his savings into setting up a new publishing company, Thames & Hudson (named for the rivers of London and New York) – launched his first, suitably patriotic title, *English Cathedrals*.

In 1952, Freud finally got his exhibition at Brausen's Hanover Gallery. In the show was *Girl with a White Dog* (1950–51), a portrait of his wife, Kitty, daughter of Jacob Epstein, whose sculpture had typified the wild side of modern art in the public imagination in the years around the First World War. Kitty sits on a grubby striped divan, a dog lolling on her tucked-up leg; she wears a yellow dressing gown, which has slipped over her right shoulder, revealing a pale breast cupped on her bent right arm. It is hard to tell whether her large eyes and lopsided mouth express sadness or just the blank endurance of the long-held pose. Either way, the staring artist is at least as strong a presence as the abstracted sitter. Freud felt that 'by staring at my subject matter and examining it closely I could get something from it that would nourish my work'. Hair, skin blemishes, fingernails – every detail is painted with the tip of a small fine brush. 'If you focus on their physical presence,' he said of his sitters, 'you capture something that neither of you were aware of before.' In this case, the strangely libidinous forensics of his gaze caught a marriage about to end.

If Moore was the face of modern British art, then the modern body, in Moore's sculptural terms, was a thing of wide flanks and pebble-smooth curves, frank and robust in its physicality but anything but erotic. Standing figures, reclining figures, figures in the landscape, landscapes becoming figures – these, with a different, more explicitly spiritual inflection, were the pleasures and revelations of Hepworth's sculpture, too. But sex? There had been no place for it in Naum Gabo's constructions either, or Paul Nash's modern megaliths, Nicholson's geometric reliefs and Ravilious's downland figures etched into the chalk. If there was something obsessive-compulsive about Freud's faces, bodies, limbs, hair and skin, it was as if that intensity of witness was imperative – as if pre-war utopian thinking, with its grand apprehension of structures, had forgotten the essential thing: the wonder and fragility of flesh, its vulnerability to dissolution, its messy urge to make again. This register of human experience could not be translated into smoothness or roundness or strung with strings.

In November 1949, Brausen gave a first solo exhibition to a self-taught Dublin-born painter, Francis Bacon, whose *Painting 1946* she'd already sold to Alfred Barr, director of collections at the Museum of Modern Art in New York, on his first European buying trip after the war (before the emergence of the so-called New York School, the museum was still actively collecting contemporary British art). Bacon had just turned forty, about Brausen's age. After spells in Berlin and Paris, he had moved to London in the 1930s, starting out as a bespoke furniture and rug designer. When he began to paint, it was images of nightmare sacrificial violence, beginning with a crucifixion in which the splayed Christ figure resembles a plucked and spitted chicken. In *Three Studies for Figures at the Base of a Crucifixion*, painted in 1944, the dreamscape whimsy of British surrealism morphed into psychosexual drama, populated by screaming faces, like the torn jaws of Henry Tonks's boyish shrapnel victims. If photographers, rather than artists, were responsible for the most unforgettable images of wartime trauma, Bacon, using photos and films as source material, recaptured that disquieting ground for painting.

Painting 1946 is another crucifixion, 6 feet tall, in which both cross and corpse are formed from the split, splayed carcass of a bull – an echo of Rembrandt's *Flayed Ox* (1655) – while a sinister male figure, the top of his head either severed or shadowed by a bat-like umbrella, stands sentinel over some kind of ringed arena. Smaller carcass sections and the splattered floor (paint, blood?) suggest an abattoir requisitioned as a courtroom. Bacon would never be drawn on the meaning of his figures, but this scene may allude to the International Military Tribunal that was in session between November 1945 and October 1946 in Nuremberg, at which twenty-four senior Nazis were indicted and tried. Bacon's first Hanover Gallery show, which launched a series of almost yearly

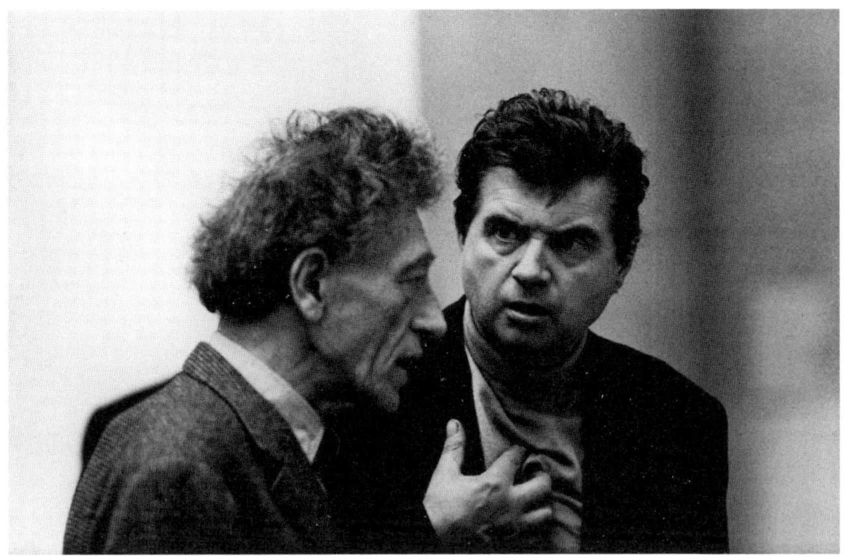

Alberto Giacometti and Francis Bacon, 1965, photograph by Graham Keen

exhibitions there until 1958, included *Head VI*, a wide-mouthed scream-ing pope, loosely modelled on a seventeenth-century papal portrait by Diego Velázquez and framed within a kind of box or cell that also echoed press photographs of the accused at Nuremberg.

Frank Auerbach, now sixteen, arrived in London in September 1947, finding lodgings in Hampstead and enrolling in art classes at Hampstead Garden Suburb Institute. Venturing downhill into the bombed city, he discovered 'a precipitous landscape' where anything felt possible: 'As you went in buses you saw the sites of bombed buildings with the pictures still on the walls, the fireplaces and so on, and great craters.' There was 'a scavenging feeling of living in a ruined city'; it seemed that 'everybody who was about had escaped death in some way, [so] there was a curious feeling of liberty. It was sexy, in a way, this semi-destroyed London.' Six years since the worst of the Blitz, since the dead and injured had been extracted from the wreckage and the fires extinguished, London's empty, ruined streets aroused complex feelings. For the urban planner and *Circle* contributor J. M. Richards:

> *The architecture of destruction not only possesses an aesthetic peculiar to itself, it contrives its effects out of its own range of raw materials. Among*

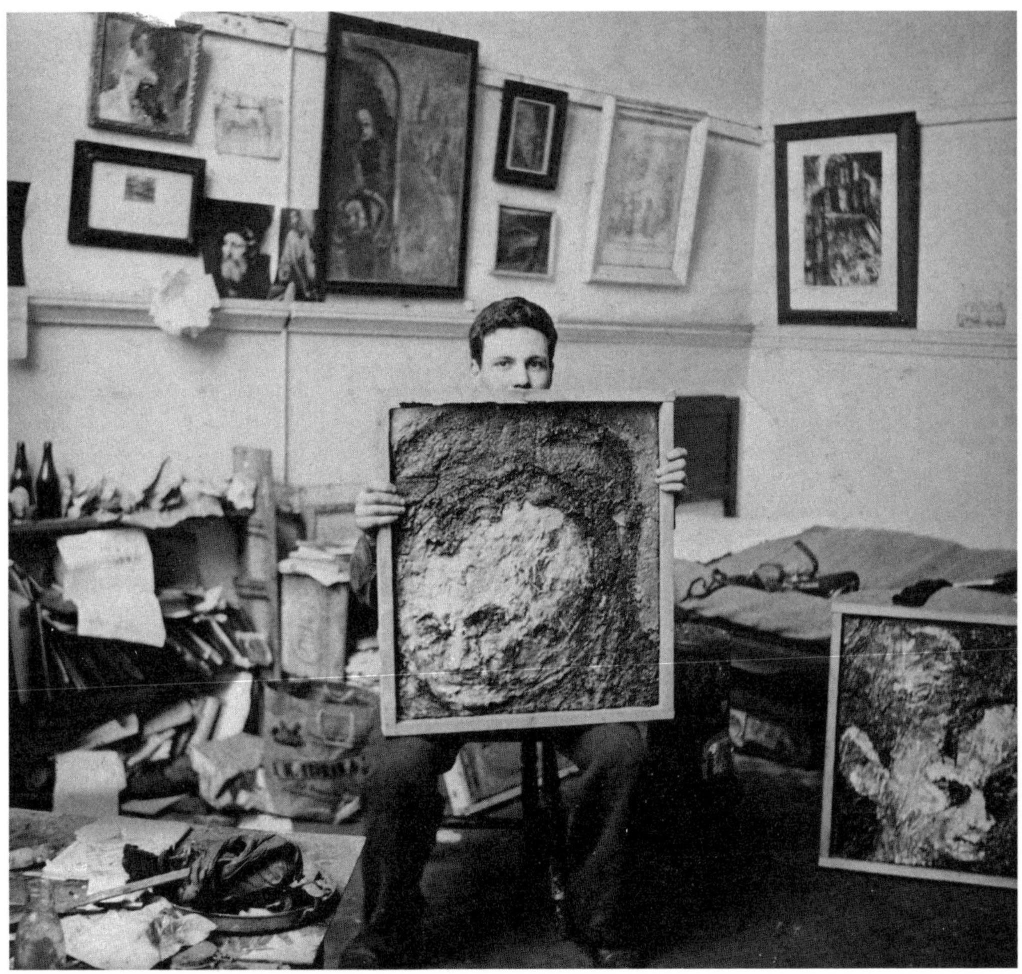

Frank Auerbach in his Mornington Crescent studio with recent portraits of the artist Leon Kossoff, 1955

the most familiar are the scarified surfaces of blasted walls, the chalky substance of calcined masonry, the surprising sagging contours of once rigid girders and the clear sienna colouring of burnt-out brick buildings, their rugged cross-walls receding plane by plane, on sunny mornings in the city.

Instinctively associating ruins with the roofless Roman temples and gap-toothed colonnades that populate seventeenth- and eighteenth-century landscape art, Clark couldn't help feeling that even the Blitz had its compensations. 'Bomb damage is in itself Picturesque,' he mused.

In the last year of war, David Bomberg had painted the City of London's gutted streets from a viewpoint in the east, not far from his childhood home in the semi-destroyed terraces of Whitechapel, with the dome of St Paul's on the horizon. A charcoal drawing of the same scene shows a sooty grid of burned-out shells. Bomberg's idea was to produce a series of these drawings – a record of blitzed but re-emergent London. These structures, the subtle, heaving life of the intersecting charcoal strokes and smudges, were the way he saw and felt – they went back to *In the Hold* and *Mud Bath* thirty years earlier – but perhaps, joined together in a panorama, they would be a commercial proposition too? Now in his fifties, he was finding it hard to scrape a living. In 1942, after several attempts, he had been commissioned by WAAC to paint an underground bomb store near Burton-on-Trent for £25, but the finished work was once again rejected. He had taught drawing to gun crews in Hyde Park and schoolchildren in Dagenham, and made scores of unsuccessful job applications. Being Jewish, obstreperous and working class did not help; he wasn't imagining it – he had been frozen out. 'I can't stand these Middle Europeans,' Freud once overheard Clark complain.

Bomberg eventually negotiated a few hours' teaching at Borough Polytechnic in south-east London. Early in 1948, Auerbach, finding the Institute a bit tame, enrolled in his class. It took place in what had been an engineering workshop, which had a heavy door that 'kept on swinging like a bar door in a Western saloon'. Bomberg set his students to scale up drawings with the aid of a grid – a method he'd learned at the Slade and adapted for his own avant-garde purposes about 1913. Probably, thought Auerbach, 'the most original, stubborn, radical intelligence to be found in art school' at that time, Bomberg 'allowed one to go for the essence at the very beginning', setting high standards of integrity: 'anything that seemed artificial or concocted or sort of false sauce and gravy on an insufficiently vital fact would be rejected'. He spoke of searching for 'the spirit in the mass', which to Auerbach expressed the relationship, for a painter, between sight and touch: 'You find yourself making gestures that imply legs, breast and so on; you begin to imply a sense of mass on the paper or the canvas simply because you felt it.'

While preparing to start at the Royal College of Art in the autumn of 1952, Auerbach made a series of drawings, not of a bomb site but a building site on Earl's Court Road. The razed city of Bomberg's abortive panorama project was entering a long, slow process of reconstruction.

Mounds of yellow sand and pale cement replaced the grimy cairns of debris. Although Auerbach had not seen Bomberg's big early canvases, the painting that emerged from these sessions, *Summer Building Site*, is constructed around a distinctly Bombergian armature of stepladders and girder forms. The earth colours of the site – ochre, browns, blacks and touches of red – glow like a new dawn. In Auerbach's series of paintings on this theme (pl. 9), London building sites represent, like *In the Hold*, bounded arenas for physical action, places vivid with the materials of their own making. Years later, when asked what he was 'hoping to be able to put on the canvas?' when he started a painting, Auerbach replied, 'What I'm not hoping to do is to paint another picture because there are enough pictures in the world. I'm hoping to make a new thing for the world that remains in the mind like a new species of living thing.' Here, as in Bomberg's phrase 'the spirit in the mass', painting is a primary creative act, but the 'living thing' it seeks to create feels different from the 'inner vitality' of which Hepworth and Moore spoke so often in the 1930s: it is a physical body rather than an abstract life force. There were moments in London in the 1940s when it appeared miraculous that anything was still standing, anyone still living at all.

In the run-down terraces of west London, other recent arrivals were soon 'hoping to make a new thing' of their lives in Britain. *Longing*: that was how Frank Bowling felt, growing up in British Guiana (now Guyana). The longing to 'just get out and go to London, and maybe… this was the plan, maybe, get lucky, right? Part-time work, study hard, and maybe get lucky, get a scholarship. And show them that I could really do it.' Sprinter, clairvoyant, teenage member of the family business Bowling's Variety Store in Berbice, initiate of the Society of Young Rum Drinkers, intent on continuing with his academic education until he had gained a qualification, whatever it turned out to be, but higher than he knew he could gain in the schools of New Amsterdam, Bowling sailed to Trinidad in the spring of 1953. Here he boarded a French ship bound for London, arriving in May, in time for the coronation of the young Queen Elizabeth II. 'I always saw London as the place,' he said; it felt 'like coming home'.

Under the 1948 Nationality Act – designed to strengthen post-war links with the former overseas empire, rebranded the Commonwealth – the population of the British Caribbean were officially British citizens. After the war, British businesses and organizations, like Marconi, London

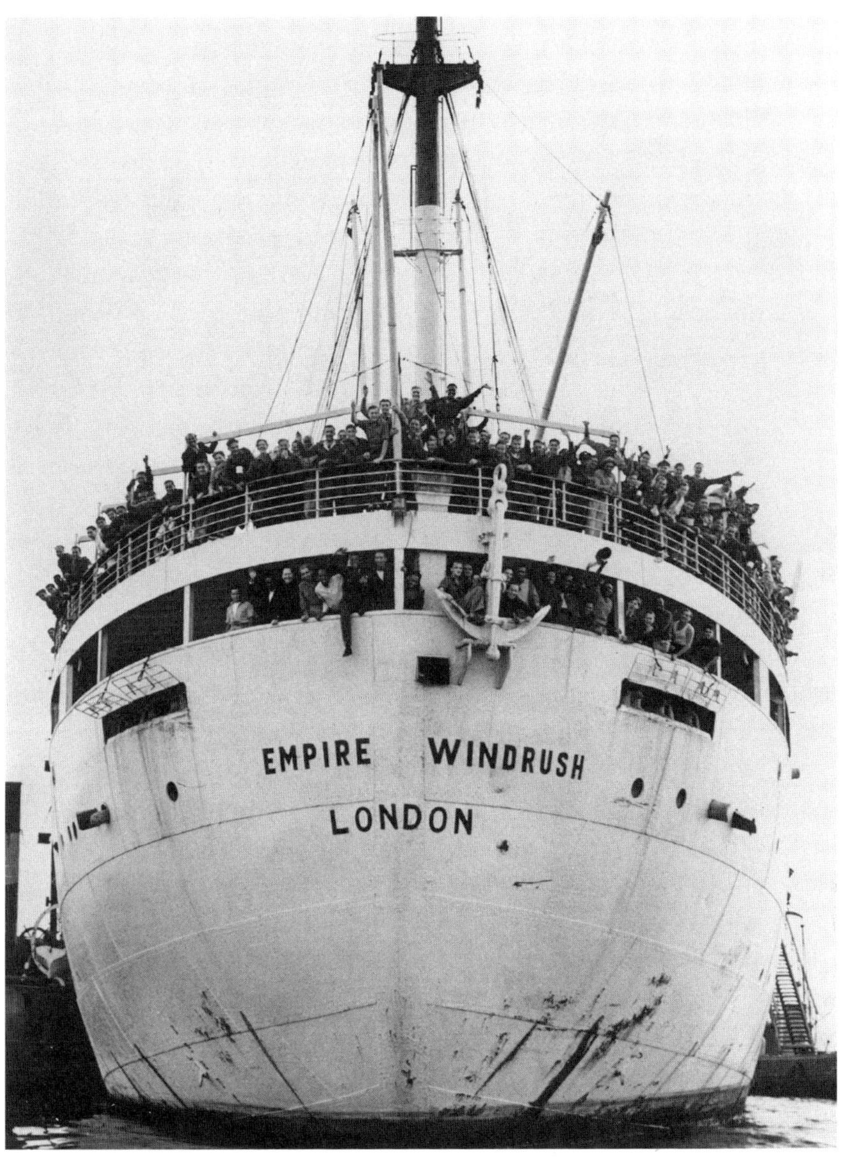

The *Empire Windrush* arriving from Kingston, Jamaica, at Tilbury Docks, Essex, 22 June 1948

Underground and the Royal Mail, began actively recruiting in the Caribbean region, offering to pay for the transatlantic fare for prospective employees. Some of the first to make the voyage in hope of a new future were the 800 West Indian passengers on the *Empire Windrush*, a former captured German troop-ship that docked at Tilbury on 22 June 1948. Many thought of Britain as their 'mother country'; about half had served in the forces or in munitions factories in Britain during the war. In the two years after Bowling arrived in London, numbers immigrating from the West Indies increased fourteen-fold, from 3,000 to 42,000. As life resumed in the war-battered city, the profound social and cultural transformation of urban Britain through immigation from the former empire was under way. At the same time, the Conservative government under Winston Churchill was actively seeking pretexts for barring legally entitled but non-white immigrants from entry. Since the memory of Nazi racist laws and all that had followed was still raw, however, race could not be made an explicit condition. Privately, Churchill opined that Britain was becoming 'a magpie society' and toyed with running for re-election in 1955 under the slogan 'Keep Britain White'.

After two years' National Service in the RAF, a 'retardation process' that left him 'floundering' for his next move, Bowling found work washing dishes, decorating ('I arrived there with no tools, no nothing.... I didn't know how to hang wallpaper') and a six-week stint as a life-class model at the Royal College of Art. 'I was in this life room with a group of girl artists,' he recalled, 'a number of really very talented women.' In between 'their giggles and pointing at me', they must surely be doing impressive work – but when he went round to look at the other side of the easels, 'They are nowhere,' he thought. 'And that kind of needled me, and...I gradually over that six weeks decided that if this is what it took to become an art student, then I would try.'

12

A different kind of life

Oxford, spring 1945

*Eduardo Paolozzi has just turned twenty-one. He is studying sculpture
at the Slade School of Fine Art, which is now housed in the Ashmolean
Museum, a palatial neo-classical building in the centre of Oxford.
The art school was evacuated from Bloomsbury, in the winter of 1940,
not long after the British Museum nearby was bombed. These days, the
students feel as if they're biding time until the war is over, waiting for
whatever is going to happen next. The Slade, it must be said, does not
provide a very exciting vision of the future. The culture is, if anything, at
least as suspicious of the avant-garde as in Henry Tonks's day thirty years
earlier. In December, at the Victoria and Albert Museum in London, the
British public will come face to face with the work of Picasso and Matisse
for the first time in a full-scale exhibition. But during the war, apart from
mixed touring shows of soft propaganda commissioned by the War Artists
Advisory Committee, few students have had much contact with actual
works of modern art. It is almost as if European movements of the past
forty years – cubism, surrealism and the rest – had never happened. Slade
principal Randolph Schwabe dislikes any kind of art that threatens 'to turn
the world upside down'. Most of Paolozzi's fellow students seem to believe
that 'you could occupy the rest of your life just thinking about English art'.
In retrospect, however, the most parochial aspect of that time will be the fact
that 'There were people at the Slade who had never seen spaghetti.'*

———

If someone had said to Paolozzi five years ago that, before the war
ended, he would be a student at the Slade, it would have sounded an
attractive prospect (he had been taking evening classes at Edinburgh
School of Art) but far-fetched. For one thing, he was locked up in
Saughton jail, where male members of Edinburgh's Italian community were interned, along with aristocratic Scottish fascists, as soon

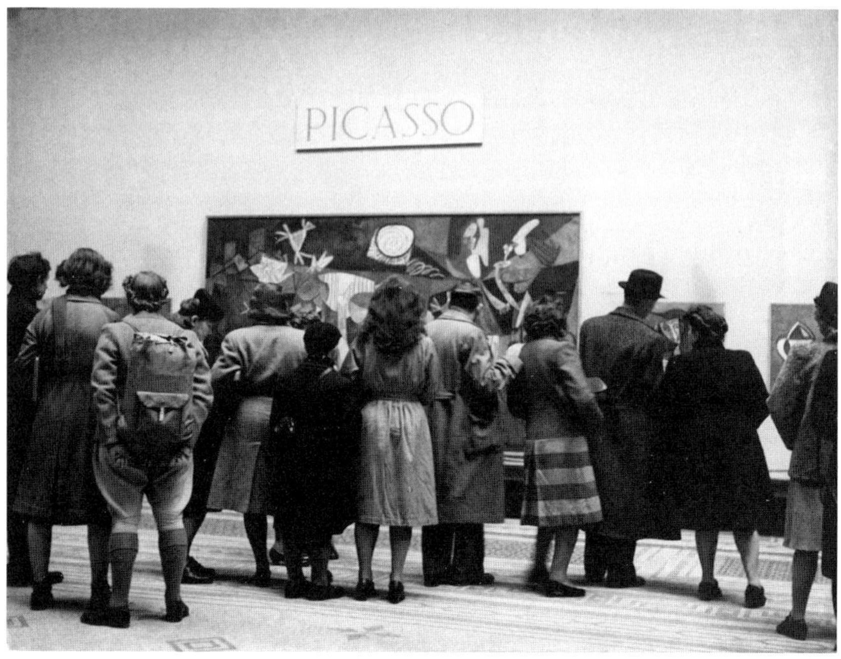

Visitors at 'Picasso and Matisse', Victoria and Albert Museum, London, December 1945

as Italy entered the war in June 1940. His father, grandfather and uncle were among seven hundred internees deported to Canada on the *Arandora Star*, which sailed from Liverpool on 2 July to be sunk by torpedo off the Irish coast the following morning. Like other Italian businesses, the family shop selling sweets and home-made ice cream in the Edinburgh docklands district of Leith had been smashed up and looted. As a child, Paolozzi had done his first drawings on the packaging in which stock was delivered to the shop. Released from Saughton, he was called up at eighteen to serve in an 'aliens' unarmed unit of the Pioneer Corps, building Nissen huts in Slough. Around the time of D-Day, with victory in the air, he managed to get himself discharged by feigning mental illness. And so to Oxford and the Ruskin School of Art, housed in the Ashmolean, together with the Slade. At the Ruskin, the emphasis was on drawing; at the Slade, to which he was able to transfer, you could study sculpture too.

In the commercial art world of the late 1940s, despite the initiatives of émigré dealers, which would change the game in the coming years, patriotism and insularity still coloured the prevailing mood. Why show Alberto Giacometti's lean, scribbly drawings, which sold 'very slowly', when British painter Matthew Smith's hint-of-tomato *hommages* to Matisse sold, Paolozzi noted, 'quite well enough'? Beyond art, widespread ignorance about domestic life 'abroad' was understandable in light of wartime rationing, which had restricted the British diet and continued to apply to some basics until July 1954. In the event, it would be on the dinner plate rather than the gallery wall – spaghetti rather than Giacometti – that a post-war expansion of British cultural horizons registered most piquantly on the senses.

'Conditions *were* awful,' observed the sometime art student and actress Elizabeth David, a Conservative MP's rebellious daughter who had finally returned to England after a peripatetic decade of love affairs and wartime Mediterranean scrapes. Marooned in a hotel in Ross-on-Wye, Herefordshire, during the big, long freeze of winter 1946–47, which the government feared would lead to famine, David could not believe what passed for food in her native country. Although 'shortages *did* make catering a nightmare', she conceded, '*still* there was no excuse, none, for the unspeakably dismal meals as in that dining room were put in front of me.' She found relief from the sub-zero ennui and depressing menus in reconstructing the recipes for dishes she'd enjoyed in Italy, Greece and Egypt: 'Even to write words like apricot, olives and butter, rice and lemons, oil and almonds, produced assuagement.' And not only assuagement; she felt she was doing something radical, almost subversive, because 'in the England of 1947, those were dirty words that I was putting down'. In 1950, David published the recipes she had recovered from the sun-soaked, amorous days of war in *A Book of Mediterranean Food* (pl. 11), with illustrations by John Minton, a former housemate and lover of Lucian Freud, now senior painting tutor at the Royal College of Art.

The general election of July 1945, called by prime minister Winston Churchill immediately after Allied victory in Europe, had delivered a Labour landslide. Churchill's scaremongering about a 'Gestapo' socialist state had disastrously misread the national mood, with its war-weary optimism and bruised hunger for change. But Labour leader Clement Attlee's vision for a social-democratic Britain had soon to make its terms with the dire economic landscape. There followed almost a decade of austerity – an economist's term for restraining public spending that had become current during the war in phrases like 'austerity clothing', 'austerity buses' and other fixes for material shortages. Attlee's government had somehow to stave off national bankruptcy precipitated by colossal war debt and the end of the US's Lend-Lease scheme in September 1945, while simultaneously pursuing the reforms in welfare, healthcare, transport and heavy industry on the promise of which, in its manifesto *Let Us Face the Future*, it had won the popular vote. The plan was to focus the nation's resources on production and exports, while restricting imports and suppressing consumer spending. Production, announced Herbert Morrison, who had crafted the 1945 manifesto, was now 'national duty No. 1'.

Austerity proved glacially slow to deliver any tangible sign of improvements in standards of living and quality of life. In many city centres, bomb sites remained unreclaimed until the early 1960s, twenty years after the Blitz, in the meantime becoming dystopian playgrounds for the post-war baby-boom generation. In Roger Mayne's photograph of a ruined building in Bermondsey, east London, in 1954, a boy clambers over rubble to vanish into a dark doorway, while another balances perilously on a stub of broken wall, and a small child smiles from a blown-out window high above the ground. Imaginative fantasy coexists with imminent bodily danger, catching the rough texture of innovation interwoven with material privation in these years. 'Grey' was the term people reached for again and again to describe the look and feel of austerity Britain. To Paolozzi, it seemed 'a world of lost souls and mental cripples', particularly during that punishing winter of 1946–47: 'whenever I read *The Secret Agent* by Conrad, that was the London that one lived, foggy, and it had moving through the fog all these lost souls somehow, it was terribly austere'. There was of course a counterargument – that present greyness was the price of future sunshine – voiced by a character in J. B. Priestley's play *The Linden Tree* in 1947:

> *Call us drab and dismal, if you like, and tell us that we don't know how to cook our food or wear our clothes, but for Heaven's sake, recognise that we're trying to do something that is as extraordinary and wonderful as it's difficult – to have a revolution for once without the Terror.*

Into austerity's 'atmosphere of damp astringency' Elizabeth David's writing infused a fertile poetry of Mediterranean warmth:

> *the oil, the saffron, the garlic, the pungent local wines; the aromatic perfume of rosemary, wild marjoram and basil drying in the kitchens; the brilliance*

of the market stalls piled high with pimentos, aubergines, tomatoes, olives, melons, figs and limes; the great heaps of shiny fish, silver, vermilion or tiger striped.

This list, as if culled from the Song of Songs, segues into a scene in a Greek kitchen, filled with 'the sound of air gruesomely whistling through sheep's lungs frying in oil'. It is the kind of image that might have suggested to Lucian Freud, with whom David briefly overlapped as a house-guest of Cedric Morris and Arthur Lett-Haines, the subject for one of his louchely morbid early drawings, like *Dead Monkey* (1944). And there is something almost Lucian Freudian – an erotic attentiveness and itemizing detachment – in some of David's early recipes ('Ripe but fine plums. Wipe and prick with a needle.... Take each one out as soon as the skin is lightly broken').

Although David admitted that when *A Book of Mediterranean Food* was first published, 'people could not very often make the dishes here described', she still felt they would find it 'stimulating to think about them'. During the austerity era, it took the British public longer to become familiar with spaghetti than its parents' generation had with Gauguin and Van Gogh. On 1 April 1957, the BBC current affairs programme *Panorama* broadcast a short feature, presented by the veteran war correspondent Richard Dimbleby, about the Swiss spaghetti harvest, a small-scale family affair compared to 'the vast spaghetti plantations in the Po Valley'. Farmworkers were filmed plucking long strands of pasta from the trees, a 'bumper crop', reported an impassive Dimbleby, made possible by 'the virtual disappearance of the spaghetti weevil'. Unaware that they had been watching an April Fool's Day edition of *Panorama*, viewers wrote in large numbers to ask how they could cultivate spaghetti at home. 'In a tin of tomatoes' was the answer.

Olive oil, too, remained hard to find, except in pharmacies, where small bottles were sold for treating blocked ears, but it was at least now possible to travel overseas for reasons other than fighting. The rediscovery of mainland Europe after years of war had happened in the 1920s, too, but the attitude and level of awareness of British art students who made their way abroad in the second half of the 1940s were different. Whereas children during the 1914–18 war often had to make sense of what was happening in terms of a single photograph of their absent father in uniform, families in 1939–45 had been presented with regular magazine photo reportage from theatres of war around the world – Europe, Russia, North Africa, South-East Asia – while perhaps following Allied fortunes on a map pinned to the parlour wall and regularly watching cinema newsreels. In a broader sense, too, cinemas, of which there were now far more than in the 1920s, had been places where a life of vivid wish-fulfilling fantasy could be maintained amid the worst fears and privations of war. 'Going to the pictures' held the simultaneous promise of grand escapism and imaginative engagement in the dilemmas facing the characters, realizing Virginia Woolf's prediction in 1926 that cinema might one day capture 'movements and colours, shapes and sounds...and convert their energy into art'.

And cinema was for everyone. In working-class Leith, Paolozzi's parents had pinned up cinema posters in their shop. From the age of five, his mother took him often to the 'flea-pits' – small cinemas 'geared to the poorest people...you could get in for a penny, and they all had the most outrageously wonderful American films. And occasionally a boring English one.' Since the 1920s, the cinema experience had been transformed by sound and, increasingly, colour. Movies had become longer and more varied, offering an 'operatic range of sound and movement, and even distortion of reality', an ability to 'dig into the unconscious'. Growing up in Bradford in the 1940s, where some forty cinemas served a population of 280,000 (in Britain today, there is about one cinema per 80,000 people), David Hockney watched wartime Hollywood releases like *Gone with the Wind* and *Citizen Kane* – movies of a scale, scope and technical quality inconceivable twenty years before. He loved the way the big screen 'as if by magic, was opening up the wall to you. It showed you another world, even in the dingiest little cinema'. Looking back at this time, he would locate his formative visual experiences in two very different towns: Bradford and Hollywood.

For ex-servicemen like Paolozzi who had not been posted abroad, and for those who were too young to have been called up, the first foray outside Britain was often Paris. Unconvinced that the Slade had much to offer him, Paolozzi left for Paris before taking his degree: 'Couldn't get there quick enough...it seemed to answer everything that I wanted in life.' On arrival, he simply found the telephone numbers of artists he wanted to meet in the Paris directory. Georges Braque said, 'Oui, come along', and opened his studio; Fernand Léger showed his new series to Paolozzi – 'eighteen canvases on eighteen easels' – and arranged a special screening of his 1924 experimental film *Ballet mécanique* (Mechanical Ballet). 'It was wonderful,' Paolozzi felt, 'these were the kinds of things one expected, this kind of sympathy, this kind of radiation, this kind of understanding'. It was the readiness to share ideas – 'the accessibility and the seriousness' – that struck him as much as the work itself, 'because this would never have happened [in England,] being invited to a studio and being shown work'.

In comparison with bombed-out central London, Paris appeared physically almost untouched by the war. To the British eye, it looked as if the experience of Nazi occupation had left far fewer scars than the Blitz. In all the years of cultural rivalry between Britain and France – the belle époque and the interwar flourishing of the Parisian avant-garde – there had never been a time like this, when Anglophone visitors could arrive, as liberators, with a certain discreet sense of moral advantage. The twenty-nine-year-old artist and critic Patrick Heron, in Paris in the summer of 1949, still considered the city 'perfectly equipped for its role as the capital of Europe's visual arts', but felt able to be more critical of the art he saw there than previous generations: there was 'a certain deadness', a 'monotony' about younger painters, and even Picasso was acting the 'inventor' a shade predictably. The philosopher Jean-Paul Sartre despaired of being able to explain that 'the Occupation was a terrible ordeal...and that there is not a single French person who has not on many occasions envied the fate of their British Allies', observing with frustration how 'English people and Americans were amazed to find us less thin than they expected.' They might even resent the French, in their elegant clothes 'that looked brand new', for 'not entirely conforming to the pathetic image they had formed of us in advance'.

Picasso had remained in Paris throughout the war; in a plaster sculpture of a bull's head, Paolozzi tried Picasso on for size (it was a success, chosen for illustration in *Horizon*, magazine of choice for enlightened British intellectuals). But he learned more from Giacometti, who, after wartime refuge in his native Switzerland, had returned to Paris, where he discovered that the public now viewed him less as an interesting maverick than as a modern national treasure. 'I'm always surprised that strangers have heard of me,' Giacometti confessed, as a stream of foreign visitors, including Paolozzi, made their pilgrimage to his ramshackle Montparnasse studio in the rue Hippolyte-Maindron. Rather than representing a sadder, wiser rebirth of the pre-war avant-garde, which in both its surrealist and constructivist incarnations had shared a sense of human nature as something deep-rooted and permanent, like a country, the hieratic, taut, stick-thin figures Giacometti was now modelling in clay and plaster struck many viewers as a disquieting totemization of the dawning atomic era. In his catalogue essay for Giacometti's exhibition at Pierre Matisse Gallery in New York in 1948, Sartre explored the realization that, after Hiroshima, peace was no longer the opposite of war: 'the little bomb that can kill a hundred thousand at a stroke, and which, tomorrow, will kill two million, brings us up suddenly against our responsibilities.... When one thinks of it, everything seems futile.' In a letter to Pierre Matisse, Giacometti had described his own 'vision of reality' as possessing 'a sharpness' like 'a kind of skeleton in space'.

In Britain, Barbara Hepworth and Henry Moore – like Giacometti in Paris – were increasingly viewed as image-makers for a modern nation, rather than creators of strange abstract forms. Both now worked in the countryside (Hepworth had stayed in Cornwall, Moore in Hertfordshire), where the primordial topography of Deep Britain, with its rhetoric of environmental process, remained part of their repertory. Futility was very much not their style. Hepworth, who became an early sponsor of the Campaign for Nuclear Disarmament, argued for a redemptive vision of humanity 'at one' with the earth, very different from Giacometti's 'skeleton':

> *I am convinced that in this 20th century we shall all become extinct unless we re-stress the living values of what are really primitive instincts in man and are the only things which really keep him alive. And we shall lose our capacity to live unless we feel at one with all the rocks and the timelessness of life with its perpetual movement and re-birth.*

Hepworth's holistic conception of 'living values' was an adaptation for the nuclear age of ideas she had expressed in her essay for *Circle*, still deeply felt and still persuasive, but it was the Sartrean emphasis on responsibility in the face of futility – a philosophical standpoint popularized by his 1946 essay *L'existentialisme est un humanism* (published in English as *Existentialism Is a Humanism* in 1948) – that resonated more strongly with the nuclear age. Existentialism stressed both the freedom and the *angoisse* ('anguish') that stemmed from acknowledgment of total personal responsibility for one's actions. It rejected the determinism implied by Hepworth's 'primitive instincts'. 'There is

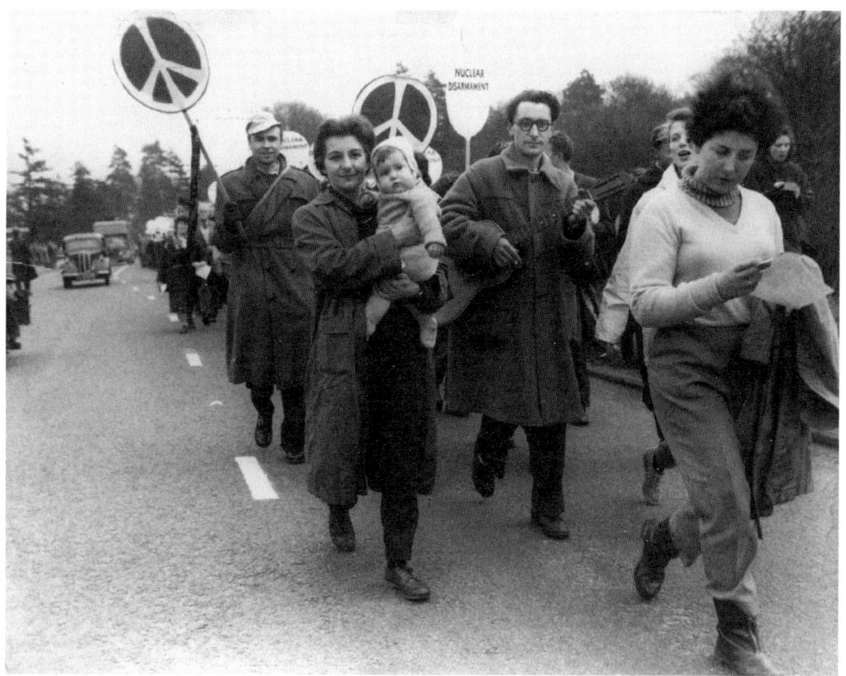

Campaign for Nuclear Disarmament march from London to Aldermaston,
site of the Atomic Weapons Establishment, Easter 1958

no determinism,' announced Sartre; 'man is free, man *is* freedom.'
Freedom was what the war was supposed to have been fought for – or
at least, freedom soon became the most precious commodity associated with the idea of peace in the context of the nuclear arms race,
although exactly what it meant to be free in any given circumstances
wasn't always easy to define. Freudian theory, for example, suggested
that life was determined by involuntary desires rather than free,
rational choices. Sartrean existentialism set the individual free from
the past but denied the validity of that kind of imaginative hope that
made freedom actually feel free. For less complex thinkers, freedom
was a stirring slogan and sure-fire rallying cry. 'Our way of life,' the
American president Harry S. Truman told Congress in March 1947, 'is
distinguished by free institutions...freedom of speech and religion,
and freedom from political oppression'. The alternative (i.e. communist) way of life, in grim contrast, relied on 'terror and oppression...and
the suppression of personal freedoms'.

The words 'free' and 'freedom' had featured heavily in the second reading of the Education Bill, presided over by the coalition government's Conservative education minister R. A. Butler on 19 January 1944. His aim was to 'completely [recast] the whole of the law as its affects education', replacing a patchwork of institutions with a national system of primary, secondary and higher education. Introducing the Bill, Butler framed it in philosophical terms:

> *An educational system by itself, cannot fashion the whole future structure of a country, but it can make better citizens. Plato said: 'The principle which our laws have in view is to make the citizens as happy and harmonious as possible.' Such is the modest aim of this Bill which provides a new framework for promoting the natural growth and development not only of children, but of national policy itself towards education in the years to come.*

In his book *The Free Child* (1953), the veteran educator A. S. Neill expounded the principles of practical and psychological freedom that informed his work at Summerhill, the best-known of the progressive schools of the 1930s. That a government minister could speak in almost rhapsodic terms of 'the natural growth and development of children' as the aim of the education system suggests that, if notions like self-realization and creativity had been associated with the experimental or eccentric fringes of education between the wars, they were now being taken seriously, not least because for policymakers Britain's children represented a natural resource to be nurtured and tapped. In the mid-1940s, a far lower proportion of British school-leavers progressed to higher education than in the USA and other rival nations. The 1944 Act was shaped by concerns that educational deficit would hamper Britain's economic recovery and technological and military competitiveness. Another factor that fed into an intense focus on children – their health, education and prospects, their psychology and life experience – was William Beveridge's assumption, in drafting his 1942 report, that Britain faced a crisis of population decline. In fact, the birth rate soared by about 50 per cent, from around 600,000 per year during the war to near 900,000 in the late 1940s.

Plato's views on education were also cited by Herbert Read in the opening pages of his *Education through Art*, published in 1943. Read's thesis, 'explicitly formulated by Plato many centuries ago', was 'that art should be the basis of education'. He argued that the purpose of education is 'to foster the growth of what is individual in each human being, at the same time harmonizing the individuality thus educed with the organic unity of the social group to which the individual belongs'. Art, Read believed, was unique among human activities in being 'permanent and indestructible, accumulative but ever free'. Although grounded in Read's anarchist convictions, *Education through Art* gained persuasive force as a counterblast to totalitarianism, emphasizing 'the development of the individual's individuality' as opposed to conformity to the demands of the state, 'insight' rather than obedience. Growth, harmony, happiness and development would also be keywords in Butler's address to the House of Commons the following year – not because the education minister had adopted the values of an anarchist critic and poet but because the ideological basis on which the war was being fought was defined in opposition to everything Nazism stood for. Read hoped that his proposals for a 'necessary revolution' in education, with art at its core, would 'reconcile discipline with freedom, order with democracy', in the cause of achieving 'individual and social harmony'.

Not all of the 1944 Act's target beneficiaries became happier citizens as a result. Fourteen-year-olds obliged to spend an extra year at school resented the blow to their prestige and potential earnings. For young people whose families would never previously have been able to afford university or art school fees, however, the possibility of state-funded study transformed their horizons. Local Education Authorities were given discretion to fund students beyond the school leaving age: by 1956–57 the proportion of assisted students in art schools had risen to 75.7 per cent from 41.1 per cent in 1938–39. With the standardization of entrance requirements and accreditation, students were no longer restricted to studying at their local college but could apply to an art school of their choice. The route to the metropolis trailblazed by Hepworth and Moore in the 1920s was potentially open to all. Although in principle this also applied to university entrance, in practice the requirement of high exam scores in academic subjects played to the advantages of middle-class applicants.

Art school, thought Derek Boshier, 'was the only way in which a working-class kid in the late '50s could get a further education'. He had grown up in Plymouth, where his father was in the navy, and started at the Royal College of Art at the same time as Hockney after two years of National Service. Among other students, he and his contemporaries still felt like a minority, 'judged on the way you spoke'. At a party in Oxford, Boshier eavesdropped an undergraduate airily advising a friend, 'Oh, you should talk to him. He's working-class, but he's *awfully good value.*' Jack Smith was in his early teens in 1944 – too young to fight, but a witness to the devastation of his hometown Sheffield by air raids on its steelworks and mines – when he pulled down a copy of R. H. Wilenski's *Modern French Painters* (1940) in the city library. The thought that he might actually one day go to Paris barely occurred, but, in blitzed, working-class Sheffield, the plates in Wilenski's book – intended, like Gombrich's later *Story of Art*, as 'a plain historical telling of the story' – were an epiphany. This voyage of the mind, in the company of 'Impressionists and subsequent adventurers in the last seventy-five years in Paris', was enough to make Smith realize, 'this is what I want to do' – that he 'wanted a different kind of life to what I saw around me'. After National Service – the rite of passage for young men of his generation – he was able to enrol at Saint Martin's School of Art in London.

Peter Blake, fourteen-year-old son of a factory electrician and a nurse, who studied at Gravesend Technical College and School of Art between 1946 and 1951, would in retrospect see himself as part of 'a whole influx of talent from an area that wouldn't have been there before...artists like myself and Hockney, who wouldn't have gone to art school before the war'. The training Blake received at Gravesend followed a pattern set in the nineteenth century of teaching students a set of technical skills, which they could put into practice either by becoming teachers themselves or in commercial art and industrial design. It included silversmithing, metalwork, woodwork, lettering, stone-carving, etching and architecture, with some practice in the fine art disciplines of anatomy, perspective and life drawing. In the Scottish pit village of West Wemyss, William Gear, a miner's son, was encouraged by 'a bright younger art master' at school, who 'had been to Paris even' and lent him art books. When he announced his ambition to study art, Gear expected his parents to object, but no. As was the case for Moore, working-class attitudes formed in the mid-Victorian self-help era ('My son's not going down the pit') could be more positive about art school as a stepping stone for their sons than those of middle- and upper-class families, who considered it appropriate only for their daughters.

Working-class men who made it to art school in the decade after the war often found themselves in the company of ex-services personnel and recently demobbed National Service recruits alongside a large cohort of younger, more privileged women. This state of affairs wasn't solely the result of class differences in families' tolerance of (and occasionally enthusiasm for) art school as a choice for sons and daughters: historian Eric Hobsbawm notes that, where universities were concerned, 'even in 1951 women students came from upper- and middle-class backgrounds to a significantly greater extent than did male students'. At Camberwell School of Art in 1947–48, the former commando and prisoner of war Terry Frost struggled to compete for tutors' attention with female students who – aside from the typically skewed pattern of gender relations with an all-male teaching staff – could afford to hand out any number of black-market cigarettes by way (Frost felt) of bribery rather than *noblesse oblige*.

The principal of Camberwell throughout the war was William Johnstone, a Scottish artist who had decided in his twenties that the best way to earn his living was to teach. He had grown up in a Border farming family and was 'determined to counteract the superior elitist notion disseminated by the Bloomsbury set that no real artist could have anything to do with art teaching'. During the 1930s, Johnstone had become interested in Bauhaus pedagogy, including the idea of teaching across different but related disciplines, such as engineering, textiles and painting, and the belief that teaching itself 'should be a really creative process'. He set about developing an innovative system of art education, first at Camberwell, then, from 1947 to 1960, at Central School of Arts and Crafts, which became known as the Basic Design course. Although more closely structured than the kind of education on offer at Bunce Court, Dartington or Summerhill in the 1930s, Johnstone's description of his approach shares their emphasis on non-hierarchical collaboration between pupil and teacher, the importance of fun and the conviction that he wasn't merely teaching a subject but assisting in a process of self-realization:

> *I taught, not as an art teacher, but as an artist, as if I were inviting the children to paint pictures with me in my studio.... We used patterns and shapes, patterns and forms, stemming from my Cubist training in Paris.... One thing dominated the situation and that was the element of fun, of play, rather than a sense of work. I was teaching these children, as a creative artist, to be more creative people.*

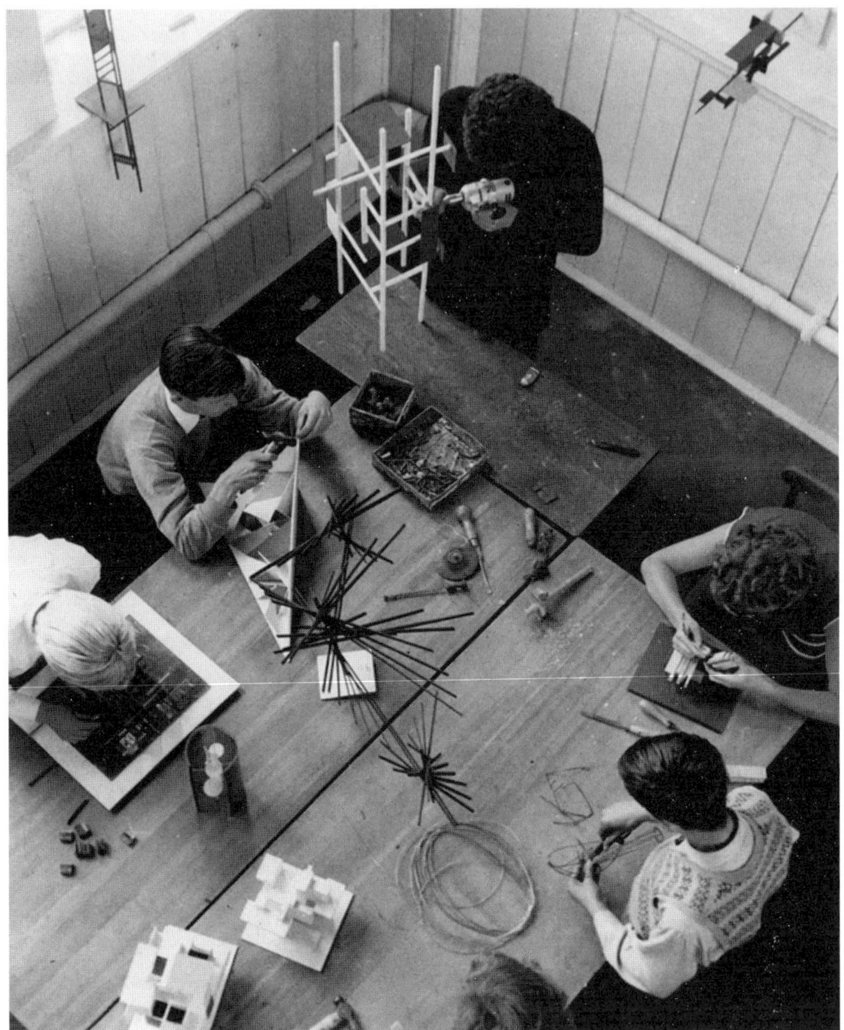

Students at Lowestoft School of Arts & Crafts, 1955, where Basic Design training was introduced by painting master Tom Hudson in the early 1950s

The purpose was not, however, simply to enable creative people to enjoy their own creativity. The aim of the Bauhaus had been to nurture applied arts – and British industry in the late 1940s badly needed new skills and fresh talent in areas like product design. Silversmithing and lettering – and the whole arts and crafts skill set enshrined in the traditional art school curriculum – addressed the needs of the first, not the present, industrial era. London County Council funded Johnstone's research trip to the USA, where he met former Bauhaus professors like Marcel Breuer and Serge Chermayeff, now in senior roles in American architectural schools.

A realignment in the understanding of the nature of art and of the artist's role in society was taking place on many levels, from educational policy to ideas of the ludic nature of human creativity. For Whistler, three generations earlier, artists were effectively an elite sect within society, who hardly cared whether the rest of the population decided to ignore or to follow their lead. Futurists and Vorticists, 'primitive mercenaries in the modern world', had seen themselves as fighting on behalf of modernity against the forces of ignorance and reaction. Forward to 1930s Hampstead and (in Read's phrase) its 'nest of gentle artists', united in a utopian endeavour to model the better future for humanity foreseen or hinted at in the *Circle* essays. Since then, through his studies of children's art and work on educational theory, Read's thinking had taken a new turn: artists now were representatives, or enablers, of a larger creative phenomenon.

Since Melanie Klein had theorized the psychology of human creativity and its sources, different interpretations had emerged. For Donald Winnicott, creativity represented 'the retention throughout life of something that belongs properly to infant experience: the ability to create the world'. The 'experience of creative living', in his view, 'is always more important for the individual than doing well'. Read felt similarly that the role of play in children's 'individuation' should be mirrored in adult life and in the workings of society as a whole, since:

> *Every man is a special kind of artist, and in his originating activity, his play or work (and in a natural society…there should be no distinction between the psychology of work and of play), he is doing more than express himself: he is manifesting the form which our common life should take, in its unfolding.*

In 1946, Read, together with the surrealist painter and collector Roland Penrose, the poet Geoffrey Grigson, publisher E. C. (Peter) Gregory, dealer E. L. T. Mesens and collector Peter Watson, co-founded the Institute of Contemporary Arts (ICA). Their general ambition was to recapture something of the energy manifested in the International Surrealist Exhibition a decade earlier and to refresh London's claim to be a centre of European modern art (American contemporary art was still, to British and European eyes, barely part of this equation). With the right kind of cultural investment (Penrose, Gregory and Watson provided money as well as ideas), young British artists, working in different art forms, could once again set about challenging the way people thought and looked and lived. Read hoped that the ICA would become a new kind of engine of social change; he thought of it as an 'adult play centre'. The first exhibition, '40 Years of Modern Art 1907–1947', opened at the Academy Hall, Oxford Street, on 10 February 1948. Featuring works by some eighty artists, many of which came from the ICA committee members' personal collections, it presented work by Bacon, Freud and Paolozzi as well as Hepworth, Moore and Ben Nicholson, together with Bonnard, Braque, Gabo, Kandinsky, Picasso, Giacometti and Mondrian. It set out to make the case – as Roger Fry had made it in 1912 in his Second Post-Impressionist Exhibition – that British artists were, like their European peers, essentially international in both outlook and spirit.

13
Cold War modern

Venice, summer 1948

To the synchronized clunk and plash of oars, the ceremonial flotilla slips away from the Giardini, bobbing back through the midsummer sparkle across the lagoon. In the grand state gondola sits the dapper figure of the elderly banker Luigi Einaudi, newly elected president of Italy. At the reception in the British Pavilion, reclaimed from the Italian army for this biennale – the first since the war – Einaudi has impressed his hosts by his familiarity not only with Turner but also with the work of Henry Moore. It is unusual, in their experience, for foreigners who are not themselves artists or critics to show the slightest interest in contemporary British art. A still bigger surprise comes with the International Jury's unanimous decision to award the Gran Premi for sculpture to Moore. The money is modest – 500,000 lire (about a year's wages for a manual worker) – but the fact that, in this first post-war test of its international standing, British sculpture takes top prize feels like a notable victory on several fronts.

———

Political art and political artists – in whose ranks few would place Henry Moore – were nothing new. Since the war, however, the arts had acquired a place in British domestic and foreign policy not seen before. One of the last acts of the coalition government in June 1945 was to establish the principle of taxpayer-funded subsidy through a new semi-autonomous body, the Arts Council of Great Britain, to be chaired by the economist John Maynard Keynes, who had previously chaired the wartime Council for the Encouragement of Music and the Arts (CEMA). Setting out the Arts Council's 'policy and hopes', Keynes invoked CEMA's spirit and success in bringing 'music, drama and pictures to places which otherwise would be cut-off from all contact with the masterpieces of earlier days: to air-raid shelters, to war-time hostels, to factories, to mining villages'. Touring productions and exhibitions had both lifted home-front morale and stirred 'newly aroused and widely diffused desires' to enjoy the fruits of civilization, without which, Keynes believed, wars were not worth winning and purely 'utilitarian and economic' capitalism incapable of fulfilling 'our notions of a satisfactory way of life'. Economists themselves should not merely serve 'the sub-human denizens of the Treasury' but act as 'trustees… of the possibility of civilization'.

The BBC, credited by Keynes with 'revolutionising the relation of the state to the arts of public entertainment' between the wars, had blazed the trail. The Arts Council, with its founding motto 'The Best for the Most', would expand this campaign by enabling a mass audience to participate as well as passively consume, attending live concerts and plays of the kind they enjoyed listening to on the radio. It would help to make 'the theatre and the concert hall and the art gallery…a living element in everyone's upbringing, and regular attendance at the theatre and at concerts a part of organised education'. A focus, too, for communities in urgent need of rebuilding, in every sense. Rather than funding artists' work, the Art Council's main concern, in Keynes's vision, would be 'bricks and mortar' – concert halls, theatres and galleries designed to 'decentralise and disperse the dramatic and musical and artistic life of the country, to build up provincial centres and to promote corporate life in these matters in every town and country'. But would it work? Keynes, who died in April 1946, did not live to see the outcome. As early as 1947, however, a confidential report for the Council detected signs that the arts of civilization as conceived by Keynes – the British regions' cultural awakening would be 'Death to Hollywood', he exclaimed – were failing to 'touch the mass of the working-class, even to the extent they did during the war'.

Abroad, the British Council had since 1936 been undertaking polite forays into cultural propaganda by staging exhibitions of British art in foreign cities. In 1938, the last time before the war that Britain had been represented at the Venice Biennale, which was still the only international art fair, it fielded a dutiful group of seven male figurative painters, including Paul Nash, Stanley Spencer and Kit Wood. Preparing for the 1948 biennale, Lilian Somerville, the British Council's recently appointed head of fine art, had more ambitious plans. As the art world gradually revived after a six-year hiatus, there was scope for reinventing and creating reputations and, beyond that, the overarching question of art's place and purpose in the post-war landscape. Keynes had made it clear in 1936 that he thought Western democracies were missing a trick in failing to tap the power of the arts in public life. The 'relations of the state to art, entertainment and ceremony' in totalitarian states might result in 'dangerous' displays of 'an aggressive racial or national spirit', but they satisfied 'the human craving for solidarity'. Democratic governments, too, would do well to recognize the social value of the arts. In the context of post-war reconstruction, in which production was 'national duty No. 1', it made sense to see how competitive the productions of home-grown artistic talent would prove in an international market.

The sculpture of Moore turned out perfectly to fit both the domestic 'craving for solidarity' and, on the international stage, the desire for modern art to express vulnerability and stoicism – the emotions of a hard-won but overshadowed peace – as well as the optimistic universals of the interwar years, the faith in 'vitality' to which Moore and Barbara Hepworth still often referred. Despite Kenneth Clark's distaste for abstract and surrealist art, he soon realized that Moore's work for the War Artists Advisory Committee (WAAC) had a unique ability to communicate. Moore's humanism was somehow both personal and generalized; it simultaneously expressed modernity and appealed to the public's more traditional tastes. After the war, those same qualities spoke equally to a yearning to recover the consoling continuities of Deep Britain – the intactness of the unbombed hills and megaliths – and the recognition of a new landscape, coloured by fears and uncertainties, for which the past provided no map. Moore's work seemed to fulfil Herbert Read's prediction, that when 'the cloud of war has passed', the artists 'in whom the spirt of modernism is embodied...will re-emerge eager to rebuild the shattered world'.

In the wake of his New York shows, at the Buchholz Gallery in 1943 and the Museum of Modern Art in 1946–47, Moore's international reputation, alone among British artists, had gathered real momentum. By the late 1940s, Moore, who had a gift for friendship and seldom got into professional wrangles, had unrivalled connections in the cultural establishment. He sat on the Arts Council's visual arts committee; Read, whose advice was listened to on every official arts body, no matter how maverick his position might be on politics or education, was a long-time friend and eloquent advocate. From every point of view, Moore was a notable asset to the British deployment of art in pursuit of soft power – an asset that Somerville knew how to make the most of. 'The Henry Moore exhibition is a matter of taste,' sniffed Sir Victor Mallet, British Ambassador in Rome, 'and although I am too old-fashioned to enjoy it' (he was five years older than Moore) 'I was glad to notice that all the many people who like, or profess to like modern art, were wildly enthusiastic.' One of the many was the poet Ronald Bottrall, the local British Council representative, who reported that Moore had, at a stroke, become 'by far the most important British artist in the world of modern art in Italian eyes'.

It's hard to imagine, before the war, an official communiqué paying much attention to European opinions of contemporary British art – a niche taste even in its country of origin. But these things mattered now. The war itself, and the tectonic geopolitical shifts that were occurring in its aftermath, had generated a need for new modes of influence and alliance, new forms of international communication and cooperation. In April 1945, fifty nations had sent representatives to San Francisco for the United Nations Conference on International Organization (the UN's charter was ratified six months later). Soon after Moore's win was announced at the Venice Biennale, the London 1948 Olympic Games opened in brilliant sunshine at the Empire Stadium in Wembley. The games, announced Lord Burghley to a crowd of 85,000, would be a 'warm flame of hope for a better understanding in the world which has burned so low'. Acute shortages of building materials meant that no new venues or facilities were constructed for the 'Austerity Games', but they demonstrated the morale-lifting, socially unifying properties of sport as public entertainment (though not of the kind Keynes had envisaged). These were the first Olympic Games to be broadcast live on television – although, since levels of television ownership, like car and telephone ownership, and indeed the fabric of most national infrastructure, had changed little since the 1930s, the sight of marathon runners jostling for position in a grainy, crumbling monochrome London was enjoyed by only a limited few armchair spectators. The idea that television would one day become a mass medium of entertainment and information was, as yet, no nearer to realization than the exercise of power through art and sport in place of money and guns.

At the same time, Moore's success at the 1948 Venice Biennale was testimony to an art that had continued to evolve in Britain since Roger Fry's two post-impressionist shows in 1910 and 1912 – the art of shaping an exhibition so as to convey a message and make a point. The involvement of artists in creating soft propaganda as well as more strident campaigns in two world wars had been managed particularly carefully in Britain, most recently by Clark at WAAC. Although WAAC had bought work from some fifty female artists (about 12.5 per cent of the total), the odds would remain stacked against any woman attempting to make a professional career in art for some time yet. Post-war public funding, however, brought openings in the field of arts administration. Organizing an exhibition – the choice of artists, the displays, the publicity, the all-important personal invitations – was a skill at which Somerville excelled, to the extent that the 24th Venice Biennale was arguably as much her triumph as Moore's. She had originally wanted to be an artist, studying at the Slade in the 1930s, then, during the war, organizing exhibitions of British art abroad for the British Council. In 1943, she had helped to set up Moore's first exhibition in the USA, with the émigré New York dealer Curt Valentin – a show that led to his full-scale, three-month retrospective at the Museum of Modern Art.

Progress had been slow and hard-won, but since the 1918 Representation of the People Act, which gave the right to vote to women over the age of thirty, there had been further landmark extensions of women's rights and opportunities. The Sex Disqualification Act of 1919 made it easier to find jobs in teaching, nursing and other occupations rather than domestic service; in 1921, the franchise was extended to women over the age of twenty-one. By 1935, about a quarter of British civil servants were women; there were nearly thirty architectural practices 'entirely run by women', reported Gertrude Leverkus, secretary of the Women's Committee of the Royal Institute of British Architects (RIBA). The patriarchal social body to which Virginia Woolf took her ironic scalpel in *A Room of One's Own* (1929) remained in rude health, however. In 1920, 1,386 women graduated from British universities, 27 per cent of the total. This dropped to 22 per cent in 1938, and 21 per cent in 1950, when there were 15,547 male graduates to 4,200 women. These numbers illustrate the 'highly masculinized' university sector that the historian David Edgerton identifies as having emerged in response to the 'warfare state' of the 1930s. This became even more marked in post-war universities, 'because the state and industry wanted men, and graduates in the most masculine of sciences – physics, engineering and mathematics'.

After 1945, while the incremental advances of the women's movement in the first half of the century seemed to crash into reverse, the focus on women's social roles and the expectations placed on them acquired bizarre intensity. The 'strengthening of masculine industries and occupations' at this time was real enough, but the relentless apotheosis of the stiff-upper-lip British male hero in the war films of the 1950s, such as *The Colditz Story*, *The Dam Busters*, *The Bridge on the River Kwai* and *Dunkirk*, hinted at underlying anxieties. As the Canadian cultural philosopher Marshall McLuhan noted in 1951 of the similar vogue that Westerns enjoyed in modern peacetime suburban life, 'The male role in society, always abstract, tenuous, and precarious compared with the biological assurance of the female, becomes obscured.'

In his analysis of a newspaper advertisement for the 'Gladiron' ironing appliance ('How to iron shirts without hating your husband!'), McLuhan made the point that the promotion of the products of masculine industries had created a quasi-industrial domestic sphere, in which a woman had 'a duty to be glamorous, cheerful, efficient, and, so far as possible, to run the home like an automatic factory'. The conflicted figure of the hero-housewife, split between radiant aspirationalism and elective servitude, was incited by adverts and exhaustively briefed by magazine articles and manuals, such as the hefty two-volume *Home Management* of 1955. Its 1,480 pages of advice, ostensibly addressed to 'happy couples', clearly targeted 'the modern woman', who 'runs her home and a full-time job, brings up her children and manages to be a very real companion to her husband, without even neglecting friends or dropping outside interests'. It was frankly admitted that to create 'a happy home', the foundation stone of the new child-focused society, was 'a major operation'. But unlike escaping from Colditz or blowing up the Ruhr Valley dams, this was essentially 'woman's work'. 'Woman', it was claimed, 'has been doing it ever since prehistoric woman succeeded in making a very passable home for her family in a cave with nothing but a few skins to furnish it. Modern woman carries on the tradition.'

The irreconcilable combination of power (the woman who can do everything) and powerlessness (everything, that is, except for leading and deciding) with which images of the modern woman of the 1950s were endowed suggests an underlying ambivalence about the still-recent war and the after-effects of Allied victory: while the war had largely been fought and won by men, it had also (as Woolf had so eloquently argued in *Three Guineas*) been exclusively caused by men. In *The Social Foundations of Post-war Building*, published in 1943 for a British readership, the American historian Lewis Mumford mused that the war represented a crisis of 'our too masculine, too life-denying society', and that 'the best slogan for the coming age is that for the life-boats: women and children first'. If home-making was woman's work, then women might have a special skill in home-building and more generally in the task of reconstruction. As had already happened with primary-age teaching, nursing and to an extent medical training, where women's accepted role as carers for the very young, the sick and the old lessened male opposition to their assuming non-menial roles in these fields, women began to make headway training and practising as architects.

Starting at RIBA in 1929, Jane Drew was one of twelve women among one hundred students. During the war there had been opportunities for this generation. Mary Crowley had worked with Ernő Goldfinger on designing an Expanding Nursery School, designed to accommodate between 40 and 120 children, and on a scheme for evacuee villages. Drew had established a women-only architectural practice in London; in 1941, she joined Judith Ledeboer, Elizabeth Denby and Jessica Albery on the RIBA's reconstruction committee (their report, *Housing*, was published in 1944). She persuaded Kenneth Clark, whom she'd met at a dance, to host an exhibition she had conceived, 'Rebuilding Britain', in the basement of the National Gallery. It was Clark who introduced her to the publisher Peter Gregory, a co-founder of the Institute of Contemporary Arts (ICA). When, in 1950, the ICA was looking for a permanent home, Drew was commissioned to convert a large townhouse in Mayfair. Working with Gregory and the ICA, she developed an interest in incorporating art-works into her plans – not as applied decoration, as in Jacob Epstein's statues for the British Medical Association or the external reliefs and foyer sculpture of *Prospero and Ariel* that Eric Gill had carved in 1932 for the BBC's headquarters, Broadcasting House, but as part of the daily experience of using and being in a building. More generally, modern art in conjunction with modern architecture was becoming routinely accepted, even expected, in the post-war public realm; certainly, none of Drew's collaborations would attract the kind of wild-side scandal that dogged Epstein's naked figures in the 1900s and, for entirely different reasons, Gill's work for the BBC, after his posthumous unmasking as an incestuous paedophile, in the 2020s.

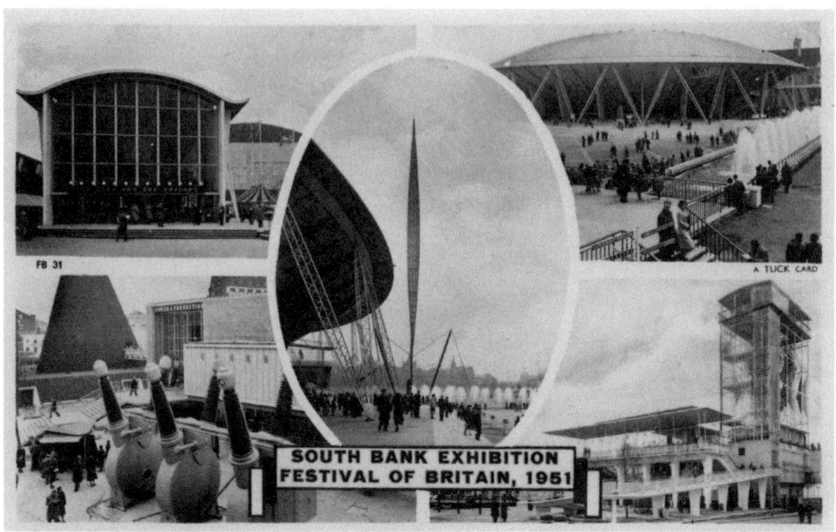

Festival of Britain souvenir postcard, showing the Skylon (centre)
and (clockwise from top left) Lion and Unicorn Pavilion, Dome of Discovery,
Viewing Tower, and part of the Power and Production Pavilion, 1951

In 1948 Drew and her husband and professional partner Maxwell
Fry were invited to join the architectural and design team for the
Festival of Britain, scheduled for summer 1951. Proposals for an event in
London to mark the centenary of the Great Exhibition of 1851 had been
through several stages when Clement Attlee and Herbert Morrison hit
on the title 'Festival of Britain'. In place of a straightforward trade and
cultural fair, the Festival would be both a national celebration and a
monumental exercise in international propaganda, trumpeting British
achievements in the past century side by side with a vision of the Britain
of the future. There would be Festival sites and events across Britain,
with an 'Exhibition of Industrial Power' in Glasgow and a touring art
show, '60 Paintings for '51', but the main action would centre on two
large sites in London.

An area of warehouses, a brewery and bombed eighteenth-century
streets between Waterloo and Westminster bridges on the south bank
of the Thames was cleared to accommodate an ensemble of more than
thirty assertively modern structures in a landscaped setting of plazas
and walkways, fountains and sculptures. The most prominent buildings,
located either side of Hungerford Bridge, were Ralph Tubbs's flying-
saucer-shaped Dome of Discovery (pl. 10) – at that date the widest

dome and the largest aluminium structure ever built – and the Royal Festival Hall, designed by Robert Matthew, Peter Moro and, putting into practice his call in *Circle* for an architecture of 'precision, economy, exact finish', Leslie Martin. Three miles upstream in Battersea, allotments and a cricket pitch became the site for a gigantic funfair. For the home audience, the themes would be educational and celebratory – British history on the one hand, British scientific and technological expertise and contemporary cultural achievement on the other – combining to suggest that the doggedly resented years of shapeless, grit-grey austerity were over and a colour-saturated, slimline, fast-paced modern future about to begin. The society photographer Cecil Beaton reported that, 'Whole walls of decoration are made of squares of coloured canvas pulled taut in geometric shapes and triangles.... A screen is made by hanging Miró-like coloured balls against the distant chimney pots of the city. Arches underneath the railways are painted strawberry pink or bright blue.'

For the world at large, the message was that Britain was back in the ring, as a producer and exporter on a global scale – products, know-how, creative energy and bright ideas. To sceptics, including leader of the opposition Winston Churchill, the Festival represented 'socialism in three dimensions'; to ordinary voters, it set out to provide industrial-scale quantities of interest, distraction, optimism and fun. For the creative team, it was a chance to test the ideas, circulating since the 1930s but not yet realized in any large public projects, that modern art, architecture and design could do more than reflect contemporary tastes: it could change them. Martin had made the case in *Circle* fourteen years earlier that the 'new aesthetic [that] exists in the motor car and the aeroplane, in the steel bridge and the line of electric pylons' was not in fact imper-sonal but 'avoids the "personal" element in order to make its "human" appeal more profound'. The designer Misha Black explained that, for him, the Festival had two main objectives: 'The first was to demonstrate the quality of modern architecture, landscape architecture and town planning; the second to show that painters and sculptors could work with architects and exhibitions designers to produce an aesthetic unity.'

'Unity' is a key term here. Arriving in Britain in summer 1951 to attend the conference in Hoddesdon of the Congrès Internationaux d'Architecture Moderne (CIAM), Le Corbusier travelled by bus and London Underground to the South Bank. 'Normally I hate exhibitions,' he confessed, but 'This exhibition is honest, it is healthy, it is solid, it is full of vigour and verve, it is full of diversity, it is full of unity.' In his formulation of 'constructive art' for *Circle*, Naum Gabo – who had sailed for America in 1946 and was about to become a US citizen – had abundantly referenced 'universal forms', 'laws', 'absolutes' and other markers of conceptual unity. To this vision, Black added the practical elements of 'quality' and production. The Festival provided the ingredient missing in 1937 – confidence that these objectives were demonstrably achievable. 'The South Bank exhibition may be regarded as the first modern townscape,' enthused *Architectural Review* in its special Festival number in August 1951, 'because its layout represents that realisation in urban terms of the Picturesque, in which the future of town planning as visual art assuredly lies.' The emphasis on public spaces, both embodying and containing visual art in the manner of the ancient Greek agora, was also part of CIAM's vision for city planning that fostered free association and free speech, the lifeblood of democracy and the opposite of totalitarianism.

Drew felt that, although the main Festival structures were not intended to be long-lasting, this would be 'a great opportunity to try out things' – one of which was incorporating art. For her Thameside Restaurant beside Waterloo Bridge, she turned to Ben Nicholson, and two younger artists, the sculptors Eduardo Paolozzi and Reg Butler. Paolozzi's *The Cage*, a tower-like, twisted, wiry construction resembling a three-dimensional maze, with echoes of Giacometti's pre-war surrealist phase, was the first sculpture he'd ever shown. Nicholson created a large curved mural. Its elegant linear geometries expressed the rebirth of optimistic *Circle*-era abstraction; the colours – soft brown, summery yellow – spoke of Nicholson's wartime home and present beach-front studio in St Ives. This was not quite visual art as town planning, but, like the roof of the Dome of Discovery, which appeared about to levitate on its tubular steel struts, or the 300-foot-high suspended needle of the Skylon, designed by Philip Powell, Hidalgo Moya and Felix Samuely, it suggested a pattern for understanding a new way of life that hadn't yet arrived – at least, not in social life and the traditional courtesies of creative patronage. Nicholson, recalled Drew, 'said to me would I please see that all the workmen who were putting up the mural wore white gloves. So off I went to Selfridges and got I think five dozen pairs.' Another young sculptor, the former architectural draughtsman Lynn Chadwick, made *Stabile (Cypress)*, a Skylon-shaped structure of steel rods and copper sheet, to stand outside Misha Black and Alexander Gibson's Regatta Restaurant opposite the Dome.

The Festival-going public was starting to get used to Hepworth and Moore, accepting that a bulky upright or horizontal shape in stone or bronze could represent a human figure and create a human kind of focus for an outdoor setting. Prominently installed in front of the Dome of Discovery, Hepworth's *Contrapuntal Forms* – a 'Group Symbolizing the Spirit of Discovery' – were unequivocally standing figures. The elliptical holes in their torsos, a feature she had introduced into her work with *Pierced Form* in 1932 as a means of expressing a solid sculpture's relationship to ambient space, now simply connoted a familiar, even slightly old-fashioned, form of the modern, set beside Powell, Moya and Samuely's techno-futurist Skylon. 'We are all fortunate,' Hepworth reflected in a short radio talk about the Festival for audiences in the USA, 'to be living at a time when new forms are being created in architecture, sculpture, painting and music'. These new forms expressed 'the particular difficulties which our civilisation presents', yet they remained 'in true accord with past tradition – springing from a profound response to life itself – from our common roots'.

Civilisation, tradition, profound, roots: despite the stress Hepworth placed on 'new', the pull of the past that had informed interwar visions of Deep Britain remained palpable. She had, she said, experienced a growing conviction,

> *that some new apprehension of basic life forces is necessary if we are to survive the mechanical destructiveness of our time. It seems to me urgent that we in Europe and you in America should, through an understanding of the art of our time as well as the art of past cultures, join hands in the great endeavour to regain our touch with the simple primeval forces which nourish mankind and which prepare the ground for a healthy vital culture.*

In words that reveal the strong community of social purpose Hepworth had felt with her Yorkshire contemporary and former Hampstead neighbour Herbert Read, carrying the tenor of their conversations in its ring of earnest yet lyrical optimism, she concluded, 'A Festival of Art allows the impact to be made upon the social structure, breaking the crust of resistance and allowing a new free growth, of interplay between the practising artist and the rest of society.' The Festival of Britain was widely experienced, and fondly remembered, as a sunny interlude in the long colourless slog out of austerity. 'There was a terrific feeling of optimism,' gushed the architect Jim Cadbury-Brown. 'It was joyous to work on.... There was a real sense of celebration, that anything was possible.'

A 'terrific feeling of optimism' was not, however, the pervasive mood in the geopolitical arena. In March 1946, Winston Churchill, freed from his responsibilities as wartime prime minister to dispense his 'true and faithful counsel' as an international elder statesman, gave a speech in Fulton, Missouri. Warming to his theme of 'the problems which beset us on the morrow of our absolute victory in arms', he spoke of 'freedom and progress', 'freedom and democracy', 'freedom and the rights of man', 'freedom of speech' and 'the title deeds of freedom which should lie in every cottage home'. Churchill drew a vivid picture of a free world, in which a nuclear-armed United States 'stands at this time at the pinnacle of world power' – words that could never have passed a British leader's lips just five years earlier. But, he continued, 'A shadow has fallen upon the scenes so lately lighted by Allied victory.... From Stettin in the Baltic to Trieste in the Adriatic, an iron curtain has descended across the Continent.' Communist states in eastern Europe were 'seeking everywhere to obtain totalitarian control'. The safety of the world required 'a new unity in Europe', and – as Hepworth would phrase it in her heartfelt advocacy of the role of the artist in a 'healthy and vital society' – a need for Europe and the United States to 'join hands in the great endeavour'. The Festival of Britain's director, Sir Gerald Barry, claimed that its collaborative character asserted 'the strength and value of the democratic way of life at a time when it was being subjected to sharp strains and challenges'.

Churchill's Fulton speech made persuasive rhetorical play with ideas of shadow and light; his 'iron curtain' was a metaphor. By the mid-1950s, however, actual steel barriers were being installed in central Europe. In order to stem the steady migration from the Communist east to the 'free' west across the inner German border – the so-called Oder–Neisse line – the East German government erected barbed-wire fencing, then increasingly permanent and formidable fortifications. Within the perimeter of the South Bank exhibition, with its smoothly engineered surfaces and visual matrix of curves, rectangles and networks, it might have made soothing sense to think of 'simple primeval forces', but there was an accumulating store and spreading consciousness of very different types of images. After the concentration camp reportage had come photos of the Hiroshima mushroom cloud and the skeletal post-apocalyptic remains of that city. The Nuremberg trials, the war in Korea and now the physical division of Europe all left after-images in consciousness that undermined any appeal, however heartfelt, to 'the beauty of life'.

In sharp contrast to Hepworth and Moore, whose 7-foot-long bronze *Genesis (Reclining Figure)* basked primordially on a plinth in front of Cadbury-Brown's Land of Britain pavilion, several younger sculptors involved in the Festival were working in iron and steel, producing open, linear sculptures without the mass and opacity of the elder modernists' work. Reg Butler's *Birdcage* in front of Drew's Thameside Restaurant, forged and welded from iron sheets and rods, resembled a dream drawing

Henry Moore in his studio, working on the plaster model for *Genesis (Reclining Figure)*, 1950, commissioned for the Festival of Britain

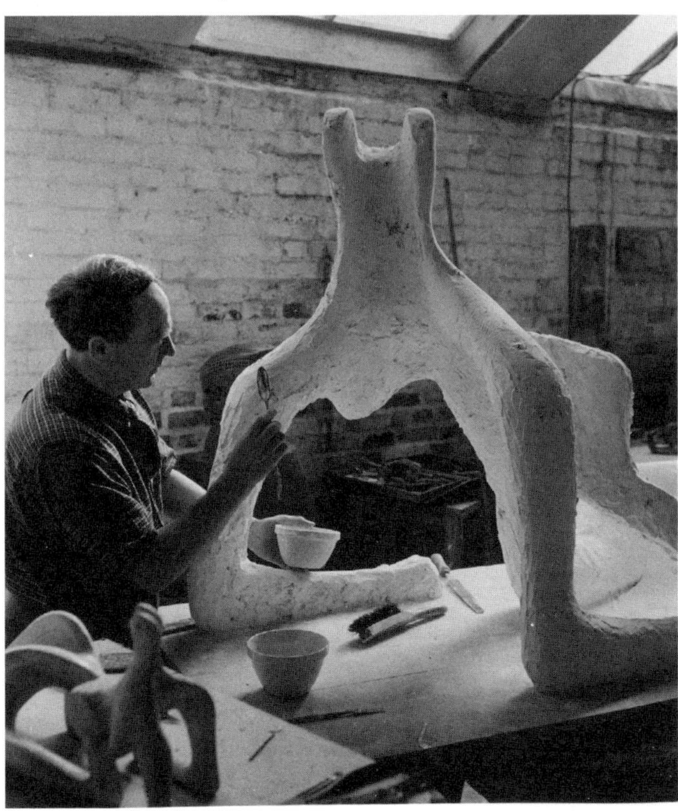

by Joan Miró, animated and ambiguously weaponized – a spiky, spindly figure, a creature or carnivorous plant colonizing the site's smooth modernist planes. In a radio conversation in September 1952, Butler went head-to-head with Hepworth. When she spoke of her feeling for 'all the rocks and the timelessness of life', he pointed out that that wasn't how modern life felt to him, with its 'clang and noisiness, the frustration and the anxiety', concluding 'however much we may think how nice it would be to live a pastoral existence in relation to them, we can't anymore – we've lost our innocence'.

This conversation was, in its way, another border confrontation – a parallel to the ideological stand-off Churchill had sketched in his Fulton speech – in which Butler's contemporary urban reality of clang and noisiness opposed the timeless 'sea-worn shapes' of Hepworth's 'pastoral' humanism. From a practical point of view, the sculptural use of steel and oxyacetylene welding gear instead of stone and chisel reflected genuine shortages of materials and the prohibitive cost of specialist art materials (the large canvases given free to the artists selected for '60 Paintings for '51' were a rare luxury). Wartime habits of improvisation and reskilling also informed Butler and Chadwick's work. Butler had trained and briefly practised as an architect in the 1930s; as a conscientious objector, he'd worked in a Sussex blacksmith's forge. Chadwick had returned from service as a Fleet Air Arm pilot to work in an architect's office: he first designed space-frame structures of the kind he employed in *Cypress* in the context of exhibition stands for the regular post-war trade fairs intended to stimulate the market for British products. More generally, twisted, tensile, skeletal forms in iron and steel took on a powerful symbolic resonance around this time: they suggested both shattered ruins and the beginnings of reconstruction; they referenced the iron-masters of Britain's industrial revolution but also had a futuristic sci-fi aura, dread and thrills combined.

When Somerville and her selection committee at the British Council were planning for the 1952 Venice Biennale, this new generation of sculptors emerged as the natural choice. After Moore's victory in 1948, Hepworth had failed to take top prize in 1950; it was time to prove that British sculpture had lost none of its vitality, that Moore had heirs, although – as Butler had rather tetchily insisted to Hepworth – they were in tune with the new iron age of Cold War and reconstruction rather than the 1930s era of wood and stone. Moore would again be represented, but outside the pavilion, on his own; inside, Paolozzi, Butler and Chadwick would be joined by Robert Adams, Kenneth Armitage, Geoffrey Clarke, Bernard Meadows and William Turnbull. As commissioner that year, Read wrote the catalogue essay, 'New Aspects of British Sculpture'. In light of his almost uncritical faith in Moore as the mid-twentieth century's pre-eminent artist, he didn't instinctively warm to the work of the 'New Aspects' crew. He managed, however, to write himself into a state of imaginative sympathy, in which he came up with the phrase – 'the geometry of fear' – that would forever define these eight artists as a group. Read had a serious interest in the Freudian basis of surrealism, and would later edit the first English translation of the works of Carl Jung. Despite the fact that the eight sculptors had originally been selected to illustrate the range of contemporary British sculpture, rather than a single tendency, Read diagnosed their work as the expression of a collective unconscious. 'These new images,' he affirmed, quoting from T. S. Eliot's 1915 poem 'The Love Song of J. Alfred Prufrock', 'belong to the iconography of despair, or of defiance; and the more innocent the

Reg Butler, *Birdcage*, 1950–51, in front of the Thameside Restaurant, Festival of Britain. Forged and welded iron, height 412 cm (162¼ in.)

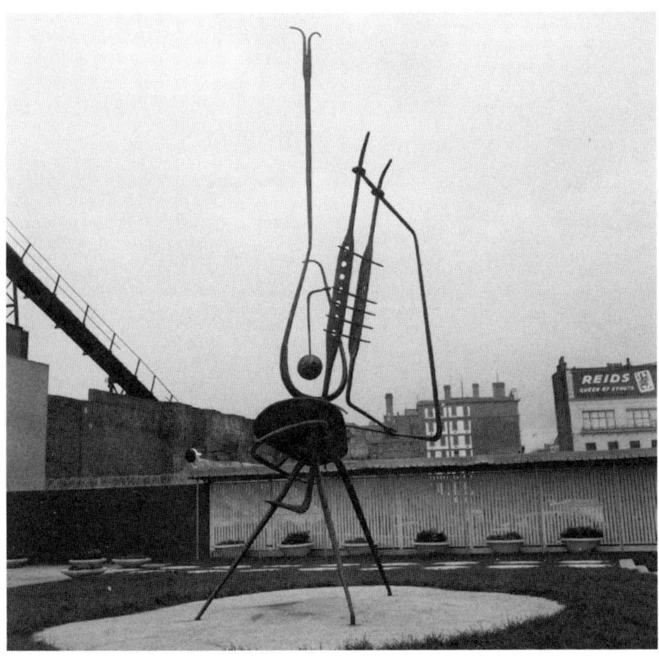

artist, the more effectively he transmits the collective guilt. Here are images of flight, or ragged claws "scuttling across the floors of silent seas", of excoriated flesh, frustrated sex, the geometry of fear.'

Despair, defiance, innocence, guilt, flight, frustrated sex and fear: into this almost nonsensical cocktail of emotions, Read stirred a Sartrean existentialist angst and a psychoanalytic reading of creative work as the release of repressed sexual desire. The 'geometry' in his final image evokes the architecture of both reconstruction and repression, as well as the circles and squares of 1930s constructivism. Some of the sculptors felt that Read's phrase travestied their work, but journalists loved it. It was a consummate exercise in finding a strapline for the spirit of the times, then identifying artists and artworks that could represent it – almost the reverse process to the futurist manifestos, in which artists announced in one way or another, 'We speak for the present moment. Our art is the new language by which the present can recognize itself.'

This was the first phase of the Cold War, a term popularized by the American journalist Walter Lippmann in his short book *The Cold War: A Study in U.S. Foreign Policy* (1947). As the opposition of Western 'freedom' and communist repression became the foundation of Anglo-American political rhetoric, contemporary art – and particularly art that was perceived to be 'free' from the weight of tradition – was seen as a vehicle for propaganda that was worth state investment (ironically, not unlike the situation for Gabo and other progressive artists in Russia for a few years after the 1917 Revolution). For a short period, the soft socialism of 'The Best for the Most' was implicated in the drive to prove to the non-aligned world that communism was wrong. In 1951, a proposal for the first ever international sculpture competition was presented to the ICA by Antony Kloman, US cultural attaché in Stockholm, where he was rumoured to have been responsible for recruiting secret agents to send to Germany in the final months of war in Europe. An 'anonymous donor' – in fact the US State Department – pledged £11,500 prize money (£280,000 today). The brief was to design a monument to the Unknown Political Prisoner, with the clear presumption that this martyr to the 'cause of human freedom' would have suffered at the hands of a repressive (communist) regime, as opposed to, say, being imprisoned as a communist or suspected communist in the USA. Predictably, the Soviet Union and their Eastern bloc allies refused to participate. At the ICA, the pacifist anarchist Read smelled a rat, worrying that, however successful the call for entries (by December 1952, some 3,500 had been received), Kloman was concealing something; he had no wish to 'sup with the devil'.

When the winners were announced, first and second places went to British sculptors – Butler and Hepworth respectively. Hepworth's maquette was a strangely compromised version of her signature holed-and-standing forms, in which the hole in one figure was criss-crossed by a prison window grille. Butler's model for the *Monument to the Unknown Political Prisoner*, largely constructed from thin steel rods, took the form of a three-legged pylon supporting a triangular platform, above which was a vertical screen-shaped aperture – shapes vaguely suggesting surveillance or a place of execution. Above this middle section projected a single tall mast, like an aerial or harpoon. What looked at first like an architectural structure, with two diminutive figures standing on its stone base, could also, like Butler's Festival *Birdcage*, be interpreted as a three-legged sci-fi alien. In March 1953, the Tate Gallery hosted an exhibition of prize-winners and runners-up; the day after it opened, Butler's maquette was vandalized by a young Hungarian refugee artist, László Szilvassy. Butler took it as a compliment: 'You take about a shilling's worth of wire and bend it about in a certain way, and it becomes a symbol powerful enough to make someone want to destroy it.' Szilvassy was arrested and charged: as someone who had experienced the brutality of both Nazi and Soviet occupation of his native country, he made a strong case in court, difficult to answer on aesthetic grounds. 'Those unknown political prisoners have been and still are human beings. To reduce them...into scrap metal is just as much a crime as it was to reduce them into ashes or scrap.' Unrepentant, he was finally released.

If the 'geometry of fear' sculptors were ever a group or a movement, this phase did not last long. Read and the journalists who adopted his phrase had so pointedly identified the eight young sculptors' work as an expression of the times that, as events supervened and the mood changed, the wiry, welded, angsty look fell out of fashion. At the 1956 Venice Biennale, Chadwick repeated Moore's coup eight years earlier by taking the International Prize for Sculpture – widely predicted to go to Giacometti. Somerville, who had organized the show and practised the necessary art diplomacy with characteristic panache, was reassured that contemporary British sculpture remained in the international limelight in a way that could barely have been imagined when she was at art school. But this was also the grand finale of British sculpture's existentialist Cold War moment.

In 1949, two students at the Slade, Nigel Henderson and Richard Hamilton, put a proposal for an exhibition to the ICA. After studying at the Royal Academy Schools, which closed for the duration of the war in 1940, Hamilton had worked as an engineering draughtsman, then as a technical designer at Electric and Musical Industries Ltd (EMI). He returned to the Royal Academy Schools in 1946, but was expelled for 'not profiting from the instruction'. He did his eighteen months of National Service and in 1948 enrolled at the Slade. Henderson had served as a naval pilot and suffered a breakdown. He had family connections with Paris-based surrealists and also with the Bloomsbury set – he was married to Vanessa Bell and Virginia Woolf's niece Judith Stephen, a Cambridge anthropologist. It was she who in the late 1940s opened his eyes and directed his camera to working-class life in the East End. If Hamilton and Henderson had been ten years older, they would have learned the standard set of art school skills – life drawing, oil painting and the rest. Instead, they arrived in the London art world – the Slade, the ICA – having picked up other ways of making images and looked at other sources from which images are made.

The exhibition 'Growth and Form' took its title from the 1917 book by Scottish zoologist D'Arcy Wentworth Thompson, which had gone the rounds of 1930s Hampstead, with its beautiful illustrations of natural geometries in the form of shells and skulls, leaves and seeds. The material to be included in the exhibition, however, went far beyond the kinds of biomorphic parallels between life and art that had occupied Hepworth and Moore. Its seventeen categories of 'growth and form' covered atomic particles and astronomy, biological and chemical processes, implicitly rejecting the notion – fundamental to the Hampstead modernists – of universal principles. 'Growth and Form' finally opened in July 1951: at the ICA's domestic-scale spaces at Dover Street, Hamilton had installed a multimedia environment, featuring photographs, X-rays, diagrams, film-loop projections showing the growth of crystals and sea urchins, and water droplets lit by stroboscope. He would later reflect that the conviction, shared by abstract artists throughout the twentieth century, that art should be 'non-allusive', 'seemed to me sad in a way – rather like pulling the plug. My ambition was to be multi-allusive! I wanted to relate to everything that was going on in the world.'

14
Tomorrow today

Bayswater, May 1955

After the Moon, Mars was easier. Venus was a waste of time...

In Magda and Frank Cordell's house, American comics lie scattered around. Galaxy Science Fiction is a favourite. In the latest issue, a spaceship lands on Dead Man's Planet.

Automatically, his hand reached for his gun...

Outside, in Cleveland Square, snow lies on the lawn, on the plane trees in full leaf. It has been a century since snow last fell this long, this thickly in London in May. At No. 52 – six storeys, tall windows, grubby stucco, steps up from the pavement, Ionic columns bracketing a double front door like all the other houses in the grand crumbling terrace – there is plenty of room for pianist-composer Frank Cordell's top-floor studio, and for the large painting room, which also serves as the studio where Frank, Magda and their lodger John McHale edit their films and McHale cuts and pastes his photomontages. While bright snatches of piano drift downstairs, sometimes whole singalong melodies from the soundtracks Frank composes for films and television, Magda works on her 'grid' paintings – networks of criss-cross lines tugged at by leaking streaks and scrawls of paint, like the tail ends of home movies. Pattern meets chaos. Logic and emotion share the same splattered armature. She is also preparing for a small show of work in progress – collages and monotypes – at the Institute of Contemporary Arts, for which Cleveland Square has become a kind of clubhouse or alternative power base for the younger members.

————

Magda Lustigova, born into a Jewish family in Hungary in 1921, fled the Nazi round-ups and exterminations of the Second World War, eventually finding safety in Palestine. Here she got a job with British intelligence, translating intercepts of enemy radio traffic, and met Frank Cordell, a military intelligence officer and local entertainment impresario for Allied troops. Before the war, Cordell had been a professional jazz pianist and a sound technician at Warner Bros film studios. Returning to civilian life in London, he worked for the BBC as a composer and conductor. In 1952, he and Magda moved into a big, old Bayswater townhouse in Cleveland Square with the idea of turning it into an atelier – an artists' workplace and drop-in community, a hive of experiment and enquiry. They had no manifesto or programme, but 'in some sense,' Magda later reflected, 'we felt that the new images might help us to prevent the repetition of the inhuman and unseemly past. It was with some excitement, then, that we approached the new and tried to erase the old.' The 'new images' were found as well as made – adverts and photos snipped out of *Life* magazine and American comics and hobby journals. The Cordells and their circle were excited by *The Mechanical Bride*, a collection of illustrated essays about American newspaper adverts by the cultural philosopher Marshall McLuhan, published in 1951. It had apparently never occurred to anyone in a British university or art school to consider popular culture, or as McLuhan termed it, 'pop kulch', as a subject for serious study – but serious he was. 'The indiscriminate cluster of items included in these images,' he proposed, 'becomes in turn a means of "popular thinking" about society and politics.'

The Cleveland Square regulars shared a magpie enthusiasm for Americana, at once spellbound and sceptical. They mocked the gurning bonehead in 'Charles Atlas' bodybuilding ads but were at the same time mesmerized by a 'dynamism which the English could never capture', as Eduardo Paolozzi put it. The modernist architects Peter and Alison Smithson, in their early twenties but already designing their first big public project, Hunstanton School in Norfolk – an expansive complex of glazed, boxlike units, making inventive use of recycled materials – had covered their kitchen walls with a collage of American food adverts. Although Hollywood movies had been a mainstay of British cinemas since the 1930s, and more than two million American servicemen had passed through Britain during the war, first-hand experience of America remained rare, even after Pan-American airline began scheduled non-stop flights between London and New York in 1947. In these bread-and-dripping austerity years, pictures in saturated sunburst colours of staple American pantry items, like Betty Crocker Golden Date Cake or Ritz Crackers ('a crisp treat in the heat' ran the slogan), felt as if they had been beamed to Britain from outer space.

Magda Cordell's exhibition in the members' room at the ICA in July 1955 ran concurrently with the main exhibition, 'Man, Machine and Motion: An Iconography of Speed and Space', organized by the architectural writer Reyner Banham and Richard Hamilton, whose 'Growth and Form' in the Festival of Britain in summer 1951 had been the first of several concept-based shows he would mastermind at the ICA, installed in such a way that visitors experienced them as three-dimensional, multimedia compendia of ideas, or labyrinths of unexpected connections, very different from the conventional art exhibition. After

Peter Smithson, Eduardo Paolozzi, Alison Smithson and Nigel Henderson, August 1956, photograph in the 'This is Tomorrow' exhibition catalogue, Whitechapel Art Gallery, 1956

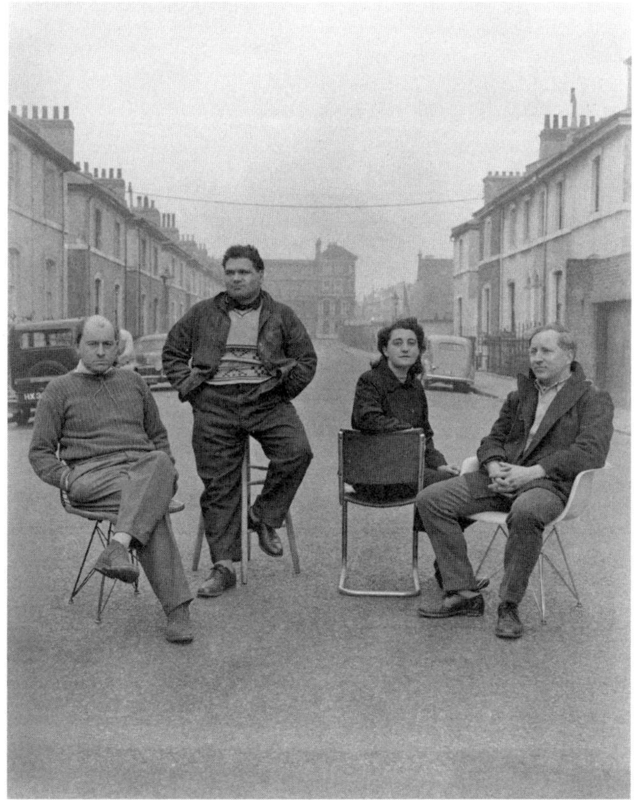

the move to permanent premises in Dover Street in December 1950, the ICA's management group embarked on a determinedly eclectic programme, with the aim of educating the public about modern art and, more ambitiously, instilling new attitudes to art in relationship to modern life. In March 1953 had come 'Wonder and Horror of the Human Head: An Anthology', in September 'Parallel of Life and Art', organized by Paolozzi, the Smithsons and Nigel Henderson, and in October 1954, 'Collages and Objects', curated by the art historian and critic Lawrence Alloway, who the following year would become the ICA's assistant director. Informing all these exhibitions was a view of art as a process of collage, drawing from all kinds of different sources rather than diving deep in search of – in Barbara Hepworth's phrase – the one 'real source'. Instead of channelling the 'inner spirit' of 'man', the artist's task, as inspired collagist, was to sample, investigate and explore.

In January 1952, Antony Kloman – the ICA's shady head of publicity who would initiate the Unknown Political Prisoner competition later that year – noted that a 'Young Group' among the membership wanted to run their own lecture series. The middle-aged board of the ICA, and particularly its first female director Dorothy Morland – our 'Guardian Angel', Banham called her – were generally supportive. This 'small, cohesive, quarrelsome, abrasive group' (as McHale described them) convened for their first session in April, when Paolozzi set up an epidiascope. Under the projector, one after another, he laid covers and spreads from American magazines he'd picked up from GIs in Paris or second-hand bookshops on the Charing Cross Road. Across the screen passed images of gleaming Chevrolets, pumped-up bodybuilders, red-lipped bikini-clad girls, aeroplanes, pineapples and explosive headlines and slogans like *BUNK!* For Roger Fry, Kenneth Clark or Herbert Read, such images could never have been considered art; for his part, Paolozzi was bored by the way 'rather bad art, bad tired art' was endlessly discussed in the same old terms. He wanted to drive home the point that, 'images might come from unexpected quarters that might be much more dynamic than the orthodox accepted form of art, and that as an artist one had to seize on one's own dynamism through the dynamic that lay about one, and not reject it'.

A new critical language in which these images 'from unexpected quarters' could be appreciated and analysed was provided by the writings of McLuhan, who had studied at Cambridge University, where the close reading of literary texts, rigorously purged of received opinions, had been pioneered in the English school in the 1930s by F. R. Leavis and I. A. Richards. McLuhan adapted their methods to a 'reading' of popular culture: any newspaper, he stated, 'is a collective work of art, a daily "book" of industrial man'. He regretted 'the failure of many serious American artists and writers to employ the rich materials of popular art'. This was the opposite of Read's position, shared by most senior British intellectuals and academics, who also, with few exceptions, shared a disdain that often shaded into hostility towards any North American claim to produce or know about art. The 'genuine arts of today', pronounced Read, 'are engaged in a heroic struggle against mediocrity and mass values, and if they lose, then art, in any meaningful sense, is dead. If art dies, then the spirit of man becomes impotent and the world relapses into barbarism.'

For the Young Group, who by November 1952 had become known as the Independent Group, the artist was not a hero-maker engaged in a struggle against barbarism, in which fascist dictators lined up B-movie directors and advertising executives on the enemy side, but a receiver and transmitter of images and ideas. Like all such groups in Britain up to that date, the Independent Group was a blokey forum, including Alloway, Banham, Hamilton, Paolozzi, Peter Smithson and surrealist artist Toni del Renzio, with Alison Smithson and Magda Cordell its only female associates. Attendance at meetings seldom stretched far beyond this small nucleus, but the ICA was serving its purpose as a place where an artist with fresh ideas could get things done.

McHale, who had shown work from his 'Transistor' series in 'Collages and Objects', alongside Salvador Dalí, Georges Braque, Picasso and René Magritte as well as a younger British cohort, had come to art – like other habitués of Cleveland Square – through an unconventional route. Rumoured to have been a streetfighter in his native Glasgow, he'd served as a naval cryptographer during the war, assembling a picture of enemy communications from disparate intercepts (a kind of codebreakers' collage). Since then, technology had moved on. Semiconductor valves, or transistors, had been developed in the late 1940s to replace the large thermionic valves previously used in radio communications; prototype transistor radios had already been built, opening up the possibility of portable private music. McHale's 'Transistors' started as coloured-paper shapes, pasted over with press clippings about bands, all torn and shuffled by hand, like tuning a radio until the sounds you want to listen to become clear. After 'Collages and Objects', early in 1955 McHale left for America on a one-year Yale Fellowship to study colour-theory with the former Bauhaus professor Josef Albers. Emigrating from Germany in 1933, Albers had taught painting at the progressive Black Mountain College before becoming head of design at Yale. When McHale returned to London the following year, he brought with him a trunk full of collage materials, a creative arsenal of American ephemera.

Following McLuhan's lead, the Independent Group and their circle always considered visuals and text as an integral whole: words were images too, and all images conveyed messages. And there was no longer (if there ever had been) any validity in the distinction, which had shadowed cultural commentary in Britain from Victorian times, between the 'highbrow' and 'lowbrow' arts. The sci-fi stories that were part of the American cult at the ICA and Cleveland Square – 'Festering swamps and carnivorous grasses. Bleak hills dipped in blood and the callous maraudings of asocial lizards' – were 'geometry of fear' material, in a way, complete with scuttling claws and silent seas, but the fantasy of battling Martians was more fun (admit it) than reading T. S. Eliot. Frank Cordell and McHale shared their cultural theories – what was the answer to the question posed by the brilliantly quotable McLuhan: 'Got any light on why our intellectuals take such a dark view of pop kulch?' Perhaps because 'pop' was a word you could never imagine issuing from the lips of Herbert Read or Henry Moore, it became Independent Group shorthand for their own intellectual concerns. McHale also talked 'pop' with Alloway, who would become an eloquent critical exponent of the post-war phenomenon of mass popular culture, not so much in the McLuhan sense of consumer products like cars and ironing boards as in the application of the epithet 'pop' (for which some gave Alloway the credit) to a new genre of art.

Read's original concept for the ICA, an 'adult play centre' where creativity could flourish in a social setting, had envisaged other such places springing up in every town in Britain, leading to the renewal of society through the nurturing of individuality. But the exemplary artist in Read's Britain of the future was still – as it had been twenty years earlier – Henry Moore. And Read's idea of what constituted art, however open-minded to new groups and movements, effectively side-lined much ordinary, everyday visual experience. Where cinema was concerned, he had little interest and nothing good to say: as Paolozzi saw it, 'he thought that the idea of American films, anything American, was unappetizing and unnecessary'. Surrealism, for Read, was as deeply rooted in eccentric-uncle whimsy of the Edward Lear and Lewis Carroll kind as in Freudian psychoanalysis. Paolozzi's method of surrealistic collage, on the other hand, led back 'to all the things that excited you in childhood, like games, secret writings...where you were able to trigger all these childhood things, which in conventional art education you were taught to forget'. Its impulse was both innocent and transgressive, embracing 'erotic drawings for example, where with this English sensibility it was simply not done, not only to do erotic drawings but even to talk about them'. And it was true that, for all the passionate talk of 'the spirit of man' that had animated the abstract camp in 1930s Hampstead, sex had featured in their work only in its de-eroticized incarnation in the mother-and-child theme, and in formalized smoothnesses and apertures. It seemed to be accepted that sex – in art, at any rate – was the preserve of the Freud-fuelled aficionados of surrealism, who saw breasts, vaginas and penises in shapes that would have suggested to Moore and Hepworth the forms of hills, 'spatial' holes and megaliths.

The one form in which American popular culture had already made inroads with the intelligentsia was music. In the interwar years, they had greeted American jazz with real enthusiasm, nothing like the distaste they often displayed towards cinema and any form of commercial art. McLuhan detected a highbrow tendency to see an equivalence between the virtuoso structured improvisations of jazz and 'the most sophisticated techniques of Mallarmé, Debussy and Picasso'; Manhattan, Le Corbusier exclaimed, was 'hot jazz in stone'. In his sleeve notes for the trumpeter Miles Davis's 1959 album *Kind of Blue*, the pianist and composer Bill Evans compared Davis's style of modern jazz to 'a Japanese visual art in which the artist is forced to be spontaneous.... As the painter needs his framework of parchment, the improvising musical group needs its framework in time.'

American popular music, especially, was a source of contagious energy and rapidly evolving genres. One evening in 1953, the Independent Group gathered round a gramophone to critique some new American records – possibly the first occasion on which British walls vibrated to a rockabilly beat. At what turned out to be the group's final session on 15 July 1955, the last in a series convened by McHale and Alloway on the theme of the relationship between the fine arts and popular art, Frank Cordell, about to take up a new job as music director at EMI, gave a talk titled 'Gold Pan Alley'. He offered an early analysis of the soon-to-be-familiar figure of the working-class rock star:

> *The transition from 'unknown' to 'star' takes place in that vague area where the common myth is shared: Although our garage-hand is now a 'star' he is still an 'available' type with the mass and as his press agent will underline, he still retains the tastes and allegiances of his group.*

Cordell, the music industry man, had grasped the cultural sea change already under way, in which the old snobberies of Bloomsbury and the British cultural elite would be flipped on their head.

In January 1956, Magda Cordell had a solo exhibition at the Hanover Gallery. Her new works were large, 7 feet high, and in contrast to her earlier grid paintings, this time the trails and stains and scabs of paint clearly, cumulatively evoked the female body. In *Figure (Woman)* (pl. 12) the fruit-like, faintly luminous full-frontal ovals of breasts, abdomen and upper thighs (the head is a vestigial red diamond), scribbled with white, appear suspended between fleshy materialization and vaporous dissolution. Both their gluey accretions of paint-marks and appearance of steamrollered flatness are effects Cordell must have enjoyed in the French artist Jean Dubuffet's work, seen at the ICA the previous year. *Art brut*, 'raw art', was Dubuffet's term for the kind of art he wanted to make, gauchely alive with the spontaneity, directness and absence of politeness and professional technique that he was drawn to in untaught artists, psychiatric patients and children. In Alloway's catalogue essay for Cordell, he took her new paintings as the cue for a word collage, in the style of psychoanalytic free association: *solar, delta, galactic, amorphous, ulterior, fused, far out, viscous, skinned, visceral, variable, flux, nebular, iridescence, hyper-space, free fall...swimming pool, contraterrene*. Art can do or be or suggest any of these things: that was Alloway's pretty confident assumption after three years of Independent Group sessions and Americana-swapping at Cleveland Square.

In a more conventional catalogue-essay vein, Alloway described Cordell as a painter who 'preserves the physical means of action painting (with its lexicon of sensuous effects)' but for whom 'the physical act of painting' was not an end in itself – there was also her search for images or 'iconographies'. He was comparing her to 'The American

Action Painters', the title of an essay in which, in December 1952, the critic Harold Rosenberg identified a new breed of artist who approached the blank canvas as 'an arena in which to act' rather than a surface for picture-making. This 'act-painting', Rosenberg proposed, 'is of the same metaphysical substance as the artist's existence. The new painting has broken down every distinction between art and life.' He did not name individual artists, but the phrase 'action painting' (like Read's 'geometry of fear') gained instant currency. Cordell's Hanover Gallery show coincided with the arrival of American action painting in London – not quite the first time it had been glimpsed, but its controversial debut in public consciousness – in an exhibition at the Tate Gallery.

'Modern Art in the United States: A Selection from the Collections of the Museum of Modern Art, New York' was a historical survey in several sections, working forwards from the early 1900s. It was one particular room at the Tate, 'Contemporary Abstract Art', that caused a sensation. Here was the action painter par excellence Jackson Pollock, with *Number 1*, an 8-foot-wide expanse of frenetic dancing drips and trails of paint, poured straight from cans or flicked with sticks on to canvas laid on the studio floor. Here were Franz Kline's *Chief* – big, freehand intersecting curves of black housepaint on the pale canvas, like industrial calligraphy – and Mark Rothko's *Number 10*, its fuzzy, translucent rectangles of colour, violet on yellow on mist-grey, stacked one above the other, more in the spirit of a prayer than a performance. Here were Arshile Gorky, Philip Guston, Willem de Kooning, Robert Motherwell, Clyfford Still, acting on canvas, it turned out, in very different ways but yet clearly a new movement – or new to British eyes (much of their work was ten years old or more). This movement, 'for want of a better term,' the curator and writer Holger Cahill explained in his catalogue essay, 'has been called abstract expressionism'.

If the British public was perplexed, artists were excited, but anxious too, because the room at the Tate felt like incontrovertible evidence that American painters had since the mid-1940s been working with a confidence and energy, and on a scale that had been all but inconceivable in austerity Britain. 'After its long tutelage to Europe and its turn toward Asia,' announced Cahill, 'American art today has the courage and the will to choose itself.' In other words, it wasn't only in the fields of cinema, popular music, advertising, consumer product design and every other domain of what McLuhan called 'pop kulch' that America had achieved world dominance; now it was moving into that traditional bastion of European superiority, fine art.

As the wartime incarnation of British fighting spirit, Winston Churchill, in his Fulton speech, had been surprisingly swift and frank in his acknowledgment of America's new geopolitical position 'at the pinnacle of world power'. In the cultural sphere, however, a subaltern role proved very much harder to contemplate. Summarizing the curmudgeonly reactions of the British press to 'Modern Art in the United States' for the New York edition of *Arts* magazine, Patrick Heron cited the *Sunday Times*'s dismissal of 'Yankee Doodles', *The Observer*'s lofty opinion that works by Pollock and De Kooning 'wear already an air of impermanence' and the *Manchester Guardian*'s failure to discern 'any seducing master or theorist likely to lead young artists ahead or astray'. For British artists, the abstract expressionists (aka action painters) were, Heron noted, a revelation, arriving in London at exactly the 'psychological moment' when curiosity about what was happening in New York was reaching its peak. Yet Heron himself, refusing to let Rothko or de Kooning dethrone the French masters of colour Pierre Bonnard and Henri Matisse, almost immediately began rowing back on his admiration of the Americans. He had been 'elated by the size, energy, originality, economy and inventive daring of many of the paintings', their 'creative emptiness' and 'flatness' had been 'a radical discovery' – and yet, 'there was an absence of worked-up paint quality such as one never misses in the French'.

American painters had taken what they had found in modern European art – the surrealist openness to accident, the impressionist confidence that the brush has a language all its own – and run with it, freely and boldly. It wasn't solely creative energy that accounted for this freedom and boldness but political and economic factors, too. In the Cold War rhetoric of capitalist-democratic freedom versus communist oppression, abstract expressionism represented the ideological opposite to the official Soviet style of socialist realism (in the 1953 international competition to design a monument to the Unknown Political Prisoner, covert US government funding had supported abstract sculpture). Where American artists painted canvases as big as they wanted, using as much paint as it took, and New York dealers had a pool of rich clients who were frankly enthusiastic about modern art, austerity-era British artists had had to make do with hardboard instead of canvas, cheaper, earthier colours and few collectors with broad enough minds and wide enough walls. Between 1952 and 1958, Frank Auerbach found that he 'could only really afford to work the way I did, which was to make a thing again and again, by using earth colours and black and white' – although in his case, the constraints liberated rather than inhibited his process.

From the standpoint of the British political left, abstract expressionism was reactionary rather than radical, an abdication rather than an act, in its failure to confront the most urgent problems facing the Cold War world. Reviewing the Tate show in the *New Statesman*, the realist painter and Marxist critic John Berger effectively accused the arm-swinging, paint-flinging makers of these 'violated canvases' of culpable irresponsibility:

> *For their own sake these slashed, scratched, dribbled-upon, violated can-vases would not be worth taking seriously. The disturbing fact is that many intelligent, talented people do take them seriously.... These works, in their creation and appeal, are a full expression of the suicidal despair of those who are completely trapped within their own dead subjectivity.... Behind these works is the same motive of revenge against subjective fears as there is behind the political policy of clinging to the 'protection' of the H. Bomb.*

The first thermonuclear bomb (hydrogen or H-bomb) – hundreds of times more powerful than the Hiroshima and Nagasaki atomic bombs – had been detonated by the Americans at Enewetak Atoll in November 1952. In 1954, against a background of cross-party consensus, Churchill had decided that Britain needed to develop a national H-bomb; the first test would take place in 1957. In Berger's view, artists who were not prepared to address this reality inhabited a disconnected world, in which 'intelligent, talented people' believed that any art that gave them pleasure must reflect some universally valid truth. Berger would himself soon stop painting, on the moral grounds that it was unlikely to accomplish humanity's more urgent task: preventing nuclear Armageddon. While the justice of Berger's cause was inarguable, Heron, who had recently been replaced by Berger as the *New Statesman*'s art critic, caught his Ruskin-like tone of crusading rectitude: 'The Berger ideals are beautifully Victorian,' he astutely teased.

Heron had plans of his own. In the winter of 1955–56, he left west London for a high-gabled Victorian mansion, perched on a granite outcrop overlooking the sea in Cornwall and aptly known as Eagles Nest. He had stayed there as a boy and had recently bought the house from the family of the Labour politician and amateur artist Will Arnold-Forster. Virginia Woolf had been a visitor; D. H. Lawrence had drafted *Women in Love* in a farmhand's cottage on the slope below; the emperor of Ethiopia Haile Selassie, deposed by Mussolini, had stared down from his bedroom window at boulder-strewn fields tumbling to the cliff edge and the sea. It was hard to imagine a remoter spot so intimately meshed with the fabric of elite metropolitan culture and politics. Where the Independent Group was intrigued by the unexpected meanings that found images and objects could connote, Heron felt that an artist's sphere of interest should be exclusively visual, uncontaminated by messages or intellectualization but cross-fertilized by experience of other art. '"Subjective" is always a term of out-and-out abuse if applied by Mr Berger to a painter's work,' he noted, writing his piece on the Tate exhibition the same month he moved his young family to Eagles Nest. On this question, he was firmly in the opposite camp. The terms had changed since Whistler – 'impressions' had become 'subjectivity' – but the question remained live: did art earn its place by reflecting contemporary society in readily recognizable form, or was art the means by which subjective experience could manifest in the wider world?

Colour was the test case. When Paolozzi cut out highly coloured American ads and cartoons for his scrapbook, the images and words were the point. Like the colour of toys or cars, this colour was illustrative, recreational. Colour didn't feature much as a subject in its own right in Independent Group debates; the illustrations in *The Mechanical Bride* – the original case studies for their exploration of pop – were all in black and white. Since the Festival of Britain, however, with its giant screen of coloured balls and other bright-and-breezy features, colour had become a powerful sign of newness and aspiration. After 'trudging through dingy Bradford streets to the cinema', the teenage David Hockney had an early intuition of what lay beyond in the 'marvellous, different world' of Hollywood Technicolor. Colour, for Heron, was absolute and real – not a matter of cultural semiotics. 'Colour is both the subject and the means,' he asserted, 'the form and the content; the image and the meaning'. He, too, felt that he was striking out into the new: 'Painting has still a continent left to explore, in the direction of colour (and in no other direction). Painting, like science, cannot discover the same things twice over.' For an artist who had little technical interest in scientific phenomena of the kind that intrigued, say, Hamilton, Heron's engagement with colour had an almost scientific precision and passion. It was as if he were seeking to recreate within the greyscale cultural landscape of mid-1950s Britain the Côte d'Azur colour-world of Bonnard and Matisse. His descriptions of the granite moorland around his Cornish home sometimes even have an air of *Galaxy Science Fiction* terrain, where the light behaves differently from elsewhere on planet Earth: 'this light seems to be travelling in all directions simultaneously so that it goes round the corners and illuminates the shadowed side of things'.

You could equally relate these kinds of kinetic, unexpected light effects to exhibits in 'Growth and Form' – the point being that Heron, like Cordell and her friends and associates in London, was on the trail of 'new images'; in his case, it was the landscape rather than comic strips or adverts that provided the found material – specifically, found colour. His 'Stripe' series – *Horizontals: March 1957* (pl. 13), for example, with its luminous overlaid strata modulating through midnight indigo, hot red, green, pink and yellow – was not, he insisted, as was often assumed a British riposte to the American titan of colour-field abstraction, Mark Rothko, but a subjective response to the western ocean sunset watched from his house. The emphasis on landscape, as a source rather than an explicit subject, linked Heron with Hepworth and Ben Nicholson as surely as the Independent Group had been determined to make a break from that generation. Now divorced, the two senior modernists were still working and living in St Ives, developing, although not fundamentally changing, the creative idioms they had honed in the 1930s. At the same time, like other artists – whatever Read's dim view of Hollywood – they watched American movies at the local cinemas, bought transistor radios and tuned in to rock 'n' roll.

'Gold Pan Alley' was not the last word from the former comrades-in-arms of the Independent Group. On 9 August 1956, the exhibition 'This Is Tomorrow' opened at Whitechapel Art Gallery. Thirty-seven artists, designers and architects had collaborated in groups of two, three or four to create twelve separate installations, each on a different theme – some more clearly defined than others but all intended to float questions, as much as provide answers, about life in the near future. Hamilton's original concept for 'Growth and Form' had involved a much larger exhibition space than the one provided by the ICA at Dover Street. Here, in the generous spaces of the Whitechapel, he found scope to organize and inspire on a theatrical scale.

Hamilton, McHale and the architect John Voelcker (Group 2), assisted by Magda and Frank Cordell, produced an outsize cut-out of the poster for the 1956 big-budget sci-fi movie *Forbidden Planet*, in which a twenty-third-century starship travels faster than the speed of light. The cut-out represented Robby the Robot – the most sophisticated film robot yet developed, endowed with ethical artificial intelligence – cradling a sensuously supine Altaira (played by Anne Francis) in his chunky metal arms. Hamilton's poster for 'This Is Tomorrow' was a collage of American ads, featuring a medley of consumer goods – a television, a tape recorder – that until recently had been the stuff of British dreams but were now coming within reach of average-earning households. This ideal home is inhabited by a bodybuilder who grasps a phallic lollipop with the word 'Pop' on its wrapper, a swooning naked glamour model

Assembling the Group 2 exhibit for 'This is Tomorrow', Whitechapel Art Gallery, London, 1956; (left to right, on ladders) John McHale, Richard Hamilton and Magda Cordell, and (holding panel) Terry Hamilton, photograph by Sam Lambert

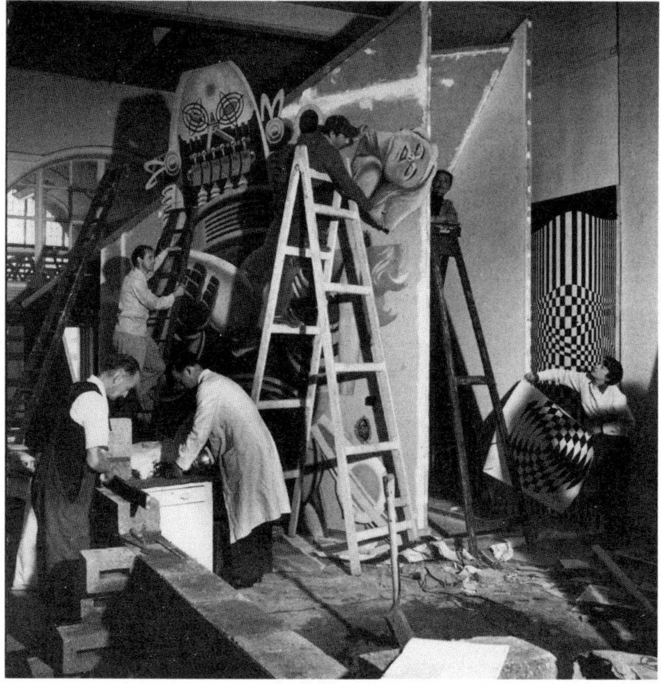

and a vacuum-cleaning housewife. Its title is a question-conundrum, pitched in an advert's chirpily cajoling tones: *Just what is it that makes today's homes so different, so appealing?* Group 6 (Paolozzi, Alison and Peter Smithson, and Nigel Henderson) created 'Patio and Pavilion', a cuboid wooden cell, part living room, part museum, in which were positioned Henderson's outsize photomontage of vegetables, stones and other raw objects configured as a human head, and fossil-like forms of various sizes described by Paolozzi as 'symbols for all human needs'.

In his catalogue introduction, Alloway explained that the twelve installations were 'display stands of ideas', collectively 'devoted to the possibilities of collaboration between architects, painters and sculptors'. In a Pathé newsreel about the show, visitors – both adults and children – are variously shown smiling tolerantly, pointing and chatting, scratching their heads. The exhibition's artists and architects 'point out that yesterday's tomorrow is not today', runs the voiceover, 'so maybe tomorrow won't be quite like you expect it'. Wide-eyed wonder or caustic scepticism – in some ways it hardly mattered. The essential thing, for Alloway, was that 'This Is Tomorrow' should be 'a lesson in spectatorship, which cuts across the learned response of conventional perception.' Or, as Group 1 (architect Theo Crosby, graphic designer Germano Facetti, sculptor William Turnbull and painter and designer Edward Wright) put it in their statement, 'The elements of this exhibition are not only the concern of the artist, they are yours. We share the same visual environment; we are all in the same boat.'

In the autumn of 1956, it felt as if the national boat was sinking. In the first week of November, against a background of economic recession, a bathetic encore to Britain's post-imperial fantasy of global policemanship played out on the banks of the Suez Canal. After attempting to retake control of the canal from the Egyptian government under President Nasser, a joint force of British, French and Israeli troops was forced to retreat after the expected American intervention failed to materialize. Conservative prime minister Anthony Eden's misstep in the Suez Crisis was decried – on the Left at least – as 'the greatest climb-down in history'. Then, in the midst of accusations of ministerial incompetence and cover-up, Eden promptly departed for a Caribbean holiday. At home, there was an impending cost-of-living crisis; petrol rationing was announced, along with a 40 per cent hike in fuel duty.

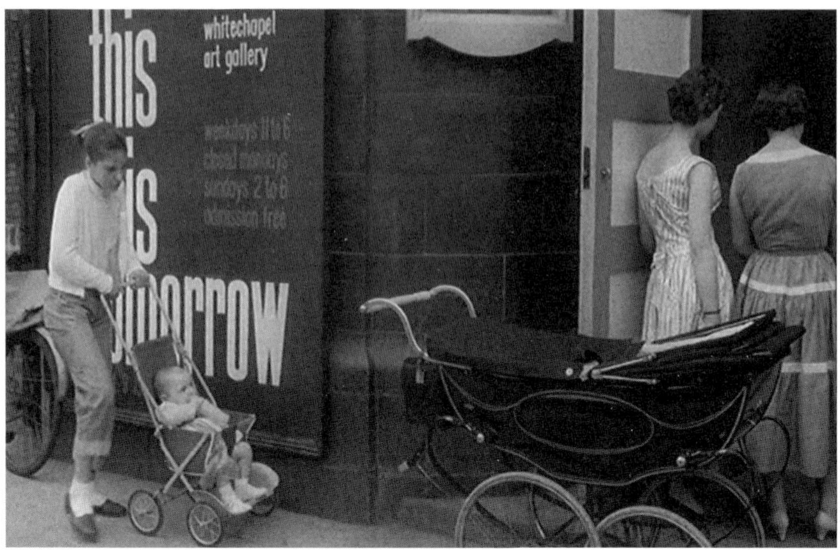

Film still from Pathé News documentary *The Face of Tomorrow*, 1956

The smoggy mood of fed-up stoicism, however, barely affected the young. People born after 1930 seemed to breathe a different air. 'What else happened in 1956?' asked *The Observer* in its round-up of this difficult year. 'Elvis Presley happened. So did Rock 'n' Roll.' The twenty-five-year-old J. G. Ballard, recently returned to England, paid a visit to 'This Is Tomorrow'. As a child in Singapore, he had been interned in a Japanese prison camp; after starting a medical degree, he had switched to English literature, then dropped that too, enrolled in the RAF and been despatched to Canada for training. His wartime experience had shown him what happens when 'The reassuring stage set that everyday reality in the suburban west is torn down [and] you see the ragged scaffolding.' When he discovered the 'wonderful exhibition' at the Whitechapel, Ballard was writing science fiction stories. The show struck him as a new kind of 'fiction for the present day' in which British society had been colonized by an alien version of itself:

I wasn't interested in the far future, spaceships and all that. Forget it. I was interested in the evolving world, the world of hidden persuaders, of the communications landscape developing, of mass tourism, of the vast conformist suburbs dominated by television – that was a form of science fiction, and it was already here.

15
Pop goes the easel

BBC television, Sunday evening, 25 March 1962

Peter Blake stands in the garden of a suburban house in Chiswick. He is sawing a door in half. Visible through the window behind him, on a washing line strung across the front room, underwear dangles. Blake is on television. While he patiently saws, a little self-conscious in front of the camera, the voice of BBC presenter Huw Wheldon gravely explains what we are witnessing. 'Blake is twenty-nine. He comes from Dartford in Kent, where his father is an electrician...his cheerful, uncompromising comments on the modern world have been exhibited at the Royal Academy, the Institute of Contemporary Arts, and so on, and he has sold pictures to all sorts of organizations, in America as well as in this country.' Against all appearances to the contrary, here is a young working-class artist who has – in terms that Monitor's *niche middle-class audience will recognize – arrived.*

———

It was seven years since Frank Cordell reported the advent of the 'garage-hand' star on the music scene. Elvis Presley, Buddy Holly – it started in America, then crossed the Atlantic; now it had spread from movies and music to theatre and art. The fact that artist Peter Blake was filmed gripping a saw instead of a paintbrush for the BBC's regular arts programme *Monitor* implied that he had graduated to being-on-television – a junior form of stardom – from the world of manual labour. The path that led from a working-class upbringing to the artistic spotlight had been travelled often before, but there was something about Blake's relationship to the camera – a feeling that, in a perfectly relaxed, confident way, he was acting a TV-friendly version of himself – that was different from Henry Moore's presence in an earlier episode of *Monitor*, solidly tweed-clad, benignly bald and wise, like modern art's cuddly headmaster.

A television was still an expensive item in 1962, costing around a month's average wage (two for women), but it was no longer an exclusive luxury. About three-quarters of British households now had one, often on rental or hire-purchase deals. At 9.55 p.m. on Sunday, 25 March, although only about 7 per cent of these sets were tuned to *Monitor*, that represented more than 1.5 million viewers. Over on the commercial channel, Independent Television (ITV) – the only alternative to the BBC – Alexander Korda's 1942 action movie adaptation of Rudyard Kipling's *Jungle Book* was in full swing. As a medium, television was widely mistrusted by those who considered themselves too highly educated to learn anything useful from it or to be leading such fulfilling lives that they had no need to resort to it for entertainment. In April 1961, the journalist and former spy Malcolm Muggeridge, one of television's new breed of celebrity eggheads, privately confessed to being 'always deeply distressed by seeing myself on television'. There was something 'inferior, cheap, horrible about television as such...only lies and insincerity will register on it'. Television made it possible, apparently, to exert personal influence on the nation's opinions while despising the means by which this was achieved. Prejudices of this kind, chiming with the earlier Bloomsbury superciliousness about cinema, had not prevented BBC television from covering contemporary art and artists in its public service remit from an early stage. In November 1936, just four years after the first television programme was transmitted from Broadcasting House, John Piper delivered an exhibition round-up, *Autumn Galleries*. From 1951, the series *British Art and Artists* presented short biographical films by John Read (son of Herbert), including features on Hepworth, Moore, Piper and Graham Sutherland.

By the late 1950s, as the Independent Group anticipated, art was in a different kind of relationship with mass media. Across the entire spectrum – art, film, music, television – more people had more choice in what they viewed or listened to. The informational narrative manner in which television had tended to cover the arts was beginning to feel wordy and wooden. *Monitor*, launched in February 1958, was designed to inject a livelier topicality and variety of content. Adopting the presenter-led magazine format pioneered for current affairs in *Panorama* and *Today*, these fortnightly forty-five-minute programmes focused on books and theatre as well as art. Like a fair-minded but conservative fellow traveller, Wheldon mediated good-humouredly between what were assumed to be viewers' traditionalist tastes and the shock of the new – or the not so new. His modus operandi, quipped his sometime assistant and successor Jonathan Miller, was that of a 'middlebrow artistic big game hunter, who went out into the veldt with a shotgun and Henry Moore fell out of a tree'. For some, like the left-wing playwright Dennis Potter, *Monitor* was a prime example of the BBC's bourgeois-paternalistic seizure of the whole idea of 'culture'. 'Culture has become too suspect for too many people,' was his take on the situation in 1962. Television should instead be working against the entrenched tastes and agendas of class: it 'can help, must help, break down these false barriers'.

Yet *Monitor* was – like television more broadly – a training ground for new directorial talent, and a vehicle that brought together visual art, social comment and elements of performance. In 1960, John Schlesinger directed an edition titled *Private View*, in which he tracked four young artists – Sonia Lawson, Anthony Whishaw, James Howie and Allan Rawlinson – through their London haunts. Opening with the literal pop of a champagne cork ('A launching ceremony, or the meeting of a secret society?' asks Wheldon's voiceover), it unfolds more like a social documentary, on the model of *Terminus*, Schlesinger's recently filmed piece about Waterloo Station for London Transport Films, than an arts feature. Although the young artists had all started to be exhibited and recognized, they appear like outcasts, making ends meet in down-at-heel lodgings, walking the dingy streets alone. When a West End dealer steps aside from her clients to glance at the paintings an unnamed young artist has brought into a gallery, he appears warily tensed for humiliation.

Early in 1962, Wheldon commissioned Ken Russell to make *Pop Goes the Easel*, a forty-minute film about another three-man, one-woman quartet – Peter Blake, Derek Boshier, Pauline Boty and Peter Phillips – all current or former Royal College of Art (RCA) students, all in their twenties. 'They're four painters,' Wheldon begins his commentary, eyeballing the viewer like a consultant about to deliver a diagnosis, 'who turn for their subject matter to the world of *pop art*.' He unfolds his hands as if to say 'bear with me', but presses on:

> *the world of the popular imagination, the world of film stars, the twist, science fiction, pop singers – a world which you can dismiss, if you feel so inclined, of course, as tawdry and second-rate, but a world, all the same, in which everybody to some degree lives, whether we like it or not…. Anyway, as far as these four painters are concerned, it's a world packed with its*

own mythology, its own heroes, its own heroines, its own poetry, and they approach it with the utmost relish.

He speaks in front of a screen or wall collaged all over with post-cards and magazine cuttings – photos of Elizabeth Taylor, Rudolph Nureyev, Elvis Presley and Marilyn Monroe, John Everett Millais's *Ophelia* and John William Waterhouse's *The Lady of Shalott*, infantas by Velázquez, Mughal miniatures, Japanese prints.... When, ten years ago, Paolozzi treated a small group gathered at the ICA to a slideshow of pages from American magazines, 'pop' was a serious thinker's subject. Wheldon still makes it sound serious, but Blake's pinboard miscellany – American stars meet pre-Raphaelite painters, famous Old Masters nudge up against cigarette cards – looks as if it has been put together by someone genuinely having fun.

The term 'pop' as a shortened form of 'popular' had been around since the nineteenth century. McLuhan's 'pop kulch' of the post-war years was a cross-generational phenomenon in which newspaper readers together with consumers of self-improvement books, shoes, cars and cod liver oil of all generations participated. 'The pop-art of today,' wrote Alison and Peter Smithson, in the November 1956 edition of the RCA house journal *Ark*, was the modern equivalent of the market-driven art of previous eras – the Dutch still life or the 'Wonder of the Machine Age' Victorian engraving – and could be found 'in today's glossies bound up with the throwaway object'. This kind of pop was conceived as modern-history-in-the-making. Around 1960, however, pop's meaning shifted: it came to define and be defined by a more specific demographic. *Melody Maker* magazine's introduction of a weekly listing of new releases head-lined 'Top of the Pops' in April 1956 signalled an increasingly exclusive association between pop and youth. Where 'pop culture' sounded aca-demic and middle-aged, pop music, pop songs, pop art, pop anything was stuff young people liked. *Pop Goes the Easel* was about art, for sure, but primarily it was about being young.

Youth had received a very mixed press throughout the 1950s. There were simmering anxieties about juvenile delinquency or 'The Trouble with Youth', commonly attributed to the replacement of violent corporal punishment by a 'dangerously soft attitude' on the part of parents and authorities, and the insidious substitution of psychological assessment for the traditional moral certainties of right and wrong. Newspapers carried regular scare stories and opinion pieces about Teddy Boys and their girls: the flick-knife 'gang battle' at St Mary Cray station in Kent in April 1954 received wide coverage. In 1956, when British cinemas screened the hit Hollywood movie *Rock Around the Clock*, in which Bill Haley & His Comets, kitted out in matching jackets and bow ties, get a sedate function-room audience jiving on the dance floor, it sparked a series of so-called rock 'n' roll riots, which sometimes spilled out on to the streets.

The same year, John Osborne's *Look Back in Anger* premiered at the Royal Court Theatre, London; its lead male character, Jimmy Porter – intelligent, working class, uncompromising in his scorn for British social norms – embodied a disruptive new figure on the scene, the Angry Young Man (or AYM). Despite the fact that National Service continued to be mandatory for young men between 1949 and 1960 (with the last recruits discharged in 1963), there was resentment on the part of war veterans, especially those who were still technically young, that men and women not much younger were enjoying youth with a freedom and (Wheldon's word) relish they had been denied. At the age of twenty-two, the sculptor George Fullard, a Sheffield contemporary and west

Jean Rayner, photographed by Ken Russell, from his series *The Last of the Teddy Girls*, 1955

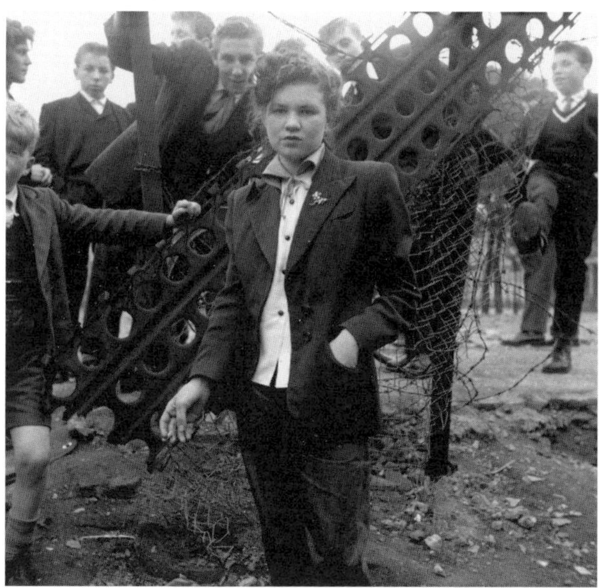

London housemate of the painters Jack Smith and Derrick Greaves, had almost lost an arm at the Battle of Monte Cassino in 1944. Trying to get his career started in the early 1950s, when the 'garage-hand' star was on the ascendant, he scribbled a Jimmy Porterish note to himself. Being working class, as Fullard was, had become less of an obstacle for an artist, but it helped considerably if you were also vigorously, youthfully young:

> As life resumes it[s] more normal course in the years after the war the natural animal energy of youth is once more manifest at home. The youth becomes a rediscovered novelty – It becomes the thing to be young and the post war youth becomes news over the war dead bodies of its immediate predecessors. The war-aged survivors of conflict, even though some of us... at the end were well under 25 years, emerged with that sense of humility and awareness that comes to the survivor of a catastrophe.

In the film *Private View*, the four young artists separately express a sense of individual determination and a touching air of existential disconnect – what the nineteen-year-old debut playwright Shelagh Delaney described in 1959 as a state of 'enraptured frustration'. They are on the threshold of the 'art world', whose 'private language' is spoken by fawning dealers and chequebook-wielding collectors. Being young in this world involves a wry acceptance that you will either be ignored and misunderstood, or – 'one of the worst things that can happen', says Whishaw – experience early success 'and not in fact go on seeking into yourself and finding out new things'. Two years after *Private View*, as the camera follows Blake, Boshier, Boty and Phillips in *Pop Goes the Easel* – through a funfair, a circus dressing room, a street market, a louche medley of bedsits and studios, and an artists' party – the foursome interact only with each other or with other artists of their own age. If contemporary art has its insider's patois, it is they, not the 'secret society' of the old establishment, who are now its native speakers.

'All of them live close to each other,' Wheldon reveals. 'They're very much a *group*.' There were pop groups, too (a term first recorded in print in 1963): just before filming started on *Pop Goes the Easel*, a group of four twenty-something musicians (all men this time), who lived close to each other in Liverpool – Paul McCartney, John Lennon, George Harrison and Pete Best – recorded fifteen songs in the Decca Studios in London. At Abbey Road Studios in June 1962, now under contract to EMI, the Beatles recorded 'Love Me Do' and 'Ask Me Why' with the same producer, George Martin, with whom Frank Cordell had worked in the 1950s. Their manager, Brian Epstein, charged £50 for a gig – slightly less than an entry-level television set and exactly half the price of one of the twenty-four-year-old Boshier's larger paintings.

Introduced and interviewed in turn, the *Pop Goes the Easel* artists all confess to being hoarders with eclectic tastes, as if they had collectively sealed a pact to transform their teenage bedrooms into living museums of art – the opposite of modernist white walls and simplicity. And if Robby the Robot was 'This Is Tomorrow''s transatlantic mascot, the bust of Queen Victoria in Blake's bedsit, along with a dressmaker's dummy customized to resemble a Victorian soldier's bemedalled uniform, set the tone here. At the same time, while youth 1962-style had its Peter Pan side, it was also – slightly coyly, as yet – more relaxed about sex than its parents' generation. In a fantasy sequence, Blake dreams about the French screen actress and sex-symbol Brigitte Bardot, of whom Dirk Bogarde, her co-star in *Doctor at Sea*, had said, 'The kind of sex she suggests is warm, uninhibited and completely natural' – making her, it hardly needed saying in 1955, 'too much for British studios to handle'. In *Pop Goes the Easel*, waking up to the after-image of a naked, smiling Bardot is all part of an artist's working day. Blake points to a reclaimed door, which he's collaged with photos of female movie stars, singers, all kinds of images of ideal women: 'This is like livin' in Girls' Town.' Without apparent irony, the softly spoken, bearded grown-up adopts the 'private language' of teenage reverie. 'This picture's called *The Girlie Door*.' He mentions other doors and pictures featuring Kim Novak, Frank Sinatra, LaVern Baker, Shirley Temple. 'They're usually entertainers,' he explains.

Americana, Victoriana, Old Masters, circus posters, junk shop finds: what stops the Old Curiosity Shop of Blake's materiel seeming 'tawdry or second-rate' is a freshness of rediscovery that feels more like the way in which fashion and history relate than history and fine art. Or modern art, at any rate, with its venerable rhetoric of radical innovation and resistance to the idea that artists might also be 'entertainers'. Like art, fashion borrows from and adapts the past, with the difference that fashion takes uncomplicated delight in newness purely for the present moment. Blake slips a single from its cardboard sleeve, which forms part of a rock-star wall.

Oh well, I gotta girl
What a girl
I don't know whatta do

The montage of music, lyrics, pictures and people speaks of the moment and nothing before or beyond. Listening to Wheldon conversing on *Monitor* with Moore, about why the sculptor had to buy Cézanne's oil sketch for *The Great Bathers*, and his sense of profound sculptural kinship with the impressionist painter, felt very different – like a window on another, earlier way of inhabiting time. 'And like the others' – Wheldon is talking about Boshier now – 'he approaches the world of the present day, the world of the teeming city, with the keenest possible enjoyment.'

For his part, Boshier sounds well versed in McLuhan: 'I'm very interested in the whole set-up of the American influence in this country,' he muses, as he prepares his breakfast,

> *I'm interested in the, sort of, infiltration of the American way of life. And I think it's through advertising and advertising techniques that this infiltration has come through. I think the Englishman probably starts with America at the breakfast table, starting with the cornflake packets, which are American in design, American in packaging and American in the whole set-up, the giveaway gifts, the something-for-nothing technique…. The mass media and the American influence occurs in many of my paintings, as in this cornflakes painting…. I'm interested in the space race and everything that's connected with it. It's something to do with what's happening now.*

Space rockets, Buddy Holly, Abraham Lincoln – Boshier's student art-cave is a world of male heroes. And, despite the proxy presence of women in the work of *Pop Goes the Easel*'s young men – Blake's deadpan Bardot-worship, Phillips's studied transposition of porn-mag nudes into a painting – all three of their studios resemble male hobby-sheds, places where a mild obsession can be methodically pursued amid its offcuts. They all collect toys – Boshier demonstrates a clockwork robot and an ice-cream-licking clockwork monkey – as if to emphasize the fact that the stories they might be telling, or the histories they might be constructing, are rooted in their own early lives.

Boty's bedsit studio is an artist's space of a different kind. It contains a wicker chair identical to the one in Gwen John's *Corner of the Artist's Room* and – another John-like touch – a cat on the bed. When the boys arrive, they make themselves boyishly at home, riffling through her record collection, questioning her about her collages (pl. 14). These are whimsical takes on German Dadaists Max Ernst or Hannah Höch – none of the bold graphic colour or fixation on badges and signs the others share. They are dreamworlds rather than toy cupboards ('I've used the kind of atmosphere of the dreams in my collages'), events rather than displays. 'I often take the moment before something has happened,' she explains. 'You don't know if it's going to be terrible or if it might be very funny.'

Sonia Lawson in *Private View* appears in an unglamorous realist setting, coping with her elderly landlady's curiosity about the incomprehensible pictures her young lodger is painting. In *Pop Goes the Easel*, Russell is much less interested in Boty's creative practice than her looks. Where Blake, Boshier and Phillips come across as self-declared fans of Elvis or pinball machines or Yogi Bear, Boty – nicknamed at art school the Wimbledon Bardot – is presented as the star of her own show. In a one-minute sequence she back-brushes her thick blonde hair. In the relationship it reveals between artist/actress/model and director, this sequence, entirely unconnected to the film's art themes, is closer to what was happening in those same early weeks of 1962 in New York, where the young British *Vogue* photographer David Bailey was doing a fashion shoot around the city with an unknown model, Jean Shrimpton.

Pauline Boty in her studio room in Addison Road, Notting Hill Gate, London, 1963, photograph by Tony Evans

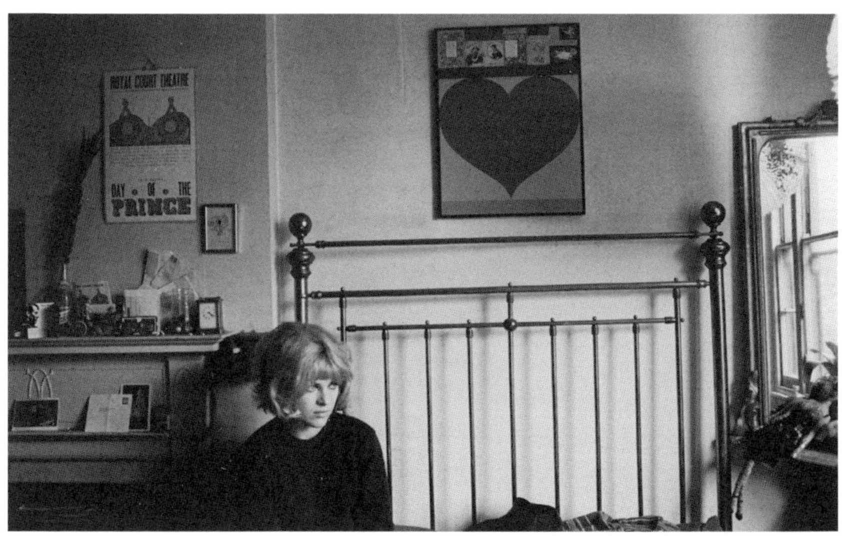

As in *Pop Goes the Easel*, a childhood toy – in Shrimpton's case a teddy bear – features in many of Bailey's shots. 'Soft', in a sneering, pejorative sense, was a term often levelled at 1950s youth and their supposedly indulgent parents, but the soft toy that accompanies 'the Shrimp' through the streets of New York, innocent but knowing, licensed for any intimacy and every kind of fun, is a kind of passport to a world in which youth can now make its own terms.

High on being young, the *Pop Goes the Easel* quartet ended their eventful day at a studio party, dancing the twist with gauche abandon. One of the guests can be seen flinging himself around in a dapper white jacket, with close-cropped, peroxide blond hair. After an unpromising start, David Hockney had become a student star (what other word was there?) at the RCA. In February 1961, he had been included for the second time in the annual Young Contemporaries exhibition at the Royal Society of British Artists Galleries, where the *Times* critic noted that 'abstraction, and particularly the improvised, American style abstraction, is "out", and...a new manner, sharply flavoured with the signs, slogans and mordant humour of metropolitan life, and emanating mostly from the Royal College of Art, is "in".' Phillips, 'with his colourful, heraldic evocations of press-button machines and amusement arcades', was the tendency's 'chief representative', but Hockney was named, too.

Youth was once again the theme. The Young Contemporaries show was, Hockney thought, the first time that there had been 'a student movement in painting that was uninfluenced by older artists in this country'. The backgrounds of Hockney's paintings shared the flat colour and graphic divisions of space adopted and adapted by Phillips, Blake and Boshier from comic books, fairground rides and other popular arts. He also incorporated handwritten and stencilled, or stencil-type, words and numbers. But his figures, whose boxed-in gestures of intimacy, isolation or abandon suggested a private graffiti world inhabited by quirkier but friendlier cousins of Francis Bacon's smeared and screaming protagonist-victims, felt as if they were not merely sign-bearers, they had a story to tell. It was, in part at least, a coded story about being gay in London at a time when any form of gay sex was still a criminal offence. The figures in *We two boys together clinging* look as if they have been chalked on a pavement by children, their togetherness somehow stronger, more out-there than if Hockney had done them as Charles Atlas he-men or Boshier-style astronauts. In *Doll Boy* a bare-legged boy, white-shirted like a martyr and labelled 'Queen', stands dejected beneath a scarlet geometric pattern suggesting both jaunty flags and prison bars. It was bought from Young Contemporaries by an art dealer, John Kasmin, who, at twenty-six, was only three years older than Hockney.

It was strange to think that people in Britain, both younger and older, looking for an alternative to the life around them – for freedom, style, sex, art, new ideas – had once been so uniquely fixated on Paris. This was still true, to some extent, in the decade after the Second World War, when Paolozzi had sought out Giacometti and Heron Braque. But by the early 1960s, the real cultural push-and-pull – the churning currents of influence and resistance – primarily took place across the Atlantic rather than the English Channel. Like attitudes to television, feelings about America polarized on the basis of age and class. 'The pursuit of happiness, which American citizens are obliged to undertake,' thought Muggeridge, trotting out a standard middle-aged, middle-class English view of America as a nation of infantile hedonists, 'tends to involve them in trying to perpetuate the moods, tastes and aptitudes of youth.' For British youth, especially art students, it was almost the reverse story: being young, like being American apparently, did mean wanting to perpetuate the moods and tastes of youth, but with a certain self-aware irony, not falling into helpless, gullible hero worship of the kind Muggeridge imagined. Blake balanced his rock 'n' roll enthusiasms with a personal image library culled from British vernacular art and the established cultural canon. Phillips hadn't caught his fascination with targets and assemblage-collage from fairgrounds so much as from the American artists Jasper Johns and Robert Rauschenberg; Russell filmed him cruising a west London flyover in a chauffeur-driven Chevrolet. At the same time, his drainpipe trousers, black polo-neck and studied, expressionless cool struck a European note of existentialist chic.

Although Americana was everywhere, it was still unusual for an art student to have had first-hand experience of New York. On 9 July 1961 – his twenty-fourth birthday – Hockney flew there for the first time. He was 'taken by the sheer energy of the place', finding it 'amazingly sexy, and unbelievably easy. People were much more open, and I felt completely free. The city was a total twenty-four-hour city…the gay life was much more organised, and I thought, "This is the place for me."' While he was watching television with friends at Long Beach one evening, an ad came on for Lady Clairol hair dye: 'Is it true that blondes have more fun?' Hockney returned to London in September with the cropped blond hair, American suit and white shoes he wore for the *Pop Goes the Easel* party early the next year. In 1966, he emigrated to the USA. 'I used to think London was exciting,' he mused, saying goodbye to the dreary lodgings and snooty galleries Schlesinger had chronicled in *Private View* and the cluttered bedsits and basement revels of *Pop Goes the Easel*. 'It is, compared to Bradford. But compared with New York or San Francisco, it's nothing.'

After returning from a visit to America, where he'd met the abstract painters Kenneth Noland and Jules Olitski, in December 1959, Moore's former assistant Anthony Caro didn't bleach his hair or don white shoes, but he did reinvent himself, both as a sculptor and as a teacher at Saint Martin's School of Art, where he found that that 'I could teach what I was discovering, not what I knew.' Noland and Olitski were younger than most of the first-wave abstract expressionists, whose work had landed with such impact in London in January 1956. They, too, worked big but with a more expansive, less furiously impulsive deployment of shape and colour. Caro, who had previously modelled his figure sculptures in a robust, demonstrably hand-formed fashion in the spirit of Moore, began constructing from welded steel sheets and girders, in the manner of the American sculptors David Smith or Herbert Ferber. At the suggestion of his wife, the artist Sheila Girling, Caro painted these constructions in bright red, yellow and green, like three-dimensional abstract paintings.

If Caro was effectively transplanting an American sculptural idiom to London, it was of a kind that stood in opposition to the British concept of American pop. The New York critic Clement Greenberg, the leading abstract expressionist theorist and kingmaker, was no friend to comic strips and television. He had nailed this kind of popular culture in 1939, in his essay 'Avant-Garde and Kitsch': compared to avant-garde art, 'the only living culture we now have', popular culture was 'rearguard'. Greenberg dismissed as 'kitsch' exactly the genres of American culture that had excited the Independent Group: 'commercial art and literature with their chromeotypes, magazine covers, illustrations, ads, slick and pulp fiction, comics, Tin Pan Alley music, tap dancing, Hollywood movies etc'.

At Saint Martin's, Caro convinced Frank Martin, head of the sculpture department, that they should urgently reform the teaching

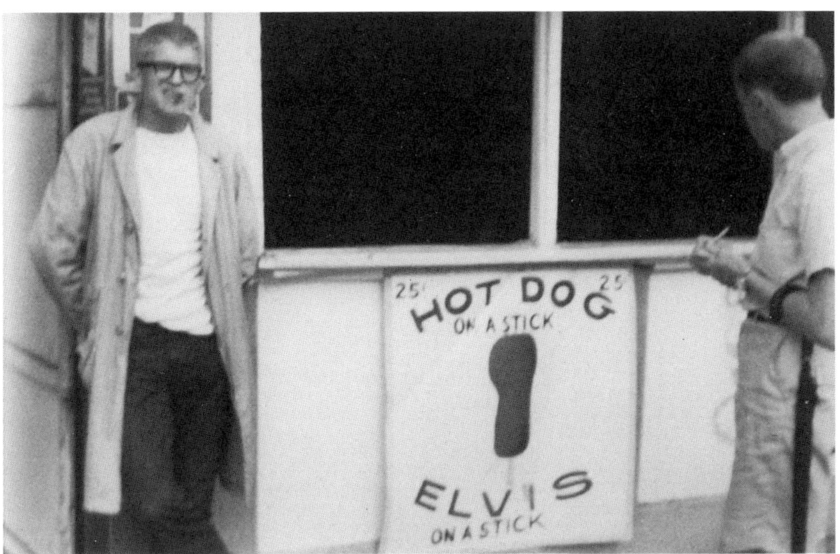

David Hockney and Billy Apple at Coney Island, New York, summer 1961

programme. From now on, it would not be founded on fixed ideas of sculpture involving solid forms but on open-ended questions about the nature of sculpture itself. Between them, they cleared the sculpture studios of every vestige of figurative art – the classical statue of Venus, the plaster casts of sculptures in the British Museum and the life-model's throne, which was 'the last thing to go but the important thing, the symbolic thing', recalled Martin. Sculpture, as debated by Caro and his students at Saint Martin's, now embraced events – the bodily sensations of walking, lying or sitting, for example – along with almost any materials or objects that could arouse feelings or stand in for events. 'Go into Soho,' he told his students, 'and find any rubbish you can and come back and make sculpture with it.... Make a sculpture of a scream, or a noise.'

Around 1960, then, America was pulling artists in Britain two ways: towards the topical appeal of pop, and towards a bold, revitalized avant-gardism, which might enlist the physical fabric of everyday life but spurned commercial imagery. What both tendencies had in common – and what made them both shout their difference from the Britain that people remembered from the 1950s – was colour. And colour, at this date, still belonged to artists. On British television before November 1969, with the exception of a BBC2 broadcast from Wimbledon tennis championships in July 1967, everything was in drizzly monochrome. In 1962, *Pop Goes the Easel* gave no hint that the colour in Blake's pictures was frank and lively. Over on ITV the same evening, *Jungle Book*, filmed in saturated Technicolor in 1942, was also in black and white. Unless you were actually standing in a gallery or studio, these were the tones of painting and sculpture on television and even in illustrated art magazines like *Studio International*. But 1962 was also the year in which this changed. In February, the *Sunday Times* published its first weekend colour supplement, 'A Sharp Glance at the Mood of Britain', including Bailey's photos of Shrimpton wearing a dress designed by Mary Quant, a former illustration student from Goldsmiths' College in London. In preparation for the new dawn of colour photojournalism, the paper had hired Antony Armstrong-Jones, a fashion photographer whose high-society connections had culminated in his marriage in 1960 to Princess Margaret, as whose husband he had been ennobled, taking the title Lord Snowdon.

In 1964–65, Snowdon teamed up with Bryan Robertson, director of Whitechapel Art Gallery and instigator of the 'New Generation' exhibitions that were proving a highly effective critical vehicle for the ascendant Youth-America-Colour spirit in British art, and the senior newspaper art critic John Russell to produce a book titled, like Schlesinger's *Monitor* film, *Private View*. Where the privacy in the first *Private View* entails a fly-on-the-wall intimacy with the trials and hopes of young artists in an austerity-tinted London, Snowdon *et al.*'s hefty, glossy book is private in the sense of behind-the-scenes glimpses of glamorous lives and exclusive friendship networks. Subtitled 'the lively world of British art', it captures a symbiosis of two generations. The post-war cultural establishment appears in the guise of middle-aged, Savile-Row-suited men, such as Kenneth Clark, the National Gallery's director Sir Philip Hendy and Tate Gallery director Sir John Rothenstein (son of the artist and former head of the RCA William Rothenstein). Art critic Denys Sutton fondles the bottom of a marble female nude. Keeper of the Queen's Pictures Sir Anthony Blunt squints expertly at a Kodachrome transparency of a head by Picasso, betraying no sign that he has just reached a secret immunity deal protecting him from prosecution as a Soviet spy. More prominent, however, is the large cast of self-possessed, camera-friendly young artists who share with their older eminent contemporaries in the atmosphere of contagious confidence, like guests at an unusually relaxed society wedding. The artists are once again overwhelmingly male, although Hepworth appears, striding a wintry Cornish beach in dark slacks and shaggy black fur coat. A thirty-three-year-old Bridget Riley is poised for New York success with her showing in 'The Responsive Eye' in February 1965, the defining moment for op art. Snowdon frames her between panels from her vast *Continuum* (1963), its shimmering, spare geometries reflected in her pale pencil skirt. How surprising, Russell remarks, to discover that paintings with such 'self-perpetuating energy' are not the work of 'a tenacious and fifty-ish she-gorilla' but a young woman 'who looks as if one could pick her up with the nearest pair of tongs'.

Pop Goes the Easel's take on the now was a do-it-yourself theatre of visual prompts assembled from American cereal packets and photos of Marilyn Monroe. As a student, Blake had improvised his first pair of American-style jeans – almost unobtainable in Britain before the 1960s – by cutting the bib off a blue boiler suit. By contrast, the images in *Private View* present a suave, well-oiled creative economy in which Britain's cultural grandees, patrons and opinion-formers, art schools and galleries and the artists themselves inhabit a social landscape through which exhibiting opportunities and money frictionlessly circulate. Hockney smokes a cigar in a bright red cardigan; Richard Smith balances in a hammock on stars-and-stripes cushions. In page after page, art renews the passport, current in London since Cave of the Golden Calf days, that allows the bearer to cross all social and geographical borders – between, say, Hockney's London of self-discovery and young fashion, and Lucian Freud's grimmer, grimier city, in which he clings on to his Delamere Terrace flat as the wrecking balls of post-war regeneration swing ever closer. New York dreams are meaningless for Freud, who believes that it is 'mad to think of travelling anywhere when there are parts of London I haven't visited'. Yet here he is in *Private View*, staring in cropped full-face straight to camera, or loitering nonchalantly beside a stately vintage car, almost the only vehicle in a once-grand but seemingly derelict nineteenth-century street. Few painters, the caption explains, 'can be more hypnotic in close-up: and as he has a habit of living by extremes, it happens that his motor car is a Rolls-Royce and his apartment one room in a condemned terrace near Paddington'.

The text of *Private View* largely consists of an extended conversation between Robertson and Russell in which they share their insiders' insights into how the cogs of the British art world turn. The promotion of artists 'who have a real chance of entering the big league' was, thought Russell, 'left to a small group of newish firms', among which he mentioned Kasmin, pictured on the facing page sitting side by side with his blue-blood bankroller and business partner Lord Dufferin in a corner of their new white minimalist space off Bond Street, surrounded by Noland's target paintings. Commercial galleries had begun, observed Robertson, 'to specialize in certain age groups as well as a particular kind of art'. Kasmin specialized in young artists, and in Hockney in particular. His private views were art-passport events par excellence – art, money (old and new), fashion, ancestry, stardom – with full-colour platforms for his artists, such as *Vogue*, the *Sunday Times* magazine and *Private View*.

In his previous job, working for Harry Fischer and Frank Lloyd at Marlborough Fine Art, Kasmin had done his best to introduce young artists, some of whom he'd met while learning his trade as an assistant at Victor Musgrave's smaller, more experimental Gallery One. John Latham, for example, a former public schoolboy and torpedo boat pilot who had studied as an ex-serviceman at Chelsea School of Art and had adopted spray-paint as his medium of choice. In 1958, Latham had made *The Burial of Count Orgaz*, a tribute to a painting of the same title by the sixteenth-century Spanish artist El Greco. Cannibalizing an old bar billiards table, he'd smeared it with plaster, into which he embedded twenty-one splayed and blackened books, along with miscellaneous other objects, including a spoon, sponge, gas pipes, wire, keys and rags. Like Blake and Boshier's collaged paintings, with their jaunty assimilation of vintage tat and Americana, Latham's *Burial* acknowledged Rauschenberg's 'Combines' – his *Bed* of 1955, for example, in which a sagging, paint-swiped pillow and quilt bulge from the upright rectangular frame. Latham built on Rauschenberg's messiness, making it messier, if anything, and his ideas were not likely to fit well with the social 'class and atmosphere' with which Fischer and Lloyd sought to infuse their business. Moving on from spray-guns, Latham was becoming interested in deforming or destroying books, because books were more often full of lies than truth.

'No,' said Fischer and Lloyd to Kasmin's suggestion. That kind of provocative junk had no place in the lively, colourful world of British art.

16
Square bashing

Braziers Park, near Wallingford, Oxfordshire, July 1964

What is that smell? Last night in the drawing-room at Braziers Park, everyone was sitting cross-legged, stoned, listening to jazz records that the American writer Clancy Sigal has brought with him to this 'weekend conference' in the country. The poet Jeff Nuttall turned in earlier than some. This morning, while they are sleeping it off, he wakes to a 'cheap, scented, chemical kind of smell'. He leaves his room to investigate, thinking vaguely he might make a start on the clearing up. As he descends the wide, wood-panelled staircase, the smell gets progressively stronger. He opens the drawing-room door. John Latham meets him with a level, manic stare. Latham has taken a book – an irreplaceable book belonging to someone else in the house, a Chinese friend of the Scottish novelist Alex Trocchi – stuck it to the wall with Polyfilla paste, then spray-painted both the book and the wall around it black. The blackest of black chemical blacks. So that was what he smelled, 'a big explosion of night'. Otherwise, Nuttall notes with some relief, the site of yesterday's chaos – the cigarette butts, the empty demijohns of home-made booze, the half-scooped cans of food and sandwich crusts – is unexpectedly tidy. 'There's something about Latham at such moments that is mad beyond madness,' he thinks. 'A staring immovable shocked and shocking inner violence.'

As it turned out, the aerosol-blackened book and wall – a development from Latham's *Burial of Count Orgaz*, where the action was contained inside a frame – was one of the more definite statements to emerge from the summer weekend in deepest Oxfordshire. In his 'Project Sigma' to establish what he called a 'spontaneous university' or anti-university – a centre for 'invisible insurrection' – Trocchi had identified Braziers Park as a potential base. This crenellated mansion in Strawberry Hill gothic style had since 1950 been home to the School of Integrative Social Research, a commune dedicated to exploring 'the dynamics of people living in groups' and fostering 'better methods of interpersonal communication'. The singer Marianne Faithfull, daughter of one of its leading members, who lived there until the age of seven, remembered Braziers as 'a bit of a mad house', where 'well-intentioned men and women…appeared to be studying Dante and the Destiny of Man and all that, but what they were also doing was fucking like rabbits'. Ten years later, the commune's 'wilder, madder, more eccentric' early phase had passed. To Nuttall, it was 'a little colony of quiet, self-sufficient middle-class intellectuals, totally square with heavy overtones of Quakerism and Fabianism'. But, all the same, Trocchi felt, a promising spot, with a building 'large enough for a pilot group (astronauts of inner space) to situate itself, orgasm and genius, and their tools and dream-machines and amazing apparatus and appurtenances'. The anti-university would perhaps resemble Black Mountain College, the experimental arts college in North Carolina that had been founded, like Dartington, in the 1930s and had similarly welcomed Bauhaus refugees on to its staff.

Together with Latham, Nuttall, Sigal and Trocchi, other 'astronauts of inner space' who assembled at Braziers in July 1964 included the radical 'anti-psychiatrist' Ronald (R. D.) Laing, the South-African psychiatrist David Cooper, playwright Tom McGrath and psychiatrist Aaron Esterson. It did not take long, however, for the 'cultural "jam session"' to self-destruct. 'Wine got into people like the sun got into butter,' Nuttall observed. In the general wooze of spaced-out anarchy, Latham alone availed himself of the opportunity to construct something. In the grounds outside, he stacked opened books on top of each other, edge-to-edge and spine-to-spine, in a 3-metre-high chimney, then lit a fire at the base, which took two hours to consume the books. Latham called it a 'skoob ceremony' ('books' spelled backwards) – an example of his use, as a matter of principle, of what he termed 'non-received language'. Although it had obvious and terrible resonance with the Nazi era, this book chimney turning to glowing ash, which Latham would re-enact in a series of skoob events over the next few years, was emphatically not intended to echo Nazi propagandist Goebbels's book-burnings of the 1930s and the crematoria that followed. It was, rather, a kind of reality check on the global situation in the mid-1960s, in which books as vehicles of knowledge and culture could no longer be enjoyed as if book culture bore no relation to the ever-growing means of mass destruction being stockpiled by 'enlightened' Western democracies. For good or ill, books are material objects with metaphysical contents. In the painting by El Greco on which Latham modelled his *Burial*, an enthroned Jesus, the Virgin Mary, saints and angels crowd the upper half, while flames and prayers ascend from the courtly funeral party below. Books, too, mediate between earth and air, matter and thought.

Books – along with easels, models, paint-scabbed parquet studio floors and the sweet and sour fug of turps and cigarettes – were, of course, a familiar, sometimes life-changing, ingredient in the art school experience, especially for students who had not grown up among well-stocked bookshelves. 'I never read a book from start to finish until I went to art school,' Derek Boshier admitted, 'and then I read voraciously for the next five years' – Albert Camus's *The Outsider*, Vance Packard's *The Hidden Persuaders*, the letters of Vincent van Gogh, 'anything by Marshall McLuhan'. Students wanted to be seen with certain titles: 'It was the time of the Penguin paperback books, orange paperback books, that you put in your back pocket and you took it everywhere.' In university academic life, books were analysed and written about; in the practical setting of art school, reading more often segued into action. When Boshier talks about his work in the *Pop Goes the Easel* film, it's clear that Packard and McLuhan's ideas are catching light in the imagination of a previously unbookish twenty-four-year-old. Paintings had played many successive roles in the rhetoric of art over the past century: they had been impressions, explosions, explorations, records, events. Now, in the topical enthusiasms of the 1960s student generation, they were taking on a new identity as messages. In sharp contrast to the abstract expressionist ethos, paintings like David Hockney's *We two boys together clinging* (1961) or Boshier's *I Wonder What My Heroes Would Think of the Space Race* (1962) were sociable, talkative works that didn't seem to mind being explained.

This sort of direct spark between reading matter and witty, topical pictures was not for Latham, for whom books, as products of the 'Mental Furniture Industry', were as liable to impose false authority as to reveal the truth. In the 1960s, the 'lively world of British art', with its photogenic cocktail of fashion, money and young, preferably authentic working-class talent, had its counterpart in 'the underground'. This term had evolved from its earlier sense of a political resistance group to designate a loosely defined transnational movement, defined by Nuttall as 'artists and alienated thinkers' and by *The Guardian*, favoured newspaper of the bourgeois left, as 'people who live outside the constraints of ordinary society', and who 'have come to the realisation of this new lifestyle through the use of cannabis and LSD'. Recreational drug use was far from being exclusive to the underground, however. Photographed by Lord Snowdon for *Private View*, Boshier found himself at parties also attended by Princess Margaret, who on one occasion 'was sitting on the floor...and she said "Have you got any dope?", and I said "I've got a joint", and we lit up'.

Nuttall traced the birth of the underground to the bombing of Hiroshima and Nagasaki. The realization that 'an evil had been precipitated whose scope was immeasurable' divided the generations: 'people who had passed puberty at the time of the bomb found that they were incapable of conceiving of life *without* a future', while those 'who had not yet reached puberty at the time of the bomb were incapable of conceiving of life *with* a future'. The result was the younger generation's loss of faith, total and irreparable, in the moral compass of its 'square' elders: 'No longer could teacher, magistrate, politician, don, or even loving parent, guide the young. Their membership of the H-bomb society automatically cancelled anything they might have to say on questions of right or wrong.' Teachers who, like Anthony Caro in the reborn sculpture department at Saint Martin's School of Art, encouraged students to question the basis of every aspect of their practice, had to be prepared for confrontation and rejections. In June 1963, Caro's student Barry Flanagan addressed a letter to him, asking:

> *Am I deluded, or is it that in these times positive human assertion, directed in the channels that be, leads up to the clouds, perhaps a mushroom cloud. Is it that the only useful thing a sculptor can do, being a three-dimensional thinker and therefore one hopes a responsible thinker, is to assert himself twice as hard in a negative way.... I might claim to be a sculptor and do everything else but sculpture.*

'This is my dilemma,' Flanagan concluded – a dilemma that confronted sculptors with particular urgency, because to sculpt was traditionally to assert the lastingness of an object and what it represented, an absurd activity in a world that might have no future.

In the context of pop, art was chic, art was fun, and America, the source of so many young artists' Technicolor dreams, existed as a purely

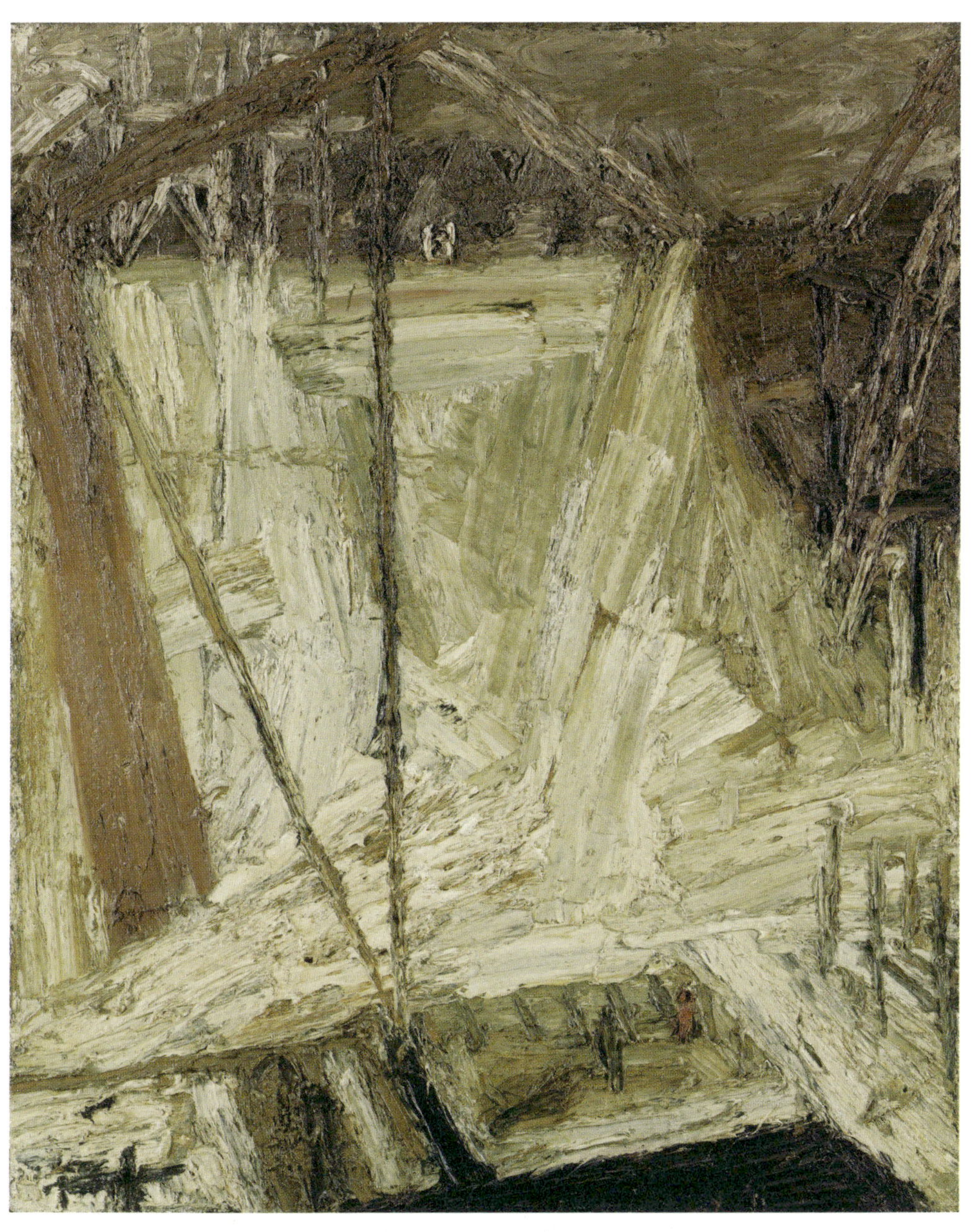

9 Frank Auerbach, *The Shell Building Site, from the Thames*, 1959.
Oil on canvas, 153 × 122.5 cm (60¼ × 48¼ in.)

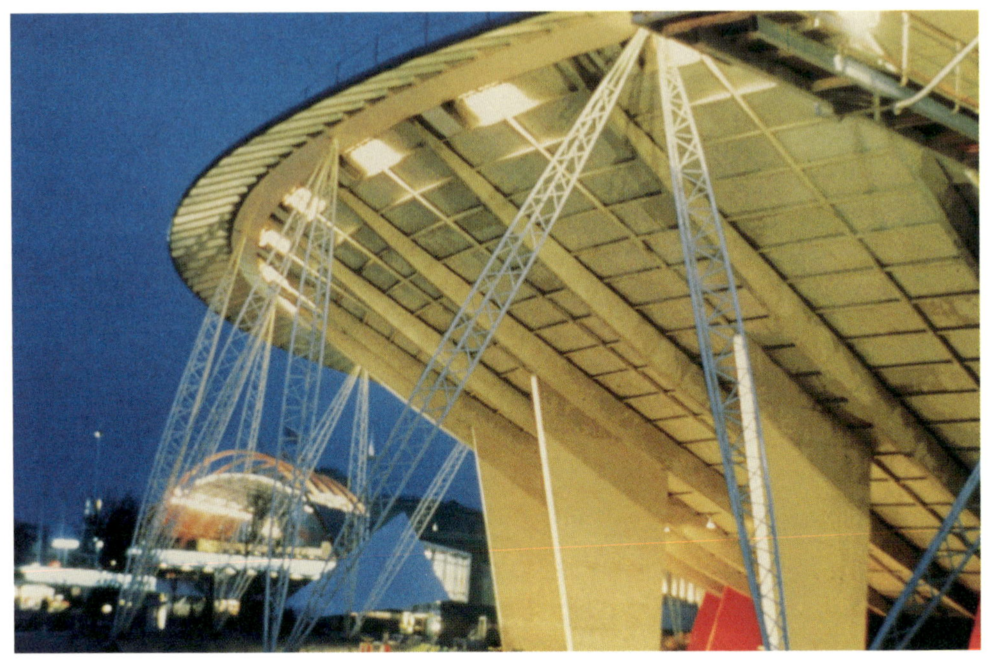

10 The Dome of Discovery on London's South Bank lit up for the Festival of Britain, 1951

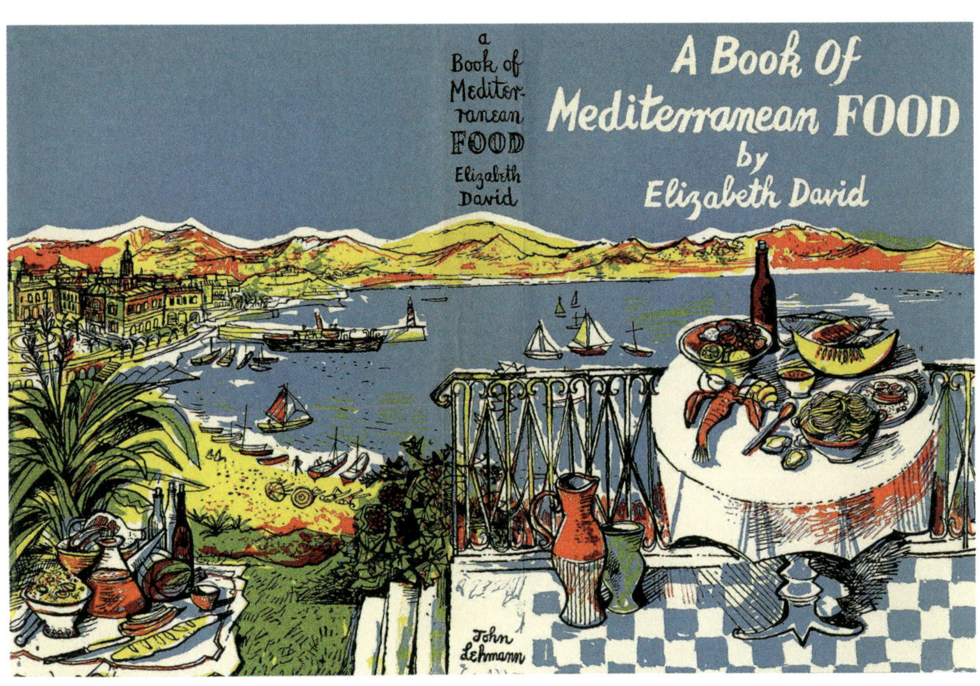

11 John Minton, cover of Elizabeth David's *A Book of Mediterranean Food*, 1950

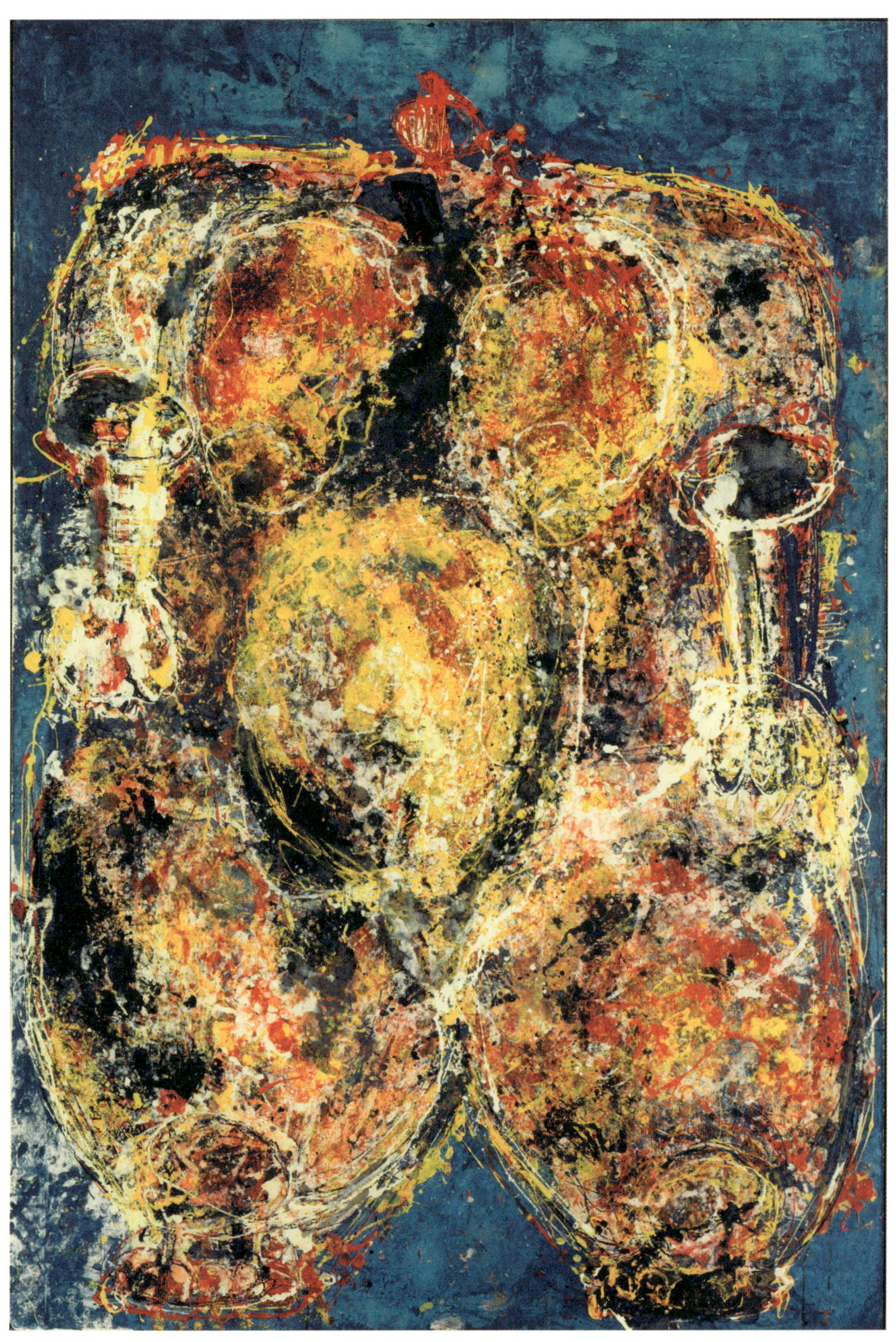

12 Magda Cordell, *Figure (Woman)*, 1956–57. Oil on hardboard, 231.2 × 152.2 cm (91⅛ × 60 in.)

13 Patrick Heron, *Horizontals: March 1957*, 1957. Oil on canvas, 122 × 56 cm (48⅛ × 22⅛ in.)

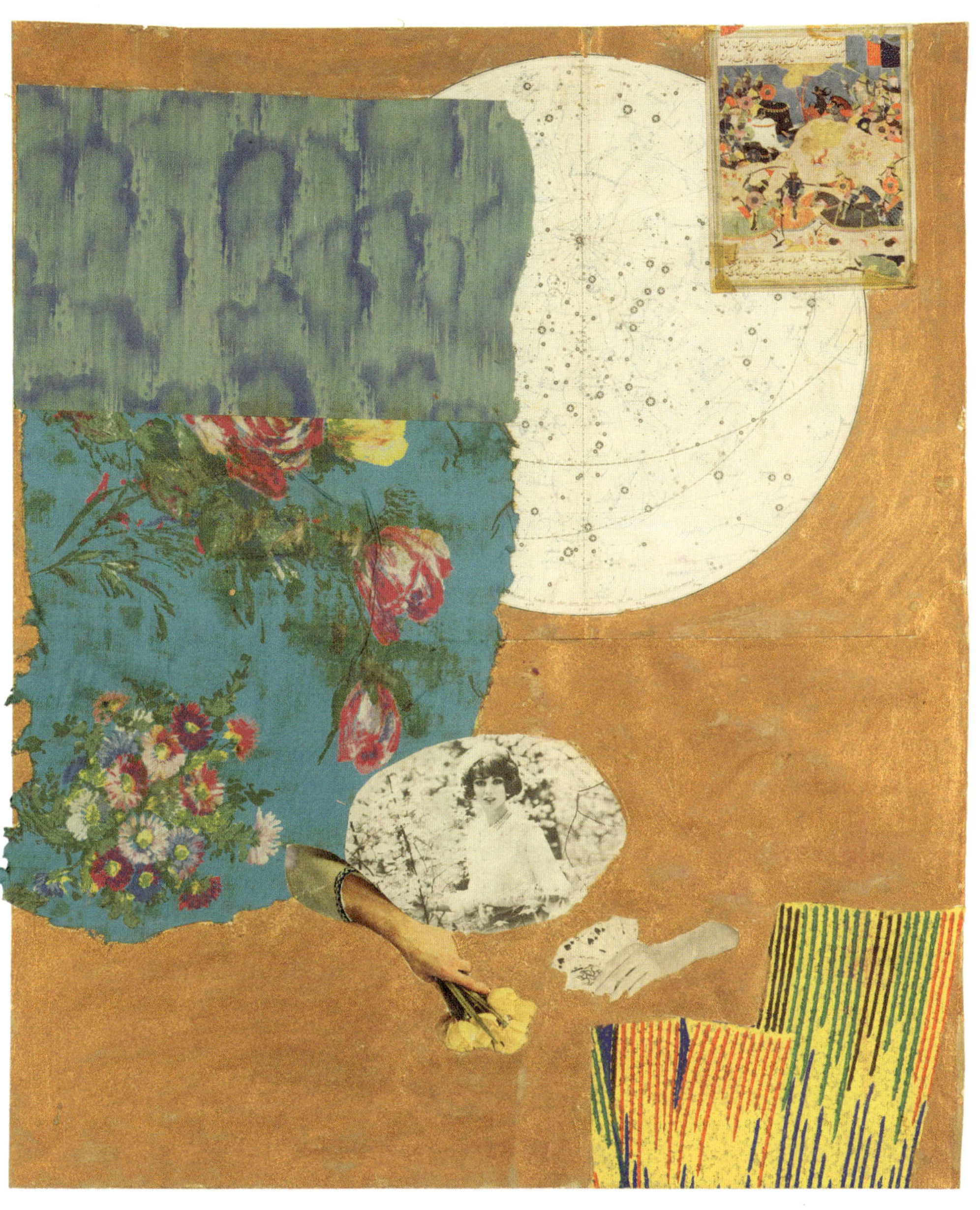

14 Pauline Boty, *Untitled*, *c*. 1961–62.
Mixed media and collage, 47.4 × 38.7 cm (18⅝ × 15¼ in.)

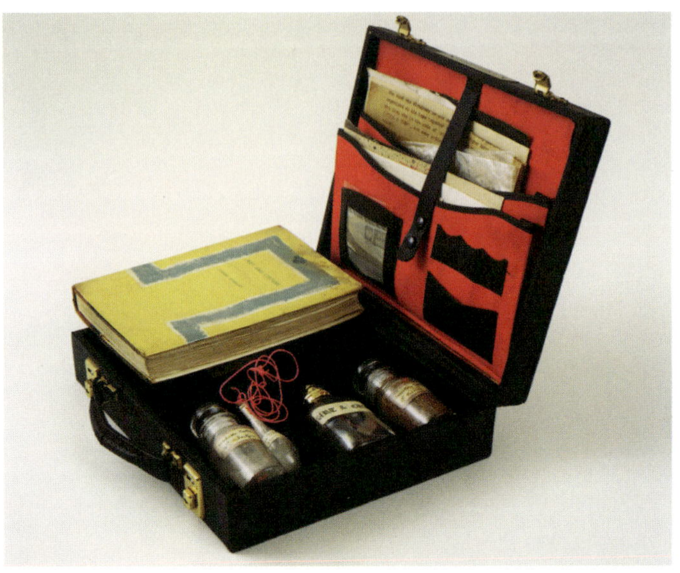

15 John Latham, *Art and Culture*, 1966–69. Book, labelled vial, flask and bottles containing liquid and powder, letters, document, invitation to the event 'Still and Chew' in leather case, 28.2 × 25.3 × 7.9 cm (11⅛ × 10 × 3⅛ in.)

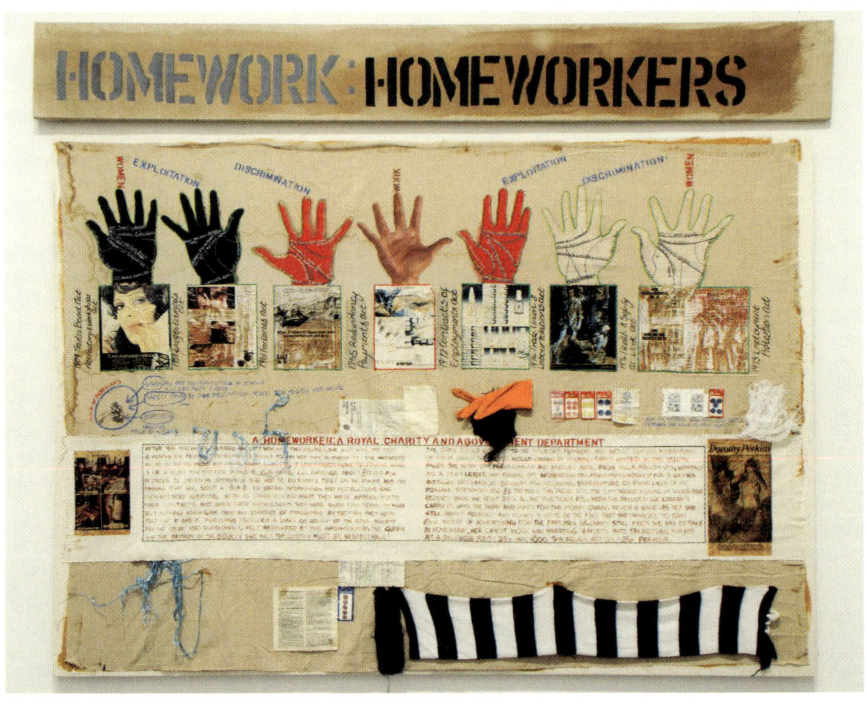

16 Margaret Harrison, *Homeworkers*, 1977. Acrylic paint, printed paper, linen, graphite, woollen scarf, 3 metal brooches, household glove, 29 plastic buttons and wool on canvas, 220 × 244 cm (86⅝ × 96⅛ in.)

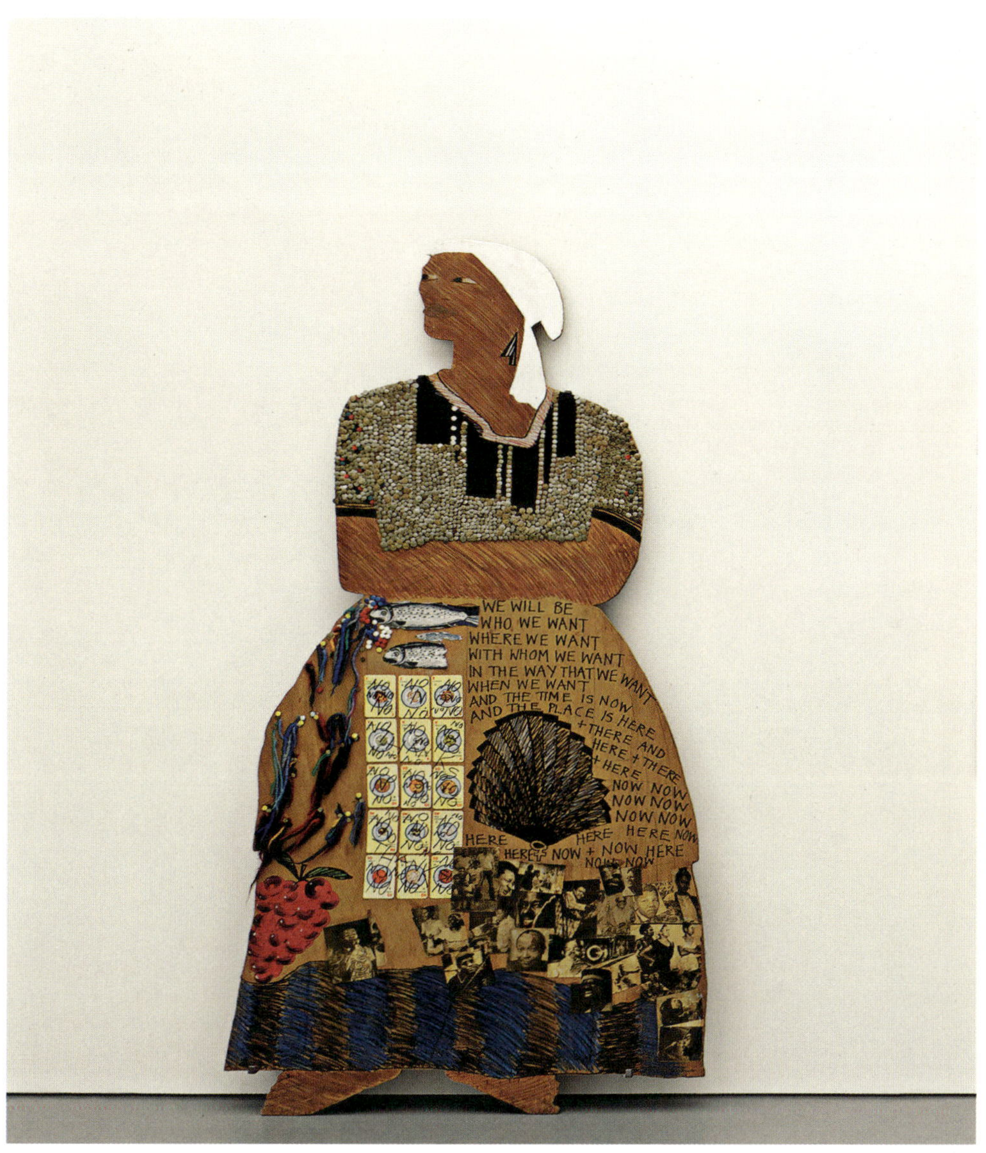

17 Lubaina Himid, *We Will Be*, 1983. Newspaper, pen, pins and acrylic on plywood, 200 × 90 cm (78¾ × 35½ in.). Installation view, 'The 1980s: Today's Beginnings?', Van Abbemuseum, Eindhoven, 2016

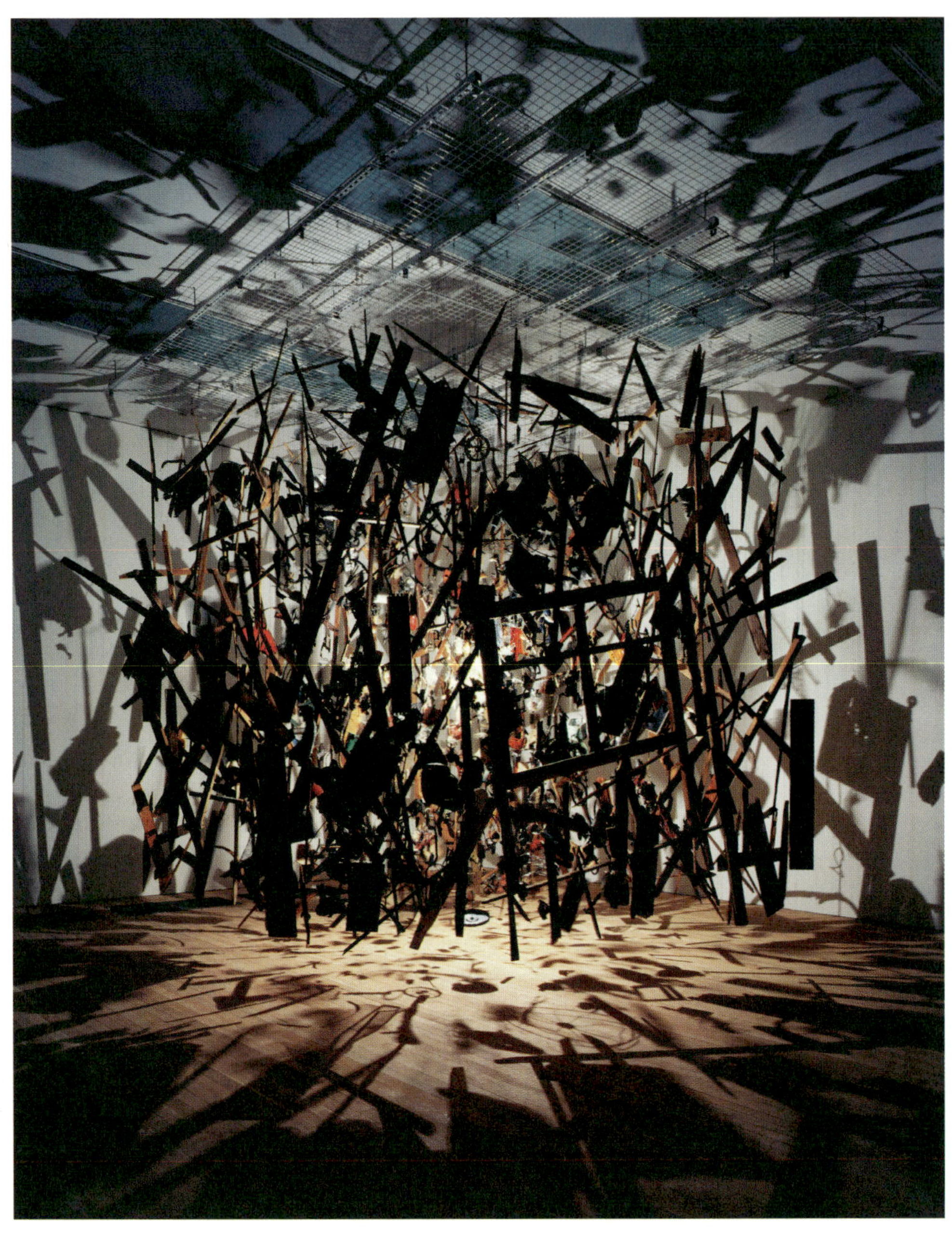

18 Cornelia Parker, *Cold Dark Matter: An Exploded View*, 1991. Wood, metal, plastic, ceramic, paper, textile and wire, 400 × 500 × 500 cm (157½ × 196⅞ × 196⅞ in.)

cultural phenomenon. To others, for whom art and the art market were by their nature political, post-war America was the opposite – a capitalist-imperialist power whose influence abroad was by its nature destructive. The McCarthy anti-communist witch-hunts, the nuclear arms race, the proxy wars in South-East Asia, first Korea and then Vietnam – if art was on the side of humanity and peace (few, apart from Italian futurists, had ever argued otherwise), then artists had to act. The underground's alternative to the status quo, retrospectively articulated by Nuttall in an eight-point agenda, included spreading 'an ego-dissolving delirium wherein a tribal telepathic understanding could grow up among men', expanding 'the range of human consciousness outside the continuing and ultimately soul-destroying boundaries of the political/utilitarian frame of reference', releasing forces 'that would dislocate society, untie its stabilizing knots of morality, punctuality, servility and property', and introducing 'a sense of festivity into public life whereby people could fuck freely and guiltlessly, dance wildly and wear fancy dress all the time'.

As an ex-forces painting student at Chelsea School of Art after the war, Latham had an early intuition that a career as a traditional painter was not for him: 'There were those that you could see going along with their easels and training themselves to be portrait painters or land-scape artists or whatever it is for the market. But not my friends, they were genuinely concerned to be doing something which would show them what was interesting and what wasn't.' By 1965, he had found a part-time teaching post at Saint Martin's, but was even further from accepting any authorized view of what was or wasn't interesting for an artist. Around the art school's corridors and studios, the authority of the older generation appeared to attract unmerited respect in the figure of the American critic Clement Greenberg. In New York, the heyday of Greenberg's influence had come more than a decade earlier, as the most eloquent advocate and theoretician of abstract expressionism. More recently, while berating post-war British sculptors such as Reg Butler and Lynn Chadwick for their 'insipidity' and 'nerveless elegance', Greenberg had become an enthusiastic supporter of Caro's constructed metal sculpture, seeing it as a development from American sculptors he had championed, pre-eminently David Smith. Caro himself frankly admitted that he owed his conversion to working in oxyacetylene-cut-and-welded metal to a conversation with Greenberg. Among Caro's students, and in consequence Latham's own, Greenberg's opinions about formal values in art retained 'persuasive power'. His *Art and Culture*, a collection of essays published in 1961, had accordingly become a favourite back-pocket book. Two more reasons for Latham's irritation at Greenberg was the American critic's dismissal of his own recent book-assemblages as 'patly cubist', and in a judgment delivered as chair of the jury for the 1965 John Moores Painting Prize in Liverpool, his lofty condemnation of almost all British contemporary painting, as being crippled by 'too good taste'.

All right then. What was the 'taste' of Greenberg's writings? Latham borrowed a copy of *Art and Culture* from the library at Saint Martin's and, with Flanagan's assistance, gathered together a group of students, critics and artists at his home to 'chew over' its contents. Each guest in turn tore a page from the book, stuffed it into their mouth and munched. Latham collected the saliva-softened pulp – about a third of the book – in a flask. He then added acid, neutralized the sugary residue with sodium bicarbonate and introduced an 'Alien Culture' to the gloopy mixture in the form of yeast, leaving it to ferment: 'several months went by with the solution bubbling gently.' Ten months later, when the library recalled the book, informing Latham that a student was 'in urgent need of Art and Culture', he returned a sealed vial containing the liquid 'essence' of Greenberg's thought. In June 1967, he was told that his teaching contract would not be renewed. Latham kept records of the experiment (a copy of the book, the overdue notice, the vials of fermented gunk), stored neatly in an attaché case (pl. 15). The Museum of Modern Art in New York bought his work *Art and Culture* in 1970, which confirmed Latham's conviction that he had no trouble communicating his ideas to audiences in America, in Europe – anywhere, in fact, outside Britain.

This wasn't the kind of story being told in *Pop Goes the Easel*, in which London appeared as a friendlier, shabbier, more relaxed home to the kind of creative energy associated with New York. Dipping into Bryan Robertson, John Russell and Snowdon's *Private View*, the impression given was that the world had fallen in love with Hockney's red cardigan and yellow hair, John Kasmin's chic white walls and Bridget Riley's zippy optical fields. 'London is the most swinging city in the world at the moment,' pronounced Diana Vreeland, editor of *Vogue*, in April 1965, in a phrase that would be endlessly echoed (by 1971, even Labour prime minister Harold Wilson's official receptions were said to have adopted 'a new swinging style'). No one seemed troubled by art's commodity status. The cycle of production and consumption – making, selling, buying, wanting more – was apparently what made art happen. Robertson observed that,

> *Young Contemporaries exhibitions during the past decade have focused our attention more and more on what very young artists are doing, and this, combined with the present cult of youth...has made us all more and more conscious of what's happening at the very source of it all, the art schools themselves.*

In *Monitor*'s *Private View*, young artists halt at the borders of the commercial world, as if sniffing its tainted but alluring air. Now the royal road to success might run – as it was doing for Hockney, Peter Blake and others – straight from art school. At end-of-term shows, Robertson reported, 'you find collectors and dealers – and certainly critics – on the prowl, eagerly intent upon a new discovery, anxious to get in on the ground floor of the career of some new and talented artist'. Or, as Trocchi put it, 'the best artists and fine minds everywhere... have usually been in revolt during their youth and have been rendered harmless by "success" somewhere around middle age'.

'Somewhere around middle age'? Not any more. In the wake of *Pop Goes the Easel*, Pauline Boty was getting plenty of offers. She played the lead role in Frank Hilton's farce *Day of the Prince* at the Royal Court Theatre in 1963, for which she also designed the poster. Boty and Boshier danced in *Ready Steady Go!*, the BBC's new pop music platform, launched that August. In September, she had a solo exhibition of twelve paintings at the Grabowski Gallery in Chelsea. It featured *Colour Her Gone*, an alter-ego-ish tribute to Marilyn Monroe, who had died in her mid-thirties the previous year, and *With Love to Jean-Paul Belmondo*, in which a portrait of the French movie star is capped with a luxuriant swollen-petalled rose and a row of love hearts. In 1965, Boty was cast as the lead in John Schlesinger's film *Darling* – or nearly. The part went to another newcomer, Julie Christie, who proceeded to win an Oscar. 'Something agreeable has happened in English life,' mused Robertson in *Private View*, citing as evidence of this sea change, 'that most native, though universally enjoyed of all poet-singer-comedian fraternities, the Beatles'. The group's hugely successful first American tour in the autumn of 1964 had made them rock 'n' roll celebrities on a level with Elvis and the other icons whose photos Blake had been filmed pasting up with wry veneration in his bedsit two years earlier. Robertson still wanted to claim the Beatles for the British scene: they were both 'very English in their words, music and wit' and living proof that a 'benevolent and quietly conducted, slowly unfolding revolution is under way, sociologically and aesthetically'. But what sort of *revolution* could possibly be 'benevolent and quietly conducted'? Was pop, with its inherent playfulness and wit, really an expression of revolutionary change – and where, if anywhere, could art and politics share a sphere of action?

Boshier, for one, didn't find this possible. After *Pop Goes the Easel* and his final year at the Royal College of Art, he travelled to India; on return in 1963, he joined the Socialist Labour League. 'I kept my political life and my art world life totally separate, and on purpose, almost, kept my work not political because my real life was political.' In 1966, he stopped painting; he went 'on lots of demonstrations for the Vietnam War', believing it 'to be more important for my life than just producing art'. In July, following news of American forces bombing civilians in Hanoi and Haiphong, four thousand protesters gathered outside the American Embassy in Grosvenor Square, chanting 'Hands off Vietnam'. The protest turned ugly; someone set fire to petrol, and there were thirty-one arrests. Kellogg's cornflake packets, model space rockets, Elvis Presley and Marilyn Monroe – all could still be found in art students' rooms, but their feelings about America and what it stood for were changing. 'Victory to the Vietcong' (the army of communist North Vietnam), the members of Youth for Peace in Vietnam shouted out on their way to Downing Street.

Boty, too, had moved into a more political phase. Painted in 1964, *It's a Man's World I* presents a Blake-style hero-wall, featuring heads of, among others, Marcel Proust, Albert Einstein, Muhammad Ali, John Lennon and Ringo Starr – novelist, scientist, boxer, rock stars, these men have all the fame. But at the base and top of this man's world – its two poles – are, respectively, a blurry but immediately recognizable panel in which President Kennedy slumps in the assassination of November 1963 and, in the upper-left corner against a holiday-blue sky, an American B-52 strategic bomber, built for Cold War service to be capable of dropping nuclear bombs. Boty's companion piece, *It's a Man's World II* is another pinboard anthology of cut-outs, this

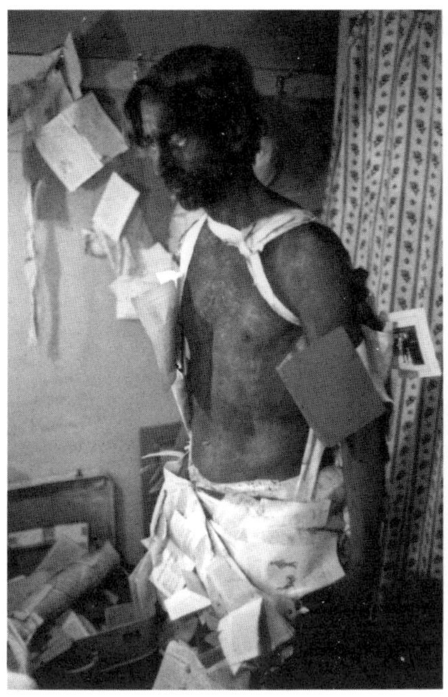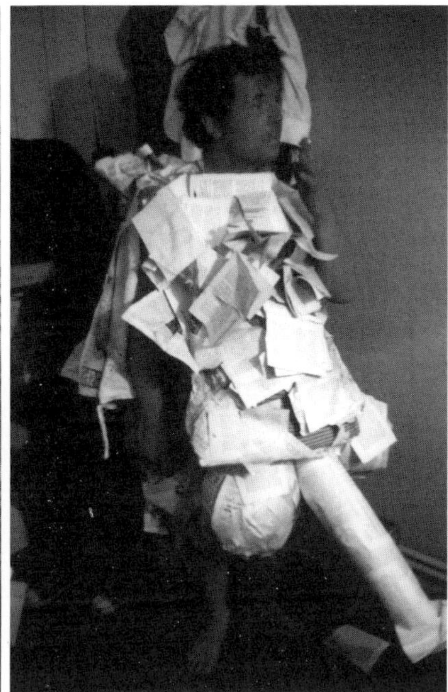

John Latham (left) and Jeff Nuttall, preparing for their unexecuted performance of *Film*, International Poetry Incarnation, Royal Albert Hall, 11 June 1965; Latham's film *Unedited Material from the Star* was to be projected on to the stage during the performance

time women – not disembodied famous heads but anonymous naked bodies, objects of male desire, dead centre a pubic bush. Although Boshier found one answer and Boty another, the question of how protest could bring its message home through the colour heraldry of pop still remained.

The underground, meanwhile, was mobilizing. The year after the International Poetry Incarnation at the Albert Hall in June 1965 – the most organized countercultural event in Britain to date – Latham and his wife, the artist Barbara Steveni, were involved in setting up the Destruction in Art Symposium (DIAS), to be convened at the Africa Centre in Covent Garden and other venues around London between 31 August and 30 September 1966. The aim of this international gathering was to 'focus attention on the element of destruction in Happenings, auto-destructive art, and other new art forms, to relate this to destruction in society'. The concept of auto-destructive art had been elaborated by Gustav Metzger, a stateless Polish-Jewish artist and former student of David Bomberg's at Borough Polytechnic, in a series of manifestos between 1959 and 1961. Auto-destructive art, announced Metzger, was 'primarily a form of public art for industrial societies', which could be created 'with natural forces, traditional art techniques and technological techniques':

> *Rockets, nuclear weapons, are auto-destructive...*
> *The drop drop dropping of HH bombs...*
> *Auto-destructive art re-enacts the obsession with destruction, the pummelling to which individuals and masses are subjected.*
> *Auto-destructive art mirrors the compulsive perfectionism of arms manufacture – polishing to destruction point.*

Metzger, who had arrived in Britain as a child refugee, was a founder member of the Direct Action Committee against nuclear war. In September 1961, he was imprisoned with thirty other committee members, including the philosopher and veteran radical Bertrand Russell, for his part in a non-violent campaign of mass civil disobedience. In court, Metzger stated that, 'My parents disappeared in 1943 and I would have shared their fate. But the situation is now far more barbarous than Buchenwald...for there can be absolute obliteration at any moment.' One of his first auto-destructive works, performed in public at the South Bank in London in July 1961, was *Acid Action Painting*. Clad in gas mask and goggles, he painted and flung acid on to white, red and black nylon sheets (the colours of the anarchist flag), arranged one behind the other, so that the acid produced a rapidly changing, coloured, three-dimensional 'painting' that, by the end of the action, had all but dissolved.

Attendees at DIAS in 1966 included artists, writers and scientists from across Europe, America and Asia. Among those hosted by Steveni and Latham at their house were the Japanese-American artist, Yoko Ono, her second husband, Tony Cox, and their young daughter. Ono, recalled Steveni, 'arrived with her stash of works that she was going to do'. For the DIAS programme, she reprised her 1964 performance *Cut Piece*, in which she sat on stage while audience members came up, one by one, to cut away her clothing in a cumulative series of small destructive acts that paradoxically liberated the artist. The outfits with which Steveni was deputed to supply her came from a trendsetting Kensington boutique, *and, she sat on this platform, and had her clothes cut off, her Biba gar-ments cut off, one by one, [and] when they had all been cut off, Yoko then had her long hair down to...her shoulders and she just sat cross-legged on the platform, and she looked very ancient, because she wasn't very ancient then, she looked like a Buddha, because she had this slightly olive skin and her hair like that.*

The American artist Raphael Montañez Ortiz performed three piano destruction concerts, two paper bag destruction concerts, and destruction rituals with a chair and a mattress. On the night of 16 September, at a meeting room next to St Bride's Church in the City of London, the Austrian artist Hermann Nitsch led an *abreaktionsspiel*, or 'reaction game', *Orgies Mystery Theater*, with audience participation, in which the carcass of a lamb was attacked, and blood, viscera and red paint strewn around the room. Tipped off by journalists, the police arrived; they issued Metzger with a summons, on the grounds that he had organized 'an indecent exhibition contrary to common law'. At jury trial the following year, he was found guilty but escaped the threatened six-year

Raphael Montañez Ortiz, *Piano Destruction Concert*, Destruction in Art Symposium, London, 1966

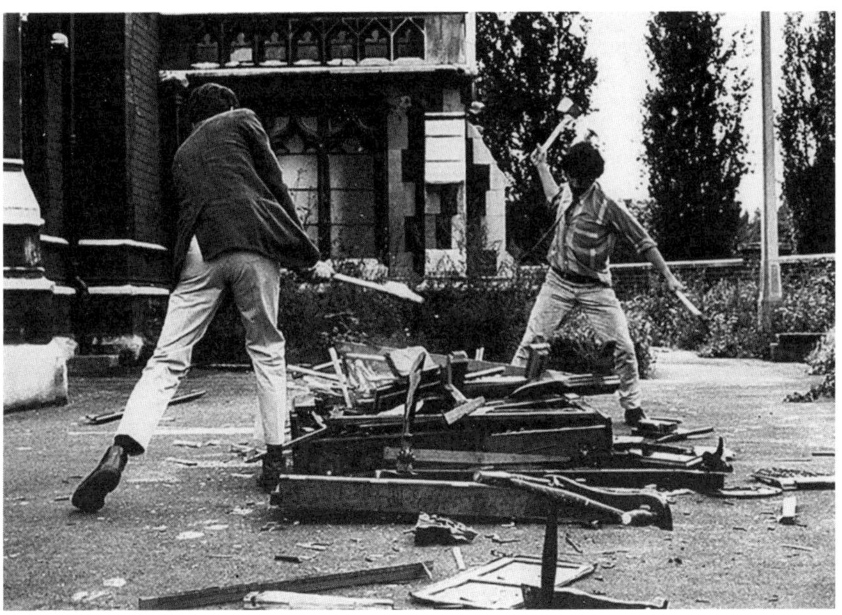

prison sentence. Latham constructed a skoob tower behind the British Museum, set fire to it and also ended up in court.

In the autumn, after the last events of DIAS had taken place, Ono stayed on in London, where the Indica Gallery had offered her a show. She was the child of fabulously rich Japanese banking families, whose first husband, the musician Toshi Ichiyanagi, had introduced her to the composer John Cage, choreographer Merce Cunningham and other members of North America's experimental arts community. When Ichiyanagi returned to Japan in 1961, Ono remained in New York, pursuing a fledgling career as a poet and performance artist – not, by some accounts, very convincingly. The beat poet Diane Wakoski surmised that Ono 'never seemed to sacrifice much for her "art" as all the avant-garders that I knew did'. For her exhibition at Indica in November 1966, titled 'Unfinished Paintings and Objects', she made a gauze-wrapped wooden chair; a painted ladder that visitors were invited to climb, in order to view through a magnifying glass the word *YES*, printed on paper attached to the ceiling; and *Painting to Hammer a Nail*, a hammer chained to a block of wood and a container of gold-plated nails. Someone had the idea of inviting John Lennon to a private preview. 'He's a millionaire, he might buy something,' Ono is said to have suggested. Lennon, apparently attracted by the prospect of 'a bit of a happening', recalled their meeting like this:

> *So, I'm looking for action, you know, and I see this thing called Hammer and Nail. It's a board with a chain and a hammer hanging on it, and a bunch of nails at the bottom. I said, 'Well, can I hammer a nail in?' and she said, 'No.'... She didn't know who I was. Anyway, she came over and said, 'Five shillings, please!' So I said, 'I'll give you an imaginary five shillings and hammer in an imaginary nail.' She said, 'All right.'*

Lennon himself was no newcomer to art, having left school with low academic grades for a place at Liverpool College of Art. Here he met Stuart Sutcliffe, who would become the Beatles' first bass guitarist, before leaving the band to study at Hamburg College of Art, where he was taught by Eduardo Paolozzi. The openness of post-war art schools to working-class students with talent and ideas, though short on exam qualifications and with no regular professional career in view, would see them become particularly fertile ground for British rock music. Richard Hamilton's students on the Basic Design course at the

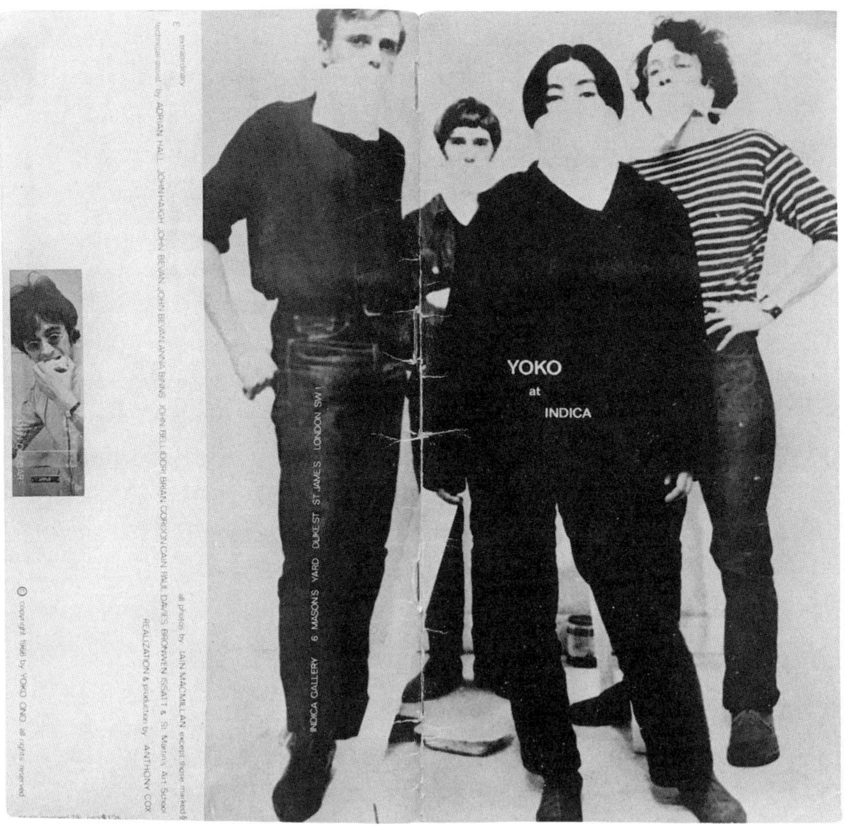

Cover of 'Yoko at Indica' exhibition catalogue, Indica Gallery, London, 1966, photograph by Iain Macmillan

University of Durham's King's College in Newcastle upon Tyne in the mid-1960s found his eclectic enthusiasms and category-dissolving sense of the connections between art, science, mass media and popular culture unlike anything they had been taught to call 'art'. In 1977, Bryan Ferry, founder and frontman of Roxy Music, would record a single titled 'This Is Tomorrow', a tribute to his former teacher and to the whole ethos of disruptive cultural enquiry that had started with the Independent Group. Hamilton himself designed the cover for the Beatles' 1968 *White Album,* a minimalist sequel to the 'hero wall' cover created by Peter Blake and his wife Jann Haworth for the band's previous album *Sgt. Pepper's Lonely Hearts Club Band.* Metzger, the doyen of auto-destructive art, created screen projections for concerts by the Who, whose lead guitarist Pete Townshend wondered whether

Metzger's belief that art 'should reflect the way we are destroying the world' had inspired his own wild-man stage act – 'So I nearly got it right with my guitar smashing.' 'One of the things that made art schools interesting places to be,' according to Ferry's Roxy Music comrade Brian Eno (Ipswich Civic College, followed by Winchester School of Art), 'is that they've always been places where people watched where the action was in culture and then moved into it.'

In their game of the imaginary money and the virtual nail at the Indica Gallery in 1966, Lennon and Ono, the musician and the conceptual artist, were comfortable on each other's ground, in a way that – whatever the sexual chemistry – it is less easy to imagine, say, a jazz saxophonist and a sculptor being ten or twenty years earlier. In the role performed by Ono as artist, *Painting to Hammer a Nail* was *con* rather than *destructive*, evoking a more optimistic, playful strand within the underground than the thoroughgoing 'insurrection' predicated by Trocchi. 'Spiritual' was a word much used to describe this type of secession from 'square' materialism and convention. And, since 'spiritual' and 'Eastern' were treated as virtual synonyms, Ono's Japaneseness fitted this role perfectly. The 'Buddha' admired by Steveni in her snipped-off Biba clothes took the form, for Lennon, of a guru in whose presence he, not she, was naked. 'She said to me, "You've got no clothes on." Nobody had dared tell me that before.' Of their later life together, he would reflect, 'it's a teacher–pupil relationship.... She's the teacher and I'm the pupil.'

In August 1967, Ono staged *Wrapping Piece* in Trafalgar Square, for which, on the pretext that she was making a film, she obtained police permission (very much not the underground way of doing business) to swathe one of the lions on the plinth of Nelson's Column in dust sheets, roped in place in the manner of wrapped structures by Christo and Jeanne-Claude. She had persuaded Lennon to sponsor her exhibition the following month at the Lisson Gallery in north London. He explained to his wife, Cynthia, that Ono 'was just a weirdo artist...wanting money for all that avant-garde bullshit'. Little more than a year later, the Lennons divorced. In March 1969, after their wedding in Gibraltar, John and Yoko honeymooned at the Hilton hotel in Amsterdam, where they staged a week-long Bed-In for Peace in their suite, inviting the press to photograph them propped in bed holding single white tulips. The Amsterdam Bed-In took its cue from the wave of sit-in student protests that followed the violent *événements* in Paris in May 1968, in which French riot police charged student demonstrators and striking workers. In sit-ins at Hornsey College of Art, Guildford School of Art and other institutions, students occupied the buildings until the authorities addressed their academic and/or political demands.

''Peace', in the Lennons' highly publicized happening, referred to the Vietnam War. The call for peace positioned the couple as celebrity protesters, but it also invoked the word's vaguer all-purpose spirituality. This chimed with Lennon's weeks in early 1968 at the Maharishi Mahesh Yogi's ashram in Rishikesh, at the base of the Himalayas, which he claimed had taken his mind 'down to that level of consciousness which is absolute bliss'. It also appeared to express Ono's embodiment, to her Western public, of all things Eastern. The wonderstruck deference with which Japanese 'simplicity' had been greeted by British artists and designers around the turn of the nineteenth century was echoed in the search for alternative lifestyles in the 1960s; like ukiyo-e prints and temple *torii*, Ono came across, even to an avant-garde insider like Steveni, as both contemporary and 'very ancient'.

Another outcome of DIAS was Steveni's idea for what became the Artist Placement Group (APG). Late one evening, while she was driving round an industrial estate in west London, on the lookout for junk props for a happening, Steveni got lost:

> *it was dark...and there was this huge, enormous industrial complex, humming away, and there was a Mars factory and a clock factory, a Timex factory. And I thought to myself, well, instead of just picking up buckets of plastic and material, why aren't we actually associated with this world that we don't seem to be touching? And, I came back with this idea in my head that...artists needed to be in this whole other area, and that was the beginning of my idea...which grew into the Artist Placement Group.*

If art could have an impact on society, Steveni and Latham reasoned, this impact must be measurable in some way. It should be possible to set up collaborations between artists who wanted their work to have a social impact and the square world of business, industry and government departments, and to evaluate the results.

On the principle that 'the context is half the work', APG artists were embedded as 'Incidental Persons' in offices and factories, and paid a regular wage. Over the past century, impressionists, futurists, constructivists and others had looked to industrial modernity for their themes; the APG was the first systematic attempt to see what happened when artists worked in tandem with employers and administrators, not merely observing and interpreting the world of work. In theory, it appeared logical; in practice, a sense of shared vision and common ground proved elusive. Artist David Hall spent his placement with British European Airways in 1970 filming surreal, slow-moving cloud formations. The Greek artist George Levantis travelled on cargo and cruise ships run by Ocean Fleets, creating an installation designed to be thrown into the sea. For three months in 1975–76, Latham would himself become an 'Incidental Person' at the Scottish Office's Development Agency, where he devised proposals for preserving a group of gigantic spoil heaps, or bings, in West Lothian created by shale oil extraction, arguing that these mounds were 'monuments to the period we live in'. The problem in quantifying the results of APG placements, Latham eventually concluded, didn't lie in the concept itself but in the limited means then available for collating and analysing all the data.

One striking feature of all this activity – indeed, about the entire British art world – was that, more than seventy years after art schools began admitting women students on equal terms to men, artists, their attitudes and their concerns remained overwhelmingly male. Ono's presence at DIAS did 'make a difference', thought Steveni, and an important one, because,

> *who were the women artists at the time?... Although I had been at art school...I didn't actually see myself as a woman artist, that came much later, because I was in a culture, and living with a quite a bit older male artist...and all artists were men at the time.*

In the same month as DIAS, Latham staged an action in Aachen, reported in *Studio International*. Leafing through their copy of the magazine, Steveni found a photo: 'there was me being burnt in a gallery in Aachen, all wrapped up in books, and just my eyes showing'. She felt that she and other women partners of male artists 'were very much participating in our men's events without thinking how much we were giving or doing or initiating or anything'. In retrospect, she came to feel that 'it took me quite a long time to pull out of that and claim what I was doing and notice myself, because I was in that culture at the time where the man was *it*'.

17

The longest revolution

Whitehall, 27 October 1968

It was only a few weeks ago that Mary Kelly said goodbye to the American University in Beirut, where she had been teaching after art school in the States. She was looking forward to London and Saint Martin's School of Art, where interesting things are happening, particularly in terms of exploring a 'conceptual' approach to making art. This autumn Sunday afternoon, she is one of 25,000 people who have joined the Vietnam Solidarity Campaign's street protest. 'Defeat US Aggression', 'UK 51st State of US', the placards read. 'We hope to show the world that the criminal policy pursued by the Labour Government does not have the support of the British people,' runs the Campaign's press statement. Starting out from Embankment Underground station at 2 p.m., the route of the march runs along Whitehall, past Downing Street, where activist and writer Tariq Ali will deliver a petition, then on to Victoria and Hyde Park, where Jean-Paul Sartre, 'the world-famous philosopher and critic of the war' has been invited to speak. Overwhelmingly, the protesters are young. And the crowd today feels like part of something even bigger. Living in London for the first time, Kelly is struck by the city's 'extremely electric' atmosphere, with its feeling of 'youthful omnipotence', the conviction that, whatever obstacles power and authority placed in your way, 'you would prevail'.

———

It was a year, *the* year, of protest, of which sit-ins at British art schools that summer had been just one manifestation. In the United States, a civil rights protest centred on South Carolina State University in Orangeburg ended on the night of 8 February in massacre, with three black protesters shot dead by police and many more injured. The assassination of Martin Luther King two months later ignited a wave of protests. Students across the USA were marching and going on hunger strike against the Vietnam War. In August, the Democratic

269

National Convention in Chicago was the focus for five days of mass anti-war demonstrations, during which police and the National Guard turned violent on protesters. In Europe, the turmoil in France in May was on such a scale that President Charles de Gaulle, fearing revolution or civil war, fled to Germany. In Czechoslovakia that August, after Soviet forces invaded to depose Alexander Dubček's reformist regime, protesters on the streets of Prague were met by tanks. There were student protests against the fascist dictatorship in Spain, and ominous signs of conflict to come in Northern Ireland, where police failed to shield civil rights marches by the minority Catholic community from attack by Protestant loyalists. In London on 17 March, when ten thousand anti-war protesters marched from Trafalgar Square to the American Embassy, there were violent clashes with police and two hundred arrests. Again and again, throughout 1968, the front pages of the newspapers were filled with banners and helmets, streets crammed with demonstrators or strewn with the running and prostrate bodies of the aftermath, lines of citizens in ordinary clothes confronting phalanxes of uniforms.

Along the Charing Cross Road, just north of Trafalgar Square, behind the modest modernity of Saint Martin's brick and glass facade, the kinds of teaching experiments that Anthony Caro and Frank Martin had introduced into the sculpture studios over the past eight years would still have been too radical for many art schools. The weekly Advanced Course evening classes, for example, featured 'situational' projects based on the sculptor's body and actions rather than objects: students might be invited to 'make use of the ideas and aims of [his or her] particular work in a physical demonstration by the use of his or her limbs in any way possible', or to 'Make a sculpture expressing a given physical emotion: i.e. "Having a hot bath".' But the teacher–pupil relationship itself could still feel rooted in an earlier dispensation. In sculptor and performance artist Bruce McLean's experience, sculpture 'crits' of students' work by staff were occasions when 'Twelve adult men with pipes would walk for hours around sculpture and mumble.' Early renegades at Saint Martin's, like John Latham and Barry Flanagan, had questioned the whole basis for making anything called 'sculpture' and then judging the result. Who, in any case, was qualified to judge? Readers of Clement Greenberg's *Art and Culture* might think they knew, but in 1968 the fallibility of authority – parents, politicians, generals, the *It's a Man's World* crew – was in the air. Conceptual art, which emphasized the idea above the material form (if any) by which it was embodied, liberated art from authoritarian spaces like art schools and galleries. If art was what happened in the audience's own minds, they were free to become participants instead of spectators. In other words – this was the theory, at any rate – conceptual art reduced the danger of someone in power telling you what to think.

The Saint Martin's graduate Hamish Fulton set off in the spring of 1967 to hitchhike from London to Andorra and back again. He intended the trip itself, which he would document in texts and photos, stage by stage, to become a piece of work. *Hitchhiking from London to Andorra and from Andorra to London, 9–15 April 1967* consists of a list of places, dates and times, neatly typed on two sheets of paper, accompanied by a snapshot of Fulton clambering out of the back of a French van and another of him walking. A few weeks later, Saint Martin's student Richard Long took a train from Waterloo Station into the countryside. Getting out at a local station, he walked into the midsummer fields, where he chose an otherwise unremarkable spot – level meadow grassland backed by a coppice or overgrown hedge – and strode up and down until his repeatedly trodden path materialized as a single straight line in the grass. He photographed the scene, giving it the title *A Line Made by Walking, England 1967*. In the random patch of grass, which at first appears uninhabited, the pale track imprinted by the artist's feet runs through the centre, a human trace that is at the same time an abstract exercise in one-point perspective, offered to the viewer in the manner of a simple but mysterious inscription. Long's photo might not have said 'sculpture' to most people in mid-1960s Britain, but it says 'England' as clearly as Eric Ravilious's smooth, uninhabited chalklands, graphically incised by furrows or criss-crossed by telegraph lines.

The conceptual ideas that interested Kelly had more to do with psychoanalytic and critical theory than tramping the green outdoors. During her time at the American University of Beirut, tensions between the liberal Western curriculum and the politics of the postcolonial Middle East were an abiding issue. 'It is the university's function,' a student newspaper had declared in 1955, 'to train us, its students and future spokesmen of our countries, to face the problems of everyday life', especially 'the basic important factors that lead to freedom from oppression'. In Britain, the late 1960s were marked by a shift in the ethos of popular protest: overtaking the hip-versus-square polemics of the underground, organized campaigns for constructive change began to take shape, notably in the women's movement. Soon after moving to London, Kelly joined the Women's Liberation Workshop and found a place to live in a west London commune. 'When people look back at that time,' she would recall, 'they often want to insist on the political description of it, or on the lifestyle description of it...either the sexual revolution, the cultural revolution, the political revolution, but all those things were very interwoven.' In the friendship groups and social circle in which she found herself, intense exchanges of ideas, books and, not infrequently, partners fuelled the sense that this was a moment of youth-generated change: 'We're all in our early and late twenties, so you can't underestimate the sort of moment that you're intensely sexually active.' In the wake the 'electric' year of protest, that commitment to change felt more serious in its objectives and more intellectually engaged than the pop youth culture of the early 1960s.

It was also during the autumn of 1968 that young Australian literary scholar, Germaine Greer, took up a part-time lectureship at the University of Warwick. She had recently gained her doctorate from Cambridge University with a thesis titled 'The Ethic of Love and Marriage in Shakespeare's Early Comedies' and was pursuing a parallel career outside academia as a contributor to the underground magazine *Oz* and a promising newcomer in television comedy. In March 1969, Greer met with a publisher, who suggested that, as an expert on Shakespeare's famously independent-minded women, she might write a book to celebrate the fiftieth anniversary of the 1918 Representation of the People Act, which had given women over the age of thirty the right to vote. Greer rejected this idea but signed up instead to write a book on 'the myth of the ultra-feminine woman'. Just over four months later, it was finished. In the United States, the 'second wave' of the women's movement had been building for some time. The publication of Greer's *The Female Eunuch* in October 1970 was the moment at which it crested and broke in public consciousness in Britain. The book sold two thousand copies in its first day and became a steady bestseller, variously hailed by its mostly male reviewers as a 'dazzling combination of erudition, eccentricity, and eroticism' and 'A manual of self-help for women kind. How to learn to stop nagging, crabbing and grabbing and make your own life.'

In *The Female Eunuch,* Greer analyses with fierce energy and well-read satirical rage the position of women – sexual, social, cultural, political – in Western society, both historically and in the present day. She shared with the critic Clive James, a Sydney friend who had moved to London in 1962, and fellow *Oz* contributor the art writer Robert Hughes, an antipodean outsider's iconoclastic take on the entrenched snobberies and hierarchies of British society, and the 'received language' of social and cultural commentary. One by one, page by page, the pillars of the bourgeois temple came crashing down. In the background, still, loomed the H-bomb mushroom cloud, but it was now augmented by other, increasingly recognized and inexorably growing threats to human survival: '*Security*, the ruling deity of the welfare state', was 'never more insubstantial than it is in the age of total warfare, global pollution and population explosion.' Although women had been admitted to the workplace, this was mainly, Greer argued, in order that they could 'help carry the can full of mess that men had made'. Freudian theory, the foundation of so much 'scientific' analysis of the female psyche, in reality failed to take account of the experience of half the human race, because, according to Freud, 'libido is invariably and necessarily of a masculine nature'. 'As far as the woman is concerned,' therefore, 'psychiatry is an extraordinary confidence trick.' If women, proposed Greer, 'are the true proletariat, the truly oppressed majority, the revolution can only be drawn nearer by their withdrawal of support for the capitalist system.' She ended with a rousing call to take '*joy in the struggle*':

Revolution is the festival of the oppressed. For a long time there may be no perceptible reward for women other than their new sense of purpose and integrity. Joy does not mean riotous glee, but it does mean the purposive employment of energy in a self-chosen enterprise.... To have something to desire, something to make, something to achieve, and at last something genuine to give.

Stirring words, but they didn't exactly map out a plan of campaign. While Greer became a reliably provocative media controversialist, women's groups were forming and mobilizing to press for practical, incremental change. On 27 February 1970, six hundred activists gathered at Ruskin College, Oxford, for the first National Women's Liberation Conference, co-organized by Kelly's housemate, mature history student and mother Sally Alexander. Debates on subjects such as socialist feminism, patriarchy and sexuality resulted in a series of resolutions to work for women's rights, equal pay and employment opportunities, access to free contraception and round-the-clock nursery provision for working mothers. Kelly joined Alexander in a London group of feminist academics and writers, the History Group, focused on 'changing our conditions – legally, practically, politically – but also trying to find a theoretical apparatus that recognized the subjective dimension of that process. And this led us to look at Freud and later [Jacques] Lacan'. Her social circle at Saint Martin's included conceptual artists such as Steve Willats and Victor Burgin, and writers associated with the Marxist *New Left Review*. Yet she sensed that, when it came to women's personal experience in a society dominated by men, there remained 'a gap in the grand narrative of Marxism' – a gap that her own conceptual practice, in whichever direction it ultimately developed, might attempt to fill.

For the moment, direct action felt like the best way forward. On the evening of 20 November 1970, Kelly participated in a protest, again co-organized by Alexander, at the finals of the Miss World beauty pageant at the Albert Hall, due to be hosted by the American comedian and movie star Bob Hope and broadcast live on television. To make the point that women should not be judged 'by their looks and their bodies', the plan, explained Alexander, was to 'disrupt the spectacle going into everyone's homes'. Smartly dressed and handbagged for the occasion, small groups of protesters infiltrated the audience, equipped with flour bombs. At the signal of a football rattle, which came unexpectedly quickly as Hope's sexist patter incensed the signaller, the protesters leaped up and launched their bombs. Hope fled backstage, 'absolutely terrified'; despite the contestants' pleas to 'Leave them alone', policemen dragged protesters by their arms and legs out of the hall. When it eventually restarted, the contest was won by Grenada's Jennifer Hosten, who became the first black Miss World. This turned out to be 'the most significant element of the night,' in Alexander's view. But for the British women's movement too, the protest was 'one of the most spectacular consciousness-raising episodes'; it reached a global audience of 100 million, and about 22 million in Britain. 'I do not think women should ever achieve equal rights,' Hosten demurred. 'I still like a gentleman to hold a chair back for me.'

'In advanced industrial society, women's work is only marginal to the total economy,' New Zealand-born lecturer Juliet Mitchell had stated in an influential article in the *New Left Review* in 1966, 'Women: The Longest Revolution':

Yet it is through work that man changes natural conditions and thereby produces society. Until there is a revolution in production, the labour situation will prescribe women's situation within the world of men. But women are offered a universe of their own: the family. Like woman herself, the family appears as a natural object, but it is actually a cultural creation. There is nothing inevitable about the form or role of the family any more than there is about the character or role of women. It is the function of ideology to present these given social types as Nature itself.

In light of the growing awareness of women's socially constructed roles, and the discussion of women's economic contribution to society – housework and childcare as unacknowledged and unpaid labour – Kelly became interested in 'woman as spectacle', particularly the ways in which the visual representation of women's lives perpetuated their state of oppression. She was constantly noticing connections 'between images of women and ideology as a system of representation', reinforcing her feeling 'that art could have political efficacy'. At the same time, she began to think of psychoanalytic theory as a means by which female sexuality in its broadest sense could 'pass into the grand narrative of social change' – 'a euphoric moment' in her search for a subject and a medium. Since the actual conditions of women's lives and the need for change would be the focus, the passage of time was integral to her project, making film the natural medium.

Women's relationship to the workplace, balancing motherhood and household work with often very poorly paid and exploitative employment, was the subject of two projects in the early 1970s in which Kelly collaborated with other artists. In 1970, she joined the Berwick Street Collective, which had been formed that year to make films about British social issues inspired by French New Wave realist cinema. *The Nightcleaners* was the result of many hours filming women office cleaners in real time, as they worked through the night, polishing desks and disinfecting toilets for absent male executives, who, after their far better paid working days, were able to return to their homes and evening leisure time. The film was intended to support the women cleaners' campaign for equal pay and conditions, which in this case ultimately succeeded. It was also, it struck Kelly, a riposte by the women's movement to the fetishization of art and the mystique of the (male) artist – Andy Warhol, for example, who in 1964 had filmed *Sleeper*, in which his lover John Giorno sleeps for over five hours, in real time. *The Nightcleaners*, joked Kelly, was a kind of campaigning equivalent – 'eight hours of someone cleaning the toilet' – which confronted serious deficiencies in the 1970 Equal Pay Act, with its exclusion of work in the home and other non-unionized workplaces, rather than appealing mainly to art world insiders. In the project 'Women and Work', she collaborated between 1973 and 1975 with artists Margaret Harrison and Kay Hunt, documenting the stories of 150 women employees in a factory in Bermondsey. Harrison would develop this strand of practice further in her 1977 visual document *Homeworkers* (pl. 16), a collage fusing the personal story of a home-worker's routine exploitation with fragments of the context in which it took place – adverts, commercial products aimed at women, words of protest, legislation, a row of hands raised in hopelessness or welcome.

In addition to low wages and poor conditions of employment, women still generally found that the demands of motherhood and home life were not acknowledged in the workplace – or, for that matter, in the cultural sphere. In traditional British bohemia, the inseminating power of the male genius was part of a creative mystique. Even in post-war British art schools, with their long tradition of welcoming female students – usually the numerical majority – women still found themselves cast in subaltern roles. In many ways, the path to a career in art was no easier for a woman in 1970 than it had been in 1900. William Coldstream, principal of the Slade between 1949 and 1975, insisted that only 'over his dead body' would a woman be appointed to teach there. Before the women's movement of the 1970s and the wide circulation of *The Female Eunuch* and other popular feminist books, women could find it difficult to articulate a compelling counterargument to traditional gender roles. The painter Sheila Girling, for example, who married Caro in 1947, looked back at her transition to motherhood in these terms:

I think it's terribly hard for a woman to be as successful as a man if she has children. I mean Bridget Riley's never married and never had children, you know. You can then be as focused as a man. And I think women are just as good as men, really. I mean you can't escape the fact you have to physically bear the child, and when you have the child you want to feed the child and all these things are so tearing you away. The men go off and the child is there somewhere and they're working all day.

Or, as sculptor Rosemary Young, married to Reg Butler, put it more graphically, 'he just sucked it away, drew all your energy away from creativity, into being part of a partnership'.

Even in the countercultural underground of the 1960s, when you scratched the radical surface, not much had changed in terms of women's liberation: 'it wasn't providing an alternative for women,' decided Rosie Boycott, journalist and, in 1972, co-founder of the feminist magazine *Spare Rib*. 'It was providing an alternative for men in that there were no problems screwing around or being who you wanted. You were still able to do it on a chauvinist level and there was still a power game going on.' A power game in which, in a straight relationship, the man would traditionally consider himself to be the primary other in his partner's life. For women who were mothers, as Michelene Wandor, poet and poetry editor of *Time Out*, explained in a piece in *Spare Rib* in 1972, the male view of sexual politics was very far from the experiential truth:

The child is totally dependent on mother for the most intimate things – she handles its whole body, cleans its vomit, can kiss and cuddle it whenever she wants to – and she is therefore the initiator of sensual contact. Babies respond instinctively, and for many women this may be the most openly sensual exchange with another human being they have ever had – or may ever have.

Yet, in 'a situation in which incest taboos are still very strong', a woman might find herself 'playing a schizoid role: with her child she is initiator, with her husband she is still the passive one'.

There was no hint of the inner conflict identified by Wandor in the mother-and-child paintings and sculptures that had such a long history in art, even in women's art – in Berthe Morisot's *The Cradle* (1872) or Vanessa Bell's tender *Julian Asleep* (1909) or Barbara Hepworth's black basalt *Infant* (1929). Women's actual, extremely mixed experiences of pregnancy and childbirth, and the highs and lows of early motherhood, barely registered as subjects of public discussion, let alone art. In its public image, pregnancy – often a far from straightforwardly or consistently joyous experience – still carried the idealized glow of

Renaissance madonnas. Few people other than close friends of Pauline Boty, for example, were aware that, after becoming pregnant at the age of twenty-seven, she had been diagnosed at an ante-natal checkup with thymoma, refused the offered abortion that would have made possible her treatment with radiotherapy, and died just five months after her daughter was born.

And what about the work involved in bearing and raising children, the skills, the labour, the long hours? Motherhood, in 1970 as in 1870, was still generally presumed to be the role for which, above all others, women were destined; it was still viewed as a biologically determined vocation rather than a full-time job. The 'celebration of mother-care as a social act' in the post-war West could, noted Mitchell, reach 'ludicrous extremes'. She quoted a pseudonymous American writer Betty Ann Countrywoman: 'For the mother, breast-feeding becomes a complement to the act of creation. It gives her a heightened sense of fulfilment and allows her to participate in a relationship as close to perfection as any that a woman can hope to achieve.' Mitchell's feminist analysis of 'the biological function of maternity' in cultural and economic terms led her to the conclusion that, as 'a universal, atemporal fact', motherhood 'seemed to escape the categories of Marxist historical analysis':

> *From it follows – apparently – the stability and omnipresence of the family, if in very different forms. Once this is accepted, women's social subordination – however emphasized as an honourable, but different role…can be seen to follow inevitably as an insurmountable bio-historical fact. The causal chain then goes: Maternity, Family, Absence from Production and Public Life, Sexual Inequality.*

This was not the first time this 'causal chain' had been questioned. Two hundred and fifty years earlier, Mary Wollstonecraft's *A Vindication of the Rights of Women* (1792) had blown the pedestal from under the Georgian patriarchy. What was different now was the size and readiness of the audience, and the extent to which previously radical ideas filtered into general awareness and mainstream journalism. Women felt able to think constructively about, and discuss in public, aspects of their experience that had previously been inadmissible. *Spare Rib* published pieces on breast cancer, abortion and, in its January 1973 issue, a call to experience 'The liberated orgasm… Make a New Year resolution to have one'.

Pregnant with her first child in 1972, Kelly decided that this was another kind of woman's work – her personal experience of the workplace of motherhood – that she would document. In her film *Antepartum* (1973), Kelly's hands repeatedly stroke her third-trimester belly, while her unborn child's kicks are visible, coming from inside, a relationship – and a future job – already taking shape. After giving birth to her son in 1973, she began assembling *Post-Partum Document*, a 'text' compiled in real time, on that classic locus of psychoanalytic theory – the mother–child relationship – but composed from ordinary objects and usually dis-

Angela Phillips, cover of *Spare Rib*, no. 1, July 1972

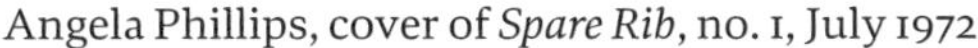

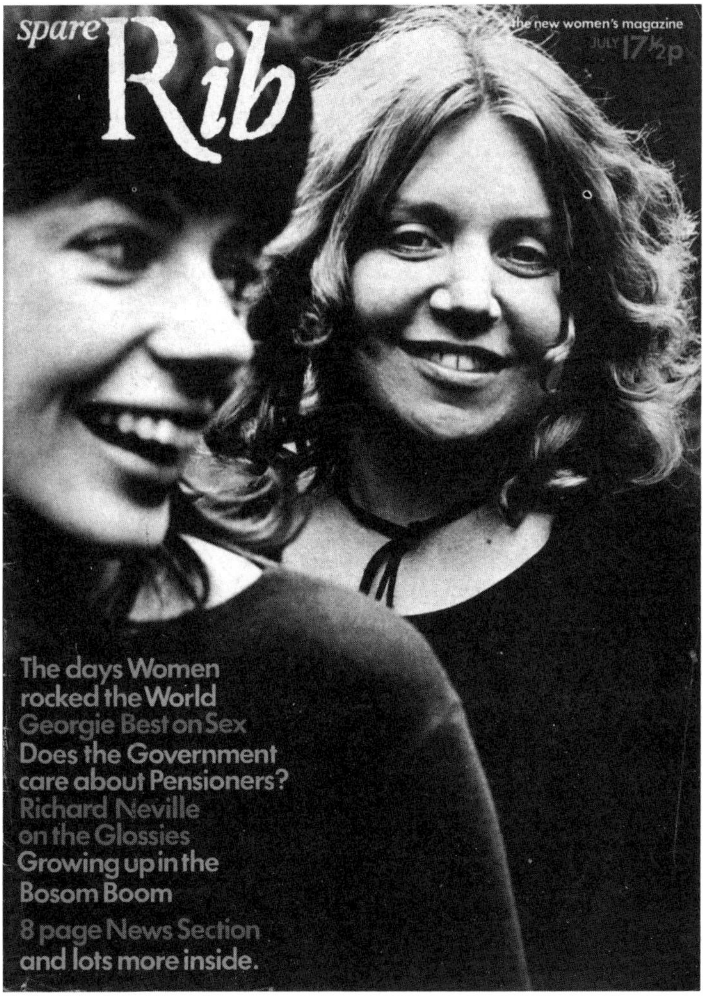

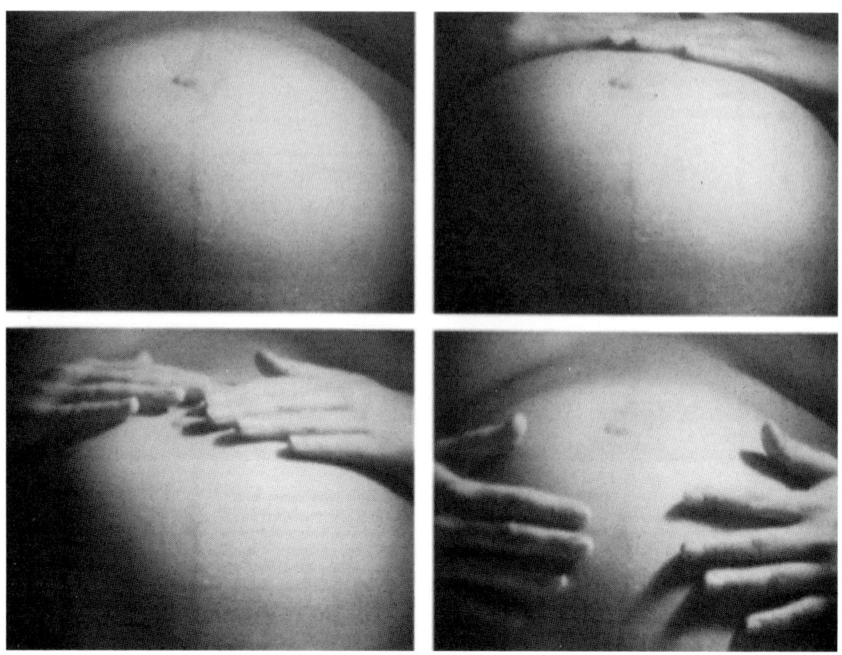

Mary Kelly, film stills from *Antepartum*, 1973. Super-8 film,
black-and-white, silent, 1:30 min

carded scraps like stained nappy-liners, baby vests and first scribblings.
For a mother, during a child's first years, these objects – worthless to
anyone else – are, in psychoanalytical terms, 'cathected' or invested
with intense feeling. At the same time, they are, as feminist thinking
made clear, tokens of a socially constructed relationship and setting.

Post-Partum Document, said Kelly, was 'located within the theoretical and political practice of the woman's movement, a practice which
foregrounds the issues of subjectivity and ideological oppression'. The
'document' format presents each piece of childhood detritus and ephemera
as an object for study, framed and recorded in a quasi-anthropological
manner, as if Kelly were a scientist objectively investigating her own
process of motherhood and her child's development. Yet, as the series
grew through successive phases over the next six years, it became inter-
active, a dialogue – almost a parody of critical discourse – between the
mother and her child. *Documentation III* takes the form of conversations
recorded between Kelly and her now three-year-old son in the autumn
of 1975, when he began to attend nursery school. Each of a series of her

son's chalk and crayon scribbles is accompanied by three typed texts representing mother and child talking to each other: transcripts of both Kelly's and her son's words, and notes of her reflections on what passed between them. What happens as *Post-Partum Document* unfolds is that a relationship conventionally taken to be instinctually maternal and located within a private, wordless domestic setting is offered – in the evidential manner of conceptual art – to public scrutiny and discussion while losing none of its intimate subjectivity. The 'document' concluded six years later 1979; in *Documentation IV*, Kelly's son began to write his own name and, in critical-theoretical terms, became 'author of his own text'.

In the book of art, however, the history of women's contribution remained almost blank. In its early editions, Ernst Gombrich's perennial bestseller *The Story of Art* contained not a single woman artist. Nor did Kenneth Clark's blockbuster 1969 BBC television series and spin-off book, *Civilisation*. In thirteen episodes, the urbane, erudite Clark surveyed European art from the Dark Ages onwards. 'What is civilisation?' he asked, quoting Ruskin in answer: 'Great nations write their autobiographies in three manuscripts, the book of their deeds, the book of their words and the book of their art...of the three the only trustworthy one is the last.' Clark's wholehearted embrace of television broke with decades of elite suspicion of the medium and made him a household name, but it popularized a masculine, heroic narrative: there was no room in the baroque for Italian painter Artemisia Gentileschi, no role in impressionism for Berthe Morisot. And it included no artist later than Vincent van Gogh. Signing off, Clark characterized himself as 'a stick-in-the-mud' who believed in strong social institutions, in genius and – with a charming touch of *noblesse oblige* – 'courtesy, the ritual by which we avoid hurting other people's feelings'. He lamented the 'moral and intellectual failure of Marxism' that 'has left us with no alternative to heroic materialism'.

Three years later, in January 1972, the Marxist critic John Berger fronted a four-part television series of his own, *Ways of Seeing*, a thoroughgoing riposte to the patrician Clark. Where Clark had sold the idea of 'genius' to his audience as the measure of art, Berger analysed the construction of images and the act of 'reading' their meanings, since 'The way we see things is affected by what we know or what we believe.... To look is an act of choice.' Berger attacked the 'mystification' of art by art historians, decoding the messages conveyed by images, captions, layouts and media with the kind of energetic irony Marshall McLuhan had brought to newspapers and advertising twenty years earlier. But, although there were plenty of female bodies in *Ways of Seeing*, Berger, too, failed to show the work of any women artists.

And so did the first institutional survey exhibition of conceptual art produced in Britain, 'The New Art' at the Hayward Gallery, London, in August 1972. Although the show was curated by a woman, Anne Seymour, the thirteen individual artists, among them Burgin, Flanagan, Fulton and Long, and the group Art & Language it presented were all men. There was, explained Seymour, no single common element in the 'new art' but instead an engagement in 'work which does not necessarily presuppose the traditional categories of painting and sculpture – involving written material, philosophical ideas, photographs, film, sound, light, the earth itself, the artists themselves, actual objects'. The ideas and attitudes contained in the work were 'equally if not more important than the media'. Keith Arnatt showed a wall inscription reading 'KEITH ARNATT IS AN ARTIST' – a statement that drew attention to the dynamics of communication, requiring the hearer's response to the speaker's intention. 'I might', he explained, 'attempt to get you to believe that I am an artist by producing "artworks" in a currently acceptable style' or alternatively 'by simply telling you that I am an artist'. Burgin exhibited a photograph of a wooden floor, identical in size to the actual floor on to which it was stapled. He wanted, he said, 'to underline the contingency of the physical object and the primacy of the observer's *act* of observation'. The duo Gilbert Prousch and George Passmore, known as Gilbert & George, described their life together as 'living sculptures' – 'our life blood, our destiny, our romance, our disaster, our light and life'. 'If there is any single attitude which binds the artists in this exhibition together,' Seymour speculated, 'it was their ability to look reality in the eye.... But reality doesn't have to be a nude lady of uncertain age sitting on a kitchen chair.'

So far, so logical, but it would be a few years yet before conceptual art – a term that acquired very vague, generally negative connotations in popular use – made headlines. That moment came in February 1976, when the *Sunday Times* published a piece about recent acquisitions of contemporary art by the Tate Gallery. These included *Equivalent VIII* (1966) by the American sculptor Carl Andre, a neat, low-level rectangular arrangement of 120 firebricks in two layers. The sculpture had been

Mary Kelly, *Post-Partum Document: Documentation VI Pre-writing Alphabet, Exergue and Diary* (detail, 1 of 18 units), 1978. Perspex unit, white card, resin and slate, 20 × 25.5 cm (7⅞ × 10⅛ in.)

on display at the Tate for four years without attracting much notice, but the revelation that the gallery had shelled out £2,297 of taxpayers' money (about £20,000 today) for a 'pile of bricks' unleashed a media storm. 'WHAT A LOAD OF RUBBISH: how the Tate dropped 120 bricks' ran the *Daily Mirror* headline. It was useless to point out that, in art-historical terms, the 'Tate Bricks' were a classic example of American minimalist sculpture. In public opinion, they symbolized an Emperor's New Clothes confidence trick that went by the name of conceptual art. In Britain, Andre's identity as their creator would always overshadow his notoriety in the United States as partner of the Cuban performance artist and sculptor Ana Mendieta, for whose death in 1985, caused by falling from the thirty-second-floor window, he was arrested and charged, though subsequently released.

As late as 1978, the American feminist critic and curator Lucy Lippard had no trouble demonstrating that the prejudice 'against women *making* art rather than being the subject of art by men or keeping house for men's art (in curatorial and critical as well as in basic domestic roles)' was alive and well. The 'Hayward Annual '78' was the first British public gallery show to be selected entirely by a panel of women artists (Tess Jaray, Liliane Lijn, Kim Lim, Gillian Wise Ciobotaru and Rita Donagh) and to feature significantly more women (sixteen, including Kelly with *Post-Partum Document*) than men (seven). In her catalogue essay, Lippard pointed out that no female artist had been given a solo exhibition at the Tate Gallery since Hepworth's retrospective in April 1968, and reeled off a list of recent statistics on gender balance: 'British Sculptors '72' at the Royal Academy (24 men, 0 women), 'Kinetics' at the Hayward Gallery in 1971 (64 men, 3 women), 'The Condition of Sculpture' at the Hayward in 1975 (36 men, 4 women), and so on. She quoted the reaction of the art journalist John McEwen to the Arts Council's announcement in 1977 that the next Hayward Annual would be selected by women: 'As for the abjectly trendy idea of having an all-woman jury as if everyone is up for rape, words fail me.' Lippard had curated a series of all-women shows in America; she made the case that a 'national group show' should represent 'artists of varied age, political and aesthetic persuasion, geographical location and – yes – sex and race'. In the wake of years of civil rights activism, the work of African-American artists was beginning to be shown more often, more widely in the States. In Britain, the Hayward controversy was all around sex: 'A BIASSED [*sic*] SHOW – WOMEN TAKE OVER THE HAYWARD' (*Observer*) was typical of the press response. Although it did not pass unnoticed, there was no public debate about the fact that, of the twenty-three artists in the exhibition, all were white.

18
Time is now

New York, February 1975

There are reasons why Frank Bowling decided to settle in New York. And there are reasons why he has decided, after the best part of nine years, to return to London. The plan is not to leave for good. He will keep on exhibiting and teaching in America, all of which has turned out better, much better, than it ever did in London. In the loft studio in SoHo, where he has lived and worked since 1967, Bowling has painted big abstract paintings – 10, 15, 20 metres in size – flooding the canvas with intense free-flowing and staining washes of colour, such as he would probably never have painted if he'd stayed in London. In New York, almost immediately, he felt able to throw himself into 'painting as total activity'. In London, he was always made to feel that, because he was black, he should be painting about black life or politics – which was where he had started as a student at the Royal College of Art – because paintings that 'speak directly of cruelty and pain, injustice and outrage', as Bryan Robertson at Whitechapel Art Gallery put it, were the kind that, in white people's opinions, best expressed black experience. It felt, for him, as if 'somebody was hanging around my neck a set of ideas'. By 1965, when he visited New York, and the artist Larry Rivers and writer Frank O'Hara encouraged him to relocate, he had had enough of that kind of reaction. When he was left out of the 'New Generation' exhibition at the Whitechapel in 1964, he was told that 'England is not yet ready for a gifted artist of colour.' Now, however, when his two sons, who still live with their mothers in London, are due to turn thirteen, he wants to be more present in their lives.

———

In the summer of 1961, Bowling and his fellow student David Hockney made their first trip to New York together. The following summer, they both graduated from the RCA. Bowling submitted his thesis on Piet Mondrian and was awarded the silver medal for painting; Hockney

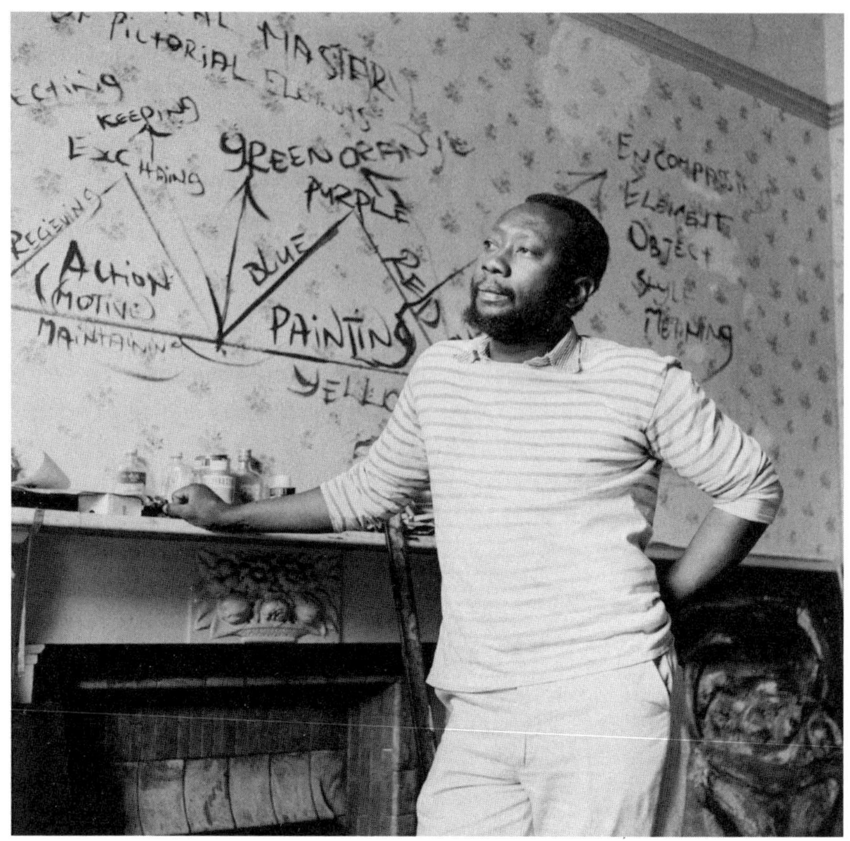

Frank Bowling in his studio, with wall inscribed with elements of his art theories, London, 1962, photograph by Tony Evans

was awarded the gold, which he collected wearing a gold lamé jacket, already something of a legend. The reason it was not the other way round was said to be because of Bowling's marriage in 1960, his first year at the RCA, to a staff member, the college registrar Patricia (Paddy) Kitchen. He later discovered that the principal, Sir Robin Darwin, had decided that the marriage breached college rules (or had made up a new rule for the occasion). He wrote to Kitchen, objecting to 'these young black people from the colonies coming here wanting to marry our girls'. What did he imagine, wondered Bowling? That 'they're going to take them back to the bush. And you know, probably eaten by tigers if not by the natives, put them in a pot or something'? Darwin's idea was to make the RCA 'a pragmatic paradise for Englishmen', where he ran the senior common room, the critic John Russell noted, like a 'mixture of High Table and grand country house'. What Bowling resented more than Darwin's pinstripe racism, however, was 'the fact that he was such a non-talented artist'. Because of his influential friends, Darwin's 'manky little watercolours' hung on the walls of West End galleries and at the Royal Academy.

In the midst of his course at the RCA, Bowling found himself, with no discussion, transferred to the Slade, where the painting studios were 'swimming around in this Bomberg mess'. At that stage, he wanted to paint pictures 'to do with what was happening in Africa and things like that…. Whereas these people were painting these pictures of a nude in a chair that was all mud, you know.' A year on, having negotiated his return to the RCA, he had two paintings in the Young Contemporaries show at the Royal Society of British Artists gallery, along with Hockney, Derek Boshier and Peter Phillips – the up-and-coming crowd. Bowling was being noticed for work that reminded people of Francis Bacon – his student hero. He was a true 'Baconian', according to the critic and Bacon-supporter David Sylvester. Bowling's subjects, however, had no obvious parallel in British art. In *The Abortion* (1962), a mixed-race couple embrace on a bed, which has an iron frame reminiscent of Bacon's theatre-y space-boxes; above the bed hover a blood-red angel and a splayed, tumbling foetus. When a tutor set the theme of 'Birthday', Bowling produced the first of what became series of paintings of a woman in labour. The 'childbirth thing' had preoccupied him ever since, soon after settling in London in his early twenties, he'd responded to the desperate cries of a woman in labour in his west London lodgings. He painted *Birthday* around the time he became an expectant father: 'I really was in a terrible state, thinking about how this child's going to come out, what it's going to look like, all those things. So, my work was anchored in personal experience.' In February 1962, a month after Kitchen gave birth to their son Dan, Bowling showed again in the annual Young Contemporaries exhibition. The Arts Council bought *Birthday* for its collection.

This was the year of *Pop Goes the Easel*. The RCA cohort, all in their twenties, were already being touted as the new face of British art. A white face, naturally. Bowling began to realize that his work was no longer being selected for high-profile group shows. He wasn't left to puzzle over the reason for long – the 'New Generation' moment in 1964, when he was kindly informed that England was not yet ready for a black artist like him, cleared up any doubt. But no one seemed to know when England *would* be ready, or what it would take for that day to arrive, or why the recognition that black jazz musicians and black writers had long been accorded could not extend to visual artists. One problem was that art was judged by values related to the idea of modern civilization, which was understood to be a Western phenomenon. The rest of the world, apparently, had 'cultures' as distinct from civilization, each having its own colourful local set of values. There were pop culture and mass culture, it was true, but these were in effect subsets of modern civilization, a joint enterprise in which, in the mid-1960s, no obvious place was open to 'a gifted artist of colour'.

There had in fact already been numerous gifted artists of colour working in Britain, although – as Bowling was discovering on his own account – their names did not often feature in the exhibitions or publications that established the distinction between artists who mattered and those who did not. In New York, as a contributing editor to *Arts Magazine* between 1969 and 1972, he explored these questions. 'Why have black artists,' he asked in May 1969, 'given their historical role in art, contributed so little to the mainstream of contemporary styles or better still, why have they contributed so little to the great body of modern or modernist art?' Henry Moore's contemporary Ronald Moody, for example, left Jamaica for London in 1923 to study dentistry at King's College. He set up in practice off Oxford Street, but by 1928 – much as had happened a few years earlier for Moore – was finding his path into sculpture via the British Museum. The hieratic, frontal stillness of Egyptian statues was the inspiration for Moody to start modelling in clay, then teach himself wood-carving – direct carving, in the manner of Moore and Barbara Hepworth. Where Moore worked with the muscularity of wood, its flexure and hollows, Moody drew out its qualities of density and stasis in heads and torsos. In 1935, the year Moore's sculpture took a more geometric turn, Moody carved *Wohin*, an 'enormous, mysterious head' in elmwood, named from a Schubert song; it was bought by the writer Marie Seton. London was not ready for Moody, but Paris was: a successful show in 1937 led him to move there. In America, he showed several works at 'Contemporary Negro Art' in Baltimore in 1939. The war brought him back to Britain and to four decades of neglect.

Aubrey Williams, eight years older than Bowling, had also grown up in British Guiana, sailing for Britain around the same time in the early 1950s. Williams started a degree in agricultural engineering at Leicester University but, restless in the face of 'British brainwashing and indoctrination', dropped out to travel. In Paris, he was complimented by Picasso – not on his dawning artistic ambitions but on his 'very fine African head'. Williams returned to London to study at Saint Martin's School of Art, and had two solo shows at the New Vision Centre Gallery. He found, however, that 'after two years all my shows were ignored', and began to ask himself 'what was wrong with me, what was wrong with my work.... I thought I had hit a level which would see me through both economically and respectably as a recognised artist in the British community.'

Recognition, it had to be said, did not necessarily equate to inclusion or acceptance. Lord Snowdon's photo of Bowling in *Private View*, published in 1965, portrayed him as primarily a family man, carrying a two-year-old Dan up to bed. The artist is shown in grainy profile, Dan face-on, wide-eyed, sleepily cute, stealing the show from the black-and-white thumbnail of Bowling's 1963 diptych *Beggars* – in reality a large-scale work – which is squashed against the margin of the opposite page. In his commentary, Robertson explained that Bowling had been raised 'on the edge of the jungle' and had crossed the Atlantic as a young man primed for an almost religious experience of Britain: 'The magical and awful impact of London on one freshly arrived from the tropics needs no description, but Bowling swam into the scene with the alacrity of a Mohammedan entering Mecca.' *Jungle*, *magical*, *tropics*, *Mecca*. Bowling apparently struck Robertson as a man who had found his natural element as an artist in London – but why did he have to underscore his point in just that way? After growing up in Bradford, Hockney experienced his first liberating immersion in London life as equally 'magical'. A few pages earlier in *Private View*, Robertson applauds him, and 'other young artists from the industrialized north', for what they 'bring to London', rather than what they've discovered there – namely 'a built-in, edgy, sceptical intelligence and a particular awareness of fashion and "what's in the air"'. This jaunty narrative of a London scene regalvanized by young, bright, attractive, rule-breaking talent from northern hinterlands of smoking factory chimneys and cobbled, washing-slung alleyways, would become the authorized version of the 1960s well into its participants' old age. Bowling, by contrast, is described as having a 'rather grim sense of life' and 'an unquenchable sense of violation'. There was grimness and violation in the background of Hockney's early gay love-paintings, too, but when this context was discussed, it was in terms of the artist's sexuality, not his skin colour or Yorkshire roots.

When, in his final year at the RCA, Bowling was offered a travelling scholarship to Rome, he persuaded the college to let him go instead to British Guiana, Barbados and Trinidad. This would be his first visit to the Caribbean since he'd left home, embarking from Port of Spain ten years before. He was conscious of 'an awful lot of attention being paid to the fact that I was born in the Caribbean, so I thought I should go and look at that. People kept talking about the light in the work, and stuff like that.' It was a homecoming without immediate resonance for his art – at that stage, Bowling 'didn't find anything that inspired me especially'. Four years later, when he moved to New York – the same year British Guiana gained independence as Guyana – Bowling took with him a set of canvases he had screen-printed with a photograph of his family business, Bowling's Variety Store – more as a personal metaphor-memory than an image of black experience in any generic sense. It was the licence that being in New York gave him to make big abstract paintings, like other young black artists there, that changed the game. And jazz, performed with an energy and edge that you didn't often find on the British scene: 'It seemed to me that, within abstraction, the black spirit, the whole thing of black, the real essence of black, [was] like jazz – jazz seemed to be the closest link I could find between the extemporizing and daring of these younger black artists.' In his SoHo studio at 535 Broadway, Bowling installed a large platform on to which he could lay a fresh canvas, then pour paint directly on to it from a height. The platform could be tilted at different angles, so that the wet paint slid and spread across the canvas. Rivers showed him how to use an epidiascope to project maps – Africa, South America – on to a canvas. In the 'map' paintings, which turned into a long series, a stain of colour could become a red continent, a yellow ocean.

Despite the deep-rooted assumptions about art and race that Bowling had encountered in London, there had been little open discussion of 'black art' or what it might mean to be a black artist in Britain at that time. 'Commonwealth artists' was the preferred label, but the term

'Commonwealth', he realized, was at best ambiguous. 'Commonwealth artists' both were and were not part of British art: their passports to serious critical consideration could be withdrawn at any time. In New York, the debate was much more energized and out-there. In 1969, Bowling curated '5 + 1' – five African-American artists plus the British-Caribbean Bowling, and there was 'Harlem on My Mind: The Cultural Capital of Black America, 1900–68' at the Metropolitan Museum of Art, a large-scale survey exhibition staged by an august national institution. In his regular contributions to *Arts Magazine*, Bowling interrogated 'black art' as a category, and the question of whether it was a label that he personally, as an abstract painter, should acknowledge. In 'It's Not Enough to Say "Black is Beautiful"', published in April 1971, he reflected,

> *Much of the discussion surrounding painting and sculpture by blacks seems completely concerned with notions of Black Art, not with the works themselves or their delivery.... And various spokesmen make rules to govern this supposed new form of expression. Unless we accept the absurdity of such stereotypes as 'they've all got rhythm...,' and even if we do, can we stretch it a little further to say they've all got painting?... For indeed we have not been able to detect in any kind of universal sense The Black Experience wedged-up in the flat bed between red and green: between say a red stripe and a green stripe.*

As Bowling readjusted to life in London in the spring of 1975 – finding a studio in Kennington, reacquainting himself with the great British artists of the past at the Tate Gallery and National Gallery – there was the question of whether, for a black artist, anything much had changed. The National Front were headline news, thrusting their Union Jacks in everyone's faces. This time the neo-fascist group was protesting against Europe rather than against immigration – in Bowling's absence, Britain had joined the European Community and Common Market, and a referendum on continued membership had recently been called. The country had somehow pulled itself out of the energy crisis and the three-day week, Labour under Harold Wilson had narrowly won the 1974 election, the coal miners had gained their 35 per cent pay rise, and the Tories now had a woman in charge, their former education minister Margaret Thatcher. Swinging London – the starry, optimistic days of Young Contemporaries – was history, and a history in which Bowling's work was seldom mentioned. Hockney, who had been based in Paris since 1973, was famous. His life had already been the subject of a movie, named for his best-known work, *A Bigger Splash*, painted in California in 1967, and he was busy now with set designs for Glyndebourne Festival Opera.

If black art wasn't yet on the British news agenda, immigration was. The Race Relations Act of November 1965 had made the promotion of hatred on grounds of 'colour, race, or ethnic or national origins' a crime. Further legislation in 1968 and 1971 outlawed discrimination in employment, housing and other fields, but it also stripped Commonwealth citizens of the automatic right to live in Britain. In April 1968, Enoch Powell, MP for Wolverhampton – where for twenty years there had been a West Indian community – addressed a Conservative Association in Birmingham. He summoned up an image of Britain in the year 2000, in which entire towns and districts would be 'occupied by sections of the immigrant and immigrant-descended population'. Comparing the children of legal immigrants to a gathering cloud, 'visible recently in Wolverhampton and…spreading quickly', he recounted the story of a local woman, terrified by 'wide-grinning piccaninnies' who followed her to the shops (Powell's offensive term for black children had slipped into seventeenth-century English from Portuguese pidgin in

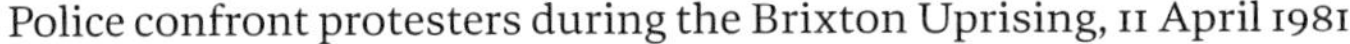

Police confront protesters during the Brixton Uprising, 11 April 1981

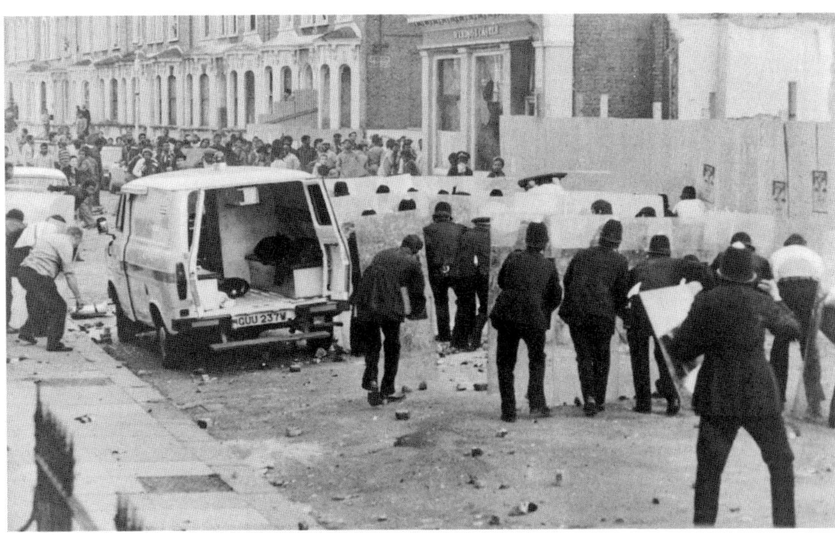

the slave fields of the Caribbean). Race relations legislation currently going through Parliament would, he claimed, enable immigrant communities to 'organise to consolidate their members, to agitate and campaign against their fellow citizens' and to 'overawe and dominate the rest with the legal weapons'. 'As I look ahead,' he concluded, 'I am filled with foreboding; like the Roman, I seem to see "the River Tiber foaming with much blood"'.

Powell's 'Rivers of Blood' speech got him swiftly sacked from Edward Heath's shadow cabinet but, however race relations law was framed, British politicians continued to tap the vote-winning properties of anti-immigrant sentiment. In 1978, Margaret Thatcher, eyeing the next general election, gave a television interview in which she asserted that 'people are rather afraid that this country might be rather swamped by people with a different culture'. On the British right, Powell's blend of Victorian racial stereotyping with classical allusion enjoyed a long posterity: in January 2002, the *Spectator* journalist and future prime minister Boris Johnson would rehash Powell's tropes – no doubt subconsciously, and for laughs this time – splicing references to 'piccaninnies', 'watermelon smiles' and the *Iliad* into a single short piece.

Attitudes of this kind, institutionally entrenched and politically exploited, fed into a febrile situation in black communities in the summer of 1981. The deaths of thirteen young black people in a house fire in New Cross, London, had met with refusal by the police to investigate the possibility of race-hate-motivated arson. Within weeks, a 'hard policing' stop-and-search operation targeting the black community in Brixton sparked rioting that spread, in similar inner-city contexts of heightened tension and distrust, to Birmingham, Bristol, Liverpool and Manchester. This was overwhelming young anger, felt by the British-born children of Caribbean-born parents of Bowling's generation, whom Powell described as 'the immigrant-descended population' and Kenneth Oxford, Liverpool Chief Constable, as 'the problem of half-castes'. As the historian David Olusoga points out, 'There was a terrible symmetry in the fact that the most serious and sustained of the early 1980s riots took place in the cities from which the slave-traders had set sail in the seventeenth and eighteenth centuries: Liverpool, Bristol, London.'

Taking inspiration from the American Black Arts Movement, in 1979 staff and students at Wolverhampton Polytechnic (in Powell's former constituency) founded the Black Artists Group, later renamed BLK

Art Group. This was the start of what Claudette Johnson, a recent art graduate and early group member, described as a 'groundswell of energy which was carrying us forward'. The Wolverhampton-born artist and writer Eddie Chambers, a Black Artists Group co-founder and at that time a student at Coventry's Lanchester Polytechnic, recalled 1979 as a year when the streets of his hometown 'were festooned with NF stickers declaring "If They're Black, Send Them Back!"' Taking an image of the Union Jack, which had been adopted by the National Front as its flag, with the NF logo in the middle, Chambers produced a sequence of four screen-prints, *Destruction of the National Front* (1979–80). In the first print, a torn-up Union Jack is reconfigured to form a swastika; the fascist emblem then progressively disintegrates into red, black, white and blue fragments, from which, perhaps, a new order could be assembled. Much as Moody and Williams had found in the 1950s, black British artists were still relegated to the edges – if visible at all – in accounts of what constituted 'British art'. For Chambers and the Wolverhampton group, it was time to articulate clearly and forcefully an alternative vision. In July 1982, he proposed that,

> *At this particular period of time in the history of Black people in Britain… the Black art student, by the very colour of his/her skin should find him/ herself drawn towards the nerve points of social and political tension and unrest choosing to respond in this situation by producing work which voices their dissatisfaction with…the police, the state, the educational system, the church, and so on.*

'Black art' needed to be activist in spirit, helping to create 'an alternative set of values necessary for better living, stronger communities, contemporary cultural identity.' 'An alternative set of values' meant just that – not assimilating into or competing within existing inhospitable cultural and political systems.

The First National Black Art Convention took place at Wolverhampton Polytechnic on 28 October 1982. In his opening address on 'Art and Black Consciousness', the British-Pakistani artist Rasheed Araeen affirmed that 'our assertion of blackness must be accompanied by a radical position in opposition to what is represented by the dominant [i.e. white European] ideology'. To be black was essentially 'to be political'. Attending from London was the twenty-nine-year-old Lubaina Himid, who had studied at Wimbledon College of Art, then joined a small theatre group and was working as a seamstress at the Royal Opera House and a waitress in a nearby brasserie. She wasn't sure what to expect of the event, but – listening to the speeches in the packed conference hall – began to feel that it was all 'very political, it wasn't very cultural or creative really, and it was very male and it was very strident, but it was exciting, it was pretty phenomenal stuff'. Claudette Johnson, too, was struck by the general tone of strident maleness. She had become aware as a student that 'I couldn't find images [of black women] that I recognised. I could find lots of parodies of black womanhood'; she 'wanted to tell a different story about our presence in this country' to 'get away from the spectrum that's most represented here in European painting'. Her response was to take the straightforward but at the same time radical step of making very large drawings of black women she knew. At the conference, Himid recalled, Johnson 'was incredibly brave, and she stood up and said, I think the women in this room have probably had enough of listening to this stuff. I think we should go into another space and discuss the issues that we want to discuss.'

The ambitions of earlier black male British artists and the context in which they had sought to position their work were, thought Himid, questionable from the point of view of a black British woman in the 1980s: they had been 'so much concerned with aesthetics and so much concerned with the world of European commercial gallery picture-making' (hence Williams's desire to be 'a recognised artist in the British community'). Yes, they were 'telling the story of Africa and the story of what it is to be African or what it is to be Indian, what it is to be from the Caribbean', but they were often doing it in 'a very exotic sort of way'. Which could be problematic, because seeing black art as 'exotic' was exactly the colonialist view. Feeling that 'the strategy hadn't worked', Himid had a sense that she and other black women of her generation now found themselves 'at year zero, that the history started there and then'.

We were confronting the issue that we didn't have quite an equal voice in the black political movement or the black art movement and we needed to be able to speak, and that it was easier to speak to each other and get a clearer idea of what we wanted to say to build a strategy if you like, speaking to each other, than we did within the wider movement, where we would have our place serving the greater good – filling envelopes, typing letters, looking after children.

In other words, very much the roles in the workplace and home that women had been expected to occupy without asking difficult questions before the women's movement of the 1970s got under way. Although things were changing – in October 1979, *Spare Rib* reported on the National Black Women's Conference in Brixton, and in October 1983 ran a 'Special Black Women's Issue' – the movement in its early days had still seemed 'too much engaged with what men were doing.... The conversation was not with each other, the conversation was with men.'

Himid was soon involved in organizing the first exhibition in Britain devoted to black women artists. In 'Five Black Women', which opened at the Africa Centre Gallery, Covent Garden, in September 1983, she exhibited alongside Johnson, Houria Niati, Sonia Boyce and Veronica Ryan. Rather than directly confronting prejudice and injustice in the way Chambers had advocated, 'Five Black Women' explored a different vein of subversion by presenting art of a kind 'that might previously have been seen as peripheral, craft-based or in some other way outside the aesthetic and intellectual parameters of "high" art'. Ryan showed a collection of gourds and other seedpods cast in lead – ordinary biological containers that carried, at the same time, a compact poetry of fertility and oceanic dispersal. Himid exhibited several large figures cut out of plywood, which could be viewed either as flat sculptures or as sculptural paintings. Intended to occupy spaces, like actors or furniture, rather than hang on gallery walls, these figures evoked the seventeenth- and eighteenth-century fashion of placing painted wooden figures, known as dummy boards or 'silent companions', around the spacious homes of the gentry and aristocracy, which were often built and run with fortunes made from the slave trade. Six of Himid's life-size dummy boards at the Africa Centre represented white men, each with an outsize penis in the form of a long, thin picture of an object of male pride and joy, wryly characterized from a female point of view – a leaping dog, a family group, a skyscraper, a paintbrush.

Within weeks, Himid was preparing for another show, again in the double role of artist–curator, this time featuring a group of fifteen women artists. In 'Black Woman Time Now' at Battersea Arts Centre, her rapidly evolving family of dummy-board figures included an Afro-Caribbean woman with headscarf, folded arms and a flaring skirt, which also functioned as a poster-wall or billboard for messages (pl. 17). It was collaged with tokens of Caribbean village life – fish, fruit, feathers – and

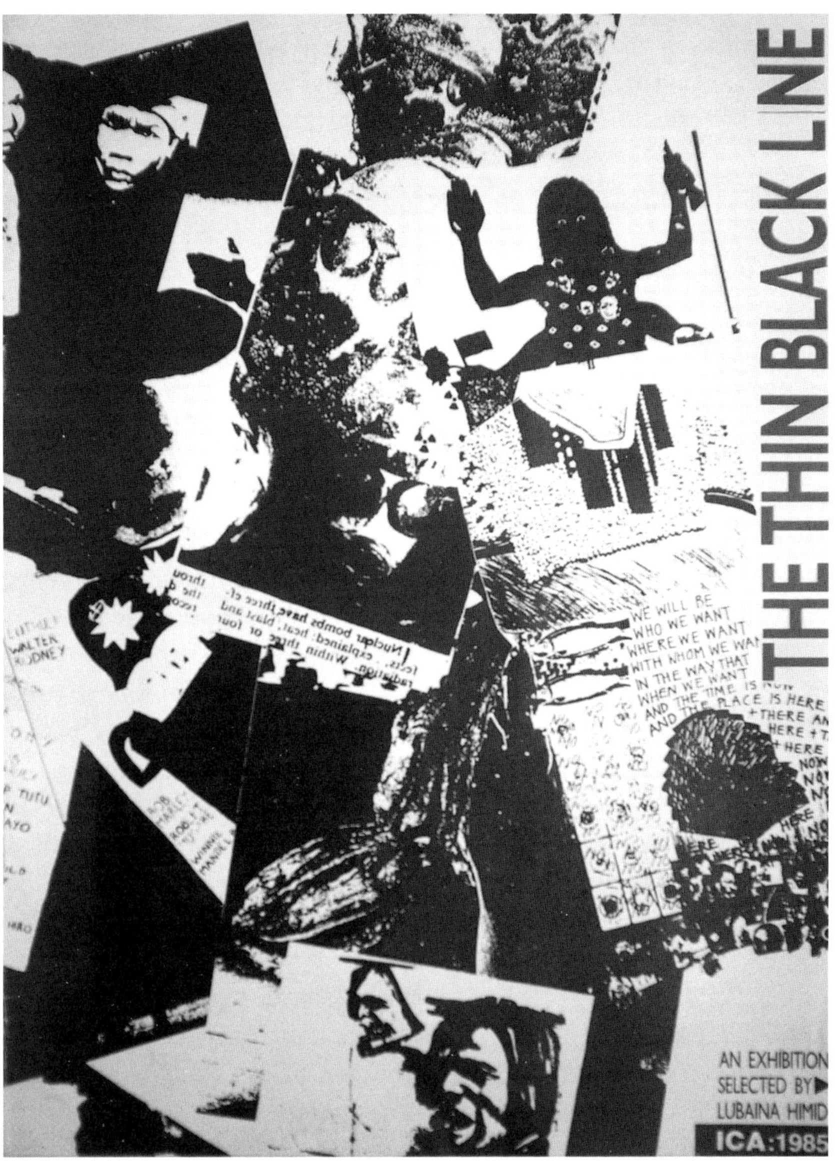

Catalogue cover for 'The Thin Black Line', Institute of Contemporary Arts, London, November 1985

press photos of Nelson Mandela, Bob Marley and other heroes of black culture and civil rights. Where the full skirt, as a marker of femaleness, might have represented a very ambivalent symbol in the early *Spare Rib* era, here its message, inscribed with capital letters, was uninhibited and assertive: *WE WILL BE / WHO WE WANT / WHERE WE WANT / WITH WHOM WE WANT / IN THE WAY THAT WE WANT / WHEN WE WANT/ AND THE TIME IS NOW / AND THE PLACE IS HERE.* The place for a third group exhibition, 'The Thin Black Line', was the Institute of Contemporary Arts in November 1985.

'In the eighties,' Claudette Johnson would recall, 'there was a whole movement, a collective that we were part of', in which 'everyone understood how powerful it was to work, to join with other people to make your voice heard'. The decade ended with what felt like, finally, the admission of black artists and black art into history, in both contemporary practice and modern art's hall of fame. Curated by Rasheed Araeen, 'The Other Story: Asian, African and Caribbean Artists in Post-war Britain' opened at the Hayward Gallery in November 1989, before touring to Wolverhampton and Manchester in the first half of 1990. First proposed to the Arts Council by Araeen in 1978, 'The Other Story' featured work by twenty-four artists, most of whom had been born outside Britain – Moody, Williams, Bowling, Chambers, Boyce and Himid among them – grouped into four themed sections: 'In the Citadel of Modernism', 'Taking the Bull by the Horns', 'Confronting the System' and 'Recovering Cultural Metaphors'. In the mainstream press, critical response was muted or hostile. Some of the invited artists were reluctant to participate: objecting to being categorized as 'Afro-Asian', Bowling took some persuading, and the young sculptor Anish Kapoor, who had been selected to represent Britain at the 1990 Venice Biennale, refused. In a sign of how much had changed in the twelve years since Araeen had originally proposed this exhibition, only four of the artists were women.

Recalling his own teenage years in the 1980s, Olusoga reflects that, in wider British life, the decade was marked by 'a strong sense among black people of being under siege, and of feeling the need to fight for a place and a future in the country'. It was a time, he suggests, when an awareness of black history and culture 'became critical to the generation whom Enoch Powell could not bring himself to see as British'. In March 1990, a new decade opened with scenes disturbingly reminiscent of the early 1980s, with street protests and rioting. This time the anger was directed against the introduction, under Thatcher's third administration, of the community charge, known as the poll tax – an attempt to shift the basis of local government taxation from property ownership to the individual. Thatcher was much quoted – on the right with admiration and with outrage on the left – on her statement in an interview in 1987 that homeless people who expected the government to house them were 'casting their problems on society'. But 'who is society?' Thatcher berated her imaginary destitute scrounger. 'There is no such thing!'

19

Shark market

Rotherhithe, July 1988

'There is a lot of work to do in the next few weeks,' reads the neatly typed memo, headed F R E E Z E. 'I am relying on everyone to do as much as possible to prepare the space.' The space is an abandoned Port of London building in what used to be Surrey Commercial Docks, on the Rotherhithe peninsula, south London, but is now a construction site in waiting. The author of the memo, Damien Hirst, a second-year student at Goldsmiths' College of Art, reckons that, if sixteen or so people put in eight days' work each, 'everything should get done in time'. Their task is to spruce up the interior of the empty building, a two-storey brick barn with rows of close-set windows along all four sides and a kind of clerestory running the length of the roof, which bathes the shabby old space in light. Hirst has negotiated with the London Docklands Development Corporation (LDDC) and the property developer Olympia & York to allow himself and his artist friends to borrow the building for a two-part, nine-week exhibition of their work. With luck and careful planning, this self-organized show will mirror as closely as possible the style of a smart contemporary commercial gallery, specifically the Saatchi Gallery in north London.

———

The docks lining the Thames between Rotherhithe and Woolwich, historically the main source of employment in this area of London, never fully recovered from the devastation inflicted by the Blitz. From the late 1960s onwards, with the growth in containerized shipping and the shift of maritime business to deep-water coastal ports, they slid into terminal decline. One after another, as the old waterfront warehouses, wharves and cranes, along with their workforce, became obsolete, the docks were closed. New housing was promised and regeneration planned, but little happened for a decade or more. Then in 1981, in a decisive early indicator of the new direction of political and economic travel, the Conservative government under Margaret Thatcher established the LDDC, giving it direct control of planning and development across an area of 8½ square miles. Surrey Docks, which had been particularly heavily bombed in September 1940, was one of the bleakest tracts in this vast urban enclave, and one of the last to be transformed by redevelopment. Islands of council housing inhabited a wasteland of rubble-filled basins and aimless roads, but in the gap between ruin and redevelopment, Hirst saw an opportunity. He persuaded LDDC to contribute £4,000 towards art materials and Olympia & York to sponsor a high-quality printed catalogue to the tune of £10,000 – a measure both of his enterprising chutzpah and of the amounts of money washing through Docklands in these years (the catalogue budget represented about a quarter of the price of a modest flat in one of the new developments).

'Enterprise' was a spirit much-trumpeted in government circles, where it was regarded as the opposite of the kinds of 'wet' attitudes that prevailed in the arts. The economic troubles of the 1970s had been exacerbated, chancellor Geoffrey Howe told Parliament in his inaugural budget in June 1979, by 'laws that stand in the way of change and stifle enterprise'. A culture of vigorous private industry, the logic ran, was essential to revitalize a society debilitated by welfare-dependency and over-generous public funding. In 1978, anticipating a general election in which levels of unemployment would be a battleground, the Conservative Party had run a billboard campaign. The poster showed an interminable queue of downcast jobless people at an 'Unemployment Office' snaking from left to right under the punning slogan 'Labour Isn't Working' (in the event, unemployment would rise from 5.4 per cent in 1978 to 10 per cent or above for most of the 1980s). The advertising agency responsible for this inspired coupling of words and image, recycled for the election itself the following spring under the slogan 'Labour Still Isn't Working' and widely credited with helping to secure a victory for Thatcher, was run by two sons of a north London Iraqi-Jewish family, Maurice Saatchi and his art-collecting brother Charles.

Central to the government's plans for stimulating the economy was the systematic transference of public assets into the enterprising hands of the private sector. The proximity of former Port of London landholdings to the financial district of the City of London created an irresistible incentive to favour office and residential developments of the kind that would make the area far more hospitable to incoming

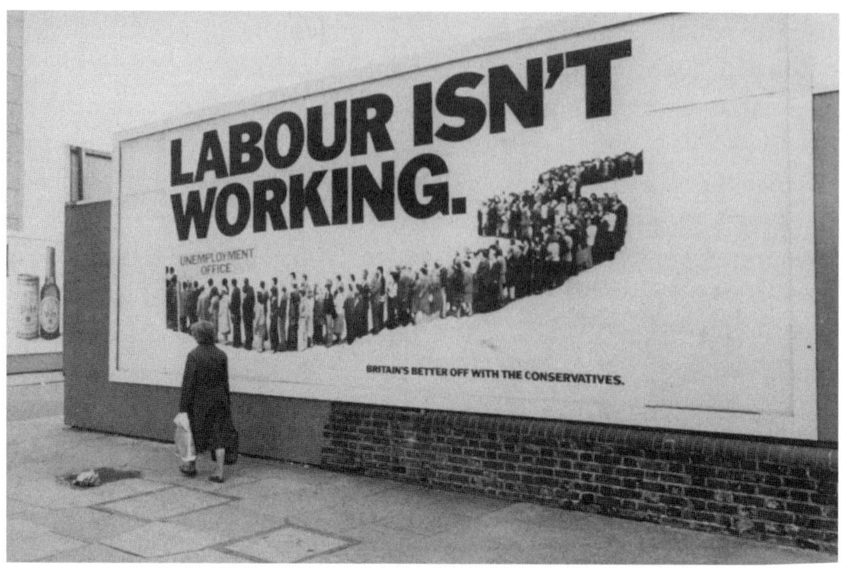

'Labour Isn't Working' billboard poster designed by Saatchi & Saatchi for the Conservative Party, 1978, photograph by Chris Ware

money than to its existing working-class population. In the wake of the deregulation of the London Stock Exchange – the 'Big Bang' of October 1986 that, among its other effects, opened up British financial institutions to foreign ownership – Docklands became the ever-higher-rising home of international corporations, attracting a fresh demographic of newly affluent young urban professionals, aka yuppies. The sense of 'being under siege' (in David Olusoga's phrase) that troubled black communities in the 1980s haunted east London's working-class communities, too, although in the case of Docklands they generally found themselves on the wrong side of history.

In 1988, the cranes and bulldozers had not yet quite reached Surrey Docks. The area was almost inaccessible by public transport – off the map for most Londoners – yet its impending regeneration, after forty years of neglect, was a symbol of the new ethos of making a roaring success of previously unthinkable schemes. The same could be said of the model on which Hirst and co. based their venture, the gallery that Charles Saatchi, who had begun seriously collecting modern American art at the age of twenty-six, opened in 1985 in a former paint factory in St John's Wood. The combined effect of the warehouse-scale space and the bright, appropriative boldness of American minimalism in the exhibition 'New York Art Now' in September 1987 – especially Jeff Koons's Hoovers, displayed in museum-style vitrines – was 'just like, boom', enthused Hirst: 'I want to show there.' In the Rotherhithe building, with its frankly industrial architecture, high white walls (they would board over the lower windows) and natural overhead light, he gauged that a comparable effect could be achieved. The building had 'the scale, the size, the impact' – the potential to become the kind of setting that contemporary art needed 'to work on an international level'.

The prospects in the late 1980s felt as bleak as they'd ever been for art students contemplating life after graduation. A period of recession in 1980–81 sapped art market confidence. Conceptual art, increasingly viewed in art schools as the area in which interesting developments were most likely to happen, was in any case inherently antipathetic to commodity culture and market forces. How an art school graduate could progress to earning a living as a professional artist was a subject frequently brushed over by tutors, like an embarrassing fact of life that ought never to form part of the creative or critical equation. In that respect at least, the modern world had kept faith with Ruskin's belief that the money motive was toxic to good art. The artist's 'state of mind', as described by the economist John Maynard Keynes, whose theories had shaped fiscal policy since the war, 'is just the opposite of that of a man the main purpose of whose work is his livelihood'. The artist friends of Keynes's youth – Vanessa Bell, Roger Fry, Duncan Grant – had of course had other sources of livelihood to tap into.

Goldsmiths in the 1980s was one of few art schools that did not tacitly endorse this unworldly view of the artist's vocation. The message Goldsmiths teacher and artist Michael Craig-Martin tried to impart to his students was that, although 'the actual motivation for people was not to become rich and famous', they needed to address the question of 'how can they survive as artists now? And for the next year?' This wasn't, it had to be admitted, a problem for which conceptual art offered any very clear solution. Craig-Martin himself was a veteran of the 1972 conceptual exhibition at the Hayward Gallery, 'The New Art', where he had shown *Faces*, a set of twelve small walk-in booths containing mirrors, in which were reflected both the face of the person in the booth and other faces and spaces in mirrors above them, posing the question – among others – of where exactly our self-image resides. In *An*

Oak Tree (1973), Craig-Martin floated a similar question: a glass of water rests on a glass bathroom shelf, accompanied by a text explaining that the glass of water is an oak tree – in other words, that the tree, like any tree, real or imagined, exists in the mind, as a word and an idea, as much (or more than) an object composed of trunk, branches, bark and leaves.

For art students in the late 1980s, who had been teenagers or younger when Thatcher came to power, the traditional expectation that the best an artist could hope for was to manage (just about) to stay afloat was not the message they'd grown up with. Following her election victory in May 1979, right from the outset, Keynesian economic theory was out. Keynes's vision of public and private investment working in tandem to create the conditions in which both national prosperity and civilized life could flourish was replaced by a thoroughgoing faith in market forces. In this model, the generation of private wealth through untrammelled commercial activity was taken to benefit society as a whole by seeping outwards and downwards from the top. No matter that Keynes had decried this kind of purely 'utilitarian and economic' approach as 'the most dreadful heresy, perhaps, which has ever gained the ear of serious people'. To Thatcher and her advisers, this was 'wet' talk – it sounded far too much like socialism. If investment didn't make money for investors, what was the point? As the regeneration of Docklands gathered pace, yielding desirable office space and smart, clean residential blocks set in shiny plazas and pleasant landscaped walks, it was viewed on the right as a triumph of the private sector incentivized by the state, and on the left as a calculated erasure of the fabric of east London's working-class community life.

Beyond a fondness for quoting Rudyard Kipling, Thatcher herself had little interest in the arts. In May 1980, she surprised an audience of Royal Academicians by announcing that she was 'not going to say that writers, painters, philosophers and actors must stand, like everyone else, on their own two feet'. But in the broader picture, she was deeply critical of the arts' taxpayer-funded bureaucratization and lack of public accountability, which she believed – not entirely irrationally – had become unsustainable during the 1970s. The government's view of contemporary arts as both a cradle of leftist agitation and an expensive but unproductive sector of the economy came to shape the horizons for young artists. The budget for the Arts Council of England, which had grown between 1969 and 1979 from £91 million to £204 million, was summarily cut by 6 per cent and flatlined for the next five years. Lord Gowrie, arts minister between 1983 and 1985, sneered at the dependence of 'subsidy junkies' on injections of Arts Council cash.

In another determined attitudinal reset, advocates of the value of creativity in any pedagogic context, from kindergarten to postgraduate research – who believed, that's to say, in the core principles of the twentieth century's most influential strands of educational theory and child psychology – were stigmatized as 'trendy teachers'. Their dangerous and irresponsible social radicalism was to be rooted out through educational reforms, which included the introduction of a prescriptive 'fact-based' national curriculum in place of 'child-centred' learning (regarded as another 'wet' delusion). The ideas of Melanie Klein, Donald Winnicott, A. S. Neill, Herbert Read, William Johnstone – that long, motley line of theorists and practitioners of ludic learning – were suddenly as out of tune with the times as the traditional strongholds of heavy industry and unionized labour on which Thatcher had also trained her sights. The bitterest and most brutal confrontation of the Thatcher years came with the miners' strike of March 1984 to March 1985, by the end of which the government had broken the National Union of Mineworkers and opened the way for mass pit closures. It symbolized a deliberate economic reorientation from manufacturing to services, strangely and, in the circumstances, ironically suggesting a parallel with the art world's shift in focus from productivist object-making to the conceptual trading-floor of pure ideas.

While the rhetoric of competitive, profit-driven private enterprise – the 'business model' – permeated every sphere, the value ascribed to individualism, which in one form or another had shaped ideas about art and artists since the Romantic era, underwent a bizarre metamorphosis. Greed, like spring rains, came to acquire an almost mystical regenerative aura. Thinkers as different as Read and Keynes were convinced of the benefits to society of the free creative individual. For Thatcher, however, because one half of this equation was missing – society ('There is no such thing') – the individual had first to prove their value to themselves, and the only really important value was that which could be quantified. 'Making lots of money – it's not hard, you know,' John Self, emblematically named protagonist of Martin Amis's 1984 novel *Money* asserts. 'Making lots of money is a breeze. You watch.' Just you watch: 'It's gonna be good!' Hirst pepped his co-exhibitors in 'Freeze' – the title of their 1988 show was apparently a riff on the frisée lettuce someone had brought along to an exhibition planning meeting in a thirteenth-floor council flat near Surrey Docks, chaired by Hirst's girlfriend Angela Bulloch and Sarah Lucas. Their project to turn an abandoned building into a convincing simulacrum of an elite commercial gallery had the air of an experiment in seeing how far the mechanisms of free-market capitalism could be hijacked for a joyride into the territory of the conceptual avant-garde.

Whatever its rationale, 'Freeze' would represent a radical departure from the ways in which artists and people in the arts, of an older generation than Hirst and his friends, had to date been responding to the realities of Thatcher's Britain. Returning to London from West Germany in February 1981 to install a solo exhibition at Whitechapel Art Gallery, the sculptor Tony Cragg had picked up on the undercurrents of social and racial tension, and the effects of recession, bringing into raw focus the economic north–south divide. Offered an unexpectedly large expanse of gallery wall to cover, he assembled *Britain Seen from the North*. A silhouette of the artist's standing figure faced an outsize image of Britain, rotated left through 90 degrees, so that Scotland was nearest the figure's face. In Cragg's sidelong but immediately recognizable Britain, composed from metal, wooden and coloured plastic junk salvaged from streets around west London, a broken country full of rubbish seems to be in clownish mood, bright with carnival debris. In the music world and sections of the media there was frank loathing for the new right: protest and satire took on a no-holds-barred battle-readiness, in songs like Morrissey's 'Margaret on the Guillotine' and Elvis Costello's 'Tramp the Dirt Down'. In the television satire *Spitting Image*, first broadcast in 1984 and eventually reaching an audience of 15 million, politicians and celebrities were portrayed in the form of latex puppets created by two artists, Peter Fluck and Roger Law. The prime minister – who claimed never to watch the show – was impersonated as the goggle-eyed, aggressively butch ringmaster of a fawning cabinet, who addressed her unanimously as 'Sir'.

The collective note struck by the participants in 'Freeze' wasn't anger or satire but rather, observed Fiona Rae, one of three painters in the show, 'cool, ironic detachment'. Through the teaching of Craig-Martin, Jon Thompson and Richard Wentworth at Goldsmiths, they had been well grounded in the theory and practice of conceptual art, in which artists generally worked with 'poor' materials or in ways that left minimal material traces. 'The New Art' had featured sand, ropes, wooden poles and sacks (Barry Flanagan), light bulbs (John Hilliard), photos of seaweed and stones (Richard Long), mirrors and fluorescent tubes (Craig-Martin), a photograph of a deserted Canadian road (Hamish Fulton), two 150-watt lamps (Gerald Newman) and the artists' own bodies (Gilbert & George). Back in the 1970s, conceptual art's ethical trump card had been its capacity to engage with a question without compromising its position by producing desirable, saleable objects – a form of detachment that could be described as committed rather than cool. But if you were going to engage with the art market of the 1980s on its own terms, in a big, white, well-lit, well-publicized gallery space, then cool irony was definitely required for the preservation of integrity. This was a balancing act that the 'Freeze' sixteen pulled off, demonstrating, for better or worse, that creativity and enterprise really could coexist.

Hirst's energies had been focused on getting the show together. His own modest contribution included a wall-mounted assemblage of brightly painted cardboard boxes. Anya Gallaccio poured a ton of molten lead across the floor, where it scabbed with the old floor-glue to form a weblike integument. Mat Collishaw's *Bullet Hole* was a technically tricky feat involving a grid of fifteen light boxes, laboriously constructed for the exhibition from sheet steel and fluorescent tubes, and bearing an enlarged backlit image of the hairy crown of a head with a pulsing puncture wound in the middle – a colour image borrowed from a book on forensic pathology, illustrating an ice-pick injury. There was no implied backstory of victim and aggressor, no context of any kind – just the glowing blow-up of a moist red hole. Another object lesson emerging through the effort and thrill of self-made self-presentation at 'Freeze' was that, in true conceptual fashion, the public could make up their own minds about a work's meaning, but also – if you succeeded in engaging the collector or curator – these people might be persuaded to add to the work the value of their own intellectual or financial investment in its significance. Craig-Martin's advice to his students was not to go scouting for potential subjects but to concentrate on something that had already caught their attention, for any reason – something that they had already, without necessarily thinking of it as art or art-worthy, made their own. 'Everything is actually more interesting than you can cope with,' he counselled. 'You have to learn, how do you limit yourself, how do you focus?' Hirst had had a student placement in a

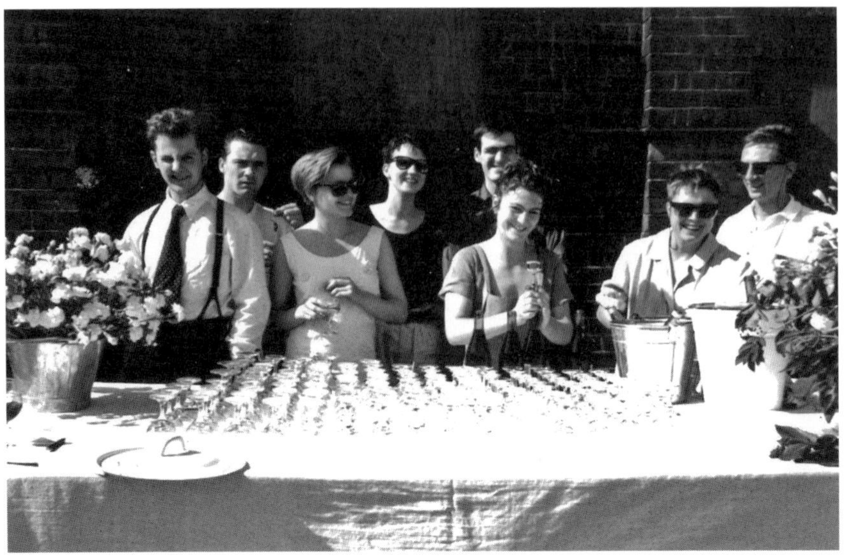

Getting ready for the 'Freeze' private view. Left to right: Ian Davenport, Damien Hirst, Angela Bulloch, Fiona Rae, Stephen Park, Anya Gallaccio, Sarah Lucas and Gary Hume. August 1988, photograph by Abigail Lane

mortuary: a good example of a subject with clear limits and strong focus, but practically unlimited possibilities, was death.

No matter that few visitors found their way through the Rotherhithe wastelands to 'Freeze', Hirst – plundering the mailing list from his part-time job at Anthony d'Offay's gallery – made sure that art world influencers were personally invited and actively courted. High on that list were Charles Saatchi, Norman Rosenthal, exhibitions director at the Royal Academy, and the Tate Gallery's newly appointed director, Nicholas Serota. Saatchi wasn't initially excited by what he saw of Hirst's work in the first part of 'Freeze' – 'a cluster of small colourful cardboard boxes placed high on a wall' – judging it 'fairly so-so'. What did impress him, however, was 'the hopeful swagger of it all'. And the swagger was extraordinarily effective: within a year, several of the 'Freeze' participants, still in their early twenties, had been taken up by commercial dealers. Saatchi himself understood the conceptual power of combining a single arresting image with a memorable strapline. Advertising, moreover, allowed a creative freedom about its means and messages of a kind that would have been disparaged in art as propaganda. The way in which you decided to give a message impact was concerned primarily with the response you aimed to stimulate in the viewer or buyer – which might or might not have much to do with truth. The unemployed people in the 1978 campaign poster 'Labour Isn't Working', for example, had in reality been acted by random members of Hendon Young Conservative Club, with the photo edited to multiply their numbers. Saatchi became a new kind of patron for British conceptual art, bringing to it a revolutionary new ingredient: serious money. Money made it possible not just to realize a concept but to stage it, blockbuster style. In 1991, he made Hirst an offer. 'Make anything you want and I'll pay for it,' he is said to have proposed.

The 'high-concept' Hollywood movie had arrived in the mid-1970s with the *Jaws* series (the fourth instalment was released in 1987), driven by one sensational idea: the terror of being eaten alive by a great white shark. Hirst commissioned an Australian fisherman to catch and ship a tiger shark – 'something big enough to eat you,' was the brief. He installed it in a room-sized vitrine filled with formaldehyde, man-trap jaws agape. As an exhibit in a natural history museum, it would have been labelled 'Tiger Shark'. Hirst's title, *The Physical Impossibility of Death in the Mind of Someone Living*, prompted other reflections about this dead fish: we are alive, the shark that wants to kill us is dead and yet at the same time disturbingly present (like a skull in a seventeenth-century Dutch *vanitas* painting) – disturbing, because the state of being dead is impossible for the living to imagine, although being eaten alive by a dead shark is not. The wording of the title, suggesting an essay by Jean-Paul Sartre or Jacques Lacan, was a conceptual coup in itself: just by reading it, you got the synaptic tingle of thinking an interesting thought. The bill came to £50,000 (about £105,000 today).

Saatchi sold off his American collection and announced that he would now collect and exhibit Hirst and his generation, whom he branded Young British Artists (yBas or YBAs). *The Physical Impossibility of Death in the Mind of Someone Living* was the centrepiece of the YBAs' debut show at the Saatchi Gallery in 1992. Hirst's shark monopolized the press coverage, overshadowing the other exhibiting artists – Rachel Whiteread, Alex Landrum, John Greenwood and the duo Ben Langlands and Nikki Bell – but buoying them in its powerful wake. The pickled shark was such a strong, clear, simple, big thing – a jolt, if not a shock, to encounter in an art gallery rather than a museum. It was impossible, however, to dismiss it as something *anyone* could have made.

From John Latham's skoob towers to Long's trodden line in grass and Craig-Martin's oak-tree glass of water, practitioners of message- and ideas-based art had generally operated in an atmosphere of monkish yet offbeat austerity. Very ordinary things, standing in their ordinary way for the real world, were reconfigured and redescribed, destroyed, deployed, dispersed, encased in ways that made you look twice and think, with an unexpected slant, about things you looked at often and took for granted. There was never the slightest hint of *swagger*, never the polished breath of money.

'Freeze' had been inspired (enterprise almost for the hell of it), but in the years that followed, with press coverage on a level only seen before at the peak of art's landmark public scandals, along with the fame and the money, it gradually dawned that, in their adoption and modification of the tenets of conceptual practice, a number of Saatchi's young British artists and their peers were actually working the other way round. Instead of employing everyday means to provoke complex, nuanced thought, artists dedicated themselves to channelling the complex resources of elite galleries and high-profile exhibitions into presenting everyday concepts, like 'everyone dies' or 'sex is messy'.

Saatchi began trawling for talent in art school degree shows and fringe venues, opening a fast track for artists at the very start of their careers. If he liked an artist's work, they didn't have to wait to be signed by a West End gallery or noticed by a curator. In January 1993, Sarah Lucas, one of the original 'Freeze' crew, teamed up with a Royal College of Art graduate, Tracey Emin, to sell work from a vacant shop in Bethnal Green. 'The Shop' was an enterprising hive of home-made merchandise – ashtrays with Hirst's face inside, T-shirts printed with slogans like 'Complete Arsehole' – with a clientele drawn from YBA social circles and gallerists curious about the bankable new youth phenomenon. 'Everyone was trying so hard to be cool,' it struck the artist Gavin Turk on visits to 'The Shop', 'it was actually quite nerve-racking.' The experience of stepping inside was more 'like a spiritual awakening' for recent Goldsmiths graduate Sam Taylor-Wood, 'suddenly feeling like, "It doesn't matter. Just put everything out there that you're thinking and feeling, and see what happens."'

This was Emin's approach to constructing a piece for the exhibition 'Minky Manky' at the South London Gallery in 1995 – it had to be larger than the ashtrays and T-shirt, she was told, large enough to stand alone.

Everyone I Have Ever Slept With 1963–1995 was a small pyramidal camping tent, on to the inner skin of which Emin embroidered 102 names – close relatives from childhood, aborted foetuses, sexual partners. Saatchi wanted to buy it, but Emin refused to sell to him, on the grounds that he had abetted Thatcher's 'crimes against humanity'. The tent was sold – then Saatchi bought it from the buyer for £40,000, three times the original price. Art transactions of these kinds of values had been happening in New York since the war, but not, before the 1990s, for young artists in Britain.

At Surrey Docks, within four years of 'Freeze', LDDC had only fifteen remaining sites for sale, all of them touted as 'first rate investment opportunities for the Nineties and beyond'. In 1994, the corporation began to wind down its activities, pulling out altogether in 1996, when planning decisions were placed back in the hands of the various local authorities. It had done its work: no one who had known that part of London twenty years before would recognize it now. The redevelopment of Docklands was the grand finale to London's protracted recovery and rebuilding after the Second World War. During much of this time, London had been a city past its peak: between 1939 and 1981, its population had declined by 21 per cent and would not approach its pre-war level for another thirty years. Throughout the twentieth century, the home ground of artists' London had been the 'semi-destroyed' or unregenerated areas of the nineteenth-century imperial city – Chelsea and Hampstead (still low-rent areas in the 1950s), Whitechapel, Hoxton, Camden Town, where Frank Auerbach, whose work was now fetching high prices, had worked in the same small studio in Mornington Crescent since 1954.

Lucian Freud had finally quit Paddington for the statelier terraces of Holland Park in 1977, and was now, in his seventies, an acknowledged grand bohemian and old master of mid-century British art, for whom, with the new appetite for art news and art celebrity, there was room alongside the reliably transgressive YBAs. In 1993, Whitechapel Art Gallery gave Freud a retrospective, which toured the following year to New York and Madrid – a rare mark of international standing for a British easel painter. Flesh, sex, the ugly-beautiful, awkward, touchable bodies of (almost) everyone he had ever slept with – these were part of Freud's repertory. At the same time, his working routine, his materials and the whole relationship of artist to sitter to studio on which his painting was based would not have seemed unfamiliar to Rembrandt. Days and weeks of intent observation, slow advances, scraping paintings back to the canvas, starting again – unadvertised and largely unobserved. Freud was now working on a series of large naked portraits of the Australian performance artist Leigh Bowery, whose act involved flamboyant drag and a lot of blood. The money made little practical difference to his working routine. He used his earnings to fuel his gambling – there was no art worth making, he felt as he had always felt, without risk.

After eighteen years of Conservative government, New Labour – another astute conceptual rebranding – won by a landslide in the general election of May 1997. This time the Saatchis' poster for the Conservative campaign, showing the New Labour leader Tony Blair with 'demon eyes' (as if 'big enough to eat you'), failed to hit the national mood for change. In many respects, the contrast between Blair's incoming administration and Conservative policies was more cosmetic than real. As Eric Hobsbawm wryly noted, 'Mrs Thatcher had a project. Blair's historic project is adjusting Us to It.' 'Labour', in historian David Edgerton's view, 'was always in part a party of protest; New Labour was nothing but a party of power.' Far from restoring high levels of public spending, New Labour would see it fall to its lowest level as a proportion of GDP since the late 1950s. All the more essential, then, to announce a cultural agenda as different as possible from the notorious Thatcherite antipathy to the arts. There would be free entry to museums, and National Lottery funding to refresh and redevelop the tired spaces of public galleries, and build new ones, although the awkward fact remained that the predominantly lower-income buyers of lottery tickets were not generally those who benefited from elegant museum extensions and stylish cafés.

Government suddenly looked younger and more in tune with contemporary culture. 'Cool Britannia' – a phrase coined in a breathless paean to enterprise London by the American journalist Stryker McGuire and first popularized in a speech by the defeated prime minister John Major – became the slogan of the New Labour moment. A 'Cool Britannia' edition of *Vanity Fair* featured Hirst, rock star Liam Gallagher and fashion designer Alexander McQueen. In July 1997, Blair hosted a reception at Downing Street for 'creative entrepreneurs drawn from across society'. Talk of the 'creative economy' become routine; it felt good to hear government ministers use the word 'creative' approvingly, although in practice it covered only the kinds of art that attracted audiences and generated quantifiable results.

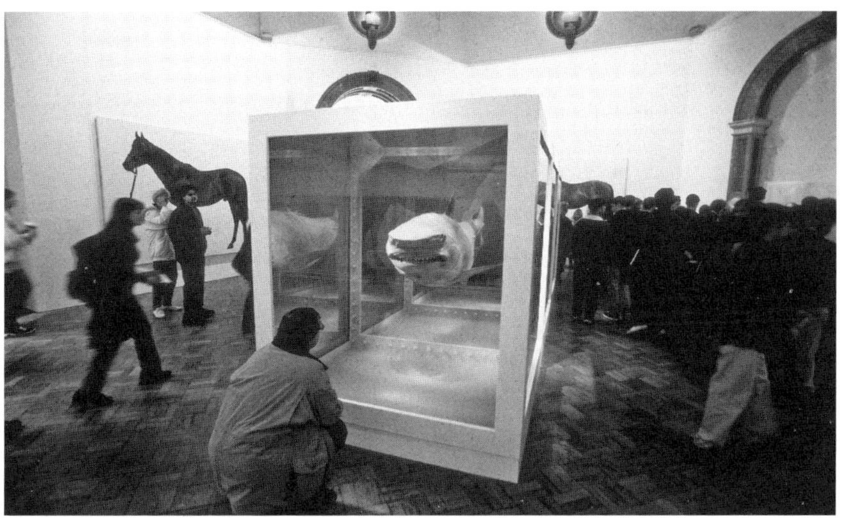

Gallery at the Royal Academy, London, during the exhibition 'Sensation:
Young British Artists from the Saatchi Gallery', 1997. Visible are Mark Wallinger's
Race Class Sex, 1992 (oil on canvas, each 230 × 300 cm; 90⅝ × 118⅛ in.) and
Damien Hirst's *The Physical Impossibility of Death in the Mind of Someone Living*,
1991 (mixed media, 217 × 542 × 180 cm; 85½ × 213½ × 70⅞ in.)

Featuring forty-two artists and more than a hundred works from
Saatchi's five-year YBA collecting spree, the exhibition 'Sensation'
opened at the Royal Academy in September 1997. Nine years on from
'Freeze', the original YBAs were approaching mid-career, but the key-
notes remained little changed, for both artists and patron. 'You know
it's Saatchi art', the painter Chris Ofili (who had work in 'Sensation')
observed, 'because it's one-off shockers. Something designed to attract
his attention.' The most controversial work at the Royal Academy was
Marcus Harvey's *Myra*, a monumental head-and-shoulders portrait
of the notorious child-murderer Myra Hindley, composed from what
appeared to be painted equivalents of the Ben-Day dots used in colour
printing but on closer inspection were children's handprints. Hindley had
been jailed for life in 1966; at the time of 'Sensation', she was appealing
against her conviction. Winnie Johnson, mother of the twelve-year-old
Keith Bennett, whom Hindley and her boyfriend Ian Brady had tortured
and murdered in 1964 and whose body was never found, wrote to the
Royal Academy, asking for the Harvey's *Myra* to be removed; when the
Academy declined, she stood in the courtyard outside, trying, with little

success, to persuade people to turn back from the door. The press storm around *Myra* had the opposite effect, pulling in 300,000 visitors – not a record but a vindication of the Royal Academy's hope that 'Sensation' would help to patch up its ailing finances.

Critical scepticism and media fatigue were setting in, however. 'High Art Lite' was the term art historian Julian Stallabrass coined for the YBAs in a book published in 1999. 'BritArt', a subset of Cool Britannia, was another label, although in the international art market of the turn of the millennium, 'Brit' and 'Art' were starting to sound a bit limiting, a shade provincial. A revolutionary aspect of conceptual practice, Craig-Martin reflected, had been its 'liberating' effect on students, artists and audiences outside the Western cultural sphere, or 'civilization' in Kenneth Clark's sense. 'Anyone could do that!' was the standard howl against conceptual art – but *anyone* was precisely the point. With conceptualism, observed Craig-Martin, art 'became so ephemeral and so disparate in its manifestations, you could have people with extraordinary imaginations participating without having to learn vast skills', with the result that it 'equalised a lot of places, it de-centred the art world'. If you had something to say, you didn't first have to learn perspective drawing or how to mix oil paints – the classical academic techniques of art that were taught in elite institutions. Nor was it essential to have access to the levels of patronage and high-cost installation on which High Art Lite, or the YBAs, had come to rely. Gallery art and museum art were no longer the exclusive preserve of nations with old-established academies and cultural institutions. And it wasn't only the art world that was undergoing a process of 'de-centring' or globalization. In its political and economic manifestations, globalization would bring insecurity and instability as well as business opportunities. One effect of the exponential spread and interconnectedness of networks and the fade-out of geographical barriers was a corresponding awareness of the individual experience of family and cultural roots, of the personal histories woven into the texture of objects and places – richer and stranger territory to explore, in many ways, than the raw smack of pure sensation.

20
Inside stories

Near Kineton, Warwickshire, 1991

Tucked into the edge of a field, screened by a line of trees, a smallish wooden shed. Inside, the kinds of things you'd expect to find if the shed stood in the back garden of someone's house instead of a field – tools, discarded toys, a bicycle, a book. What is a shed, after all? A shelter in which to make, to hoard, to hide. A place of well-worn ordinariness and modest obsession. It exists in its own liminal, personal dimension between indoors and out. What is it doing here? There is not much time for questions, because plastic explosives have been laid and...Whoomph! No fireworks, no flames, just a short disoriented after-pause, then a spaced-out confetti of splintered wood, wheels, pedals, a handle-less spade, ice skates, the whole scrambled jigsaw returning to earth. Stillness returns to the rural scene. Cornelia Parker and a group of young soldiers from the Army School of Ammunition scour the field, gathering up as many fragments as they can find.

———

There could have been good reason to hide in a faraway field. In London, bombs had been going off again and again. Through the summer of 1990, almost every week there had been another bomb. On 16 May, the Wembley bombing, when a minibus outside an army recruiting centre was blown up, killing a soldier. In June, twenty people injured by a bomb at the Carlton Club, a favourite with MPs, then on 20 July, a much bigger explosion, which blew a ten-foot hole in the London Stock Exchange, although no one was hurt this time – the Provisional IRA, who planned this campaign as a brutal reminder to the mainland British public about Northern Ireland, telephoned a warning. Another attack came on 7 February 1991, this time targeting Downing Street. Three 140-pound mortar shells were fired at No. 10, one of which landed in the back garden. Prime minister John Major and his war cabinet were meeting at the time to discuss the campaign in the Middle

East, where Britain and America had sent troops to repel the Iraqi invasion of Kuwait. Any night on television, you could watch explosions and the bulging black columns of smoke from burning oil wells.

It was a fact of life in Britain in the early 1990s, observed Parker, that 'you couldn't turn on the news without there being yet another explosion'. Yet it was not – at least, not directly – because of the IRA bombing campaign and the Gulf War that the shed had been placed in the field. Since her art school days in Gloucester and Wolverhampton in the 1970s, explosions as events had interested Parker. In an interview, she spoke of the 'imminence' of explosions in society and in our worldview, 'from the violence of the comic strip, through action films, in documentaries about Super Novas and the Big Bang'. The shed was to do with an exhibition she was planning for September 1991 at Chisenhale Gallery in east London – in its way, another story of Docklands in the early Thatcher era. It had been established alongside studios in a derelict veneer factory by artists evicted to make way for the conversion of Butler's Wharf into luxury flats. At thirty-five, however, Parker was a bit older than the Young British Artists and not at all in their garrulous, media-savvy mould, although death was her subject, too. What she called 'cartoon deaths', enacted with 'cartoon violence', had been a feature of her early work – running over household objects like silver spoons, knives and forks, with a steamroller, for example. In cartoons, violence has no permanent consequences: characters are squashed flat, then pop up as themselves again, with reinflated vigour. But, even if we never experience it, we are also familiar with images of what real violence – a tank or a bomb – or the threat of violence actually does to people and to homes. Explosions both create and destroy; they shape the world that comes after. The blast itself, though, is over in a moment. Unless you photograph, or even paint, it – as Whistler once painted fireworks over the nocturnal Thames – only the fallout has a continued existence.

In her researches about how to blow up a garden shed, Parker took advice from an expert, Major Doug Hewitt at the Army School of Ammunition, a complex of about a hundred serried bunkers amid Warwickshire farmland near the village of Kineton. He demonstrated how plastic explosives can be laid to blow up a car or a table, or any kind of object that needs exploding. This was an unusual meeting of means and ends: the British army doesn't often work with artists ('artist' is old

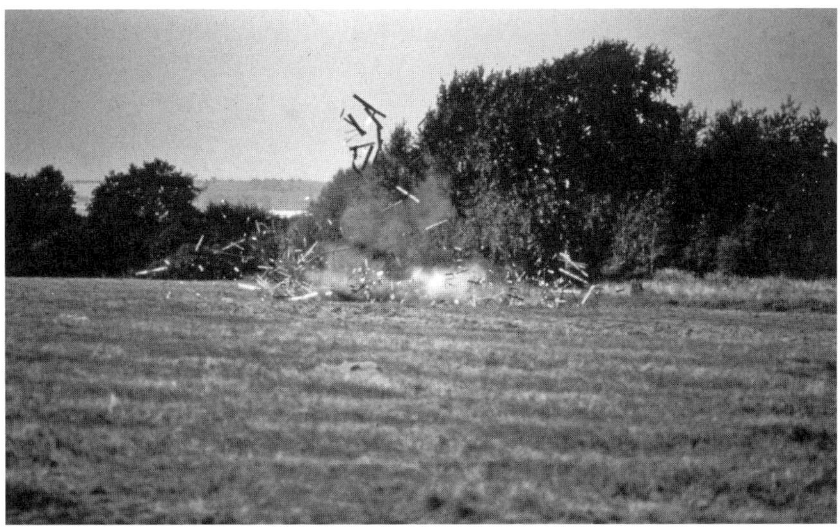

Explosion destroying a shed in a field in Warwickshire,
during the making of Cornelia Parker's *Cold Dark Matter:
An Exploded View*, 1991, photograph by Hugo Glendinning

army slang for a total incompetent, as in 'What *artist* wired this up?').
After scouring allotments for the right kind of shed, Parker decided
that most existing examples were too 'biographical' for her purposes.
A life story, in this case, must not upstage the objects. In the end, she
commissioned a Suffolk carpenter to make a brand-new shed, which
was then assembled in the chosen field.

After as much as possible of the explosion debris had been salvaged, she reconfigured the fragments, hanging them on wires, in a
kind of spherical formation – a freeze-frame of perpetual detonation
to which she gave the title *Cold Dark Matter* (pl. 18). 'As the objects
were suspended one by one, they began to lose their aura of death
and appeared reanimated, in limbo', as if the shed were a model of the
universe (which, in their purely biographical dimension, sheds often
are), 're-exploding or perhaps coming back together again'. It was both
an end and a beginning. Illuminated from inside by a single bulb, *Cold
Dark Matter* created a looming shadow-play of fragments on the gallery
wall, like a forest in a fairy tale. The whole thing felt like a still from a
film – an art film in this case rather than a 'high-concept' Hollywood
movie – but it also recalled a phrase John Berger had used in his 1972
television series *Ways of Seeing*, in which he spoke of the 'stillness and

silence' of a painting. If *Cold Dark Matter* was about violence, it was the violence of an orchestral chord, shaking the senses but not making the ground tremble or the ceiling fall.

When artists like John Latham or Gustav Metzger had burned things down or smashed them up in the 1960s, their actions took place in a context of protest against institutional authority in all its destructive manifestations, most powerfully symbolized by the H-bomb and the war in Vietnam. In a more general, metaphorical sense, blowing up meant exposing cover-ups and hypocrisy, as in Michelangelo Antonioni's 1966 thriller *Blow-Up*, whose title refers to a photographer's discovery of a possible murder through an enlarged (blown up) detail of a photo he's taken in a park. Parker's explosion was not an act of protest; it was, rather, a contemplative conceptual exercise, a kind of ballet of ideas to do with origins, intimacy, exposure, safety and its loss – an equivalent for a state of mind in which the private and outer worlds can meet. When the Tate Gallery bought *Cold Dark Matter* in 1995, there was no outcry about public money being wasted on 'rubbish', or on a gesture of support for the Provisional IRA. It almost seemed possible that the public had at last, after twenty years of encounters with conceptual art, started to read it as poetry as much as provocation. Or was this kind of acceptance a sign that, in the realm of art, political content had by the 1990s been replaced by sensation? The fact that a national art collection was now buying and displaying work by young British artists, and helping to expand the audience for them, had brought what was once the powder keg of protest inside the walls of the institution, where it could be – if not fully defused – set up for calculatedly controlled explosion.

In the first six years of the Turner Prize, inaugurated in 1984 to recognize achievement in British art and presented annually at the Tate Gallery, some conceptual pioneers of the 1970s Saint Martin's generation had been honoured: in 1986 the prize went to Gilbert & George, in 1989 to Richard Long. In 1988, Lucian Freud and Richard Hamilton were nominees (Tony Cragg won); Freud was on the list again in 1989, with Gillian Ayres and Paula Rego, all in their sixties. From the outset, the Turner Prize had been intended to generate publicity, but it attracted only moderate media interest until 1991, when an age limit of fifty was imposed and Channel 4 took over the sponsorship, doubling the prize money to £20,000. That year, three young artists who had featured either in the original 'Freeze' show or in the various group exhibitions that followed – Ian Davenport, Fiona Rae and Rachel Whiteread – were on the shortlist (the prize went to Anish Kapoor). In 1992, Hirst was shortlisted, going on to win the prize in 1995. The average age of nominees fell steeply, from fifty in 1989 to thirty in 1991, after which it remained below forty, edging upwards only as the YBA generation itself aged. In another tweak to the format, each shortlisted artist was given a solo display at the Tate, with the result that the countdown to the award became a mini-survey of what younger artists were up to. These attracted wide publicity, allowing the gallery-going and television-viewing public to become familiar with little-known artists whose reputations were (thanks to the Turner) likely to rise fast. The judging process might be opaque, but with the annual routine of shortlisting, exhibition and televised award night, the emergence of the artist from the chrysalis of obscurity to the sunshine of fame became a new national sport.

The avant-garde, in order to regard itself as – and continue actually to be – avant-garde, had always had a testy ambivalence about institutional recognition. In nineteenth-century Paris, Gustave Courbet nursed his contempt for his high-society patrons like a lethal dose he reserved the right to slip them at any time. Tracey Emin, her career on the ascendant, a Turner nomination around the corner, felt the need to reassert the authenticating pain that informed her work. 'On the outside it might look like my life is very comfortable, but inside my heart is still in turmoil over things,' she explained. 'I still curl up in a small foetal shape and cower from the world and those feelings never change.' The early 1990s were not a particularly comfortable time for many people in Britain: along with background anxieties about IRA terrorist attacks, the economy went into a recession that lasted from autumn 1990 until the end of 1991, accompanied by rising unemployment and high inflation (9.5 per cent in 1990). On 16 September 1992, dubbed Black Wednesday, a precipitous fall in the pound's value forced the government to pull out of the European exchange rate mechanism; within hours, in an attempt to stem the sell-off of sterling, interest rates were hiked twice, from 10 to 15 per cent. This fiscal catastrophe did more than any artists' protest to blow apart the Conservatives' hopes of re-election.

All the while, media interest in young British art – the sheer volume of coverage and the consensus that, even if not everyone agreed that this was great art, it was lively and relatable – injected a certain energy into an otherwise gloomy scene. In contrast to the strong strand of social

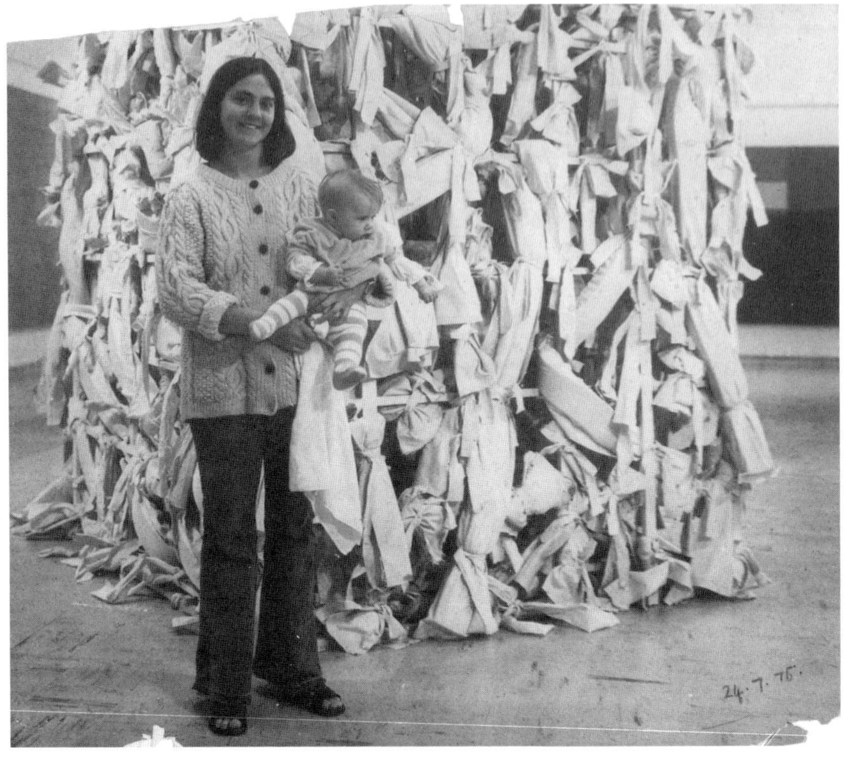

Phyllida Barlow with her daughter Clover in front of *Shedmesh*, Camden Arts Centre, London, 1975

and political engagement running through many artists' work between the 1960s and the 1980s, even Hirst's death-art acquired the aura of a recreational alternative world. Had *The Physical Impossibility of Death in the Mind of Someone Living* symbolized international corporate finance about to maim the debt-burdened, job-insecure British public – the physical impossibility of life in the mind of someone dying – the debate around it would have been very different. And what sort of a legacy, in the end, had the campaigning spirit of previous decades left? How much, for example, had changed for women artists since the women's edition of the Hayward Annual Exhibition in 1978 and the election of Britain's first female prime minister the following year? Margaret Thatcher's rise to top spot in the patriarchal world of politics appeared to have complicated the argument without helping the cause. 'Feminists hate me, don't they?' Thatcher was sure. 'And I don't blame them. For I hate feminism. It is poison.' In the roster of Turner Prize nominees before 1997, when the first all-woman shortlist was announced, men outnumbered women more than four to one. Among the winners it was twelve to one, with the sculptor Rachel Whiteread becoming the first woman to take the prize in 1993.

The sculptor Phyllida Barlow, who taught Whiteread's year group at Brighton Polytechnic in the 1980s, has reflected with unusual frankness on the problems of working out a professional route for which, even at that time, there were still no maps – how to combine 'the complicated life demands that lots of people have' (including in her case five young children) while trying to work, constantly on the lookout for 'the chink where I could get into the studio'. 'Who was I', she asked herself, 'and where was the art/life divide? Did it have a divide, or was the *making* a continuation of what was happening in my home next door?' Barlow's solution was to work at night, while her children slept. She made sculpture from cardboard, textiles, plastic wrapping, wooden crates – any ordinary materials that came to hand, 'trying to find ways of constructing that were outside the kind of laborious techniques that I had been taught at art school'. This impulse to use materials that had been discarded or trashed must be connected in some way, she felt, to a childhood visit with her father, perhaps five or six years after the war, to a heavily blitzed area of the East End. This 'strange tour' had always remained 'fixed in my mind', as if – as Frank Auerbach had found, arriving in London as a sixteen-year-old in 1947 – the 'semi-destroyed' fabric of the city contained the seeds of the future:

> *the constant changes inscribed within the urban environment form a particular archaeology which absorbs present, past and future: damage, reparation, renewal, reconstruction – these are in an ever-evolving lifecycle which mirrors the decay and renewal of the natural environment.*

After training at Chelsea School of Art, then, from 1963 to 1966, at the Slade, Barlow was teaching part-time, with a growing family at home, and few opportunities or encouragement to show her work. Eventually, as 'a way of getting them out into the world', she carried her sculptures into the streets. She wedged one between a pair of lampposts, balanced another on a dustbin and, at two o'clock one morning on Waterloo Bridge, threw one into the Thames. Through a cycle of 'reparation, renewal, reconstruction', she transformed a pile of old wooden canvas stretchers thrown out from the Slade into the foundation for *Shedmesh*.

This consisted of a set of roughly nailed-together criss-cross panels, about 6 to 8 feet wide, which she assembled into a cube, then threaded through with strips of canvas padded with foam rubber. In Barlow's descriptions of trying to balance childcare and artistic practice, the idea of home takes on a certain ambivalence. In a photo in which she cradles her daughter Clover in front of *Shedmesh* at Camden Arts Centre in 1975, the sculpture itself has the double aspect of a looming domestic obstacle and a beckoning refuge.

On a visit to London in April that same year, the young Palestinian graphic designer Mona Hatoum found herself stranded. In her hometown of Beirut, massacres in a church and on a bus would be followed by fifteen years of civil war. Hatoum, who was not a Lebanese national, wasn't authorized to return. Her own family had arrived as refugees from Palestine in 1948, at the time of the Arab–Israeli war; thanks to her father's job in the British Embassy, however, she held a British passport and was able to stay on and study at the Byam Shaw School of Art in London, then at the Slade. Hatoum's art, too, would address the ambivalent reality of what it means to inhabit a place or a space, for the body to feel at home. At the Pompidou Centre in Paris in 1994 she showed a video work, *Corps étranger* (Foreign body), composed from films taken by endoscopic and colonoscopic cameras inserted into her own body through different orifices, while an echograph recorded her heartbeat and breathing. Projected on to the dark floor of a small white room that visitors were invited to enter, it presented a video tour, with a pulsing cardiac soundtrack, of the viscous, roseate channels and caverns of the artist's insides, like a diver's exploration of an undersea cave. To the accusation that *Corps étranger* objectified the female body in the manner of pornography, Hatoum responded that there was 'nothing seductive about seeing green slime flowing inside the intestinal tubes'. Where Barlow was testing what she called 'the art/life divide' in the setting of stable family life, Hatoum's sense of the borderline between inside and outside, subject and object, was more disturbing; she spoke of 'how we are watched and scrutinised constantly and how our boundaries are constantly invaded'.

From the physical body itself, her attention turned to 'objects that we encounter in our everyday life', like tables, chairs, beds and kitchen utensils – objects with which 'we already have an established relationship'. Yet the contents of a home *are also very much about the body, so they can refer to the body even when it is absent. And when those familiar objects are transformed in such a way that they become strange and sometimes threatening and dangerous objects – revealing an undercurrent of hostility, danger and threat – by implication they make reality itself questionable and full of uncertainties.*

Hatoum reflects here on her 1996 sculpture *Divan Bed*. Taking the upholstered-sandwich form of a two-piece divan – a standard item of soft furnishing – she constructed the piece from thick metal floor-plates with knobbly non-slip treads. The contrast with Tracey Emin's *My Bed*, made two years later, is striking: where Emin's bed is a tangle of slept-in sheets, with its surrounding scurf of intimate personal jetsam, there is no sense of privacy or refuge about Hatoum's bed, no shadowed folds of cloth, no hint of the residual heat of an absent body. The 'lifecycle' of objects here is in a state of arrest, perhaps literally. But even the metal bed, suggesting a prison cell or interrogation room, is possessed by both artist and viewer as a possible place for the body to inhabit – very different again from the role played by furniture in the events of the 1966 Destruction in Art Symposium, the pianos and chairs smashed to splinters by Raphael Montañez Ortiz. The 'destruction concerts' were about dismantling rather than inhabiting – an assault both on the objects themselves and on what John Latham termed 'Mental Furniture', the ideas that needed to be thrown into a skip (or 'chewed over') in order to clear a space for fresh thinking.

After *Divan Bed* came *Home*, a piece Hatoum assembled in 1999. She placed metal kitchen equipment – a colander, a ladle, scissors, a hand-cranked pasta machine – on a long table with a heavy wooden top and metal legs. Everything on the table was wired up – a nervous intermittent current made tiny lights go on and off inside the objects, like signals or sprung traps, with the crackle and buzz of the electrics relayed by speakers. The table stood behind a row of electric wires, as if imprisoned or restrained. These things were all so ordinary, they wouldn't usually be noticed; in *Home* they became unreachable yet impossible to ignore. Hatoum intended *Home* to be 'a work that shatters notions of the wholesomeness of home, family, and the nurturing that is expected'. No space, she seemed to be saying, was so intimate or 'wholesome' as to be safe from surveillance or invasion.

As a student in Brighton in the 1980s, Whiteread had made wax casts of flotsam gleaned from the pebbly beach. She'd pressed a spoon into a tray of sand and poured molten lead into the simple mould to make a solid, small, curved mass – the inverse of Parker's steamrollered cutlery. A few years later, she was casting larger everyday things – a rubber hot-water bottle, an old mattress, the inside of a bath, the undersides of chairs and tables: 'These were all very particular pieces of furniture – cheap, post-war furniture,' she said, 'which I somehow wanted to immortalise, to give it a kind of grandness. I was trying to make spaces that I was very familiar with, and that a lot of people would be very familiar with.' In other words, the physical components of a home and of a historical time. She moved on in 1990 to making a plaster cast of the entire living room in a Victorian house in the Archway Road, not far from her childhood home in north London. When the plaster sections were removed and reassembled, what had been 'negative' spaces – the alcoves either side of the chimney breast, the window recess – became positive, protruding from the flat sides of a plaster cube. The little charred cave of the iron grate stuck out like a navel. Whiteread called this sculpture *Ghost*, referring to its tomb-like marmoreal pallor and also to her original desire to 'mummify the air in a room' – to preserve the life of a domestic space. It is a ghost, too, in the sense of a revenant, who revisits a familiar place from 'the other side'. *Ghost* was shown at Chisenhale Gallery in 1991, a month before *Cold Dark Matter*; it was snapped up by Charles Saatchi.

Whiteread likened her plaster-casting process to 'embalming a body' – a bricks-and-mortar entity through which time and life had flowed, leaving a charged but vacant space. On 2 August 1993, in the company of a group of engineers, builders and assistants, she entered an empty house at the end of Grove Road, Bow, in east London. The terraced streets all around had been built in the 1860s, in the rapid expansion of the Victorian city; for a hundred years, the London docks had been big local employers. In June 1944, where the railway bridge crossed Grove Road, the first of two thousand V-1 flying bombs to fall on London had exploded. Now No. 193, with its view towards the redeveloped Docklands and the skyscrapers of Canary Wharf, was the last house standing in a row to be demolished to make space for a park. The presence of its last tenant, who had held out while houses to either side came down, was still palpable, among the 'fitted cupboards, cocktail bars and a tremendous variety of wallpapers and floor finishes'. It took about six weeks for

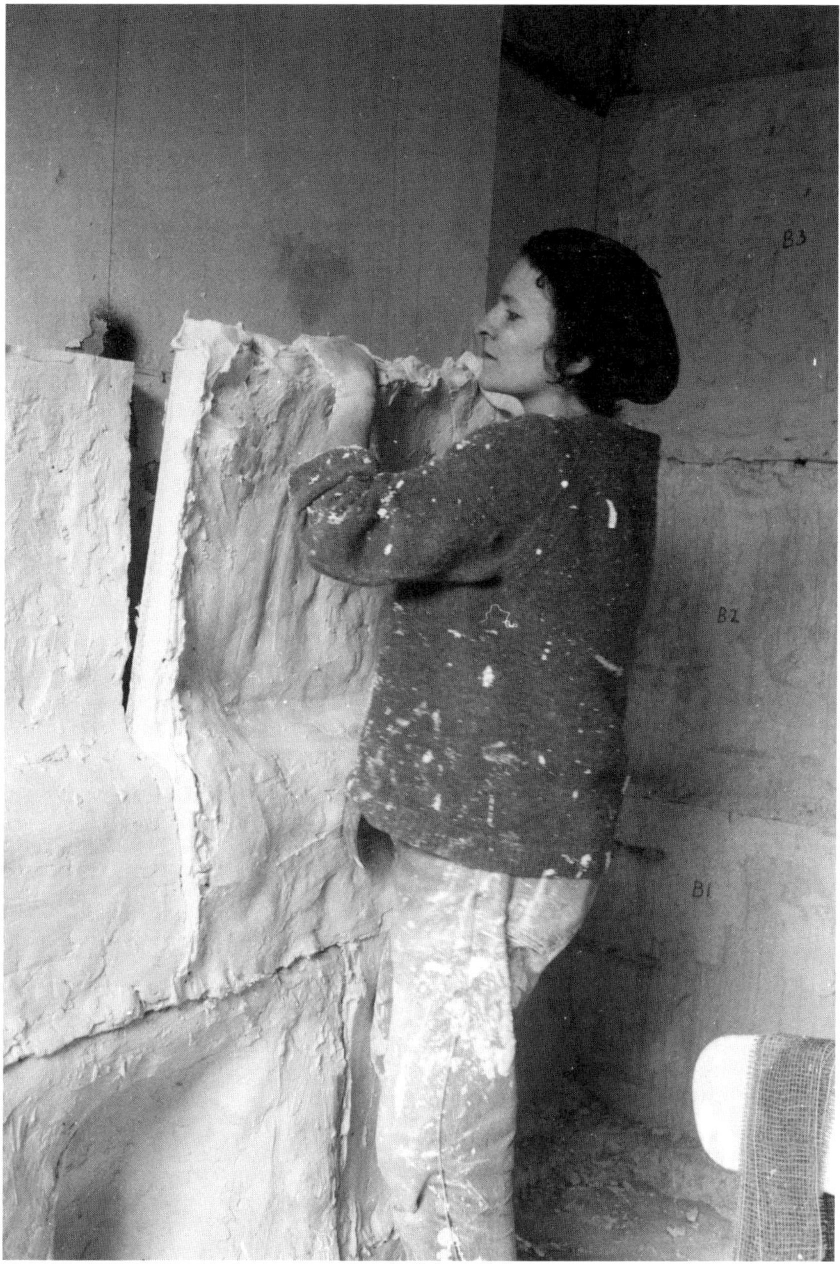

Rachel Whiteread removing a plaster panel from the interior of 486 Archway Road, London, during the making of *Ghost*, 1990

Whiteread and her team to strip out all the internal spaces and prepare the house for casting. This involved applying a release agent to every surface, spraying on a first thin coat of concrete, then constructing a metal armature to support a heavy layer of concrete. By late October, they were ready to demolish the house, breaking away the outer shell of walls, windows and doors to reveal the hollow but impenetrable concrete cast, which Whiteread named after the thing it no longer was, whose ghost now stood in its place – *House*. The following month, she won the Turner Prize. And then, in January 1994, *House* itself became a ghost, when Bow Council's bulldozers moved in.

The high-water mark of the YBAs might have passed, but the popular audience they had helped to win for contemporary art, along with the New Labour narrative of the creative economy and the confident, burnished brand of internationalism that had been seeded in London by the transformation of the City and Docklands, all contributed to the most monumental art project of those years. Opposite St Paul's Cathedral, on the down-at-heel south bank of the Thames, Bankside Power Station had closed in 1981 and stood derelict since then. Plans to convert it into, among other proposals, an opera house, an industrial museum or a hotel had come to nothing. Designed in the 1940s by Giles Gilbert Scott, architect of Battersea Power Station and designer of the ubiquitous red telephone box, it took the form of a gigantic brick basilica with a soaring central chimney, like a modern campanile answering the baroque dome of St Paul's. In 1994, it was identified as the site for a new Tate Gallery that would display twentieth- and twenty-first-century international art. The Tate at Millbank would become Tate Britain – the place where you could see work by James McNeill Whistler, Henry Moore and the Turner Prize nominees. The new gallery, Tate Modern, was to be an ambitious corrective to the Tate's long track record of being sluggish to recognize and even slower to acquire art being made outside Britain, no matter how striking or likely, in years to come, to express the spirit of its times (hence the vestigial presence of, for example, cubism and American abstract expressionism in the Tate collection). The Bankside gallery was also a recognition that contemporary art of all kinds was increasingly being exhibited and interpreted in global rather than national frames of reference. The label 'BritArt' – the last claim for a national art movement in Britain – had not worn well.

In converting the power station, the Swiss architects Jacques Herzog and Pierre de Meuron retained its industrial grandeur. Between the nave-like brick internal walls of the former turbine hall they laid an industrial-scale concrete entry ramp. Creativity rather than oil, it was strongly implied, was powering the invisible turbines now. But the public appetite for modern and contemporary art had never been tested on this scale – almost a quarter of a century after the furore surrounding Carl Andre's *Equivalent VIII*, the 'Tate Bricks' remained a running joke. Yet it soon became clear that something had changed: in the year after it opened in May 2000, Tate Modern received 5.25 million visitors. And there was no longer any form of art so radical or transgressive as to rule itself out from appearing there. Even artists whose work was an explicit form of protest could find a welcome in the institution. In the language of New Labour, 'The important thing is not their politics, but the fact that they are part of a new and exciting cultural renaissance in this country.'

For the first headline work of contemporary international art in the Turbine Hall, the eighty-nine-year-old French-American sculptor Louise Bourgeois was commissioned to produce a colossal spider – the latest iteration of her *Maman* (Mother) series. It arched over visitors, more than 30 feet high, on eight spindly steel legs, with a meshed egg sac containing seventeen marble eggs. Bourgeois thought of the spider as 'a friend', because, she said, 'my best friend was my mother and she was deliberate, clever, patient, soothing, reasonable, dainty, subtle, indispensable, neat'. There was nothing soothing, dainty or maternal, however, about Bourgeois's 3,600-kilogram, sci-fi monster *Maman*. Whether fearsome or friendly, it also unquestionably stood for success – of the new building, the international artist, the whole activity of presenting and encountering modern art.

But what of the studio, the private space where art is made? Success has a different meaning there. 'A work of art doesn't have to be explained,' said Bourgeois. 'If this doesn't touch you, I have failed.' Failure, reflects Phyllida Barlow, who would find international fame in her seventies, with a Tate Britain Commission in 2014 and at the 2017 Venice Biennale, is 'a very positive thing, a whole process towards finding out about something', because

if something doesn't work it carries an enormous amount of information with it.... So the failure of it is that it hasn't quite happened yet, but I don't know what it should be. And that not-knowing state is often deemed a kind of failure; you must know what you want, you must know what your intentions are, you must know what your aims and objectives are. It's such a harsh, unforgiving language. And yet the not-knowing can often be that, as an artist, you're not working necessarily with very vivid visual, cerebral processes. You're actually trying to find those, and that's why you want to make the stuff, or draw the stuff, or paint the stuff. So the failure thing to me is very much associated with that striving for, and that struggle.

'Striving' and 'struggle' are, she admits, 'words that I know are very unfashionable'. Even so, 'there is something for me in the striving to find the visual thing that isn't yet in one's head.'

Not yet, not today, but – maybe – tomorrow.

The silence of mirrors

Bankside, June 2019

A humid midsummer afternoon. 'It's okay to go in now.' The gallery attendant moves the barrier aside. She holds open one half of the door. We go in. A corridor filled with mist or fog, lit gently from above. As we walk along, the light changes colour. I can't see to the end – just soft-toned, shadowy figures a few yards ahead. Two girls immediately in front stop to take photos of each other. Back there, in the coloured clouds, I hear some more of us, the public, being let in.

———

It is like one of those summer days that starts misty before the sun burns through. Blue mist, green mist, pink mist. An unreal, new-born feeling that passes even as you breathe it in. And we're out. Another room. A silver tunnel up some steps, big enough to walk through. The curved inside surface is shiny and densely faceted. I hear the word 'kaleidoscope' and remember that this was mentioned in a leaflet I picked up. I stare at my kaleidoscoped self, the constructed scatter of the cubist me. No time to muse, however. I feel the pressure of people behind having somewhere they want to get to.

Who are we all, moving from room to room this afternoon with a vague shared sense of expectancy? Am I really the public? The point of being here is surely about individual experience as distinct from collective identity. *Audience* doesn't sound right either. We know that each of us is – or is meant to be – a small, cumulative part of what is happening. If we declined to participate, would it still be what we agree to call it? Art.

Pink mist, kaleidoscope people. Now I'm in a small, high room in which the entire ceiling consists of a mirror. I stand in one corner, while other visitors walk through – sometimes pausing, often not. There is more noise than you usually hear in an art gallery. Everyone seems to be finding something to talk, laugh, even shout about in this exhibition by the Danish-Icelandic artist Olafur Eliasson. Pushchairs jitter past. It's busy, in a way that makes it hard to stay still or focus for long.

Look up at the ceiling, though. There we all are, defying gravity, going our various upside-down ways, but so quietly, seemingly with endless, effortless courtesy. It's a mime show, a ballet – organized, that is, as if in accord with certain unspoken rules. Not like it is on the floor, in real life, although of course the mirror reflects only reality, the things that are actually here.

Why are mirrors so quiet? A good question. A thought. An *art* thought, which I might not have had, or at least not caught hold of, if I hadn't come to Tate Modern this sultry afternoon.

In the final room a film plays. Eliasson walks around, between shelves full of stuff from which art is going to be made. He talks about how, when we're walking, our paces simultaneously measure time and space. On the wall, photographs of ice sculptures and ice sheets melting because of climate change. The seas are rising, space and time are running out. The climate emergency is reality, too, even though we cannot touch or see it, or even begin to imagine it, here in the art gallery where everything feels normal and well behaved, like an interesting lesson in school. At the end of the film, Eliasson says, 'art is holding out the possibility of things being different'. It's a considered statement – a bit of a rallying cry. But the thought I leave with is this: *the silence of mirrors*.

Paintings, too, are 'silent and still', John Berger wrote, 'in a way that information never is'. Back home, I look up that quotation in *Ways of Seeing*. The silence and stillness, he goes on to say, 'permeate the actual material, the paint'. I can't explain this, but think it is true: information is restless, paint is still. How useful this reflection will be for the book I am planning to write about artists in a noisy, turbulent century I am not sure. Too much talk of art-induced reverie might undermine my case.

———

This story almost ended where it began, beside the Thames in central London. Along the Victoria Embankment still stand the glossy cast-iron lampposts in the form of writhing dolphins, whose lights were sensationally electrified in the month after the Whistler–Ruskin libel trial, the faraway winter of 1878. Almost...

In February 2022, we are coming out of another winter and I have been walking on Porthmeor Beach beside a very different body of water, the Atlantic rather than the Thames. I spoke at the beginning of art's continuities – the passing on of one kind or another that takes place across all kinds of barriers and often in unlikely circumstances. But it is disjunction, not continuity, that has been the theme of the past two virus-dominated years – a severance (among other kinds) from the people we thought we were and the tomorrows we imagined in that pre-pandemic summer of 2019. If ideas travel fast, germs travel faster. Writing a book during this period has felt more than usually like constructing a desert-island raft. For much of the time, galleries, museums, libraries and archives were closed and travel complicated by rules and risks. So this quarter-mile curve of sand and its flanking headlands have been an intermittent thinking-path, where I made virtual visits – rather than the actual ones I'd anticipated – to James McNeill Whistler's old Chelsea stamping-ground, David Bomberg's Whitechapel and other places, remembered and imagined. I was lucky, of course, whether it was legal at the time or not, to be able to escape so easily from my desk. And today, the quiet of those weeks of lockdown feels unrecapturable as distant history. If, that is, history ever goes away. Suddenly, people in Kyiv and other Ukrainian cities are sheltering sleeplessly in basements and metro stations, while Russian bombs destroy their homes and lives, as Londoners sheltered during nights of the Blitz more than eighty years ago – as Henry Moore watched and drew them, no one knowing what daylight would bring.

It was at about this spot, I'm guessing – where this morning's high tide has dumped a Medusa's head of seeping, tangled wrack – that on a late summer's day in 1883, a young woman and three small children sat on the sands, unaware, maybe, that Walter Sickert was painting them, quickly, uncharacteristically brightly, on a wooden cigar-box lid. He noticed then, as I notice now, how the sea darkens towards the horizon – the sea, which is as full of art as of other life forms. Listen to John Ruskin insisting again and again on how Turner's pictures very nearly *are* the sea, with their 'great iron waves', 'dancing waves', 'slow waves upon the sand', the sea in every state from 'grey and lightly broken' to 'shadowed', 'heaping', 'trembling', 'the run and the leap of it', the 'toss and writhe'. Closer to our time, I am trying to remember exactly how the twentieth-century Spanish-Basque sculptor Eduardo Chillida phrased this idea in an interview: the sea, I think he said – with an air of lighting on an observation which was also a metaphor that might contain his art, his family life and the history of his times – is both the most ancient thing and the most modern. The source and the breaking wave.

Sources and further reading

I have listed here the main publications and other printed and online sources consulted for each chapter. As standard reference works, I have used the regularly updated online versions of the *Grove Dictionary of Art*, *Oxford Dictionary of National Biography* and *Oxford English Dictionary*. Many of the direct quotations from artists in the later chapters come from interviews recorded for the National Life Stories project *Artists' Lives*, which are listed separately. General histories of the period to which I have referred include David Edgerton, *The Rise and Fall of the British Nation: A Twentieth-Century History* (London: Penguin, 2019); Eric Hobsbawm, *Age of Extremes: The Short Twentieth Century, 1914–1991* (London: Michael Joseph, 1994) and *Fractured Times: Culture and Society in the Twentieth Century* (London: Little, Brown, 2013); David Kynaston, *Austerity Britain, 1945–51* and *Family Britain, 1951–57* (London: Bloomsbury, 2007 and 2009), and *On the Cusp: Days of '62* (London: Bloomsbury, 2021); and Dominic Sandbrook's *Never Had It So Good: A History of Britain from Suez to the Beatles* (London: Little, Brown, 2005) and *White Heat: A History of Britain in the Swinging Sixties* (London: Little, Brown, 2006). For contemporary press coverage, I have used the British Newspaper Archive (britishnewspaperarchive.co.uk), *The Times* Digital Archive (www.gale.com) and theguardian.newspapers.com. With the exception of Naum Gabo and Anton Pevzner's *The Realistic Manifesto*, quoted from Gabo's own English translation, I have used translations in Alex Danchev (ed.), *100 Artists' Manifestos: From the Futurists to the Stuckists* (London: Penguin, 2011).

Introduction

I have quoted from Lawrence Alloway, *This Is Tomorrow* (exhib. cat., Whitechapel Art Gallery, London, 1956); Niall Ferguson, *War of the World: History's Age of Hatred* (London: Allen Lane, 2006); Naum Gabo, in Martin Hammer and Christina Lodder (eds), *Gabo on Gabo: Texts and Interviews* (Forest Row, East Sussex: Artists.Bookworks, 2000); Eric Hobsbawm, *Fractured Times: Culture and Society in the Twentieth Century* (London: Little, Brown, 2013); Alison Light, 'Behind the Green Baize Door', *Guardian* (8 Nov. 2003); and Susan Sontag, *On Photography* (London: Penguin, 2019).

Chapter 1

Quotations from the proceedings of the Whistler–Ruskin trial are taken from Linda Merrill's reconstruction in *A Pot of Paint: Aesthetics on Trial in Whistler v. Ruskin* (Washington and London: Smithsonian Institution Press, 1992). Whistler published his own account, *Whistler v. Ruskin: Art & Art Critics* (London: Chatto & Windus, 1879).

For James McNeill Whistler, I also consulted Lisa N. Peters, *James McNeill Whistler* (New York: Smithmark, 1996); Stanley Weintraub, *Whistler: A Biography* (London: William Collins, 1974); and contemporary press coverage, such as the unsigned account of a studio visit in *Kilburn Times* and *Western Post* (24 May 1878).

The Library Edition of the Works of John Ruskin, ed. E. T. Cook and A. Wedderburn (1903–1912) is available at The Ruskin, Lancaster University (lancaster.ac.uk/the-ruskin/). Ruskin expressed his views on railways in his preface to Robert Somervell, *A Protest against the Extension of Railways in the Lake District* (London: Simpkin, Marshall & Co., 1876).

Henry James's essays on art and culture in 1870s London and Paris are reprinted in Leon Edel and Ilse Dusoir Lind (eds), *Henry James: Parisian Sketches: Letters to the New York Tribune, 1875–76* (London: Rupert Hart-Davis, 1958); and John L. Sweeney (ed.), *The Painter's Eye: Notes and Essays on the Pictorial Arts* (London: Rupert Hart-Davis, 1956).

For the 'cultus of Impressionability' debate, see Walter Pater's 'Preface' in Pater, *The Renaissance: Studies in Art and Poetry* (Oxford: Oxford University Press, 2009); and Robert Tener and Malcolm Woodfield (eds), *A Victorian Spectator: Uncollected Writings of R. H. Hutton* (Bristol: The Bristol Press, 1989).

Chapter 2

For Walter Sickert's life and his extensive journalism, see Anna Gruetzner Robins (ed.), *Walter Sickert: The Complete Writings on Art* (Oxford: Oxford University Press, 2000); and Matthew Sturgis, *Walter Sickert: A Life* (London: HarperCollins, 2005).

For Sickert and London music halls, see Anna Gruetzner Robins, 'Sickert "Painter-in-Ordinary" to the Music Hall', in *Sickert: Paintings* (exhib. cat., Royal Academy of Arts, London, 1992); and Robert Upstone, '*Minnie Cunningham* 1892 by Walter Richard Sickert', in Helena Bonett, Ysanne Holt and Jennifer Mundy (eds), *The Camden Town Group in Context*, Tate Research Publication, May 2012, tate.org.uk.

Other sources include Michael Baker, *The Rise of the Victorian Actor* (London: Routledge, 2015); Frederic Daly, *Henry Irving in England and America, 1838–84* (London: Fisher Unwin, 1884); James H. Rubin, *Courbet* (London: Phaidon, 1997); and Oscar Wilde, *The Picture of Dorian Gray* (London: Penguin, 2003). Wilde's 1882 North American tour is comprehensively documented at oscarwildeinamerica.org.

Chapter 3

For the Clydebank shipyards and the Japanese connection, see W. H. Brock, 'Engineering in Tokyo, London, and Glasgow at the End of the Nineteenth Century', *British Journal for the History of Science*, vol. 14, no. 3 (Nov. 1981); Christopher Dresser, *Japan: Its Architecture, Art, and Art Manufactures* (London: Longmans, Green & Co., 1882); Neil Jackson, 'Found in Translation: Mackintosh, Muthesius and Japan', *The Journal of Architecture*, vol. 18, no. 2 (2013); and 'Shipbuilding on the Clyde', clydewaterfront.com. Elizabeth Hawksley's 'The Strand Magazine: Child Acrobats and Stage Dancers' (11 Oct. 2020, elizabethhawksley.com), casts light on the Yokohama Troupe.

A wealth of documents relating to the work of Charles Rennie Mackintosh can be accessed online via Glasgow School of Art Archives and Collections; the Charles Rennie Mackintosh Society; Mackintosh Architecture, University of Glasgow; and the Hunterian, University of Glasgow, which also holds examples of Margaret Macdonald's work and archival material.

For the garden city movement, see Brett Clark, 'Ebenezer Howard and the Marriage of Town and Country', *Organization & Environment*, vol. 16, no. 1 (March 2003); Ebenezer Howard, *To-morrow: A Peaceful Path to Real Reform* (London: Swan Sonnenschein, 1898); Barry Parker and Raymond Unwin, *The Art of Building a Home: A Collection of Lectures and Illustrations* (London: Longmans, Green & Co., 1901); and William Morris, 'Art Under Plutocracy: A Lecture Delivered at University College, Oxford, 14 November 1883', *The Collected Works of William Morris* (Cambridge: Cambridge University Press, 2012).

The final quotation comes from Virginia Woolf, *A Room of One's Own*, ed. Anna Snaith (Oxford: Oxford University Press, 2015).

Chapter 4

For Gwen John's life and work, see Michael Holroyd, *Augustus John: The New Biography* (London: Vintage, 1997); Augustus John, *Chiaroscuro: Fragments of Autobiography* (London: Jonathan Cape, 1954); Cecily Langdale and David Fraser, *Gwen John: An Interior Life* (exhib. cat., Barbican Art Gallery, London, 1985); Sue Roe, *Gwen John: A Painter's Life* (New York: Farrar, Straus and Giroux, 2001); and the 1975 BBC television documentary *Augustus and Gwen: The Fire and the Fountain*, archived on BBC iPlayer.

For Whistler in Paris, see Cyrus Cuneo, 'Whistler's Academy of Painting, Some Parisian Recollections', *The Pall Mall Magazine*, vol. 38, no. 163 (Nov. 1906); and William Rothenstein, *Men and Memories*, vol. 2 (London: Faber and Faber, 1932).

For Auguste Rodin, see Frederic V. Grunfeld, *Rodin: A Biography* (New York: Holt, 1987); and the online collections of the Musée Rodin, Paris (musee-rodin.fr).

I have quoted from Rainer Maria Rilke's *Selected Letters 1902–1926*, Eng. trans. R. F. C. Hull (London and New York: Quartet, 1988), *The Notebooks of Malte Laurids Brigge*, Eng. trans. Stephen Mitchell (New York: Vintage, 1990), *Letters to a Young Poet*, Eng. trans. Reginald Snell (London: Sidgwick and Jackson, 1945) and 'The Rodin Book: First Part (1903)', *Rodin and Other Prose Pieces* (London: Quartet, 1986).

Leslie Stephen's 'In Praise of Walking' is reprinted in his *Studies of a Biographer*, vol. 3 (London: Duckworth, 1902).

For Vanessa Bell, see Frances Spalding, *Vanessa Bell: Portrait of the Bloomsbury Artist* (London: Bloomsbury, 2018).

Chapter 5

For Roger Fry's life, work and correspondence, see Roger Fry, *Vision and Design* (London: Chatto & Windus, 1920); Frances Spalding, *Roger Fry: Art and Life* (Norwich: Black Dog, 1999); Denys Sutton (ed.), *Letters of Roger Fry*, vol. 1 (Chatto & Windus: London, 1972); and Virginia Woolf, *Roger Fry: A Biography* (London: HarperCollins, 1976).

For New York in the 1900s, see Stephen N. Broadberry, 'How Did the United States and Germany Overtake Britain? A Sectoral Analysis of Comparative Productivity Levels 1870-1990', *Journal of Economic History*, vol. 58, no. 2 (Jun. 1998); Henry James, *The American Scene*, ed. Peter Collister (Cambridge: Cambridge University Press, 2019); Library of Congress, 'Immigrants in the Progressive

Era', *U.S. History Primary Source Timeline* (www.loc.gov); and *Metropolitan Museum of Art Bulletin*, vol. 8, no. 4 (Apr. 1913).

Translations of futurist manifestos by Filippo Tommaso Marinetti, Umberto Boccioni, Carlo Carrà *et al.* are cited from Danchev (ed.), *100 Artists' Manifestos.*

For futurism in London, see Giovanni Cianci, 'Futurism and the English Avant-Garde: The Early Pound Between Imagism and Vorticism', *Arbeiten aus Anglistik und Amerikanistik*, vol. 6, no. 1 (1981); Penelope Curtis (ed.), *Dynamism: The Art of Modern Life Before the Great War* (exhib. cat., Tate Liverpool, 1991); F. T. Marinetti, interview in *Daily Mail* (6 May 1914); and Jamie Wood, '"On or about December 1910": F. T. Marinetti's Onslaught on London and Recursive Structures in Modernism', *Modernist Cultures*, vol. 10, no. 2 (2015).

Anna Gruetzner Robins, *Modern Art in Britain 1910–1914* (London: Merrell Holberton, 1997) provides a detailed, well-illustrated commentary on nine exhibitions between 1910 and 1919, including Fry's two post-impressionist shows.

Chapter 6
Anthony Julius's *Trials of the Diaspora: A History of Anti-Semitism in England* (Oxford: Oxford University Press, 2010) provides information on nineteenth-century pogroms in the Russian Empire. The Jewish community in London's East End is richly documented online, e.g. at spitalfieldslife. com and British History Online (www. british-history.ac.uk), and in the *Jewish Chronicle* Archive (archive.thejc.com). I am indebted to Richard Cork's work on David Bomberg, Jacob Epstein, Percy Wyndham Lewis and the art scene in the early 1900s, especially *Art Beyond the Gallery in Early 20th Century England* (New Haven and London: Yale University Press, 1985), *David Bomberg* (exhib. cat., Tate Gallery, London, 1988) and *Young Bomberg and the Old Masters* (London: National Gallery and Yale University Press, 2019).

Christabel Pankhurst is quoted from *Suffragette Manifestos* (London: Penguin, 2020).

A digital scan of *BLAST*, no. 1 can be viewed at bl.uk (British Library Collections).

Chapter 7
For Isaac Rosenberg's letters, poems and art, see Ian Parsons (ed.), *The Collected Works of Isaac Rosenberg* (London: Chatto & Windus, 1979).

On German military theory, see Friedrich von Bernhardi, *Germany and the Next War*, Eng. trans. Allen H. Powles (New York: Longmans, Green & Co., 1914) and *On War*

of To-day, Eng. trans. Karl von Donat (New York: Dodd, Mead & Co., 1914); and Heinrich von Treitschke, *Politics*, vol. 2 (New York: Macmillan, 1916).

Official propaganda is discussed in Florian Altenhöner, 'War Propaganda Bureau', in 1914–1918 Online, International Encyclopedia of the First World War (11 Oct. 2017, encyclopedia.1914-1918-online. net); and John Mueller, 'Changing Attitudes Towards War: The Impact of the First World War', *British Journal of Political Science*, vol. 21, no. 1 (Jan. 1991).

For artists' war experiences, see Roger Berthoud, *The Life of Henry Moore* (London: Faber and Faber, 1987); Henri Gaudier-Brzeska, 'Vortex (From the Trenches')', *BLAST*, no. 2 (Jul. 1915); David Haycock, *A Crisis of Brilliance: Five Young British Artists and the Great War* (London: Old Street, 2010); Robert Hewison, 'Edward Wadsworth and the Art of Dazzle Painting', *Stages*, 4 (Liverpool Biennial, Dec. 2015); Percy Wyndham Lewis, 'War Notes: The God of Sport and Blood', *BLAST*, no. 2 (Jul. 1915) and *Blasting and Bombardiering* (London: Eyre and Spottiswoode, 1937); and Kathleen Palmer, *Women War Artists* (London: Tate Publishing, 2011).

Rupert Brooke's 'Peace' is quoted from *Poetry: A Magazine of Verse* (April 1915), Marina Tsvetaeva from 'Poets with History and Poets without History', in *Art in the Light of Conscience: Eight Essays on Poetry by Marina Tsvetaeva*, Eng. trans. Angela Livingstone (Bristol: Bristol Classical Press, 1992); and Clive Bell from *Peace at Once* (Manchester and London: National Labour Press, 1915). 'Speeches by Members of the Women's Social and Political Union' is reprinted in *Suffragette Manifestos* (2020).

Chapter 8
Dora Carrington's letters to Gerald Brenan, Noel Carrington, Mark Gertler, Christine Kühlenthal and Lytton Strachey are quoted from Anne Chisholm (ed.), *Carrington's Letters: Her Art, Her Loves, Her Friendships* (London: Chatto & Windus, 2017).

For Paul Nash, see Andrew Causey, *Paul Nash: Writings on Art* (Oxford: Oxford University Press, 2001); and Simon Grant, 'A Landscape of Mortality, Paul Nash', tate.org.uk.

For Winfred Nicholson (Roberts), see Christopher Andreae, *Winifred Nicholson* (Farnham and Burlington, VT: Lund Humphries, 2009); Andrew Nicholson (ed.), *Unknown Colour: Paintings, Letters, Writings by Winifred Nicholson* (London: Faber and Faber, 1987); and Jovan Nicholson, *Winifred Nicholson: Liberation of Colour* (London: Philip Wilson, 2016).

I have quoted from T. S. Eliot, *The Waste Land and Other Poems* (London: Faber and Faber, 1940); and D. H. Lawrence, *Women in Love* (London: Heinemann, 1921).

For women in the 1920s, see Robert Graves and Alan Hodge, *The Long Week-End: A Social History of Great Britain 1918–1939* (London: Hutchinson, 1985); and Marie Carmichael Stopes, *Married Love: A New Contribution to the Solution of Sex Difficulties*, 6th edn (London: A. C. Fifield, 1919).

For Dartington, see Dartington Trust, 'Our History', dartington.org; and David Parsons, 'Dartington: A Principal Source of Inspiration Behind Aldous Huxley's Island', *Journal of General Education*, vol. 39, no. 1 (1987).

Melanie Klein's 'Infantile Anxiety-Situations Reflected in a Work of Art and in the Creative Impulse' is reprinted in Klein, *Love, Guilt and Reparation and Other Works, 1921–1945* (London: Hogarth Press, 1975).

Chapter 9

Barbara Hepworth quotations are from Sophie Bowness (ed.), *Barbara Hepworth: Writings and Conversations* (London: Tate Publishing, 2015); and Eleanor Clayton, *Barbara Hepworth: Art & Life* (London: Thames & Hudson, 2021).

D. H. Lawrence's essay 'Nottingham and the Mining Countryside' is reprinted in A. A. H. Inglis (ed.), *A Selection from Phoenix* (Harmondsworth: Penguin, 1979).

For the coal industry, see David Greasley, 'Fifty Years of Coal-Mining Productivity: The Record of the British Coal Industry before 1939', *Journal of Economic History*, vol. 50, no. 4 (Dec. 1990).

For Henry Moore, see Roger Berthoud, *The Life of Henry Moore* (1987); Henry Moore, 'Primitive Art', *The Listener*, vol. 25, no. 641 (Aug. 1941) and *On Being a Sculptor* (London: Tate Publishing, 2010); and Henry Moore and John Hedgecoe, *Henry Moore: My Ideas, Inspiration and Life as an Artist* (London: Collins & Brown, 1999).

For Eric Ravilious, see Andy Friend, *Ravilious & Co: The Pattern of Friendship* (London: Thames & Hudson, 2017).

For the reception of Freudian theory, see Sally Alexander, 'Psychoanalysis in Britain in the Early Twentieth Century: An Introductory Note', *History Workshop Journal* (Spring 1998); and Robert Graves and Alan Hodge, *The Long Week-End* (1985). Texts by Paul Nash and Herbert Read about 'Unit One' are reprinted in *Unit One: Spirit of the 30's* (exhib. cat., Mayor Gallery, London, 1984).

Chapter 10

For Naum Gabo, see Martin Hammer and Christina Lodder, *Constructing Modernity: The Art & Career of Naum Gabo* (London: Yale University Press, 2000) and Hammer and Lodder (eds), *Gabo on Gabo: Texts and Interviews* (2000); Sara Matson and Giles Jackson, *Naum Gabo: Constructions for Real Life* (exhib. cat., Tate St Ives, 2020); Natalia Sidlina, *Naum Gabo* (London: Tate Publishing, 2013); and *Gabo: The Constructive Idea* (exhib. cat., Museum of Modern Art, Oxford, 1988).

Lenin is quoted from *Materialism and Empirio-Criticism; Critical Comments on a Reactionary Philosophy* (Moscow: Zveno, 1909), in *Lenin: Collected Works*, vol. xiv, Eng. trans. Abraham Fineberg (Moscow: Progress, 1972).

A facsimile edition of *Circle* was published by Faber and Faber in 1971.

Virginia Woolf is quoted from *Three Guineas* (Oxford: Oxford University Press, 2015).

For Kenneth Clark, see Clark, 'The Future of Painting', *The Listener*, vol. 14, no. 351 (Oct. 1935); and Chris Stephens and John-Paul Stonard (eds), *Kenneth Clark: Looking for Civilisation* (London: Tate Publishing, 2014).

For concentration camp photography, see Cornelia Brink, 'Secular Icons: Looking at Photographs from Nazi Concentration Camps', *History and Memory*, vol. 12, no. 1 (Spring/Summer 2000); Mark Haworth-Booth, *The Art of Lee Miller* (London: V&A Publications, 2007); and Susan Sontag, *On Photography* (2019).

Chapter 11

For Frank Auerbach, see Catherine Lampert, *Frank Auerbach: Speaking and Painting* (London: Thames & Hudson, 2015); and *Frank Auerbach* (exhib. cat., Hayward Gallery, London, 1978). See also Martin Gayford, *Modernists & Mavericks: Bacon, Freud, Hockney & the London Painters* (London: Thames & Hudson, 2018), which also contains much material on Lucian Freud and Francis Bacon.

The experience of refugees in Britain is discussed in Arifa Akbar, 'Pop Art Pioneer [Kurt Schwitters] is back in the Picture', *The Independent* (27 Jan. 2013); Monica Bohm-Duchen (ed.), *Insiders Outsiders: Refugees from Nazi Europe and Their Contribution to British Visual Culture* (London: Lund Humphries, 2019); Rachel Pistol, 'Refugees from National Socialism Arriving in Great Britain 1933–1945', *Refugees, Relief and Resettlement* (Gale, a Cengage Company, 2020); and Cherith Summers, *Brave New Visions: The Emigrés Who Transformed the*

British Art World (exhib. cat., Sotheby's, London, 2019). See also schwitters-stiftung. de and hutchinsoncamp.com.

Primo Levi is quoted from Elizabeth Scheiber, 'The Failure of Memory and Literature in Primo Levi's *Il sistema periodico*', *MLN*, vol. 121, no. 1 (Jan. 2006).

For Lucian Freud, see David Dawson, *Lucian Freud: Monumental* (New York: Rizzoli, 2019); William Feaver, *The Lives of Lucian Freud: Youth* (London: Bloomsbury, 2019); and Hugh St Clair, *A Lesson in Art & Life: The Colourful World of Cedric Morris and Arthur Lett-Haines* (London: Pimpernel Press, 2019).

For Francis Bacon, see Mark Stevens and Annalyn Swan, *Francis Bacon: Revelations* (London: William Collins, 2021); *Francis Bacon: Man and Beast* (exhib. cat., Royal Academy of Arts, London, 2021); and francis-bacon.com.

Ernst Gombrich discussed the genesis of *The Story of Art* (London: Phaidon, 1951) in his 1999 interview with Cathy Courtney for *Artists' Lives* (see details below).

For the landscape of austerity Britain, see Lynda Nead, *The Tiger in the Smoke: Art and Culture in Post-War Britain* (New Haven and London: Yale University Press, 2017); and J. M. Richards (ed.), *The Bombed Buildings of England* (London: Architectural Press, 1942).

For the experience of West Indians arriving in Britain, see Frank Bowling's interview for *Artists' Lives* (see details below); and David Olusoga, *Black and British: A Forgotten History* (updated edn, London: Picador, 2021).

Chapter 12
Eduardo Paolozzi describes his early life in his interview for *Artists' Lives* (see details below).

For Elizabeth David, see Artemis Cooper, *Writing at the Kitchen Table: The Authorized Biography of Elizabeth David* (London: Faber and Faber, 2011); and Elizabeth David, *A Book of Mediterranean Food* (Harmondsworth: Penguin, 1955). Clips from BBC *Panorama*'s 'Spaghetti-Harvest in Ticino' (1957) can be accessed on youtube.com.

For cinema in interwar Britain, see Christopher Simon Sykes, *Hockney: The Biography*, vol. 1 (London: Century, 2011); and Virginia Woolf, 'The Cinema', in David Bradshaw (ed.), *Virginia Woolf: Selected Essays* (Oxford: Oxford University Press, 2008).

I have quoted from Alberto Giacometti's 'Letter to Pierre Matisse', in Herschel B. Chipp, *Theories of Modern Art: A Source Book for Artists and Critics* (Berkeley, Los Angeles and London: University of California Press, 1968); and from Jean-Paul Sartre, *The Aftermath of War*, Eng. trans. Chris Turner (London, New York and Calcutta: Seagull Books, 2017) and 'Existentialism Is a Humanism', Eng. trans. Philip Mairet, in Walter Kaufmann (ed.), *Existentialism from Dostoevsky to Sartre* (New York: Meridian, 1989).

Barbara Hepworth's 'Conversation with Reg Butler recorded on 28 September 1951' is reprinted in Sophie Bowness (ed.), *Barbara Hepworth: Writings and Conversations* (2015).

For educational theory, practice and legislation, see Hansard vol. 396 c.208, House of Commons Debate 19 Jan. 1944; Nigel Llewellyn and Beth Williamson (eds), *The London Art Schools: Reforming the Art World, 1960 to Now* (London: Tate Publishing, 2015); and Herbert Read, *Education through Art* (London: Faber and Faber, 1970). Donald Winnicott is quoted from 'Living Creatively', based on talks given to the Progressive League in 1970, in *Home Is Where We Start From: Essays By a Psychoanalyst* (London: Pelican, 1986).

Peter Blake, Derek Boshier and Jack Smith are quoted from their interviews for *Artists' Lives* (see details below).

For the early years of the Institute of Contemporary Arts, see Ben Cranfield, 'All Play and No Work? A "Ludistory" of the Curatorial as Transitional Object at the Early ICA', *Tate Papers*, no. 22 (Autumn 2014); Herbert Read, unpublished speech at the opening of the exhibition 'Forty Years of Modern Art: 1907–1947, A Selection from British Collections', Institute of Contemporary Arts, Feb. 1948, Tate Archive; and 'Complete ICA Exhibitions List, 1948–July 2017', archive.ica.art.

Chapter 13
For the 1948 Venice Biennale, see Roger Berthoud, *The Life of Henry Moore* (1987); and Sophie Bowness and Clive Phillpot (eds), *Britain at the Venice Biennale 1895–1995* (London: The British Council, 1995).

For John Maynard Keynes, see James Heilbrun, 'Keynes and the Economics of the Arts', *Journal of Cultural Economics*, vol. 8, no. 2 (Dec. 1984); and Donald Moggridge (ed.), *The Collected Writings of John Maynard Keynes*, vol. 28: *Social, Political and Literary Writings* (London: Macmillan, 1982).

Lynne Walker's 'Golden Age or False Dawn? Women Architects in the Early 20th Century' is published by Historic England (historicengland.org.uk).

I have quoted from Alison Barnes (ed.), *Home Management*, 2 vols (London: George Newnes, 1955); Marshall McLuhan, *The Mechanical Bride* (New York: Vanguard

Press, 1951); and Lewis Mumford, *The Social Foundations of Post-war Building*, Rebuilding Britain Series (London: Faber and Faber, 1943).

For the Festival of Britain, see Mary Banham and Bevis Hillier (eds), *A Tonic to the Nation: The Festival of Britain* (London: Thames & Hudson, 1976); and Elain Harwood and Alan Powers (eds), *Festival of Britain* (London: The Twentieth Century Society, 2001).

Winston Churchill's speech 'The Sinews of Peace', 5 March 1946, can be accessed at winstonchurchill.org.

Herbert Read is quoted from 'New Aspects of British Sculpture', in *The British Pavilion: Exhibition of Works by Sutherland, Wadsworth, Adams, Armitage, Butler, Chadwick, Clarke, Meadows, Moore, Paolozzi, Turnbull* (London: The British Council, 1952).

Richard Hamilton is quoted from Michael Bracewell's *Roxy: The Band that Invented an Era* (London: Faber and Faber, 2007).

Chapter 14

I have quoted from Gerald Pearce's 'The Dreaming Wall', in *Galaxy Science Fiction* (May 1955).

For Magda Cordell, see Giulia Smith, 'Painting that Grows Back: Future Past and the Ur-feminist Art of Magda Cordell McHale, 1955–1961', *British Art Studies*, 1 (30 Nov. 2015).

Herbert Read, speaking at 'Documenta III' in 1964, is quoted from Huw Wahl's film *To Hell with Culture* (2014). Frank Cordell's talk 'Gold Pan Alley: A Survey of the Popular Song Field' was published in *Ark* (London: Royal College of Art, 1957).

For debates around American abstract expressionism, see Holger Cahill, 'American Painting and Sculpture in the Twentieth Century', in *Modern Art in the United States* (exhib. cat., Tate Gallery, London, 1956); Clement Greenberg, *Art and Culture: Critical Essays* (Boston: Beacon Press, 1961); Patrick Heron, 'The Americans at the Tate Gallery' and 'A Note on My Painting', in Mel Gooding (ed.), *Painter as Critic: Patrick Heron, Selected Writings* (London: Tate Publishing, 1998); and Harold Rosenberg, 'The American Action Painters', *The Tradition of the New* (New York: Horizon Press, 1959).

For the Independent Group, see Martin Harrison, *Transition: The London Art Scene in the Fifties* (London: Merrell, 2002); Anne Massey, *The Independent Group: Modernism and Mass Culture in Britain, 1945–59* (Manchester: Manchester University Press, 1995); and *This Is Tomorrow* (exhib. cat., Whitechapel Art Gallery, London, 1956).

J. G. Ballard is quoted from David B. Livingstone, 'J. G. Ballard: Crash – Prophet with Honour', *Spike Magazine* (1 Aug. 1999).

Chapter 15

Pop Goes the Easel, directed by Ken Russell for BBC *Monitor*, first broadcast in March 1962, can be viewed on BBC iPlayer.

For the *Monitor* series (including embedded video of John Schlesinger's *Private View*), see Michael Clegg, '"The Art Game": Television, *Monitor*, and British Art at the Turn of the 1960s', *British Art Studies*, no. 8 (Jun. 2018); and Mary M. Irwin, '*Monitor*: The Creation of the Television Arts Documentary', *Journal of British Cinema and Television*, vol. 8, no. 3 (Oct. 2011).

Malcolm Muggeridge is quoted from Craig Brown, *One Two Three Four: The Beatles in Time* (London: 4th Estate, 2020).

For post-war youth, see Marcel Danesi, *Forever Young: The 'Teen-aging' of Modern Culture* (Toronto: University of Toronto Press, 2003); Shelagh Delaney quotation, from a letter to Joan Littlewood, Apr. 1959, in Michael and Orlando Bird (eds), *Writers' Letters* (London: Frances Lincoln, 2021); and George Fullard quotation, in Michael Bird, *George Fullard: Sculpture and Survival* (Chalford: Pangolin, 2016).

For the American scene, see Clement Greenberg, *Art and Culture* (1961); Louis Menand, *The Free World: Art and Thought in the Cold War* (London: 4th Estate, 2021); and Christopher Simon Sykes, *Hockney: The Biography*, vol. 1 (2011).

For the 1960s London art scene, see Bryan Robertson, John Russell and Lord Snowdon, *Private View: The Lively World of British Art* (London: Thomas Nelson, 1965).

Derek Boshier is quoted from his *Artists' Lives* interview (see details below).

Chapter 16

Braziers Park is recalled by Marianne Faithfull, *Memories, Dreams and Reflections* (London: 4th Estate, 2007); and Jeff Nuttall, *Bomb Culture* (London: Paladin, 1970). See also Alexander Trocchi, 'A Revolutionary Proposal: Invisible Insurrection of a Million Minds', *Internationale Situationniste*, no. 8 (Jan. 1963).

Barry Flanagan is quoted from 'A Letter and Some Submissions' in his student journal *Silâns*, no. 6 (Jan. 1965), and John Latham and Barbara Steveni from their *Artists' Lives* interviews (see details below).

Bryan Robertson is quoted from Robertson, Russell and Snowdon, *Private View* (1965).

For the Destruction in Art Symposium and related events, see Danchev (ed.), *100 Artists' Manifestos* ('Auto-destructive Art'); Nigel Llewellyn and Beth Williamson (eds),

The London Art Schools (2015); Kristine Stiles, 'Synopsis of the Destruction in Art Symposium (DIAS) and Its Theoretical Significance', *The Act*, vol. 1, no. 2 (Spring 1987); and Andrew Wilson *et al.*, *Conceptual Art in Britain, 1964–1979* (London: Tate Publishing, 2016) and Wilson, 'Gustav Metzger obituary', *Guardian* (3 Mar. 2017).

For John Lennon and Yoko Ono, see Andrew Barker, 'John Lennon's Art College Days', liverpoolmuseums.org.uk; and Craig Brown, *One Two Three Four: The Beatles in Time* (2020).

Chapter 17
Mary Kelly is quoted from her *Artists' Lives* interview (see details below). The Beirut student is quoted from 'We Want to Learn', *Outlook*, vol. 12, no. 4 (19 Nov. 1955). *Vietnam Solidarity Campaign Bulletin 18* can be accessed at ucpi.org.uk.

For early conceptual art in Britain, see *British Sculpture in the Twentieth Century* (exhib. cat., Whitechapel Art Gallery, London, 1981); *The New Art* (exhib. cat., Hayward Gallery, London, 1972); and Wilson *et al.*, *Conceptual Art in Britain* (2016).

For the women's movement of the 1970s, see Sally Alexander, in conversation with Poppy Sebag-Montefiore, 'Beyond "Misbehaviour"' (11 Mar. 2020), historyworkshop.org.uk; Germaine Greer, *The Female Eunuch* (London: MacGibbon & Kee, 1970); Lucy R. Lippard, 'The Anatomy of an Annual', in *Hayward Annual '78* (exhib. cat., Hayward Gallery, London, 1978); Juliet Mitchell, 'Women: The Longest Revolution', *New Left Review* (1 Nov. 1966); Joanna Moorhead, '"I heard the signal and threw my flour bombs": why the 1970 Miss World protest is still making waves', *Guardian* (26 Feb. 2020); and Michelene Wandor, 'Family Everafter', *Spare Rib*, 5 (Nov. 1972).

Sheila Girling and Rosemary Butler (Young) are quoted from their interviews for *Artists' Lives* (see details below).

For art on television, see John Berger, *Ways of Seeing* (London: Penguin, 1972); and Kenneth Clark, *Civilisation* (London: British Broadcasting Corporation, 1969).

Chapter 18
I am indebted to David Olusoga's *Black and British: A Forgotten History* (2021).

Frank Bowling is quoted from his *Artists' Lives* interview (see details below), and 'Discussion on Black Art II', *Arts Magazine* (May 1969) and 'It's Not Enough to Say "Black Is Beautiful"', *Arts Magazine* (April 1971). See also Melissa Chemam, 'Land of Many Waters: An Interview with Frank Bowling', ArtUK (artuk.org, 11 Aug. 2021); Elena Crippa (ed.), *Frank Bowling* (exhib. cat., Tate Britain, London, 2019);

and Courtney J. Martin, 'They've All Got Painting: Frank Bowling's Modernity and the Post-1960 Atlantic', in *Afro-Modern: Journeys through the Black Atlantic* (exhib. cat., Tate Liverpool, 2010).

For artists of colour in twentieth-century Britain, see Eddie Chambers, *Black Artists in British Art: A History Since the 1950s* (London and New York: I. B. Tauris, 2014), 'Black Artists for Uhuru', *Moz-Art: The Arts Magazine of the West Midlands*, no. 5 (Mar.–Jul. 1982) and archived articles at eddiechambers.com; and Jean Fisher, 'The Other Story and the Past Imperfect', *Tate Papers*, no. 12 (Autumn 2009).

A recording of the First National Black Art Convention, Oct. 1982, can be accessed at blkartgroup.info.

Lubaina Himid is quoted from her *Artists' Lives* interview (see details below) and Claudette Johnson from her *TateShots* interview 'Giving Space to the Presence of a Black Woman' (2021).

The text of Enoch Powell's 'Rivers of Blood' speech can be accessed at anth1001. files.wordpress.com. Boris Johnson's 'If Blair's So Good and Running the Congo, Let Him Stay There' appeared in the *Spectator* (10 Jan. 2002). For Margaret Thatcher's interview with *Woman's Own* ('No Such Thing as Society') (23 Sept. 1987), see Margaret Thatcher Foundation, 'Speeches, Interviews and Other Statements', at margaretthatcher.org.

Chapter 19
For 'Freeze' exhibition and the YBAs, see Elizabeth Fullerton, *Artrage! The Story of the BritArt Revolution* (London: Thames & Hudson, 2016); and Julian Stallabrass, *High Art Lite: The Rise and Fall of Young British Art* (London and New York: Verso, rev. edn 2006).

For Geoffrey Howe's first budget statement, see Hansard, vol. 981, 26 Mar. 1980.

John Maynard Keynes is quoted from Donald Moggridge (ed.), *Collected Writings*, vol. 28, *Social, Political and Literary Writings* (1982).

For the political context of the 1980s, see John Harris, 'How Thatcherism Politicised the Arts in Britain', *Guardian* (9 Apr. 2013); Charles Moore, *Margaret Thatcher: The Authorized Biography*, vol. 3 (London: Allen Lane, 2019); and Margaret Thatcher, 'Speech at Royal Academy Banquet', 27 May 1980 (margaretthatcher.org).

I have quoted from Martin Amis, *Money: A Suicide Note* (London: Penguin, 1984). London Docklands Development Corporation's sales brochure from the

early 1990s can be accessed at lddc-history.
org.uk.

Michael Craig-Martin is quoted from his
Artists' Lives interview (see details below).

Chapter 20
Cornelia Parker is quoted from 'The Story
of Cold Dark Matter', tate.org.uk. For the
London bombs of 1990–91, see Mia Bloom
and John Horgan, 'Missing Their Mark:
The IRA's Proxy Bomb Campaign', *Social
Research*, vol. 75, no. 2 (Summer 2008).

Tracey Emin is quoted from Mark
Gisbourne, 'Life into Art', *Contemporary
Visual Arts*, no. 20 (1998), and Margaret
Thatcher from Paul Johnson, 'Failure of the
Feminists', *Spectator* (12 Mar. 2011).

Phyllida Barlow is quoted from her
Artists' Lives interview (details below). See
also Fiona Bradley (ed.), *Phyllida Barlow:
Sculpture 1963–2015* (Ostfildern: Hatje Cantz,
2015); Gary Carrion-Murayari (ed.), *Phyllida
Barlow: siege* (exhib. cat., New Museum, New
York, 2012); Jennifer Higgie, interview for
Hauser & Wirth, 'Phyllida Barlow: The Edges
of Things', 11 Feb. 2021 (www.hauserwirth.
com); and John Reardon and David Mollin
(eds), *ch-ch-changes: Artists Talk About
Teaching* (London: Ridinghouse, 2009).

Mona Hatoum is quoted from H. G.
Masters, 'Domestic Insecurities: Mona
Hatoum', *ArtAsiaPacific*, no. 59 (Jul.–Aug.
2008) and 'Nothing Is a Finished Project',
TateShots, May 2016; her *Corps étranger* (1994)
can be viewed at fourthree.boilerroom.tv.

For Rachel Whiteread's *Ghost* and *House*,
see Charlotte Mullins, *Rachel Whiteread*
(London: Tate Publishing, 2004).

Artists' Lives recordings
Artists' Lives is a continuing oral history
project initiated by National Life Stories
in 1990 to record the experiences of British
artists, art critics and other art world
professionals. These long-form interviews,
which are typically recorded in a series
of sessions, range across many areas of
life beyond the art world, from childhood
and family background onwards. Original
recordings are held in the British Library;
many can be accessed online, sometimes
also in transcript form, at sounds.bl.uk.

Phyllida Barlow, interviewed by Kirstie
Gregory, interview in progress, 2018, *Artists'
Lives*, British Library reference C466/335
(quoted on pp. 321, 327–28)

Peter Blake, interviewed by Linda
Sandino, Apr. 2003, *Artists' Lives*, British
Library reference C466/168 (quoted on
p. 198).

Derek Boshier, interviewed by Hester
Westley, May 2007–Mar. 2009, *Artists' Lives*,
British Library reference C466/262 (quoted
on pp. 197–98, 255–56, 260).

Frank Bowling, interviewed by Mel
Gooding, Mar. 2001–Mar. 2007, *Artists' Lives*,
British Library reference C466/127 (quoted
on pp. 184, 186, 285–87, 290).

Anthony Caro, interviewed by Paul
Moorhouse, Oct. 1993, *Artists' Lives*, British
Library reference C466/16 (quoted on
pp. 248–49).

Michael Craig-Martin, interviewed by
Melanie Roberts, Jul. 1998–Feb. 2002, *Artists'
Lives*, British Library reference C466/109
(quoted on p. 314).

William Gear, interviewed by Tessa Sidey,
Jul.–Aug. 1995, *Artists' Lives*, British Library
reference C466/33 (quoted on p. 198).

Sheila Girling, interviewed by Hester
Westley, Aug. 2009, *Artists' Lives*, British
Library reference C466/296 (quoted on
pp. 266–67).

Ernst Gombrich, interviewed by Cathy
Courtney, Sept. 1999, *Artists' Lives*, British
Library reference C466/89 (quoted on p. 178)

Lubaina Himid, interviewed by Anna
Dyke, Sept.–Nov. 2006, *Artists' Lives*, British
Library reference C466/249 (quoted on
p. 295).

Mary Kelly, interviewed by Lydia O'Ryan,
Sept. 2004, *Artists' Lives*, British Library
reference C466/194 (quoted on pp. 269, 272,
274–76, 280–81).

John Latham, interviewed by Melanie
Roberts, Mar. 1998–Jul. 2000, *Artists' Lives*,
British Library reference C466/69 (quoted
on p. 258).

Frank Martin, interviewed by Melanie
Roberts, Aug. 1997, *Artists' Lives*, British
Library reference C466/58 (quoted on p. 249).

David Nash, interviewed by Denise
Hooker, Jun. 1995, *Artists' Lives*, British
Library reference C466/32 (quoted on p. 6).

Eduardo Paolozzi, interviewed by Frank
Whitford, Jun. 1993–May 1994, *Artists' Lives*,
British Library reference C466/17(quoted on
pp. 187, 189–90, 192–93, 222, 224, 226).

Jack Smith, interviewed by Cathy
Courtney, Nov. 1999–May 2001, *Artists' Lives*,
British Library reference C466/96 (quoted
on p. 198).

Barbara Steveni, interviewed by Melanie
Roberts, Jun.–Oct. 1998, *Artists' Lives*, British
Library reference C466/80 (quoted on
pp. 262–63, 267–68).

Rosemary Young, interviewed by Gillian
Whiteley, Sept. 1999–Jun. 2000, *Artists' Lives*,
British Library reference C466/94 (quoted
on p. 277).

Acknowledgments

Thank you, first, to my agent Catherine Clarke at Felicity Bryan Associates for believing in this book and guiding its passage from first thoughts to publication. Thank you, too, to the brilliant team at Thames & Hudson – to my editors Ben Hayes and Jen Moore for their enthusiasm and efficiency; to Nikos Kotsopoulos for his creative picture research; to Jo Murray, whose sensitive and scrupulous copy-editing has much improved the final text; and to Howard Watson for his vigilant proof-reading. For their support, patience, interest – everything, really – I thank my family, especially Orlando, for his comments on the manuscript, and Felicity, in whose studio several chapters were written and to whom I owe the best of the insights a wordsmith can gain into an artist's life.

Sources of illustrations

1 The Hill House, National Trust for Scotland; **13** Harvard Art Museums/Fogg Museum. Bequest of Mrs Alfred Mansfield Brooks. Photo President and Fellows of Harvard College; **19** Library of Congress, Washington, D.C. Prints and Photographs Division; **26** Liverpool John Moores University Library; **30** Photo Science Museum Group; **33** The Metropolitan Museum of Art, New York. Gift of Paul F. Walter, 1985; **40** Photo 12/Alamy Stock Photo; **47** Boston Public Library; **51** Glasgow School of Art; **52** Private collection; **56** Private collection; **60** National Portrait Gallery, London; **65** The Metropolitan Museum of Art, New York. Gift of Auguste Rodin, 1912; **68** Private collection. Photo Bridgeman Images; **74** Library of Congress, Washington, D.C. Prints and Photographs Division; **82** Beinecke Rare Book and Manuscript Library, Yale University Library, New Haven; **86** Private collection. © Estate of Vanessa Bell. All rights reserved, DACS 2022 and © Estate of Duncan Grant. All rights reserved, DACS 2022; **90** Photo Heritage Image Partnership Ltd/Alamy Stock Photo; **92** Photo Topical Press Agency/Stringer/Getty Images; **100** British Library, London. © Wyndham Lewis Memorial Trust. All rights reserved 2022/ Bridgeman Images; **107** Photo DeAgostini/ ICAS94/Getty Images; **112** Published in Encyclopædia Britannica, vol.30, 1922. © Norman Wilkinson. All rights reserved, DACS 2022; **116** UCL Art Museum, London. Photo UCL Art Museum, University College London/Bridgeman Images; **125** © Imperial War Museum (Q 2943); **128** Photo courtesy Gavin Stamp/C20 Society; **132** Tate. Photo Tate; **145** Photo by Imagno/Getty Images. Barbara Hepworth © Bowness. Skeaping © The estate of John Skeaping/Tate; **150** Shell Art Collection. Courtesy the Shell Heritage Art Collection. Photo Shell Art Collection; **151** Albright-Knox Art Gallery, Buffalo, New York. Room of Contemporary Art Fund, 1948; **157** Tate. Photo Tate. The Work of Naum Gabo © Nina & Graham Williams; **158** © Edith Tudor-Hart; **169** Photo Popperfoto via Getty Images; **181** Photo Graham Keen/ TopFoto; **182** Photo courtesy Marlborough Gallery, London; **185** Photo Daily Herald Archive/SSPL/Getty Images; **188** Photo by Keystone-France/Gamma-Rapho via Getty Images; **195** Photo Keystone/Getty Images; **200** National Arts Education Archive at Yorkshire Sculpture Park. Courtesy Tom Hudson Archive; **210** Photo Chronicle/ Alamy Stock Photo; **215** Photo The National Archives/SSPL/Getty Images. Reproduced by permission of the Henry Moore Foundation; **217** Photo Heritage Image Partnership Ltd/Alamy Stock Photo. © The estate of Reg Butler; **223** Tate. Photo Tate. © Nigel Henderson Estate; **234** Photo Sam Lambert/Architectural Press Archive/ RIBA Collections; **236** Photo courtesy British Pathé; **241** Photo Ken Russell/ TopFoto; **245** Photo Tony Evans/Timelapse Library Ltd/Getty Images; **249** Courtesy the Billy Apple® Archive; **261** © The John Latham Foundation; **263** Courtesy Raphael Montañez Ortiz; **265** © 1966 Yoko Ono. Photo by Iain Macmillan; **279** © Angela Phillips; **280, 283** © Mary Kelly. Courtesy the artist and Mitchell-Innes & Nash, New York; **286** Photo Tony Evans/Timelapse Library Ltd/Getty Images; **292** Photo Bettmann/Getty Images; **297** Courtesy Lubaina Himid and Hollybush Gardens,

Index